MW00805144

HEART AND SOUL OF FLORIDA

UNIVERSITY PRESS OF FLORIDA

Florida A&M University, Tallahassee
Florida Atlantic University, Boca Raton
Florida Gulf Coast University, Ft. Myers
Florida International University, Miami
Florida State University, Tallahassee
New College of Florida, Sarasota
University of Central Florida, Orlando
University of Florida, Gainesville
University of North Florida, Jacksonville
University of South Florida, Tampa
University of West Florida, Pensacola

HEART AND SOUL

of FLORIDA

Sacred Sites and Historic Architecture

ELSBETH GORDON

Foreword by Herschel Shepard, FAIA

UNIVERSITY PRESS OF FLORIDA

Gainesville/Tallahassee/Tampa/Boca Raton/Pensacola
Orlando/Miami/Jacksonville/Ft. Myers/Sarasota

A Florida Quincentennial Book

Copyright 2013 by Elsbeth Gordon

All rights reserved

Printed in the United States of America on acid-free paper

This book may be available in an electronic edition.

18 17 16 15 14 13   6 5 4 3 2 1

Library of Congress Cataloging-in-Publication Data
Gordon, Elsbeth K.
Heart and soul of Florida : sacred sites and historic architecture / Elsbeth Gordon;
foreword by Herschel Shepard.
p. cm.
Includes bibliographical references and index.
ISBN 978-0-8130-4400-2 (alk. paper)
1. Sacred space—Florida. 2. Mounds—Florida. 3. Indians of North America—Florida
—Antiquities. 4. Church architecture—Florida—History. 5. Church buildings—Florida
—History. 6. Architecture—Florida—History. 7. Religious architecture—Florida.
I. Shepard, Herschel E. II. Title.
BL2527.F6G67 2012
203'.509759—dc23
2012031971

University Press of Florida
15 Northwest 15th Street
Gainesville, FL 32611-2079
http://www.upf.com

To Kathleen Deagan, Michael Gannon, Eugene Lyon,

and Charles Tingley

In archaeology, history, and the library, each makes the

pursuit of historic architecture a joyous journey.

Contents

Illustrations

FIGURES

Arranged topically according to chapters.

Foreword

IN A REMARKABLE and well-illustrated journey through extensively documented examples of Florida's architectural landscape, Elsbeth Gordon has carefully chosen the adjective "sacred" in describing sites that she argues are symbols of the beliefs and aspirations of the people who created them. In this context, "sacred" encompasses Native American, European colonial, and later American religious and secular sites. Drawing from a broad range of recent archaeological and historical research as well as many earlier sources, she argues that there are universal symbols reflected in Florida's architecture. Although the events and many of the early beliefs that shaped our heritage are irretrievable, Gordon emphasizes that the artifacts shaped by those events and beliefs can be experienced *today*—whether archaeological sites, landscapes, or structures, these artifacts are the visible, tangible evidence of the activities that have led us to this moment in space and time. In a word, they are "sacred"—and they should be saved.

Before embarking on this journey with Gordon, the reader may find a brief discussion of architectural symbolism and proportional systems helpful. The built environment is surely symbolic of the activities, beliefs, and abilities of its builders. Gordon is particularly interested in meanings attributed to the forms, colors, geometries, and other distinguishing characteristics of historic architecture. The meaning and symbolic significance related to the cultural values of a historic period that are assigned to architecture are ambiguous, often arbitrary, and sometimes misunderstood. The early architects of the white Greek Revival buildings would be astonished by later research revealing that Greek temples were highly decorated, often with bright colors.

As symbols of particular beliefs, structures and sites can be positive symbols to the believers and negative symbols to those with different views, as found in African American and English opinions of Fort Mose. Furthermore, viewpoints and meanings may change from generation to generation. For instance, the word "gothic," originally a pejorative term applied to medieval structures meaning "barbarous" or "uncivilized," over time changed to one of admiration for remarkable spaces and structures that could represent the mystery and glory of religious belief. Not surprisingly, when beliefs and tastes change over time, function often follows form. Thus, worship can be adjusted to fit the gothic nave as well as the Greek and Roman temple. Also, some forms are symbolic of an attribute common to different functions; the columns, pediments, and domes of the Classical and Renaissance Revivals signify civic as well as religious authority and have served both functions. However, as the eclectic mixture of historic architectural styles increased, the academic and symbolic significance of individual styles decreased. Religious and civic buildings built in the eclectic Mediterranean Revival style combined many elements in an often stunning but bewildering mixture of historical motifs. These buildings reference historic sources in general as romantic interpretations of the past. They have become symbols of particular places, times, events, construction methods, materials, and architects' abilities.

Different cultures often attribute meanings to colors that are fairly consistent throughout history because the meanings are drawn from universal natural events to which colors are related. For instance, fires are red, and red is symbolic of heat and passion. Similarly, geometric figures have attributes that are universally understood in mathematical terms. However, certain attributes are assigned to geometric figures that are not geometric or mathematical, but are related to the geometric shapes. For instance, the circle is often a symbol of eternity, for it has no end. These universal attributes are not difficult to discover and understand. However, other attributes may have been arbitrarily assigned to colors or shapes by a society or belief system. An example is the use of the five-pointed star, or geometric pentagram, in the American flag to signify one of the fifty states. The meaning of the star in the context of the flag cannot be understood without knowledge of certain events in the history of the United States, but the meaning of the star as a pentagram in geometry is universally understood. If a social or belief system assigning arbitrary attributes is lost, the attributes are almost impossible to interpret and understand, as seen in Gordon's examination of Native American sites.

The unchanging relationships among the circle, square, triangle, and other geometric shapes were known to many early civilizations. Certain relationships are called proportional when shapes and spaces are similar or geometrically related regardless of size, and together form a harmonious whole. There is evidence that proportional systems were used in the design of Egyptian, Greek, Roman, and possibly Native American structures, and there is certainty that they were used to design important buildings of the Gothic, Beaux-Arts, and Modern movements. Geometry and proportional systems have been viewed as evidence of a universal, eternal, and perfect order or the work of a supreme being. Thus, proportional systems can be used to create buildings and sites that represent this perfect order, or the cosmos, or the work of a supreme being. Furthermore, the "most perfect" or "godlike" must be the "most pleasing" or "most beautiful." In this way, proportional systems and geometry have been linked aesthetically to belief systems and religions, but over time this link has disappeared as the study of aesthetics developed as a separate discipline. Whether or not the famous "golden section" or other proportions are related to an abstract standard of beauty remains an open question. In any event, proportional systems had an important practical use in societies where there was no standard unit of measurement. By establishing an arbitrary unit locally, lengths and shapes of materials could be determined in proportion to that arbitrary unit during planning and construction, and materials could be accurately fabricated in remote locations.

The properties of the "golden section" were related to the proportions of the human body by several artists and architects during the Renaissance, and possibly much earlier by the Greeks. More recently, in the 1940s the French architect Le Corbusier combined these ratios with metric dimensions, suggesting that man could indeed be the "measure of all things." Designers during the Romantic movement attacked the use of geometric proportional systems by asserting they cannot be seen or experienced in constructed buildings, but these systems continue to have their supporters.

In *Heart and Soul of Florida*, Gordon deals consecutively with selected sites in precolonial, colonial, and American occupations of Florida from ca. 6000 B.C. to ca. A.D. 1950. In part 1, she discusses supernatural beliefs linked to a water underworld and the cycles of time that appear to be present at the Windover and similar early sites, as well as at the later Belle Glade Fisheating Creek site, where extraordinary carved effigies of small animals and birds are accompanied by a mound that remained in ritual use through the early historic period. Symbolism that may be related to astronomy, numbers, and geometry appears in the Weeden Island–era McKeithen Mounds. The processional way and large mound at the Mount Royal ceremonial center as well as the McKeithen Mounds may have links to the beliefs of the southeastern Indians of the Mississippian Period and possibly to the Mexican Maya. Part

1 ends with a discussion of the universal symbolism of the circle found in the Glades-era Miami Circle and seventeenth-century Apalachee council house at Mission San Luis, Tallahassee. In addition, Gordon addresses the mystery of Native American practices that were observed and recorded by the Europeans and the possible symbolic meaning of mounds and seashells.

Part 2 addresses the history and symbolism present in Florida's colonial settlements and religious architecture. The symbols associated with colonial European structures are less mysterious and more easily identified than the Native American. The 1573 edition of the Royal Ordinances addressing town plans in the New World speaks not only of Renaissance order, but also of Roman military planning and mud-brick villages known to the Moors. This edition of the Ordinances was preceded by several others, one as early as 1513, and the plan of St. Augustine was surely affected by these efforts to bring order to the natural world. Gordon makes clear the origins and importance of the several Catholic churches and later English church to this plan, and also addresses the construction and symbolism of the Cathedral Basilica. Another town plan, the free black settlement of Fort Mose, is described in detail. During the First Spanish Period, Fort Mose was a symbol of sanctuary to escaped slaves and an irritating symbol of lost property to the English. In addition, Gordon records the fitful history of Catholic and Protestant churches in Pensacola and describes the Catholic mission sites of Nombre de Dios and Mission San Luis, which stand as reminders of this nation's oldest mission system, established shortly after 1565 and ended in 1704 by the British and their Creek allies. Unlike the later Spanish missions constructed in the western United States, the early missions of La Florida were built of impermanent materials and survive only as archaeological sites except where reconstructed.

Part 3 addresses landmarks from 1821 to 1950, including churches, courthouses, city halls, post offices, the Florida Capitol, Bok Tower, the Overseas Highway, fortifications, and several other civic structures. As in parts 1 and 2, Gordon's documentation throughout this period is broad in scope and rich in detail, clearly defining the place of Florida architecture in national and international movements. The evolution of church and civic design and symbolism is traced from the frontier vernacular wooden structures to the Greek and Classical Revival buildings of the territorial period, the post–Civil War Gothic Revival, and the many other revival styles popularized by the Chicago 1893 World's Exposition and the Panama-California Exposition at San Diego in 1915. By the advent of the Great Depression in 1929, the Mediterranean Revival reigned as a major motif in Florida architecture. However, the seeds of Art Deco and the Modern movement had been planted in the nineteenth century. A number of European and American architects rejected the associative symbolism of "romantic eclecticism" and searched for new architectural expression growing from advances in technology, science, the arts, and changing cultural attitudes. Gordon cites the Bok Tower at Lake Wales as the combination of a Gothic-inspired tower with exceptional Art Deco décor. Wright's chapels at Florida Southern College and churches by later Sarasota School architects and others are cited as harbingers of things to come. Following the Great Depression and the end of World War II, American schools of architecture supplanted the principles of the École des Beaux-Arts with those of the modern movement, but this work is beyond the scope of this book. By ending with a strong argument and urgent plea for the preservation of historic sites, Gordon echoes the sentiments of Abraham Lincoln, who stated, "If we could first know where we are and whither we are tending, we could better judge what to do and how to do it."

Herschel Shepard, FAIA
Professor Emeritus, University of Florida
School of Architecture

Preface

WHEN MY Connecticut-born husband announced we were making a move to Florida with his new professional degrees in hand, a Connecticut friend who was a descendant of one of New England's first families said: "I can understand if you move as far as New York, or maybe even Philadelphia, but if you move to Florida—you can *never* come back!" Four hundred and fifty years have passed since Pedro Menéndez de Avilés and eight hundred Spanish colonists landed in St. Augustine, Florida, and built the nation's first permanent European settlement. Our friend neither recognized nor appreciated Florida's history and humanity. And he is not alone.

Traveling beyond Florida's borders, I am frequently asked where I come from. I reply, "St. Augustine." Seldom do I meet someone who knows about America's oldest city and its sixteenth-century Spanish founding, or more than very little about Florida history in context with that of the United States. And so, with a long-standing interest in architecture and buildings, the humanities, and how we remember history, I set out to prove that there are truths to be told about Florida in the state's architectural landscape that are far richer than we knew. I soon discovered that proof lies in what people invest of themselves in their buildings, their numerous religious and public buildings that have stood in every community from the start.

I had recently completed *Florida's Colonial Architectural Heritage,* which revealed little-known treasures by Florida's colonial-era builders. Its reviewer, Michael Gannon, kindly wrote: "This first-ever book on Florida's colonial architecture will be an eye-opener to readers who identify American colonial buildings solely with the powdered-wig states of Virginia and New England." Researching that first book filled my file drawers with many more "eye-opening" constructions, both before and after the colonial period. The overflowing files and newer discoveries led to this illustrated book.

Heart and Soul of Florida is a journey that starts in about 6000 B.C. and passes through the cultural lives of Indians, European colonists, and American pioneers to discover the Florida of today. It will look at their sacred sites, architectural activities, and historic buildings up until about 1950 (a building must be at least fifty years old to be considered for listing in the National Register of Historic Places). The purpose of this overview approach is to tell a story about today's built landscape, the buildings that dominate our daily paths and our views, who designed them, what shaped their facades and floor plans, and what inspired their colors, materials, and aesthetics. If we look more closely at Florida's sacred sites and public buildings, we will see that they *visually* record many material and spiritual things, including the state's history, its flourishing moments, its growth, and its diversity. But architecture does not just happen. The journey herein seeks Florida's cultural and artistic wellhead in its landmarks that mark the passages of cultural and human time.

The pursuit of architecture in *Heart and Soul of Florida* begins in prehistoric times, and moves forward with discoveries in archaeology and history, myths and religious beliefs, ancient testimonials and documents, maps, and old and new drawings and photographs.

At the end of the journey, there is a Florida that is so worth knowing. It may make my Connecticut friend want to move here.

HEART AND SOUL OF FLORIDA

In Pursuit of Florida

The fairest thing we can experience is the mysterious. It is the fundamental emotion which stands at the cradle of true art and science.

ALBERT EINSTEIN

EIGHT THOUSAND YEARS, more or less, have passed since people near Cape Canaveral selected a pond in which they created a ritual that had great meaning to them and their tribe, and to the generations that came after them. As the centuries advanced, and more and diverse peoples arrived in Florida, they too expressed themselves, their material situations, and things of the spirit, in richly human landmarks. *Heart and Soul of Florida* seeks their expressions in architectural activities, and how these activities from about 6000 B.C. to 1950 tell a continuous Florida story.

This book was originally intended to describe a selection of architectural landmarks listed in the National Register of Historic Places or designated National Historic Landmarks. However, the selection soon promised much more than backward glances over roads traveled fifty years or more ago, the age a site or structure must be for listing. The landmarks demonstrated that a larger important story lies in how preserved sacred sites and historic buildings relate to *today's* built landscape, how they and their stories of people, places, and events express certain foundations or fundamentals about the state's cultural identity. A thesis explored in this book is that we seldom think about the built landscape as the state's visual biography. We rarely think about the buildings that surround us every day: who designs them, how they are designed, and what they express about us and our community, and what we value.

As the manuscript progressed, I discovered that Florida's religious and public structures are two types of architectural activities that exhibit a continuous story of humanity, of extraordinary creative expressions, and of the public's ideals.

This discovery led to a second thesis, that if landmark sites and buildings offer exceptional revelations about Florida and its cultural ways, they should be thought of as *sacred* to our collective memory of Florida. Religious sites and houses of worship are generally considered sacred spaces, but why not also those civic monuments that are the visual landmarks of Florida's founding history, of growth, of flourishing moments in its development, and of the public's democratic ideals? To know who we are and what we are a part of, should we not protect these landmarks "gainst the teeth of time and razure of oblivion"?[1] I was persuaded in this thesis after reading an interview in *Preservation* with Pulitzer Prize winner David McCullough:

> I think having no sense of the story of your country is not greatly removed from having no sense of the story of your life. It's a form of amnesia and can be as detrimental to society as to an individual. If you have no story, I don't think you have a soul. If we lose our collective memory, our story as a society and as an ongoing experiment, we are going to be in big trouble.[2]

To capture Florida's spirit of place in the built landscape, the storytelling must begin in the deep shadows of time to see how and what the built landscape sequesters of architectural origins, diversities, changes, continuities, and connections. Thus, this book is an overview of architectural activities described in three parts—three parts meant to be read as one. It proceeds chronologically, beginning with the sacred/secular landmarks of people living in Indian Florida beginning about 6000 B.C. (part 1). Next explored are the religious and civic constructions of the Spanish and English colonists during 1565–1821 (part 2), followed by a look at the architectural decisions of the people who arrived after Spain ceded Florida to the United States in 1821 (part 3). What this book is not is a narrative about religion or government, or a critique of nuts-and-bolts construction practices, or of good, bad, or ugly architecture. It is written to capture the essence and soul of Florida through the visible record found in historic sites and architecture, to show that the state's history and cultural heritage are far richer than we knew. *This* is a story never told before.

The world gets smaller as the book progresses. With the arrival of Europeans, Christianity, democracy, slavery, a civil war, the Great Depression, and tourism, Florida's religious and public buildings record changing cultural ways, tastes, and values, and expanding connections and kinships with other places and people. The architectural picture grows larger and more complex after 1821. Many historic parts of Florida's built landscape must be set aside, and a number of constructions will be treated briefly, or left out, in order to present an expansive view that is interesting, informative, and entertaining. The selections and illustrations, therefore, should be considered samples of the many more that the reader might identify with, before and after 1950.

Peering into archaeological trenches, poring over ancient maps and documents, paddling down rivers, or traveling newly laid rails or brick roads to capture histories and compare vintage and more recent photographs, *Heart and Soul of Florida* probes the mysteriousness of human creativity and sees architectural activities as cultural signposts. They read like a census of Florida's population and economic growth. They are high-water marks of social eras and historic events, of arriving peoples with diverse cultural backgrounds, of local influences, and of national trends and technologies in the arts of architecture. The illustrating plates and figures were selected to record the passage of cultural time.

Regardless of the adopted construction material, be it mud, sand, cactus, palm fronds, oyster shells, coquina, wood, concrete, glass, tile, or steel, it documents people expressing what is meaningful in their lives in a given time and location. From this viewpoint, we discover that Indian burial mounds are more than "cemeteries," and that historic houses of worship and public designs are about more than religion, power, and politics. We also discover that civic adornment and preservation profit the state. Moreover, Florida's sacred sites and historic architecture tell us why we should stop thinking that the cultural history of these United States of America began with the arrival of the English.

Walt Whitman (1819–1892) stepped into this fray a century ago: "We [Americans] tacitly abandon ourselves to the notion that our United States have been fashion'd from the British Islands only, and essentially form a second England only—which is a very great mistake."[3] However, Tony Horwitz in his recent best seller, *A Voyage Long and Strange on the Trail of Vikings, Conquistadors, Lost Colonists, and Other Adventurers in Early America,* reveals that there are Americans who still believe in the English creation myth. When he questioned a clergyman who preached at the Harvard Club in Cambridge about the New England origin myth of the United States—and about the "Pilgrims" and "first Thanksgiving," which are nineteenth-century terms—the clergyman pointed out that myth is more important than history or facts, and that even if the myth is created and not correct, the myth transcends truth.[4] Does it?

Only if you believe the England-misted historians who wrote the first histories that proclaimed the Pilgrims founded America. Succeeding generations of American schoolchildren crayoned the seventeenth-century *Mayflower* and English pilgrims in their black hats and buckled shoes. No children colored the *San Pelayo* and its Spanish colonists. The *San Pelayo* was the flagship of Admiral Pedro Menéndez de Avilés. Menéndez, with some eight hundred men, women, and children, settled St. Augustine and La Florida in 1565 while the *Mayflower*'s timbers were still sprouting in the ground (fig. 1). The sixteenth-century Spanish colony and its town plan, governor's house, parish church, hospital, and fort are important "firsts" in the genesis story of the United States (plate 6). Before Spanish explorers and colonists arrived, however, there were pre-Columbian settlements in Florida established by peoples who also had origin myths and "firsts."

Florida has always been a frontier and an "ongoing experiment." But why is the richness of its cultural prism overlooked in context with that of the nation? Because its ancient pre-European people left no writings? Or because its founders and early builders were Spanish, African, Cuban, Mexican, Portuguese, and not English? Or because its late nineteenth- and twentieth-century residents are described by some writers as land speculators with "new" money, or as "transients," or "winter snowbirds," if not "Parrot Heads" in Margaritaville, condo time-sharers, or dealers in Miami's vices? Or is it because we have lost touch with our own history?

Florida is colorful, sometimes bizarre, but in addition to its beloved Jimmy Buffett songs, Hemingway look-alike contests, Weeki Wachee mermaids, and Disney characters, there is a bounty of historic sites and architectural gems stretching from the state's forested north to its Caribbean south that tell us how Florida got to be what it is. Religious architecture consecrated in its own time, and public buildings made sacred by time, are stepping-stones to the undiscovered and mysterious reasons why Florida's built landscape looks like it does.

Ponce de León arrived in Florida in 1513. A little over fifty years later, in 1565, the Spanish settlement in St. Augustine was established. This volume, however, begins with cultural landmarks that were created before the Spanish arrived. Why? Because on a cold winter morning in Washington, D.C., I stood at the research entrance to the National Archives and read carved in stone: "Study the Past; What Is Past Is Prologue." It became obvious to me that the

FIGURE 1. Pedro Menéndez de Avilés, 1519–1574, Adelantado, first governor of La Florida. On September 8, 1565, Menéndez and some eight hundred Spanish settlers stepped ashore in Florida and officially established St. Augustine, and began building their houses, headquarters, armory, and defenses. The settlement of St. Augustine endured through the centuries and today is recognized as the first permanent continuously occupied European settlement in North America. Photocopy courtesy of Florida State Archives.

"past" in Florida did not begin with a European ocean voyage. Thus, in this book it begins in a pond. It is called Windover Pond by archaeologists, and is the creation of people some 7,000–8,000 years ago. Excavations in the pond reveal evidence that generations of people made Windover a destination to express their sacred/secular beliefs in a ceremonial ritual in water that sent off their dead beyond this world with selected cultural materials. Water and its associated beliefs may be a prologue to later Indigenous architectural symbolism.

Windover takes place in an ancient landscape before there were enclosed sanctuaries and altars (plate 1). After Windover, part 1 looks inside three burial-mound centers built in the first millennium A.D. and finds that Indian builders used architectural symbolism to express intangible ideas. The ritual centers and symbols are the creation of people whose subsistence was primarily harvested in water. Mammoths and mastodons were long gone, and maize was not yet cultivated or ritualized. If maize and agriculture were not venerated in the burial tombs, what was? We cannot decode the motives or the symbolism of Florida's pre-agricultural seafood-eating people who buried their dead in mounds because they left us no written explanations or oral histories. But we can sense that Florida's sand-capped burial mound architecture was meant to express a coherent and sophisticated set of sacred/secular beliefs, of which the mound was the essential symbolic monument (plate 3).

Part 2 begins with St. Augustine's sixteenth-century town plan. It is the bedrock of the Spanish foothold and its architectural wellhead. It is also the nation's first comprehensive town plan and oldest set of building codes. Its principles are found in the Spanish Royal Ordinances published in 1573, evolving from or respecting European Classical ideas and Spanish experiences in laying out new towns in the West Indies. A half century passed before any town in the English colonies was rationally planned. St. Augustine's structured grid was characterized by logic and order, and addressed the welfare of its citizens, the town's local environment, defenses, religious and humanistic necessities, as well as the needs for important public and private spaces, cleanliness, and health. The Ordinances and their suggested applications in St. Augustine reveal clues to sixteenth-century Spanish decisions about the town's layout and architecture. Four and a half centuries later, the town plan has little changed despite the arrivals of diverse peoples and governments (fig. 2). Even after 450 years, however, there is need for more archaeology and discoveries in documents to tell St. Augustine's true story.

Part 3 begins in 1821, only 192 years ago. It is the shortest period but has the greatest number of architectural activities. Historic buildings in this period are presented topically and chronologically in context with Florida history after it became a U.S. territory in 1821. They reveal peoples' architectural decisions before and in the aftermath of the Civil War, as well as during an industrial revolution and a Gilded Age, two world wars, the Great Depression and post-Depression, and at the beginning of an age of nontraditional modernist and regional ideas. Buildings on Florida's new frontiers—first in the agricultural Classically minded north and almost a century later in the subtropical exuberance of the eclectic-minded south—tell the unique story of Florida's growth and diversity.

Part 3 departs from its chronological presentation when it relates the stories of the Spanish-built Governor's (or Government) House and Castillo de San Marcos in St. Augustine. They are among the most significant landmarks of Florida's Spanish heritage, but herein their architectural stories are more about their future and relevancy, and their architectural roles in sustaining the city's cultural tourism as well as the nation's memory of its Spanish beginnings (fig. 3). They have been in American hands some 190 years, and the future is about how to conserve their walls, interpret and renovate their spaces, raise public and private financing, and stay relevant to future and younger visitors who increasingly download history on the latest, coolest lighted screen.

Each of the book's three parts has an introductory chapter that sets the stage for the cultural period in which the described architectural activities took place. Thus, part 1's introductory chapter, "Mysteries in Water and Earth," wades into a virtual water world of the pre-European period and how it might have influenced Indian burial-mound architecture. The introductory chapter of part 2, "Planting Spanish Architectural Roots," draws attention to influences on Spanish architecture such as the Catholic Church, the Royal Ordinances, Indian, French and English hostilities, the local materials, climate, and environment. "The Magic of Architecture" introduces part 3, explaining the route taken to view architectural topics in the rapidly changing built landscape that have a story to tell about the making of the fourth-largest state.

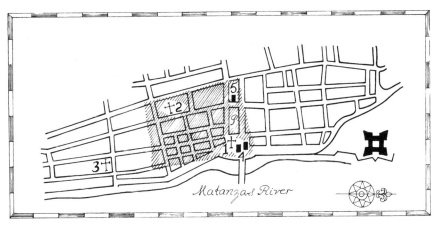

Sixteenth Century San Agustín

FIGURE 2. Sixteenth-century St. Augustine superimposed on today's street plan. The shaded area marks the street plan of the early 1570s. Today's street plan is that of the sixteenth-century plan, which appears to have followed principles set forth in the Spanish Royal Ordinances that were published in 1573 following practices established earlier in the Spanish New World. The principal buildings laid down in the sixteenth century are: 1. Nuestra Señora de los Remedios, parish church; 2. Nuestra Señora de la Soledad, shrine and hospital; 3. Franciscan Monastery; 4. Guard House and Armory; 5. Governor's House; P. Plaza. Drawing by E. Gordon.

No large Stonehenges or pyramids greet us in this book. The first architectural landmarks were created in the simplest ways without monumental pretense. Florida native stone of construction quality was limited: coquina (the Spanish name for the stone composed of tiny shells) was quarried along the edges of the Atlantic Ocean, and a coral rock (keystone) was quarried in the Keys. A native limestone is found in north central and southwest Florida.[5] Coquina blocks are the material of St. Augustine's seventeenth-century Castillo de San Marcos (plate 9) and eighteenth-century Cathedral Basilica, and crushed coquina is the hallmark of Henry Flagler's nineteenth-century concrete buildings in St. Augustine (fig. 4; plates 26–29). A native limestone gives character to two twentieth-century Mission Revival style churches (figs. 17.12, 17.13), and keystone (or coral rock) is the marine fossil material of several WPA buildings (fig. 18.21; plate 51). The lack of a native granite or basalt did not prevent Indian, Spanish, or American designers and builders from being creative with indigenous Florida materials. Any serious study of Florida's built landscape must start with the indigenous, the expedient, the vernacular. They are to the art of architecture what folklore is to literature, or folk songs are to music. Earths, sands, clay, logs, oyster shells, wood planks, thatch, cactus, bricks, and coquina form Florida's earliest historic architecture.

Standing constructions are the subjects of this book, with exceptions: important Indian landmarks, the Spanish missions Nombre de Dios and San Luis (the latter has been re-created), the free black sanctuary fort-village Gracia Real de Santa Teresa de Mose (commonly called Fort Mose), the hermitage/hospital/church Nuestra Señora de la Soledad, and the parish

---

FIGURE 3. Seventeenth-century Castillo de San Marcos, St. Augustine. The coquina stone castillo (castle, defensive fort) was begun in 1672 and completed in 1695 and 1763. Its thick walls were never breached; its defenders never surrendered. The old castillo stands as an icon of Florida's and the nation's Spanish heritage. On its ramparts, re-enactors and Park Service rangers fire its cannon and bring it to life in the twenty-first century. Today, this magnificent architectural landmark lives on as a tourist destination challenged by changes in the ways an increasingly indoors social networking public retrieves and enjoys history. No longer a bulwark against military attackers, the old castillo is now defending itself against the effects of time, climate, and competition in the newer world of cultural tourism. Photograph 2011 by Kenneth M. Barrett Jr.

churches in St Augustine and Pensacola. Their wood-and-thatch architecture has perished, but not their history. Their preserved sites are now tourist destinations, and because their histories are important in context with the history of Florida and the United States, they are recalled in reconstructions conjectured with archaeological evidence and historic documents. They enable

Heart and Soul of Florida

us to arrive in the twenty-first century with Florida's cultural prism intact. In this volume, the accounts of eyewitnesses describing their original constructions are presented in italics to distinguish their Spanish viewpoints from current scholars' perspectives, which are presented in quotes. Descriptions straight from the Spanish mouth (or quill) convey the reality in which these constructions took place, even if the documents are not always accurate. Biases and prejudices are a human continuum, and are themselves revealing.

Frank Lloyd Wright admonished Floridians in 1950 at a founders week address at Florida Southern College in Lakeland, where he designed twelve of the campus buildings between 1938 and 1958: "I don't see how we can consider ourselves as civilized, cultured people if we live ignorant of the nature of our environment; if we do not understand what we do to make it. Where the buildings that we live in are false, where they do not represent truth and beauty in any sense, where they are merely stupid or merely copying something that's not understood, we have no true culture."[6]

When Wright began to design the Florida Southern campus in 1938, he had finished his now-famous Fallingwater residence in Pennsylvania, and he would soon turn to New York City's famed Solomon R. Guggenheim Museum. Few Americans know that he designed the Florida Southern buildings, the largest collection of buildings designed by the man *Time* magazine chose for its cover of January 17, 1938, and identified as "the greatest architect of the 20th century."[7] Wright's Annie Pfeiffer Chapel (1941) at Florida Southern is one of Florida's many sacred spaces—Indian, Spanish, and American—that tell the story of Florida's religion-inspired constructions.

People expect their sacred and secular temples to be of high quality and exceptional design. Religious and public constructions are often a community's most intellectual and artistically ornamented buildings, and were frequently designed to be the tallest landmark. Whether they recall the world's best architectural traditions or demonstrate exciting innovations, they reveal how the congregation and the public thought of themselves. Moreover, religious

---

FIGURE 4. Interior courtyard, Ponce de Leon Hotel, 1887, now Flagler College, St. Augustine. Carrère and Hastings, architects. The Ponce de Leon architecture was the first eclectic combination of Mediterranean architectural traditions designed to create an allusion to Spain for themed tourism. Carrère and Hastings ornamented the entrance facade with scallop shells, after the House of Shells in Salamanca and the Knights of the Order of Santiago; reproduced the traditional Andalusian ceramic frogs in the fountain; and emboldened the entrance door with a terra-cotta Richardsonian Romanesque arch. Photograph 2011 by Kenneth M. Barrett Jr.

FIGURE 5. Miami Daily News Building, 1925, now the Freedom Tower, Miami. What began as a commercial building with a La Giralda–style tower (the minaret and Renaissance bell tower of the Cathedral of Seville) is today the symbolic Statue of Liberty for the Cubans who fled from a dictator and arrived in Florida in the 1960s and 1970s. Rescued from development, it is now part of Miami Dade College. Photocopy courtesy of Florida State Archives.

and public buildings reveal the use of architectural symbolism. Symbols add layers of meaning to the selected materials, ornamental schemes, colors, shapes, and floor plans. Symbols are a human universal. Not recognizing architectural symbolism, we miss a building's meaning, and the common threads that connect humanity. Indian ritual mounds were intentionally swathed in red or white sand. Now shorn of the colored material, they look like plain mounds of dirt. When the Castillo de San Marcos in St. Augustine was completed in the eighteenth century, its presence was magnificently enhanced in red and white stucco, the colors of the Spanish flag and symbol of Spanish dominion. The stucco is gone—and with it the sense of Spanish pride. Do modern courthouses without colossal white columns appear less impressive if bereft of the stirring Classical temple-front that has long been a leitmotif of America's democratic ideals? Symbolism is part of the magic of Florida's historic sites and architecture.

Today's preservationists are making sure that Florida's story perseveres, and that we do not become ambivalent about our surroundings and our identity. They fight to save cultural landmarks despite the ravages of age, hurricanes, fires, termites, treasure hunters, progressive politicians, bulldozers rushing to grow the state, and the changing tastes and ambivalence of youth. The stories of a few of the more dramatic hard-won rescues from impending destruction are told in the pages to come, including those of the Miami Circle, the Old State Capitol, the 1916 Palm Beach County Courthouse, and the symbolic Cuban Freedom Tower (fig. 5). Without these successes, Florida's cultural biography would be about holes in the ground.

Each year, as Florida's population grows, the financial incentive to tear down and build bigger increases. When Florida became a state in 1845, the population was about 70,000. The census of 2011 records a population of 18.9 million. Inevitably, Florida's tomorrows will exert pressures on the older architectural landmarks that are the keepers of Florida's flourishing moments, and visible truths of the state's founding and growth, change and diversity. Change is a continuum that provides vibrant new opportunities, but change also lends a special urgency to the work of historians, preservationists, conservationists, archaeologists, architects, photographers, city and county planners, and state politicians in whose charge is the identity of Florida, past and future. To the adage "We are what we build" should be added, "We are what we preserve."

The journey herein is its own reward: it promises that we will not lose touch with our own history.

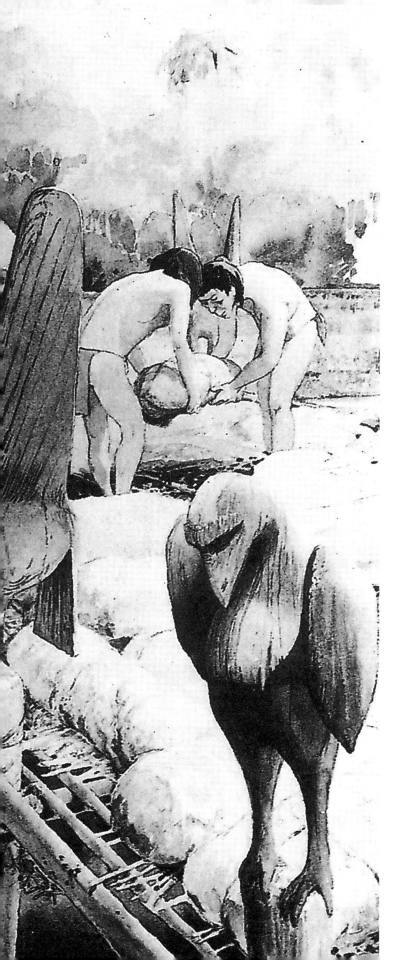

PART 1

Indian Florida

6000 B.C. to Early
Colonial Period

1 ✢ Mysteries in Water and Earth

Native American faiths have been co-opted by New Agers and so simplified by Hollywood that they can seem from the outside like a vague, spiritual environmentalism. . . . But this view, however sympathetically intended, is a simplistic caricature of religions that usually have creation stories and cosmologies as complicated and resonant as any of the world's larger faiths.

REED KARAIM

PREDATING SYMPATHETIC NEW AGERS, the sixteenth-century Spanish, eighteenth-century British, and nineteenth-century Americans were equally unknowing about Florida Indians.[1] They were biased as to religion and prejudiced as to race in their writings about, and actions toward, native peoples and their cultures. Indian architectural landmarks were thus wantonly erased from the landscape. Crews preparing a site for Henry Flagler's Royal Palm Hotel in 1896 at the mouth of the Miami River leveled a large pre-Columbian Indian burial mound and carried off barrels of human bones, depositing them "into a large solution hole off the site" that is now under an office tower.[2] Bulldozers were still knocking down Indian ritual burial mounds well into the twentieth century: Sarasota Bay Mound in the early 1970s for a condominium; Grant Mound on the St. Johns River in 1989 for house lots. In 1998, the Miami Circle was about to be wrenched from the ground by a developer before it was dramatically rescued and researched (fig. 6.1). Indian shell mounds containing cultural materials were mined for construction materials, roadbeds, and septic-tank drainage fields (fig. 1.1). These Indian landmarks and many more were destroyed without conscience.[3] Not a good start for a cultural biography of a state that prides itself on its diversity.

Fortunately, a number of intact Indian burial mounds survived into the twentieth century and are now protected by state law and conscientious property owners. Advances in scientific technologies, archaeological methods, and archival discoveries have made it possible for us to peer deeper into ceremonial Indian architecture and observe and speculate about what was not known before. The oldest burial mounds are Florida's first religious and public monuments. They may be the oldest in the United States.[4]

Florida's burial mound architecture suggests the Indians used symbolism to convey religious beliefs, myths, and social values. However, they left no written clues or explanations of any symbols and their meanings. It is nevertheless worthwhile to point out some uncommon assemblages of materials and construction practices that accompanied human remains in Florida's sand mounds. They appear to have been essential to the prehistoric architect-builder or religious specialist in order to convey the importance of the ritual, the mound, and the spiritual beliefs if not the identity of the tribe associated with the burial mound.

FIGURE 1.1. Mining Turtle Mound in the early twentieth century, New Smyrna Beach, Volusia County. Turtle Mound, ca. A.D. 800–1565, might have been the tallest shell mound in Florida. One adventurer estimated it to be 80 feet tall. The Spanish used shell mounds as lookouts; early cartographers depicted them as mountains; and early Americans thought they were built by a "lost" race of people. One postcard writer in 1910 attributed the mound to the "appetites of the aborigines and Spanish adventurers," noting that they were mined "to form the beautiful shell roads so prevalent throughout Florida." Shell mounds are now known to contain valuable archaeological data about Florida's first residents. Photocopy courtesy of Florida State Archives.

Three burial mound centers in Florida will speed us back in time to see how architectural symbolism might have been intentionally used to convey some kind of message. They are as follows: Fisheating Creek's Fort Center (ca. A.D. 100–500 in central Florida in the Lake Kissimmee watershed and Lake Okeechobee Basin); McKeithen Mounds (ca. A.D. 350–475 in a north Florida band of aquatic and hammock resources); and Mount Royal (ca. A.D. 900–1350 in eastern Florida on the St. Johns River). These are not their original names. When their ritual construction activities were completed (sometimes after several hundred years), the mounds were intentionally mantled with white or blood-red sand brought to the site. They were not meant to be impermanent—there was no failure of materials. These three examples were selected because they were built in different cultural regions and times, were more or less intact at the time of their excavation, but are little known outside academic circles.

Although burial mounds vary in many ways, they show enough similarities across Florida over many centuries to suggest that they exhibit a widespread religious belief that gives the mound sacred status. Mound similarities seem to transcend the different languages and artistic traditions of their geographic locations and times. One common practice, for example, was to entomb not only the deceased but all signs of the mortuary preparations—including the paraphernalia used in body preparation, as well as the platform mound on which the deceased were prepared. Another common trait was the mantling (or capping) of the completed entombment mound with a white or red-dyed sand. Additionally, specific shells were commonly placed in the mound in context with the deceased.

Part 1 explores some examples of burial-mound architectural practices and raises questions about them in context with the water-world subsistence of Florida's Indians. To do this, it looks at various ancient myths about "magic" mounds, "First People" origin myths, and the universal use of shell symbolism in other early religions that *are* explained in writing. But before we climb into an excavation trench, there is something of cultural value to be discovered in water and burials in water at Windover Pond near Cape Canaveral. It is the oldest sacred site to which science can take us in Florida today. It is described by archaeologists as a charnel pond where more than three hundred people representing many generations were buried with similar rituals beginning about 6000 B.C. What the archaeologists found preserved in the pond's muck makes this site one of the most unusual mystical places anywhere in the New World.[5] Chapter 2 will bring us to its water's edge. Could watery burials be a prologue to the burial mounds?

Burials in water were followed by burials in sand mounds that contain building materials and cultural items suggestive of the importance of water resources and its harvested foodstuffs. If what lived in water was particularly important to survival and leadership, did water, its sources, resources, and riverine-estuarine or offshore harvesting techniques spawn religious beliefs, myths, and heroes? The successes of the fishers in the waters in and around Florida suggest to some scientists they may have contributed to a cycle of depletion of aquatic resources still felt today. Startling reminders of part of this seafood subsistence industry are the huge ancient shell mounds along the Gulf and Atlantic coasts. One mound was described at Mound Key in Estero Bay (near Naples) in Frank Hamilton Cushing's diary in 1895 as 60 feet high. Turtle Mound (A.D. 800–1565) in New Smyrna Beach was said to be 80 feet high before it was mined for construction material (fig. 1.1).[6]

Until recently, it was commonly believed that agriculture—particularly the cultivation of maize—gave rise to permanent settlements and was the prerequisite and the catalyst for complex spiritual beliefs and symbolic architecture. However, agriculture and maize cultivation were not widely practiced in Florida until a couple of centuries before the Spanish arrived.[7] If agricultural rituals and the likes of corn gods were not important to the fishers and divers who harvested food from water and who built Florida's burial mounds, what was?

To walk up the large and numerous shell mounds at the University of Florida's Randell Research Center on Pine Island with Dr. William Marquardt is to see and experience one aspect of the amazing fishing heritage of the Charlotte Harbor Calusa. His research reveals that they had sedentary villages that harvested aquatic species, and that fishing provided the primary source of protein (plate 4; fig. 1.2).[8] Archaeologist Barbara Purdy similarly notes that fishes and turtles were probably the most important species in all time periods to the people of Hontoon Island in the St. Johns River watershed, which raises a question about a carved pelican found nearby. Does it symbolize anything associated with water myths and harvests or anyone in the Hontoon burial mound?[9] At the Crystal River burial mound complex (plate 3) on the Gulf Coast, what is the meaning of the carved stone plummets placed near the dead in the circular embankment? Are they fish-net weights needed in an afterlife, or, in context with the mortuary mound monument, do they transcend practical or ornamental uses to symbolize a supernatural power that can mediate between the good and bad gods controlling water resources?[10]

Ask any fisher today how difficult it is to live by harvesting what lives in water. Fishing can be a dangerous, unpredictable business, even with fast boats, GPS, depth-finders, weather reports, published fishing guides, and a large variety of manufactured nets, hooks, reels, and baits. Florida's ancient Indians had multiple harvesting techniques and tools they made from parts of fish, shells, animals and plants. They made nets of different sizes, and weirs, sinkers, floats, hooks, and spears; they dug canals and fabricated oceangoing canoes. They depended on local knowledge of climate, tides, currents, marine habitats, seasonal spawns and migrations. Did they look to traditional ancestral myths about the spring moon, and to supernatural Neptunes and Poseidons? Did they "talk" with their deceased ancestors as suggested in the sixteenth-century accounts of Father Juan Rogel (chapter 7)?

FIGURE 1.2. *People of the Estuary*, Pineland, 2,000–1,700 years ago. Lee County. Pre-Columbian Florida Indians (ancestors of the Calusa encountered by the sixteenth-century Spanish) lived along the Gulf Coast near today's Fort Myers. They had sedentary villages and subsisted primarily on seafood. Surely some of their religious beliefs, myths, and creation stories contained heroes and villains that controlled the seas, tides, currents, storms and water harvests. Are such beliefs symbolized in the cultural and construction materials of their burial mounds? Art by Merald Clark, courtesy of the Florida Museum of Natural History.

Surely Florida's Indians had gods and heroes under the water surfaces and in the day and night skies that were connected to tides, seasonal runs, water temperature, and storms. Did they believe malevolent lords of the hurricanes plagued them seasonally? Did they believe gods threw lightning bolts and sent powerful winds and water surges into fishing villages, and closed or opened new ocean inlets? Did they believe a benevolent god could calm the seas and renew aquatic foodstuffs? Did they also believe their sea gods waged battles? One look at Albrecht Dürer's fifteenth-century *The Battle of the Sea Gods*, or at Giovanni Stradanus's sixteenth-century depiction of Columbus's ship surrounded by sea monsters and gods, tells us that such beliefs were widespread before our time (chapter 7). What archaeologists have excavated in the mounds described in part 1 suggests that Florida's burial-mound architecture was not simplistic.[11]

In most of the world's cultures, sacred constructions immortalize gods, earthly rulers and priests, divine powers and metaphysical spaces. Profound beliefs are expressed in paintings, in gold and silver, marble and stained glass. Pyramids, spires, and domes soar above kingly and priestly crypts. Tangible symbols of altar-throne powers and divine or earthly lineages are human universals. They may also lurk in Florida's burial mounds but are difficult to recognize in Florida's organic sand mound materials and shell accoutrements. Perhaps they exist at Fisheating Creek's Fort Center in the placement of an adult human skull and child's skull cap in the *east* side of a mortuary platform mound that was built beside a man-made body of water? They were placed there together with "seven *Busycon* dippers, three *Venus* clam shells, a set of nested clam shells consisting alternately of four clam and four scallop shells, and two bird-bones."[12]

And perhaps they exist in the tomb of an elite female who in death was laid on an east-west axis in a mound built at the apex of an isosceles triangle at the McKeithen Mounds ceremonial site, her head in the west, her hair dyed red with ochre and nesting an anhinga bone, her feet toward the eastern sunrise accompanied by a ceramic bird's head painted red?[13]

The chapter "That's Not Just a Work of Art—That's Our Godhead" ponders possibilities and raises questions. It is intended to bestow a past on the elite warriors, chiefs, and priests who might lie in the burial mounds swathed in the symbols of their creation and lineage myths that are lost. In its mysteriousness, their tumulus landscape is no less sacred to Florida and American history.

2 ✣ Windover Pond

They Entered the Water

Water, which moves like a living being, has always been an image of the life of the spirit.

JOHN M. LUNDQUIST

WINDOVER POND is the earliest *sacred site* described in this book. Beneath its shallows, some 7,000–8,000 years ago, more than three hundred bodies of men, women, and children in successive generations were pinned down with prepared stakes in shallow graves in the pond. They were ritually wrapped in woven fabrics, and wood branches were stacked over them in conical piles. This charnel pond became a destination for repetitive similar burial activities.[1] Are its spiritual implications suggestive of beliefs about water or its sources, and are such beliefs a distant prologue to beliefs in burial-mound architecture that has implications of water symbolism?[2]

When discovered in 1982 in Titusville, near the Kennedy Space Center at Cape Canaveral (Brevard County), and excavated during 1984–86 by archaeologists Glen Doran and David Dickel, the dead were well preserved in the neutral pH and anaerobic saturated peat, even as to their brain tissue, fabric threads, and accompanying cultural materials. Each person had been wrapped within forty-eight hours of death in handwoven fabrics and intentionally positioned. The majority were flexed (knees drawn to chest, arms folded) on their left side, heads to the west, faces to the north. There were no signs of unusual violence (as in sacrificial burials). The pine stakes had been smoothed, pointed, or fire-hardened, and driven into the peat so as to project above water. They might have marked clusters of burials or lineage affiliations. Some burials were completely covered by conical piles of wood. Selected items of value accompanying or adorning the deceased were gathered from nature—gourds, bones, fish vertebrae, sharks' teeth. Some of these items were changed by artistic endeavors, crafted into shell beads or incised with meaningful marks we cannot interpret (fig. 2.1).[3]

Archaeological data show the charnel activities took place in rhythm with nature's calendar—they occurred only during July to October, even though the pond held water year-round. Many generations returned to the same place to perform the same burial ritual in the same season.[4] Windover Pond was a destination. It implies that there were supernatural beliefs about water or water sources, and about a ritual linked to a concept of cyclical "time." Were they related to seasonal cycles in nature's foodstuffs? Windover people were semi-nomadic hunter-gatherers. Their subsistence was riverine, between two major river systems: the St. Johns River and the Indian River. Ducks, catfish, and turtles were important sources of their protein, supplemented with small animals and gathered local edible plants, from prickly pear to persimmon, elderberry and wild grapes.[5] We can imagine their need for tangible rituals that might express beliefs about death, and communicating with unseen supernatural powers that controlled the cyclical renewal of the plants, animals, and aquatic species.

Science is mute as to who these Archaic Period people were, where they came from, and when they arrived in Florida. Their relationship to American Indians is also unknown. Windover awaits advances in scientific studies and techniques to discern the origins of North America's populations. DNA, for example, revealed that the 9,200-year-old "Kennewick Man" discovered in the state of Washington was related to the Ainu, a Caucasoid people of the Japanese archipelago. More recent studies suggest in addition to people walking across the Bering Strait land bridge, others from western Europe arrived in North America some 26,000 to 19,000 years ago by coastal waters.[6]

The fabrics wrapping the human remains have received much attention. There are shrouds, blankets, clothing, caps, hoods, or bags—laboriously made by stripping the native palms and using various twining methods. They are the oldest-known of their type in the New World, and the largest collection of Archaic Period woven fabrics in North America. Also of growing interest are the ingested seeds and some nineteen medicinal plants. Windover's mysterious water ritual and its human cultural discoveries make it one of the most unique sites in the New World.[7]

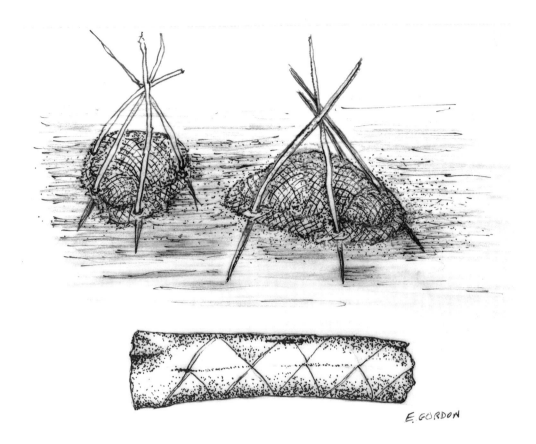

FIGURE 2.1. Windover Pond burial, ca. 6000–5000 B.C., Titusville. Brevard County. Some three hundred men, women, and children representing a number of generations were intentionally buried with ritual in water. The deceased were sent off on their death journey with various cultural items, including etched bird bones and woven fabrics, the oldest known in North America. Who these people were and where they came from are unknowns. Also unknown is whether the water site and its cyclical ritual had spiritual implications. Sketch by the author based on *Windover*, edited by Glen Doran.

But this pond was not alone. Archaeologists have discovered that similar aquatic burial activities took place during the millennium following the burials at Windover: in south Florida at Warm Mineral Springs, Little Salt Springs, Bay West, and Republic Groves. At Little Salt Springs, about 200–400 human beings were placed on biers of wax myrtle, wrapped in grass and placed in the peat muck of a pond slough or drainage, secured and marked with fire-sharpened wood stakes. A forty-year-old female was buried in a plant-fiber shroud with her head to the west and wood markers or supports for a protective cover. At Bay West, in a cypress pond, individuals were buried with poles intentionally shaped, and at Republic Groves, originally a bayhead swamp with three springs, charred stakes had been hammered into the peat where impressions of matted cordage and incised ornaments were found. Hundreds of everyday items accompanied these water burials. Archaeologist George Luer suggests that some of the water locations might be ancient flooded sinkholes, and that early people might have thought they led to a mythological underworld.[8]

Beliefs about water in some of the world's ancient religions are thought-provoking. Water in rivers, springs, and sinkholes was generally believed to be the first source of life. But water was associated with more than a single quality. It was both life-giving and life-destroying; it could induce fertility and germination, as well as resurrection and divinity. For example, in the proto-Shintō religion of the ancient Ainu, water purified, and purified humans could come near to the Divine. Coastal-dwelling Arctic Eskimos of the past depicted water as female, and had a Mother of the Sea Creatures who was recognized as the source of life, regeneration, and fertility as well as the devouring mother in her role as mistress of the underworld.[9] In nineteenth-century Cherokee belief, springs and rivers represented the underworld in the tripartite universe of sky, earth, and underworld. James Mooney collected a Cherokee story in the late 1800s that described another world under this world, reached by trails that are the streams that come down from the mountains—the springs at their heads are the entrance doorways to the underworld.[10]

At Chichen Itzá, Yucatan, the Maya ritually sacrificed humans by flinging them into the mouth of a sinkhole to appease the god of rain. A terrifying full-page painting of a young girl hurled 80 feet into the sacred natural limestone water pit appeared in a 1936 edition of the *National Geographic Magazine*, illustrating the Itzá ritual designed to intercede with the gods during droughts. Human bones, carved jade, gold disks, copal incense, and idols have been dredged from the sacred *cenote* (Spanish corruption of Maya *dzonot*, sinkhole).[11] Classic Period (A.D. 200–900) Maya believed the "Underworld" was "a watery world that could only be entered by sinking beneath water," a place of darkness and death where there would be rebirth. Maya words for "bone" and "seed" were homophonous; bone was the seed for resurrection. Two Maya tombs illustrate this belief in stone carvings accompanied by glyphs for bone, seed, and waterbirds: one depicts the death of a king in A.D. 378 at Tikal (Guatemala) with the words, "he entered the water"; the other depicts the death of King K'inich Janaab' Pakal at Palenque (Chiapas, Mexico) in A.D. 648 on a magnificent stone sarcophagus carved with his image sliding in death into the watery underworld on his path to rebirth.[12] Cormorants or anhingas were the "Water Bird" that "symbolized the watery surface of the Underworld."[13]

In Florida's excavated burial-mound sites, many types of shells and images of fishing waterbirds (ducks, pelicans, anhingas, spoonbills, osprey, eagles) have been found. In addition, there are net sinkers (carved from stone and whelk and conch shells), caches of whelk, conch, and oyster shells, freshwater snails, sharks' teeth, and shell drinking cups. Are they symbolic? Do they suggest a distant link to earlier burial rituals in water, or to the harvest of foodstuffs in water and the underwater gods that controlled supplies and the harvest? A monk who accompanied Christopher Columbus on his second voyage in 1493, Fray Ramón Pané of Catalonia, was the first New World missionary and the first to record Caribbean religious beliefs. His written report describes the fish-eating Taino believing in two supreme gods: one was Yúcahu, god of salt water; the other was Atabey, his mother, goddess of freshwater and fertility.[14] A number of the world's early religions included similar beliefs and ways to express those beliefs with symbolic water-related materials (chapter 7).

On the other hand, archaeologist Robert Hall presents some later interpretations of beliefs and myths about water thwarting ghosts, unwanted witches, and other supernatural beings. He drew his theory from the nineteenth-century Omaha, Iroquois, and Ojibwa beliefs that water was a protective barrier that skeletons and ghosts dared not wade through or cross. Jesuits in eighteenth-century south Florida had indeed noted that Florida Indians so feared the powers that the dead could exert on the living that they did not permit the names of the dead to be pronounced. They made pilgrimages to "cemeteries" placed beyond towns with offerings to placate them.[15]

Florida's mound builders, however, lived centuries before those of the myths just described. And Florida's mound builders were dependent on foodstuffs in water. Whether water was a portal to divine powers, had ghost-busting magic, or defied predators, its connection with and symbolism in sacred ceremonial architecture in Florida remains unknown. The discussion of the Fisheating Creek architects in the next chapter will only deepen this mystery.

In 1987, in recognition of its significance, Florida's Windover Pond was designated a National Historic Landmark.

3 ✛ Pre-Columbian Architects on Fisheating Creek

Man creates to complement nature, and nature has its effects on man's creations.

I. M. Pei

About the time barbarian invasions were taking place in Europe, and Christianity was crystallizing in the Near East, people living on Fisheating Creek just west of Lake Okeechobee (Glades County) began to build a mysterious ceremonial complex. Its original name is unknown. In an unfortunate twist of fate, this Indian site has received the name "Fort Center" after a nearby nineteenth-century U.S. Army blockhouse built to rid Florida of the Seminole Indians following the 1830 Indian Removal Act.[1]

Humans occupied the area beginning about 1000 B.C., but architectural activities at the ceremonial complex did not begin until about A.D. 100–200. The finished complex consisted of a man-made pond, two mounds, and an earthen enclosure. Other earthworks of mysterious use were nearby outside the complex enclosure. The ceremonial complex was located in the Okeechobee Basin along a substantial creek that was called "thlathlopapka-hatchet" in the early nineteenth century according to a large map, *The Seat of War in Florida* (Seminole War), drawn in 1839 by U.S. Topographical Engineers by order of General Zachary Taylor. Today the surrounding region had been drained and farmed, and the creek is smaller and better known as "Fisheating Creek." Archaeologists refer to the region's culture as "Belle Glade." At some time, the region was part of the far-reaching Calusa empire of ca. A.D. 500–1700, when it controlled the southern peninsula from its center on the Gulf coast near today's Fort Myers, east-ward to Lake Okeechobee and Cape Canaveral, and south to what is now Miami and the Keys. Agriculture did not define the Belle Glade–Fisheat-ing Creek culture or that of the Calusa.[2]

The Fisheating Creek ceremonial complex was built in the midst of a large and diverse watery environment. Close by was Lake Okeechobee, which meant "Big Water" in the nineteenth-century Miccosukee lan-guage, but before that it was "Lake Mayaimi," an earlier Indian name that also described it as a large body of water.[3] It is the largest lake in Florida. Surrounding it was an extensive marsh system that was the drainage of this lake, and of Lake Istokpoga, Lake Kissimmee, and the Kissimmee River to the north, all meandering naturally southward to Lake Okeechobee. The lake in turn overflowed into the liquid expanse that flowed continu-ously southward to the Gulf of Mexico and Florida Bay. General Taylor's map referred to this living sheet of water as "pay-hai-o-kee or grass water," and "Everglades." Indian canoes could pole southward in the *agua dulce* (freshwater) to the Miami River and Biscayne Bay, and to the Gulf coast by a series of natural drainage systems, rivers, and Indian-built water ca-nals for canoes. Trade goods and ideas could flow southward, and east to the Atlantic and west to the Gulf coast, if not north as far as the contem-poraneous Adena-Hopewell region in Ohio. Florida's vast watery world of plants, birds, fish, animals, and human passages was unlike anywhere else in North America.[4]

Fisheating Creek's ceremonial architecture story begins in 1926, when an extraordinarily large (62-inch-high) carved wooden bird was pulled out from under 3 feet of muck at the edge of a mound. It was headless. A head was fashioned for it, and the "eagle" became a yard and grocery-store decoration. In 1932, it was donated to the Florida Museum of Natu-ral History. In the 1960s, a new eagle head was conjectured and carved to replace the 1926 head.[5] Some forty years later, archaeologist William Sears and his team excavated the muck and mound. They discovered the muck was a human-made "pond" in which were remnants of more than a hundred carved birds and animals. Sears conjectured the wood carvings were attached to a wood charnel platform that had been constructed in the water to hold bundled human bones, presumably to await a later and final ritual. His concept of the charnel platform in water was drawn and published and has been widely accepted since 1982 (fig. 3.1).[6] A one-third scale model of the charnel platform was installed at Dickinson Hall at the Florida Museum of Natural History, University of Florida, in Gainesville.

According to Sears's theory, the wood platform in the water burned

FIGURE 3.1. Conjectured charnel platform, Fisheating Creek–Fort Center, ca. A.D. 300–400. Glades County. Excavating archaeologist William Sears conjectured that bundled bones awaiting final burial were placed on a platform in a man-made water pond. Carved life-size birds and animals were associated with the platform and/or the deceased. Sears theorized that the platform and the bundled bones slipped into the water, and that later a number of the bundles were retrieved and entombed in an adjacent burial mound. The mound was capped with 17 feet of clean white sand. Photocopy by Merald Clark courtesy of Anthropology Division of the Florida Museum of Natural History.

and collapsed, and the wood effigies and bundled human bones slipped underwater. At an unknown later time, he conjectured, about half of the bones were retrieved and placed with wet earth on the adjacent mortuary platform (low earth mound) where the deceased had initially been prepared and bundled. This retrieval constituted a burial ritual for about 150 people in a conical earth mound 28–29 feet high, capped with 17 feet of clean white sand brought to the sacred site. In the mound were entombed the deceased and all evidence and paraphernalia of the mortuary ritual.

This monument was highly visible, rising out of the landscape as a symbol of something more than its earth, bones, and sand.[7]

The second mound in the complex had begun as a midden, but was converted into the house foundation for those who prepared the dead and masterminded the architectural activities and ceremonial rituals. They lived in a circular pole-and-thatch lodge (rebuilt a number of times) surrounded by many of the materials of their profession—sharks' teeth and shell tools, quantities of river mussel shells, marine conch and *Venus* clam shells, prepared lime, and pipes and bone fids.[8] These residents may have been religion specialists who lived close to their profession, a tradition we recognize to this day—from Spanish Franciscan friars who lived in monasteries attached to or close by their churches and cemeteries, to American clergy living in the manse next door to the house of worship, with its funeral ceremonies and cemetery.

Sears described the excavated carved birds and animals in three categories: large birds and beasts; two-legged-style small cat or animals carved in pairs; and a third category of portable tenoned birds that could be fitted into sockets in the tops of poles for use in ceremonial processions. All the figures were sculpted in pine with amazing skill and creative talent, using tools made from shells and sharks' teeth and taking advantage of knots and grains. These gifted unnamed artists would rank high among the best animalists in the world. A loss of detail and paint from exposure to the elements occurred before the figures were immersed in the water.[9] Some closely resemble the carvings found at the Belle Glade Mound near the southeast shore of Lake Okeechobee, and those found at Key Marco on the Gulf coast near Naples by Frank Hamilton Cushing.[10] The Fisheating Creek birds and animals are conserved at the Florida Museum of Natural History at the University of Florida in Gainesville.

What were the architects and sculptors conveying in their ritual constructions and carved images? With penetrating observation of the animals and birds in their local wetlands environment, the sculptures are realistically rendered with an emphasis on physical attributes (speed, flight, strength, keen eyesight, hooked and long beaks). As conjectured by Sears, a number are fish-catching waterbirds. Were these attributes intentionally associated with the culture's subsistence, with deceased individuals, and/or with tribal identities? Were they effigy markers symbolizing "other selves" or guardian spirit-protectors in death's journey? Possibilities are endless. Archaeologist Ryan Wheeler sees the pond as a ritual charnel pond similar to Windover and Florida's other aquatic burial sites, where burials were placed underwater and marked with the carved posts.[11] Archaeologist Jerald Milanich wonders if the bundles of bones might have been actually attached to effigy marker posts instead of laid on a platform.[12]

As to mystical powers, one would be remiss not to mention analogous bird representations in prehistoric times and places, if only to stretch the mind as to possibilities in architectural symbolism in Florida. Bird-on-pole symbolism, for example, is as old as the Paleolithic Cave of Lascaux in France, where a shaman is depicted with a staff surmounted by a bird symbolizing the flight of the spirit. In the second century, Romans worshiped their ceremonial signas (standards), which were wood poles topped with golden eagles as emblems of the empire associated with their supreme god.[13] A bird on top of a graveyard post was recorded in nineteenth-century Canada as a symbol of the vertical arrangement of the universe and ascent to the sky-world.[14] In Florida, a carved wooden bird's head resembling a vulture was seen in 1743 by two Jesuits at Tequesta (Miami) and was identified by the Indians as the God of the cemetery.[15] An eagle image has long been a significant symbol of the American spirit, appearing on courthouse flagpoles, not to mention on currency and military buttons. But why were the effigy creatures, carved with such effort, conviction, and obvious importance to the ritual ceremony, left in Fisheating Creek's pond when the bones were retrieved and buried in the mound in Sears's theory?[16]

The pond excavated in the 1960s was roughly 5 feet deep, 70 feet long, 40 feet wide, and partially filled in by the slump of the adjacent burial mound. Its bottom had originally been flatly contoured below the water table and kept wet by clear water from underground seepage. Wet mud from this pond was used to build the mortuary (body-bundle preparation) mound, the earth enclosure wall, and the final burial mound. In some Woodland cultures, wet earth was pulled from river bottoms for ritual constructions. Was this wet architectural material symbolic? Fisheating Creek's wetland environment provided a subsistence of fish, turtles, and mussels, but did the pond's source of underground freshwater introduce a layer of religious symbolism—a belief about water's source in an underworld? Was there an ancient connection to burials in water holes?[17] On the other hand, wet earth might have been a firm building material and the "pond" a borrow pit that filled with water, and protected the bundled bones on a platform from predators—or ghosts.

The ceremonial center's enclosure was a low U-shaped earth embankment extending from the residential workshop around the burial mound and pond. Human bones were buried in this "wall" during its construction.

It was not high enough to discourage intruders or predators, but it might have protected the mortuary complex from Fisheating Creek floods. Or did it cordon off the elite burial rituals, or mark a spiritual zone? We might conjecture that it protected the dead from evil spirits outside, or conversely kept the ghosts of the dead and their feared putrification inside.[18] A similar enclosure was found at Crystal River, a National Historic Landmark on Florida's Gulf coast (plate 3), and at Adena–Hopewell sites in Ohio, but they, too, remain mysterious.[19]

However, what was excavated in the *eastern* wall of the body-preparation platform that abutted the pond suggests the designing architect-builders had expressed something of importance in a symbolic language. In the wall they had placed the following: "A single adult human skull [no gender identified] with the skull cap of an infant with traces of cutting on its margins, seven Busycon dippers, three Venus clam shells, a set of nested shells consisting alternately of four clam and four scallop shells, two bird-bone tubes, and the cut and worked mandible of a small carnivore."[20] They were placed there for a reason.

Belief in the burial mound's spiritual powers long outlasted the original builders. In the sixteenth and seventeenth centuries, human remains and offerings were placed at the top of the burial mound, and later still, a deceased Seminole in a cabbage palm "coffin" was interred in what was left of the center's 1,500-year-old human-made "pond."[21]

The Fisheating Creek complex has been leveled, and the Belle Glade wetlands region has been drained of the marshes and river sheds by nineteenth- and twentieth-century canals, managed rivers, and cattle ranching. In 1975, a house was permitted on one of the last remaining Belle Glade burial mounds.[22] Except for William Sears's work, the story of the architectural complex in Florida's natural wetlands that had existed for many centuries would be unknown, erased from the landscape. Its story awaits more telling in laboratory analyses of its excavated remains.

4 ✢ McKeithen Mounds

A Priestess in a Burnt Temple

The past is everywhere, if one only knows where and how to look. Nowhere in the United States is this more true than in Florida, where twelve thousand years of human history lie beneath our feet in archaeological sites.

JERALD MILANICH

AFTER A FINAL RITUAL, when the purification fires had spirited away all signs of death and putrefaction, the builders of the McKeithen Mounds in Columbia County capped the third of their three ceremonial mounds with white sand and walked away from their ritual complex. The year was about A.D. 475. For some 1,500 years, this sacred site lay hidden in north Florida, camouflaged by the grass and trees that had reclaimed it. Its conservation-minded twentieth-century owner, Lex McKeithen, has protected the site from vandals and development—except for one incident. While he was in Vietnam, grave robbers hit one of the mounds.[1]

During 1977–79, with Lex McKeithen's permission, archaeologist Jerald Milanich and his University of Florida team investigated the site and discovered four architectural surprises: (1) there were three mounds that formed an isosceles triangle in what appeared to be a comprehensive plan; (2) the apex mound (Mound B) had a commanding view of a central plaza and the village, and a line of sight toward the rising sun at the time of the summer solstice; (3) Mound B contained the tomb of an elite female whose body and burial were rife with supernatural symbolism; and (4) the mortuary (body preparation) platform (Mound A) due east of the entombed elite female had been constructed with a mysterious inner section of seven precise layers of specific earths known only to its builders. At their concluding ceremonies, each domical mound was capped with white sand that entombed within the mounds all traces of the dead, the mortuary paraphernalia and preparation mound, and concluding feast. These architectural activities took place between about A.D. 350 and 475 (fig. 4.1).

Adding to the mystery of the ritual architectural complex is the revelation that the village itself had taken shape earlier, about A.D. 200. Furthermore, despite the fact that ritual mound construction and ceremonies ended in the fifth century, the McKeithen village continued to exist until approximately

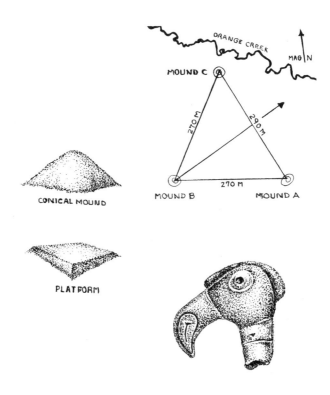

FIGURE 4.1. McKeithen Mounds Complex, A.D. 350–475. Columbia County. Archaeologists in 1977–79 discovered that the three McKeithen Mounds form an isosceles triangle. The apex mound had a commanding view of the plaza and village with a line of sight toward the rising sun at the time of the summer solstice. In that mound was the tomb of an elite female, perhaps a priestess. Her body and burial were rife with symbolism, including the red ceramic head of a raptorial bird placed at her feet in the east, and an anhinga bone in her red-ochred hair in the west. There are no written words or oral histories to explain the ritual mounds or their multiple symbols. Sketch by the author after Milanich et al., *Archaeology of Northern Florida a.d. 200–900*.

A.D. 750. It is unknown why a unique triangle of earthworks sprang forth and ended in the middle of the village's life span.[2]

This village was adjacent to a permanent creek, Orange Creek, which in A.D. 200 was in the middle of a band of water bodies and mesic hammocks, ideally situated for both aquatic and hammock resources. The freshwater aquatic habitat was larger than it is now, strung together by lakes, ponds, creeks, marshes and swamps that provided a variety of fish, turtles, reptiles, clams, mussels, mink, muskrat, otter, wading birds, and aquatic plants. Marine resources were available from the not-too-distant Gulf of Mexico and Atlantic Ocean. Deer and small terrestrial animals, nuts and fruits existed in the wooded areas between. There is no evidence that McKeithen villagers practiced maize cultivation or maize-related religious rituals.[3] Archaeologists identify their culture as Weeden Island; it preceded the development of the better-known Mississippian agricultural cultures north of Florida in the tenth century.[4]

According to the team excavating the site, Mound A was the "funeral parlor" where the deceased were ritually prepared. Mound A began as a raised rectangular earth platform (31 × 42 m) with a mysterious 12 × 14 m section that was composed of seven layers of specifically collected earths. They were systematically laid down behind a screen of pine posts. Each earth layer was 2–4 cm thick. A layer of organic matter was first, followed by three layers of dark-gray sand that alternated with two layers of yellowish-tan sand, and a final layer of organic matter that was identical to the first. On top of this seven-strata section, the builders spread a 25-cm layer of topsoil that hid the mysterious section from view. Milanich and his team conjectured that the deceased were placed in pits dug only into the special layers (to be defleshed by natural organisms). They also conjectured that the pine posts that screened the mysterious section might have been surmounted by ceramic effigies.[5] It is unknown what they might have marked or symbolized, such as the ritual's significance, or the metaphysical space, or the identities of the deceased.

Proceeding with the archaeologists' suggested ritual sequence, the defleshed long bones and skulls were exhumed from Mound A and coated (purified?) with red ochre. Almost the entire floor of the mortuary area had some red ochre on it. Bones and skulls were bundled and stored on Mound C in a wood-and-thatch charnel house to await the scheduled final ritual. Mound A's platform was then ritually purified: a layer of clean sand was spread over it, and the pine post screen was pulled down and set on fire. Fine-grained white sand (more than 1 meter thick) "taken from the meander belt of Orange Creek" capped and entombed all the evidence of the ritual, including the preparation mound and the ashes of the fire. When discovered after fifteen centuries of settling and weathering, Mound A was an elliptical domical mound 45 × 80 meters and 1.6 meters high—its architectural image reduced and grassed over similar to today's Crystal River mound (plate 3).[6]

Mound B was constructed on the highest elevation in the village, 3 meters higher than the plaza. It began with a rectangular flat-top platform (14 × 10.5 m), on which was constructed a wood structure (6.9 × 10.2 m, oriented 62.5 degrees east of north) that had the commanding view of the village and the rising sun. Inside the wood-and-thatch building, the archaeologists discovered several hearths and benches, and the shallow grave of a female in her mid- to late thirties. She was originally assumed to be a "gracile male," but with further osteological analyses, "he" became "she."[7] Over her grave a log tomb had been erected, and over the tomb was piled a layer of "insulating" earth that protected the tomb during the next ritual, in which the house of the deceased was set on fire and burned to the ground. Sand was brought to the site to cover and entomb the house ashes, the burial chamber, the platform mound, and all cultural accompaniments, including ritual ceramics, creating a circular sand mound 27 meters in diameter. She lies there today in her sepulcher, a skeleton with an arrowhead in her leg—a lady with no name.[8]

Who was the deceased? She was obviously important. Her body was not cremated, but was protected by the earth-insulated log tomb. Her mound abode was part temple and part astronomical observatory, and her body and burial ceremony were rife with symbolism. She lay on her back, on an east-west axis, her head to the west and the descending sun, but if she were to rise and take a breath of life, she would face east and the rising sun at the summer solstice. Her hair was colored with red ochre, and she wore a headdress ornamented with a leg bone of an anhinga, a black waterbird that can dive underwater to great depths and is associated in Maya religion, for example, with the underworld of water and death (see chapter 2). A small hole dug near her feet held a clay head of a crested raptorial bird that was painted red (fig. 4.1).[9] Lady McKeithen represented or impersonated something of value associated with accumulated symbols: bird imagery, black and red colors, and the cardinal directions west and east, which generally refer to the setting sun, death, and the underworld, and the sunrise and renewal.

Little is known about the status of women in precontact Florida. One was found buried at Jones Mound (Hillsborough County) with a precious stone duck or spoonbill effigy plummet.[10] Almost a thousand years after Lady McKeithen, a woman of similar age and status was buried at the Lake Jackson

Mounds (built ca. 1200–1500) near today's Tallahassee. On her breast was a very large copper gorget depicting a winged female bird-impersonator, a falcon dancer-warrior that incorporates design elements of the Mississippian belief system to the north. Sixteenth- and seventeenth-century Timucua women achieved the rank of chief (*cacica*), according to sixteenth- and seventeenth-century Spanish documents.[11] Late nineteenth- and early twentieth-century ethnohistoric studies in the American Southeast document matrilineal descent, and women as shamans as well as warriors. Women were also mythical symbols of good and evil, and of "earth mother" in control of natural forces. Cherokee myths in the early twentieth century depicted the sun as female and the source of light and life; she was called "the apportioner"—she could divide night and day, life and death.[12]

Lady McKeithen's mortuary architecture suggests she was a priestess/chief who was buried with symbols of her culture's supernatural beliefs. In 1564, René de Laudonnière, the commander of Fort Caroline (today's Jacksonville), recorded that *the body of the priest is also buried inside the house, and then they set fire to it.*[13] In addition to the fire ritual, the color red on the McKeithen platform floor and in the priestess's hair, as well as on the bird head, suggests intended symbolism. Red is associated with bloodlines and the sun deity in a number of early religions. Her anhinga headdress might be a symbol associated with the realm below the water's surface and the underworld, and her body's east-west axis might refer to her supernatural death journey as a metaphor for the sun. Her spirit will "die" in the west, travel through the underworld, and be reborn in the east with sun god attributes. Mound A, in other words, might have been about renewal: renewal of the sunrise, food resources, and of Earth.[14]

Mound C climaxes the ritual theater at McKeithen. It was the northernmost mound of the triangular complex. It began as a circular flat-top platform 15.7 meters in diameter. On it stood a wood-and-thatch charnel house where bone bundles were temporarily stored until their final ritual. Milanich and team conjecture that the bundled bones were removed to the edge of the circular platform, and the charnel house was set on fire. In every instance, they report, the bone bundles were deliberately placed on a layer of clean sand. A feast was prepared on top of the charnel house embers: one fish, one mud turtle, a liquid, and some medicinal plants were among the ceremonial ingredients. When the ritual feasting ended, sand was brought to the site and mounded over the charred remains of the charnel house, the platform mound, the bone bundles and all feast remnants—including the ceramic effigy vessels "killed" with a hole punched in the bottom to release spirits.

Buried under 4 feet of sand today are some seventy-two individuals, men, women, children. The oldest were in their sixties; the youngest was two.[15] Had the priestess's death preceded or follow theirs?

The seven layers of earths in Mound A are particularly intriguing. Did they symbolize a concept of the universe? In some of the world's religions and inspired architecture, the universe is depicted in layers. Eleventh-century architects at Angkor Wat in Cambodia depicted an underworld and six heavenly layers; the Maya depicted seven to thirteen celestial layers (depending on how one counts them) and four layers in the underworld; Hindus believed that the universe was divided into twenty-one cosmic zones, six heavens above earth and fourteen realms below; and in some American Southeastern Indian cultures, there were seven levels between the underworld and upperworld.[16] Mound A's inspiration, however, remains a mystery.

Mounds A, B, and C as described above formed a complex with integrated rituals. Even with its ancient mysteries obscured by antiquity, we sense that its architecture has tangible expressions of the culture's unseen beliefs.

5 ✠ Mount Royal

"A Magnificent Indian Mount"

The historical past was real, but the evidence that survives of it can be distorted and disconnected like a shadow cast on a field of rocks. The evidence includes . . . the bones of Indians whose deaths silenced personal stories that still await telling; buried artifacts that speak of technologies long forgotten; and earth constructions that speak of rituals long abandoned.

ROBERT HALL

IMAGINE PADDLING A CANOE up the St. Johns River about 240 years ago with William Bartram, and *fifty yards distance from the landing place,* seeing through the trees a huge conical mound, *a magnificent Indian mount.*[1] Six hundred years ago it would have startled even the most adventurous traveler: it was then mantled with blood-red sand, the final architectural activity on a highly visible landmark that had been some five hundred years in the making. With the last basket of red sand, the mound rose to a height of more than 20 feet from a base some 300 feet in diameter.[2] It was a holy place then, and it remains one now. Entombed within are generations of people, unknown by name, age, or gender (plate 5). Today, after five centuries of weathering, invasive trees growing from its top and sides, some plowing, illegal treasure hunting, and a well-meaning amateur archaeologist digging into it, the mound is still an immense and sacred landmark. Now it is owned by the State of Florida, donated in part by the owner with an additional section purchased. But it is caged in a protective chain-link fence, cut off from its oneness with the riverine landscape.

Mount Royal was named by the British. James Grant, the newly arrived British governor of East Florida, traveled the St. Johns River in 1764 with Martin Jollie, agent for John James Perceval II, the Earl of Egmont and Lord of the

Admiralty. Grant and Jollie were looking for acreage on which to locate a plantation for Egmont. Grant chose the site with the mound for the Lord of the Admiralty's "Noble House," and stayed two days selecting which trees to cut to open a "fine view" of what he saw as "one of the finest Rivers in the World." He told Lord Egmont: *The Mount is certainly the work of former inhabitants, but it must have been raised a hundred years ago, for the oak trees upon it are of that age.* One oak tree was so large that Governor Grant refused to cut it down, even though it blocked the view. And so the Indian "mount" on Lord Egmont's plantation became known as "Mount Royal."[3]

It is much older than Grant thought. Construction of the Indian "mount" had begun sometime in the ninth or tenth century in what was a very old architectural continuum along the St. Johns River drainage. Millennia-old burial mounds have been found at Tick Island, and at Thornhill Lake recently investigated by Jon Endonino (south of Mount Royal) and at Hontoon Island.[4] Grant was also unaware there had once been a precontact Indian village on the riverbank adjacent to the Mount Royal mound, or that the village was later the site of a Franciscan mission founded in 1595 according to documents found in Spanish archives by John Worth.[5]

Mount Royal rose with accumulating episodes of burials and material deposits. Its building sequences and cultural history, however, have not been investigated with modern archaeological technology. Its strategic location on the St. Johns River just north of where it intersects with Lake George suggests the builders' livelihood depended mostly on the resources and trade routes of the St. Johns River watershed and surrounding woodlands, as well as marine resources to the east. Freshwater fish and shellfish, marine animals, waterfowl, turtles, and aquatic plants are conjectured to have been the villagers' primary foodstuffs, supplemented with deer, small animals, nuts, and herbaceous plants. Artifacts retrieved in the nineteenth century from the upper (later) parts of the mound reveal that late in its history Mount Royal people were trading far and wide and with formative Mississippian cultures north of Florida. Evidence of local maize cultivation does not exist.[6]

Mount Royal's European discovery begins with oblique colonial references by the French of Fort Carolina in 1564 some two hundred years after the cessation of the mound's construction. They called a village near the mound Eneguape and described it as occupied by Timucua. The village is variously spelled in French and Spanish documents: Anacape, Enecape, Enacape, Anacapi, Enecaque, Anacabila. A Spanish mission was established there in 1595 known as San Antonio de Enecape, combining the Indian village name with that of the saint. In 1951 and 1956, with shovel tests and surface collections, archaeologist John M. Goggin found evidence of the mission structures near the burial mound. B. Calvin Jones found five structures in 1983, 1994 and 1995, one of which he interpreted as a convento. Mission San Antonio de Enecape (or Anacapi, Anacabila) was mentioned in Spanish reports in 1655 and on a 1683 map when it was occupied by immigrant Yamasee from coastal Georgia.[7]

In 1766, two years after Governor Grant's trip to Mount Royal, two intrepid exploring botanists from Philadelphia, John Bartram and his son, William (Billy), made an extraordinary journey by foot and boat through north Florida and came across the startling ceremonial mound. John made note that it was *nearly round* and conical shaped, 20 feet high, rising from a base 300 feet in diameter. It had live oak trees 3 feet in diameter growing from the top. When William revisited the site a decade later, its wild state, which he remembered as having *an inexpressible air of grandeur,* had changed. The live oaks and palms had been shorn away by Lord Egmont's slaves. He made a sketch of the *magnificent Indian mount* (which he captioned as rising 40 feet) as well as the *great highway or avenue sunk below the common level of the earth.* Mount Royal differed from the Cherokee ceremonial centers he had visited, particularly in respect to the causeway, one end of which terminated at the mound, and the other either in a vast savanna or natural plain, or in an artificial pond or lake (fig. 5.1).[8]

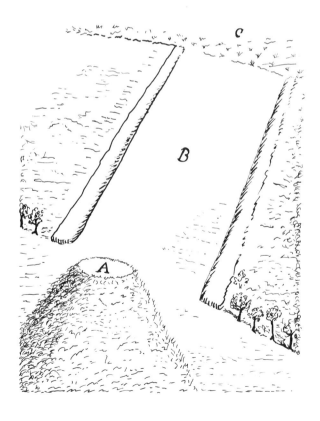

FIGURE 5.1. Mount Royal, Indian burial mound, ca. A.D. 800–1300, eighteenth-century sketch by William Bartram. Welaka, Putnam County. In the sketch of the "magnificent Indian Mount," Bartram illustrates "A," the mound (later discovered by archaeologists to have been capped with sand dyed blood-red); "B," the "noble Indian highway"; and "C," the human-made pond or natural lake. After centuries of trees growing out of the mound, erosion, and plowing, this burial mound is still impressive. Entombed within are generations of the deceased who lived by and harvested the St. Johns River. Redrawn by the author after Edwin H. Davis, National Anthropological Archives, Smithsonian Institution.

Mount Royal was excavated by Clarence B. Moore from March 31 to April 17, 1893, and from February 20 to March 14, 1894. It is easy to have a love-hate relationship with Moore, who dug, trenched, and extracted artifacts from the mound before today's scientific era. He disturbed the mound's cultural matrix, moving materials that today could date and tell the larger story of Mount Royal. However, he did record his finds with meticulous notes, and he beat the grave robbers who would have pillaged the mound in secrecy. Moore sent his observations and materials to the Academy of Natural Sciences of Philadelphia. Mount Royal was but one of many hundreds of Florida burial mounds that Moore dug into, including eighty-three on the St. Johns River. Moore was a wealthy, Harvard-educated Philadelphian who was driven to explore. He outfitted several steamboats with an office, photographic factory, and artifact laboratory. He arrived at sites "with his cook, steward, engineer, and captain," but hired his waiters locally and "colored gentlemen" to excavate.[9]

Moore's 1894 report begins: *On the east bank of the St. Johns, just below where the river leaves Lake George, in a great grove of bearing orange trees not 300 yards from the water's edge, stands Mt. Royal.* Moore measured Mount Royal at 16 feet high (slumped by tree removal, rain, and plowing after the Bartram visits) and its circumference at 555 feet, but noted *evidence of a much greater height in former times.* He found the base was a mixture of sand and charcoal, and he discovered that layers and pockets of yellow, white, and red-dyed sand held the deposits of pottery and human remains. They were *in every portion of the excavation.* These architectural features were common at other sites excavated by Moore and later archaeologists in the St. Johns River region. Mount Royal was unique in its deposits of *Busycons* (whelks) grouped in unusual numbers: 136 in one group, and 1,307 in one trench.[10]

After the last deposits of human remains and cultural items (a century or two before the Spanish settled St. Augustine), the huge completed mound was mantled with red sand up to 7 feet thick on the northeast side. Archaeologists working in the region have reported finding similar red mantles: Ryan Wheeler reported one mound with so much red ochre that "it ran red like blood when it rained." Jerald Milanich wrote, "the first time I saw red-dyed strata I was blown away."[11]

Among the Indians of the Americas, the color red was used in architectural symbolism with various overlapping ideas, including blood and bloodlines, the sun deity and death and rebirth, and the cardinal direction east. Red ochre was smeared across mound floors, painted on surfaces, applied to ritual paraphernalia, hair, bodies, and bones of the dead (see chapter 4). In the *Popol Vuh,* the sacred book of Maya myths and history (written before the Spanish arrived), and the Maya story of the world's creation, the founding town of the Maya is described as having a large mound painted red. In Mexico, the Pyramid of the Niches at El Tajín, Veracruz, ca. A.D. 600–800, was entirely painted red and associated with beliefs about death and supernatural rebirth.[12] In Florida, Mount Royal's red has unknown meanings.[13]

Among Moore's finds in the upper (later) levels of Mount Royal were numerous copper trade items. Copper was highly esteemed by American Indians. Two copper plates (about 11 inches square) were discovered 5 feet under Mount Royal's surface, wrapped in reeds with woven vegetable fibers and backed with bark and wood. They are embossed with images of forked or winged-eyes, concentric circles, and geometric figures, imagery linked with the Southeastern Ceremonial Complex of the Mississippian cultural region (ca. A.D. 1000–1300). A similar plate was found in Spiro, Oklahoma. Mount Royal's plates were not made locally, and it has been suggested by archaeologist Keith Ashley that Mount Royal in later years had become a center for trade, such as whelks for copper.[14]

Mount Royal's mysterious "avenue" and "pond" were described in three separate visits: the first in 1766 by John Bartram, the second by William, his son, in 1774, and the third by Clarence Moore in 1893. John Bartram wrote:

> directly north from the tumulus is a fine straight avenue about 60 yards broad; all the surface of which has been taken off, and thrown on each side, which makes a bank of about a rood [rod, 16.5 feet] wide, and a foot high, more or less, as the unevenness of the ground required, for the avenue is as level as a floor from bank to bank, and continues so for about three-quarters of a mile to a pond of about 100 yards broad and 150 yards long, N. and S. seem to be an oblong square and its banks 4 feet perpendicular . . . by its irregularity it seems to be artificial.[15]

William (Billy) Bartram, revisiting the mound, in 1774 described it as

> a noble Indian highway, which led from the great mount, on a straight line, three quarters of a mile, . . . on the verge of an oblong artificial lake, which was on the edge of an extensive green level savanna. This grand highway was about fifty yards wide, sunk a little below the common level, and the earth thrown up on each side, making a bank of about two feet high.[16] (fig. 5.1)

About a hundred years later, in 1872, Jefferies Wyman had also seen the "avenue" to the pond, but it was overgrown with trees. Two decades later, however, Clarence Moore described the avenue as still readily traceable, though its point of union with the mound is no longer visible. Its course is north about half a mile to the pond, where water lilies were in flower at the time of our visit. It consists of a depression from twelve to twenty yards in width at different points, between embankments of sand with an average height of 2.5 feet, and 12 feet in breadth.[17]

Mount Royal's "avenue" in aerial photographs is estimated to be 820 yards long and 12–15 feet wide.[18] Other precontact "avenues" in the St. Johns watershed are suggested at Shields Mound, Grant Mound, Murphy Island, Thursby Mound, and possibly Drayton Island.[19] Drayton Island, located near Mount Royal, is thought to be "Edelano," a sixteenth-century Timucua village with an avenue described by René de Laudonnière in 1565, and possibly by Solís de Merás in 1567, and by William Bartram in the eighteenth century.[20]

Avenues or processional ways have long been used in spiritual practice. The Great Cursus at Stonehenge was a long white avenue that was banked on each side about five thousand years ago. The Maya had their *sacbe,* and Europeans and Americans alike have processional aisles in their cathedrals and churches.

Mount Royal is still with us, and still impressive even shorn of its riverside village and mortuary grandeur with its symbolic red mantle. It had been a temple of ritual interments for centuries, and it had witnessed a Spanish mission; a failed English plantation whose seventy-three slaves plowed its sides and cut trees from its top; several orange groves planted around its periphery; C. B. Moore digging; and of late a housing development. It is an enduring organic sacred space with cultural mysteries awaiting more telling.

6 ✛ Round, Because the Circle Is the Perfect Symbol?

Whether the product of an eastern or a western culture, the circular mandala or sacred diagram is a familiar and pervasive image throughout the history of art . . . whether in the form of paintings or buildings or dances. . . . They are most often in some way cosmological: that is, they represent in symbol what is thought to be the essential structure of the universe.

ROBERT LAWLER

A CIRCLE IS MANY THINGS beyond its geometric figure. A circle is the universe, the sun and earth, the pupil of the eye and the navel. In all times, cultures have observed circular forms in nature and sky and the human body and found in them their symbols of one and center, unity and creation, of cosmos and life's cycles, of deities and their abodes, of divinity and power. In North America, the Lakotas believe that "all things spiritual are within the circle." In Europe, the halo, nimbus, or aureole encircles the head of Christian saints. Bramante's design for St. Peter's in Rome was round and domed—"round because the circle, without beginning or end, is the perfect symbol of God."[1]

Could two architectural circles created in ancient Florida invite speculation as to these sacred principles? One was carved in the bedrock limestone at the mouth of a freshwater creek (now the Miami River) where it met the saltwater bay (now Biscayne Bay); the other was laid down in pine poles in the earth on a hilltop (now Tallahassee). They were separated by a thousand-some years, hundreds of miles, and different languages and cultures. Yet, in their stories as told below, there is a sense that they are both in their own way connected to beliefs about the circle that are simultaneously old and new and beyond the limits of the geometric figure.

The Miami Circle

Some two thousand years ago, people carved a circular feature in limestone at Miami's Brickell Point (Dade County). It was discovered in 1998, and since then has been known as the "Miami Circle" (fig. 6.1). Its circumference is composed of twenty-four semi-rectangular basins cut into the bedrock. Within each basin are circular and ovoid holes pecked into the basins' bottoms. The circle's diameter is 11.6 meters; the basins are some 56–74 centimeters long by 30–45 centimeters deep. Who the builders were and where they came from are unknown, but in theory the site was occupied by people from about 750 B.C.–A.D. 1200, a cultural period described by archaeologists as Glades I–Glades II. They might have been ancestors of the Tequesta, who occupied the site during the Spanish colonial period. Their cutting tools were made from the columella of the whelk (*Busycon*) hafted to a wood handle. Many of its mysteries remain unsolved, but it is currently thought that the holes in the basins held wooden posts: they may have elevated a structure, or defined a ritual, or an open-air enclosure that was part of a larger settlement hugging the ancient shorelines of Biscayne Bay and the Miami River.[2]

Rescuing the Miami Circle was almost as dramatic as the find itself. It was saved from a developer's backhoe at the last minute by a public that, according to one newspaper, cherished "its very own Stonehenge." The developer had attempted to restrict archaeological investigations in order to construct two commercial and residential high-rises on top of the circle, and failing that, he planned to cut the circle into blocks and wrench it from the site.[3] Today, the circle's Brickell Point site is owned by the State of Florida, 2.2 acres in downtown Miami whose preservation is made possible by the state's CARL program (see appendix 2) and private funds (plate 2).[4]

Archaeologists have recently found a second circular feature. It is across the Miami River to the north, about opposite the Miami Circle. It has three concentric circles composed of holes cut into the oolite limestone. Its site is called the Granada Site, and the circle itself is called the Royal Palm Circle, named after the site that was once the elegant Royal Palm Hotel, built by Henry Flagler in 1896. Before the Flagler era, the shores of the Miami River might have been inhabited by the Tequesta, who were occupying the region when Europeans arrived in the sixteenth century, but their connection, if any, with the people who created the two circles two thousand years ago is unknown.[5]

Numerous ancient human burial areas have been found in proximity to both circles. Burial mounds noted in the nineteenth-century diaries of several explorers were destroyed during the development of Miami before they

PART 1. Indian Florida: 6000 B.C. to Early Colonial Period

FIGURE 6.1. Archaeologists investigating the Miami Circle, Miami. Dade County. Pecked into the limestone some 2,000 years ago, the circular figure is conjectured to have held wood posts that might have elevated a structure or defined a ritual. In many cultures the world over, mankind has observed circles and cycles in nature and in the sky, and has practiced the ritual making of circles as a way to transfer a circle's perceived powers and divinity. Photocopy courtesy of HistoryMiami Archives and Research Center Collection.

could reveal their cultural information. One large, centuries-old mound near the mouth of the river, described as 20 feet high and 100 feet wide, stood out like a small hill and contained many bones. The centuries-old mound was unceremoniously leveled to make way for the veranda of Flagler's Royal Palm Hotel, which lasted only thirty years before being destroyed by the 1926 hurricane. Another sand-capped mound described as 10 feet high and 120 feet in diameter with numerous burials was also leveled, most likely when the Brickells subdivided their property. Still another was destroyed to make way for a church that no longer stands.[6] Scientific and historical curiosity was overrun by the enthusiasm to build Miami.

When mapping the newly discovered circle, archaeologists noted that the pattern of the large basins composing its circumference may have been reversed in the north and south halves during its construction. Two complementary opposites in stone-chipping techniques appear to each side of its east-west axis.[7] Was this intentional, reflecting a sacred principle? Beliefs in reversal behavior and duality have been documented in studies of the Maya and later North American Indians. Their bipolar stories told how nothing could exist by itself. Sacred ritual clowns of the Pueblo, Sioux, and Cheyenne sustain ancient beliefs in alter egos and second selves, and express the virtues and flaws of various gods who reverse behavior and say and do the opposite of what is meant. Day and night are thought to represent reversals of the upperworld and underworld (with complicated beliefs and rituals about the reversal of the sun, the renewal of nature, and weather magic). Among the Osage, an east-west axis regulated clan membership and social control, dividing villages to the south from villages to the north, where behavior and possessions had opposite characteristics. Through opposites, polar forces were generated and mediated and the proper balances in nature and cosmos were maintained. Thus, the "great mother" of the underworld sea, for example, is capable of yielding bounty as well as withholding it.[8] We may never know if similar symbolic thinking was involved in creating the Miami Circle.

Material artifacts at the circle site that is so close to the shoreline are few. Among them are items from freshwater and saltwater resources: sharks' teeth, stingray spines, barracuda and sawfish teeth, *Busycon* (whelk) and *Strombus* (conch) shells—as well as some items traded from Lake Okeechobee and Fort Center, and as far away as Georgia and Missouri.[9] Later, between A.D. 1530 and 1680—long past the time of the circle's makers—a sea-turtle carapace, a dolphin cranium, and a shark were laid east to west within the Miami Circle.[10] How had the spirit of this site lingered or come to be reinterpreted a millennia beyond its ritual inception?

While archaeologists pursue scientific answers to its mysteries, a virtual view of the circle's natural environment and aquatic subsistence might suggest some of its spiritual underpinnings. Brickell Point was then naturally contoured with none of today's bulkheads or tall buildings (plate 2). Its eastern shoreline was lapped by the saltwater bay, and its northern edge was washed by the fresh waters descending from the river of grass, the Everglades. These salty and sweet waters were the primary sources of the circle builders' food and transportation routes. The circle makers looked eastward unimpeded at the great circle of light and warmth of the sun rising from underneath the edge of the world to begin its daily journey over earth before descending in the west. Similarly, they watched the cycles of the moon grow into a full circle and send lunar tides and a beam of light across the night waters that must have equally weakened many a knee. In many prehistoric religions, the sun and moon were believed to have mystical powers, and this belief had its effects on ceremonial rituals performed in circles (fig. 6.2). At Brickell Point, did circle making have a ritual connection to a sky god, particularly to the sun that "died" in the west and had to be brought back to life? Surely the circle form was not incidental. The discovery of the Miami Circle enables us to

PART 1. Indian Florida: 6000 B.C. to Early Colonial Period

FIGURE 6.2. Sixteenth-century Indians dancing around posts set in a circle with carved faces. Unsigned engraving published in 1590 by Theodore de Bry that is the reverse of a painting by John White illustrating a Carolina Algonquian ceremonial ritual that he observed in 1585. The ritual, the circle, and the carved images suggest religious implications in the making of a circle. Photocopy courtesy of Florida State Archives.

contemplate Florida's natural world, its effects on early religious beliefs, and human creations that complemented nature and belief—and how we might treat their meaningful creations.

In 2009, Florida's Miami Circle was designated a National Historic Landmark.

Apalachee Council House

More than a thousand years after the making of the Miami Circle, a set of concentric circles was laid down ca. 1656 to give shape to an Apalachee council house (or *bujío,* the Spanish descriptive word brought from the Caribbean),[11] a building with religious and secular purposes. It was discovered by archaeologists in 1983 as they excavated the Spanish-period Mission San Luis in Tallahassee (Leon County). The council house was re-created in 2000 by the State of Florida on the mission's 50-acre site acquired by the same state program (Conservation and Recreation Lands, or CARL) that helped acquire the Miami Circle. Its representation was in accordance with the archaeological data and meticulous research, but using modern tools, equipment, and materials. Its breathtaking size and circular substance forces twenty-first-century Americans to rethink their views of Indian architecture (fig. 6.3).

FIGURE 6.3. Circular Indian architecture, ca. 1656, Apalachee council house framework, Mission San Luis, Tallahassee. Leon County. The ground plan of the enormous seventeenth-century Apalachee council house, replicated in 2000 at Mission San Luis according to archaeological evidence, had a number of circular features, including the outermost posts set in a circle, several seating circles, and the circular hearth at the center of the great circle. Above the circular hearth was the circular eye-in-the-sky smoke hole. That the ritual making of such circles might have spiritual meaning is suggested in Indian myths recorded elsewhere in the United States. Photograph 2000 by the author.

Excavations revealed the seventeenth-century circular footprints and conical form. Concentric circles (defined by postholes) move toward the center, the hearth and sacred fire, above which is another circular form, the eye-in-the-sky opening. The outermost circle has an exterior circumference of 376 feet; its diameter is 120 feet. Inside of this circle, the next three circles support encircling benches, the innermost bench of which was for the ruling elite. A fifth circle is made up of the eight large weight-bearing timbers that support the massive 50-foot-tall conical framework. At the center of the council house, the large circular hearth is 14 feet in diameter, and towering above it is the large circular opening and smoke hole about 45 feet in diameter. These seven circular elements that compose the form and substance of the council house structure may or may not have symbolic significance.[12]

Spanish documents hint of spiritual concepts in the council-house architecture. Eyewitnesses report the seventeenth-century Apalachee continued to believe in their own spiritual leaders and healers despite their conversion to Catholicism. This is borne out in the discovery that they erected their council house at the mission without Spanish tools or building practices even though they were available—the Apalachee remained faithful to their own ancestral building traditions. They would, however, employ Spanish tools, fasteners, and methods to build the European building, the Spanish church. They felled the enormous council-house timbers with fire, and joined the circular framework together with plant and animal cordage. No wrought-iron spikes or nails were used. According to archaeologist Bonnie McEwan, some 56,000 palm fronds covered the framework. In 1674, Gabriel Díaz Vara Calderón, bishop of Cuba, visited the Florida missions and wrote Queen Mariana of Spain that the council houses were capable of holding some 2,000–3,000 people.[13]

The council house was the only building in which the ritual tea (casina) was drunk, and in which the sacred-secular dance ceremonies were held. A special seat was reserved for the principal chief, who might also have traditionally been the supreme religious leader. His seat was higher than all the rest, and faced *east,* the direction generally linked to the sun and divine powers. Florida's Indians were described as worshipping the sun in sixteenth-century Spanish and French reports.[14] Also of note is the ball game itself played by the Apalachee, which hints of supernatural powers and origin myths. During pre–ball game ceremonies, new fires were lighted between the chief's and the ball players' benches in the council house and were used only to light the chief's tobacco.[15] Seven might have been a magic number in the ball game. One account of the mythic origin of the ball game associated winning with seven points.[16] It is highly speculative, however, that the council house's seven circles are intentional symbols of ancestral myths. More obvious is that its size symbolized the Apalachee chief-priest's powers. But, is its resemblance to the conical burial mound form a coincidence of its construction? (fig. 7.1).

American Indians in North America in general believed that powers vested in the circle could be magically transferred by the ritual making of circles. They inscribed circles in sand and stamped their pottery and copper amulets with circles and spirals; they built round kivas, sun-dance and medicine lodges, and encircling earthen enclosures. Natchez people walked in spirals as they bore their dead leader of the Sun Lineage to the temple. Circles that imitated cosmic bodies did not disturb the natural order or offend supernatural powers.[17] A Pawnee myth explains much more—and illustrates Florida's loss when its Indian cultures came to their early end during colonization. Pawnee lodges are generally 50-feet-tall conical thatched structures. They are begun with a large post placed in the center of the house site. An Indian at its top draws together the vertical structural poles that are set in the ground to form the lodge's circumference. When all is secured, the center post that had marked the center is removed, and a hearth is made in its place. This traditional construction is explained by the creation myth in which the first Pawnee lodge was built when the daughter of Morning Star and Evening Star, and the son of Sun and Moon, were created. An ash tree magically grew where the center of their lodge was to be built. When the lodge was complete, the Sun sent down fire to consume the ash tree, leaving the central hearth, sacred fire, and a smoke hole in the center of the lodge roof.[18] Did a similar myth guide the builders' hands in Florida?

There are also "First People" myths recorded among nineteenth-century Southeastern American Indians that stir up the imagination about links between magic mound/mountains, burial mounds, and council houses. They describe people emerging from earth womb-mounds to receive their culture, knowledge, and first sacred fires, and hollow chambers made inside mounds for creation and purification rites (chapter 7).

American Indian archaeologist Daniel T. Panton summarizes the commonality of beliefs in things circular among American Indians: "Power is thought of as an impersonal force that permeates all creation; this force is often represented as circles or spirals, signs observed in nature (sun and moon, spiraling flights of birds, seasonal rounds), and that in these signs they found a world-view and religion."[19]

Beliefs in the principles of center, sun, and the divine in sacred circles in architecture are universal. Symbolic circles have been created in great quantities and with dazzling diversity: Stonehenge in England; Angkor Wat in Cambodia; Borobudur in Java; rose windows in Europe; and the magnificent dome in St. Peter's in Rome. There is a circular labyrinth in the floor of the Cathedral of Chartres in France that symbolically leads upward to heaven. The coronation of English kings and queens takes place in a circle embedded in the floor of Westminster Abbey. If such circles conveyed religious beliefs, origin myths, or kingly or supernatural powers, why not at the edge of Biscayne Bay or in the hills of Apalachee Florida?

7 ✦ "That's Not Just a Work of Art— That's Our Godhead"

If translated into ritual . . . a good myth showed you how to cope with mortality, discover an inner source of strength, and endure pain and sorrow with serenity.

KAREN ARMSTRONG

WE STAND OVER archaeological pits to discover Florida's first people. This chapter is written to convey a sense of the mysteriousness of their burial mounds beyond the artifacts. It looks at myths, whale bones, Earth Divers, magic mounds, and universal shell symbolism to bestow on the mound builders a cultural past imagined through their existing, little-understood architectural activities.

Sixteenth-Century Whalebone Ritual in Chief's House

Jesuit and Franciscan friars and Spanish officials observed and recorded a few revealing Indian spiritual ways and verbalized beliefs. In 1568, Father Juan Rogel described the Calusa in southwest Florida as expressing to him that the Spanish *should let them be*, because they desired to live under their own belief systems, and because their forebears had lived under them *from the beginning of time.*

> *They [Calusa] say each man has three souls. One is the little pupil of the eye, another is the shadow that each one casts, and the last is the image of oneself that each one sees in a mirror or in a calm pool of water. And that when a man dies, they say that two of the souls leave the body and that the third one, which is the pupil of the eye, remains in the body always. And thus they go to the burial place to speak with the deceased ones and to ask their advice.*

When the Calusa challenged him about the Spanish belief that God cannot be seen, Rogel wrote to his superiors: *They say they have heard it said by their forebears that they saw God in their burials.*[1]

Along the same line of thought, Juan López de Velasco, a Spanish cosmographer, noted in 1569 the following Tequesta ritual in which the larger defleshed bones (skull and long bones) of their dead chief were placed in a box, which was placed in the dead chief's house. Upon killing a whale, they pull it in until it runs aground on the sand. *And the first thing that they do to it* [is that] *they open the head and extract two bones that it has in the skull and they throw these two bones in this box in which they place the deceased* [chief] *and in this they adore.* Hernando de Escalante Fontaneda similarly describes the Tequesta whale bone custom, and concludes his memorial with the following: *Then the whole village comes there and they hold these bones as their gods.*[2]

In the Tequesta ritual, their dead chief becomes divine. His deification translated into ritual thus became real, tangible, and visible. Did the chief's house substitute for the burial mound of more ancient times? (fig. 7.1). One wonders if his divinity and mythic supernatural powers were associated with the sea mammal because since the beginning of time their ancestors were dependent on fishing and diving for survival. Escalante Fontaneda, a Spanish captive of the Calusa since he was shipwrecked at age ten, was freed by Pedro Menéndez de Avilés in 1566 and wrote ca. 1575 that certain seafood separated the elite hierarchy from the common people and was central to their concept of power: *The common food is fish, turtle and snails (all of which are alike fish) and tunny and whale. Some eat sea-wolves; (manati, dugons) not all of them, for there is a distinction between the higher and the lower classes, but the principal persons eat them.*[3]

In north Florida, according to the correspondence of Governor Menéndez Marquez in 1579, the Timucua similarly *showed no sign of abandoning their ancestral religion.*[4] A few of the ancestral supernatural beliefs about fish and fishing may be apparent in the following observations. Fray Francisco Pareja, a Franciscan who arrived in 1595 at Mission San Juan del Puerto (Fort George Island), where he served for decades, wrote that Timucua Indians *refrained from eating fish after a death,* and *prayed to the first fish caught.* Jesuit Joseph Javier Alaña in 1760 described an Indian shaman-healer in south Florida as *accustomed to calling the winds with certain whistles* and able to ward off the hurricanes with growls. People of the Keys, Alaña noted, kept a principal *idol* in the form of a wood tablet in the image of a fish. He described it as resembling a barracuda. He also noted they had a ritual mask called *sipi,* which possibly meant "stock, impale, harpoon."[5]

FIGURE 7.1. Conical Apalachee council house (1656) re-created at Mission San Luis (2000), Tallahassee. Leon County. Excavation data reveal that the council house was constructed in the seventeenth century according to ancestral practices, without using the Spanish tools and fasteners that were available. In addition, myths recorded and practices observed by Spanish friars in sixteenth- and seventeenth-century Florida support the suggestion that the chief's house had spiritual significance, if not a link to the ancient conical burial mounds. Photograph by Merald Clark, courtesy Anthropology Division of the Florida Museum of Natural History.

Scant as these references are, they may be vestiges of ancient beliefs held in pre-Columbian Florida. Some of these beliefs might be symbolized in the precontact burial mounds built when Florida's Indians subsisted on seafood. Effigy plummets (fish-line sinkers and net weights shaped from the conch or whelk columella), for example, might be symbolic when buried with the deceased Indian leaders.[6] What do the utilitarian fishing-tackle objects rendered artistically in other materials, including stone, mean when worn by dead chiefs and priests in their ritual burial mounds? Do objects with seafood-subsistence connotations take on new meaning in death rituals? Items like the anhinga bone (a diving waterbird) placed in the priestess's hair at McKeithen Mounds, and the whale bones placed next to the Tequesta chief's bones in the same box suggest they are symbols of supernatural powers bestowed on priests and chiefs in their death-rebirth journey.

Mythic Mounds

In *Archaeology of the Soul,* archaeologist Robert Hall makes the point that American Indian rituals are seldom without their origin myth.[7] Many origin myths worldwide begin with water and earth-mound principles. In some places, they come together in architectural symbols that affirm divine connections. We will explore this line of thinking first in a water-earth origin myth, then in a mound origin myth, followed by architectural examples. They were collected in the nineteenth century and found to be widespread among various American Indian cultures.

The water-earth myth is thought to have migrated much earlier from eastern Europe through the Balkans eastward across Russia to Mongolia and into Canada and the United States. In its various versions, water covered the universe in the beginning, and Earth was formed when clumps of mud were brought up from under the water by creatures known as "Earth Divers." Earth Divers were crawfish in the mythology of the Creek, Shawnee, and Osage. The Cherokee Earth Diver was a water beetle. The Ojibwas, Ottawas, Foxes, and Onondagas believed it was a muskrat. The Cheyenne had a mudhen. The Arikaras had a duck, and the Arapahoes a red-headed duck. Is it a coincidence that the bones or carved images of diving-fishing waterbirds appear in sacred context exclusively with female burials in Florida's ancient mounds? At McKeithen Mounds (chapter 4), the anhinga bone was placed in the red-ochred hair of the elite female. Waterbird bones are not found in middens (domestic trash heaps), suggesting that they might have had sacred status and were a food taboo.[8]

Another origin myth casts an interesting light on Florida's burial mounds. "First People" myths collected in the nineteenth century in the American Southeast frequently depict people emerging from human-made mounds, or receiving their culture, their laws, and their sacred fire on a mountain or its symbol, the earthen mound. In the Smoky Mountains of western North Carolina, Kituwah is a great earthen mound that is still widely held to be "sacred ground, the place where the people we call Cherokee began." It is described as the "storied birthplace of the Cherokee" where they received "their laws and first fire"—the fire is a symbol of the sun, their main deity. A Cherokee descendant refers to it as the "holiest of holies."[9]

Choctaw people in Mississippi recently participated in the excavation of their own sacred mound. According to their beliefs, "newly formed humans emerged from the birth cave [together with locust], and after drying out atop the sacred Nanih Waiya mound, scattered across the land, becoming the various Muskogean tribes." Coweta-Kashita and Creek myths had sacred mountain symbols representing the "foundation of all things." In the Coweta-Kashita version of the mound myth, a hollow chamber was made inside a mound for creation and purification rites. Chickasaws referred to artificial human-made mounds as "navels" with a concept of the center of man and center of Earth, using words (*bokko, nånih*) that equally meant hills and mountains. James Mooney in the late nineteenth century collected Cherokee stories in which "the streams that come down from the mountains are the trails by which we reach this underworld, and the springs at their heads are the doorways by which we enter it."[10]

Human-made mounds exist around the world in the form of ziggurats, temples, and pyramids that were historically believed to be "magic mountains," expressing many of the sacred principles that make up "religion" and holy sites. They were endowed with accumulative symbolism of upward paths to life in higher places. They served as burial chambers of god-kings and affirmed divine connections—and they were the landmarks of community identity.[11]

Two thousand years ago at Teotihuacan, central Mexico, the mound now known as the Pyramid of the Sun on the Avenue of the Dead was known as "the place where man becomes divine." Teotihuacan's most famous mural depicts a personified mountain from which flows a river with images of abundance.[12] Maya legends compiled in the sixteenth-century sacred book *Popol Vuh* spoke of mountains as metaphorical places where sacred bundles were kept to represent their ancestors as symbols of their powers and sovereignty as founding fathers. In this same sacred book, the founding Maya town had a large mound painted red.[13] Angkor Wat, Cambodia, represents a mountain rising out of a body of water, and the Babylonian ziggurat El-Temen-An-Ki meant "house of the Foundation of Heaven and Earth." The Ptolemaic Temple of Edfu ("Foundation Ground of the Gods of the Beginnings") had an inner sanctum, known as the High Seat, or "mythical mound of primordial creation," under which ran a stream of holy water.[14]

Shells: A Form of Symbolism?

Shells are placed in numerous ways in the architectural compositions of Florida's pre-Columbian burial mounds. Did the conchs, whelks, Venus clams, oysters, and scallop shells, for example, symbolize something beyond their utilitarian uses as drinking cups, dippers, fish-net weights, and jewelry when ornamenting and bedding the kingly bones? Did they connect the dead to origin myths, or invest the dead and the mound with divine powers as to the harvests of aquatic species that were the staple foods?

What archaeologist William Sears found on the east side of the mortuary platform at Fisheating Creek (chapter 3) was not a random grouping of shells. The "adult human skull" and the "skull cap of an infant" were placed with a purpose with "seven *Busycon* (conch) dippers, three *Venus* clam shells, a set of nested shells consisting alternately of four clam and four scallop shells."[15]

In northeast Florida, when a Timucua chief died, according to René de Laudonnière (commander of Fort Caroline in 1564), the ceremonial cup from which the chief *always used to drink* was placed on his burial mound. An engraving (attributed to a drawing by the fort's artist, Jacques le Moyne), published in Frankfurt, Germany, in 1591 by Theodore de Bry of Liège, depicts a shell placed on a chief's burial mound (fig. 7.2). Did the shell, like the whale bones in the burial ritual described above, symbolize a chief's divinity? De Bry's depiction uses the South Pacific nautilus that was prized by Renaissance Europe rather than the Florida whelk, which was then little known, but has since been found in abundance in Florida's burial mounds.[16]

Exploring the universal uses of conch shells as symbols of religious beliefs, creation myths, supernatural powers, and communications with ancestors reveals the following. Conch shells were ritual cups for consecrated water in Hinduism and Buddhism; the dancing Shiva of Hindu myth holds the shell in one hand as an instrument through which he initiates creation. Conch shells were directly associated with fertility and the god of water in Minoan art in ancient Crete (ca. 3000 B.C.), and in the murals of the people of Teotihuacan, Mexico (ca. 100 B.C.–A.D. 1000), as well as in the arts of the Aztecs (ca. 1200–1500). Triton, the Greek god and son of Poseidon, who lived at the bottom of the sea, was characteristically depicted with a conch shell in his hand with which he convened the river deities.[17] Classic Period Maya (ca. A.D. 200–900) depicted conch shells as trumpets that called forth supernatural powers. They also depicted conch shells in the watery underworld with emerging human heads.

In addition to the conchs and whelks, other types of shells have been used to symbolically depict the spirit world. An oyster shell with a piece of jade placed inside was found in a Maya tomb in Copan, Honduras, where it symbolized the underworld and the king's soul. An image carved on the tomb of King Pakal (K'inich Janaab' Pakal) at Palenque, Mexico, shows him sliding into a watery underworld in A.D. 648 symbolized by shells and accompanying explanatory glyphs.[18] Sandro Botticelli in 1480 painted the birth of Venus in a scallop shell, and in Spain, the scallop shell is still the symbol of Saint James and his miracles, and of the Knights of the Order of Santiago (St. James), and the pilgrims and pilgrimages to his holy site, the Cathedral of Santiago de Compostela in Galicia (fig. 4).

If shells in documented examples speak of origin myths, underworlds, divine powers, heroes, gods, and saints, why not in shells like the "left-handed" lightning whelks (*Busycon sinistrum*) that were the principal drinking cups placed in ritual context in the Calusa burial mounds with a hole punched in them after the tea ceremony?[19] The more one ponders such possibilities and comparative examples, the more questions are raised. However, shells were more than cultural adornments. In Florida, shells and shellfish may have been a symbol of the Indian godhead.

FIGURE 7.2. Timucua chief's shell drinking cup on circular burial mound, ca. A.D. 1564. Theodore de Bry's engraving published in 1591 illustrates a Timucua chief's burial ritual observed by the French who built Fort Caroline in Jacksonville in 1564. The chief's shell drinking cup is depicted as a nautilus (sixteenth-century Europeans were not familiar with the Florida whelk or conch). The burial mound and shell iconography suggest the drinking cup is symbolic of the chief's powers and perhaps his divinity. Shells were symbolically used worldwide in ancient religions with many spiritual implications. Photocopy courtesy of Florida State Archives.

ORIE

OCCIDENS

10

PART 2

Colonial Florida

A.D. 1565 TO 1821

8 ✢ Planting Spanish Architectural Roots

And on the following day, the day of Our Lady of September [September 8], *the said Adelantado*
[Pedro Menéndez de Avilés] *landed near noon, and when he found many Indians awaiting him there,
as they had had tidings of him from the other Indians with whom he had spoken four days before; he
had a solemn mass said in honor of Our Lady, and when that was ended, he took possession of the
country in the name of his Majesty.*

GONZALO SOLÍS DE MERÁS, 1567

IN THIS WAY, in the words of an eyewitness 450 years ago,
St. Augustine was founded on September 8, 1565 (fig. 8.1).[1]
Its settlement unleashed momentous immediate local consequences for the arriving Spanish, the Timucua on whose
land they settled, and the French who had built Fort Caroline (1564) 40 miles to the north. Pedro Menéndez was a
licensed Spanish entrepreneur whose focus during the next
seven years assured his enterprise in Florida was a success.
While his followers constructed the campsite's first buildings and defenses with wood and palm fronds, he led soldiers north and captured Fort Caroline, after which he led
them south and massacred French stragglers in the sand
dunes at Matanzas ("massacre") Inlet. Within eight months
of landing, conditions pushed Spanish soldiers to mutiny
and the Timucua to become hostile, forcing the settlement
to relocate to Anastasia Island in May 1566.[2]

On Anastasia Island, the Spanish built an expedient fort
and a new town, and *casa fuertes* (blockhouses) to guard the
river inlets. Menéndez also established forts near today's St.
Lucie Inlet, Miami, and Tampa, and founded a settlement
at Santa Elena (now South Carolina), which he intended
to be the capital of Florida. Meanwhile, the procurement
of food and supplies and relationships with Indians was of
paramount concern. Spanish architecture in the first years
can only be described as expedient. By 1572, the Jesuits had

FIGURE 8.1. Conjectured place of Spanish landing, St. Augustine, 1565. St. Johns County. A giant stainless-steel cross and a sculpture representing the settlement's first parish priest, Francisco López de Mendoza Grajales, stand opposite the inlet, the "arm of the sea," through which Pedro Menéndez led his eight hundred Spanish settlers. Cross and priest commemorate the planting of the Spanish settlement and its Catholic religion in Florida. The sculpture is by Ivan Mestrovic, of Notre Dame University. Photograph 2011 by Kenneth M. Barrett Jr.

arrived and left (having failed to establish a successful Indian mission), and the sea was eating into the Anastasia Island presidio. The Spanish moved back to the mainland and laid out the town that is now the city of St. Augustine. Many perished in the founding of the nation's first permanent European colony. We are walking on their bones.

Part 2 tells the story of architectural activities that are central to colonial Florida.

The Spanish settlers' Roman Catholic religion—its beliefs, architectural traditions, and symbolism—contributed greatly to Florida's built environment. It starts with Ponce de León sighting and naming the peninsula in 1513 during Easter Week, la Pasqua de la Florida. He named the land "La Florida," honoring his religious beliefs in much the same way that Christopher Columbus, with similar devoutness, named his landfall "San Salvador" (Holy Savior), and the island "Trinidad" after the Holy Trinity.[3] In 1565, the mysticism of Pedro Menéndez de Avilés led him to name the colony he founded "San Agustín de la Florida" after Saint Augustine, theologian and bishop of Hippo (A.D. 354–430), on whose feast day (August 28) Menéndez first sighted Florida. Many Florida place-names to this day reflect the names of Catholic saints. Anastasia Island, for example, across from St. Augustine, was originally Santa Anastasia. Historian Susan Parker's research leads her to believe it was the name of the patroness saint of a chapel at the island's lighthouse: "You would not believe how many individuals I have told that the island is not named for the missing grand duchess of Russia." The Spanish coquina lighthouse was raised higher by the British and by the Americans, but in 1880 it slipped into the sea and oblivion—except for the name of its patroness saint. The new lighthouse, a 165-feet-tall conical brick tower painted black and white, is now the island's striking landmark and headquarters of an active maritime history and archaeology program.[4]

When Menéndez initially dropped anchor a league off St. Augustine's harbor entrance, he sent his captains ashore, but he himself did not disembark and claim the land for his king (Philip II) until September 8, *the day of Our Lady of September.*[5] "Our Lady" was the Virgin of Covadonga, patron saint of Asturias, Menéndez's home region in Spain, where she is called "Our Lady of September." Her holy feast day on September 8 is symbolically important in Spain's history: it marks the beginning of Christianity's ascendency over the infidels. According to Spanish legend, Don Pelayo, a Visigothic nobleman and first king of Asturias, led a small band of outnumbered Christians that defeated the Moors in 722 with the help of the Virgin, who appeared and gave them great hope and courage. Their victory is said to have inspired Christians to begin the Reconquest of the Iberian Peninsula. Pelayo and his Asturians took refuge in a cave in the Picos Mountains at Covadonga, today a beloved pilgrimage shrine dedicated to the Virgin and the tomb of Don Pelayo.[6] Menéndez likely had the Christian victory in mind as he landed among the Indians in Florida. And perhaps he thought about another legend when he chose the name for his flagship, *San Pelayo,* after a tenth-century boy who chose martyrdom after he was captured by Muslims.[7]

St. Augustine's sixteenth-century town plan and buildings were laid down during the glorious age of Europe's Renaissance, the age of the printed book and adventures of the mind, and of Spain's golden age of arts, literature, and architecture—and of gold and silver flowing to Seville from the New World. Michelangelo had died only the year before Menéndez landed. St. Augustine was founded when Spain's Catholic missionary work was expanding in the West Indies, and when the Protestant Queen Elizabeth I reigned in England (1588–1603). Catholics and Protestants were massacring each other in Europe (1562–90s). France and Spain were enemies in competition for claiming Florida. Challenges to the Catholic Church were not taken lightly: sixty-eight years after Menéndez landed, Galileo would be tried for heresy (1633) for expressing belief in Copernicus's view that the earth revolved around the sun in opposition to church teachings that the earth was the center of the universe.[8]

Menéndez defeated the French Protestants (Huguenots) at Fort Caroline in 1565 and gave us Spanish Florida. From the French, however, came some of the earliest descriptions and published images of Florida. The images were attributed to Fort Caroline's artist, Jacques le Moyne de Morgues. One drawing of a palisaded Indian village has been used for years in textbooks and other publications to illustrate Chief Seloy's village as the place where the Spanish landed and founded St. Augustine. A growing number of scholars today, however, doubt the accuracy of this and other Le Moyne drawings of Florida. They had to be redrawn from memory in Europe after Le Moyne escaped from the Spanish attack by swimming to a French ship. Further complicating their accuracy is the fact they were not engraved and published until 1591 in Frankfurt by Theodore de Bry of Liège—and that Le Moyne's "re-created" drawings have disappeared. De Bry's published images are now thought to have been composed by the engraver based on the French reports and images made elsewhere in the New World by other artists.[9] During the next two centuries, imaginary depictions of architecture in Florida were published by artists who had never set foot in Florida, but whose imaginations captivated a European public eager to know about the New World.[10]

Fort Caroline National Memorial (Duval County) was established in 1953. A fort representing the French fort was constructed with wood and earth berms in 1964 on a St. Johns River bluff, based on the de Bry etchings and French descriptions (fig. 8.2). Its original site had washed away after the river channel was deepened and widened in the 1880s. Remains of the fort still elude archaeologists. However, the twentieth-century Fort Caroline (now

FIGURE 8.2. French Fort Caroline, 1564, Jacksonville, depicted in a 1591 engraving by Theodore de Bry of Liège. Duval County. The French built their fort on a riverbank near the mouth of the St. Johns River. Soon after the founding of St. Augustine forty miles to the south, the Spanish marched north, defeated the French, captured the fort, and renamed it San Mateo, after the saint on whose day the fort was captured. The remains of the fort have not been found, but a hypothetical fort commemorating the French in Florida was built in 1964 based on de Bry's etching; it is now an "outdoor exhibit" in the Timucuan Ecological and Historic National Preserve administered by the National Park Service. Photocopy courtesy of Florida State Archives.

called an "outdoor exhibit") is a visual monument recalling the first decisive battle for Florida, and of Pedro Menéndez's victory that set in motion the permanent Spanish settlement and imprint on Florida's built landscape. Fort Caroline's story today is enlarged as part of the present Timucuan Ecological and Historic National Preserve, administered by the National Park Service, that tells the European arrival story in context with that of the Native American Timucuan people who populated the Atlantic Coast before and during the Spanish settlement.[11]

Philip II, king of Spain (1556–1598), also had an impact on colonial Florida architecture. He was the son of Charles I (Holy Roman Emperor Charles V), and was married (1554) to Catholic Mary Tudor, queen of England. His palace, El Escorial, was designed by Juan Bautista de Toledo and Juan de Herrera, the latter Spain's leading architect known for his restrained Renaissance Classicism (*desornamentado*) that established a new architectural style in Spain. In 1573, King Philip compiled and published a set of ordinances for planning new Spanish towns in the West Indies. It is suggested that his ordinances for laying out new towns influenced the planning of St. Augustine (chapter 9). Concerns and principles enumerated in the ordinances with respect to the street grid, the plaza, climate and environment, religious well-being, public health, home defense, and community aesthetics appear to have been implemented in St. Augustine's sixteenth-century town plan. It is the first comprehensive urban plan in the nation (fig. 2), and is the plan of the historic city today. The town plan is designated a National Historic Landmark.

Where there were once a hundred-some Spanish parish and mission churches, stretching north and south of the capital city of St. Augustine and west to San Luis (Tallahassee) and Pensacola, today there is only one, the stone Cathedral Basilica in St. Augustine, constructed during 1793–97 (plate 13). The church at Mission San Luis (late 1600s) has been replicated on its original site in wood and palm thatch according to the archaeological data (fig. 10.3). It resembles the 1586 and 1594 depictions of the first St. Augustine parish church Nuestra Señora de los Remedios, and the 1594 depiction of the church at Mission Nombre de Dios, north of St. Augustine, the first and longest surviving mission in what is now the continental United States (figs. 10.1, 11.1). Mission Nombre de Dios's last church was ornately carved in stone and stood until 1793. Nombre de Dios's architecture is no longer visible, but the site is a tourist destination that compels its little-known story to be told as conjectured from documents and archaeology (chapter 11).

The Cathedral Basilica story descends from those of the two previous parish churches, Nuestra Señora de los Remedios and Nuestra Señora de la Soledad. In its walls and entrance facade are the recycled stones and

Neoclassical-style portal surround of the last stone church at Mission Nombre de Dios. In 1887–88, following a fire, the cathedral was restored by James Renwick, one of America's best-known architects. In 1965, sweeping changes altered the interior. The Historic American Building Survey (HABS) is an important tool for studying the changes (fig. 14.5).

The Castillo de San Marcos and the Governor's (or Government) House, like the cathedral, were rooted in Florida soil in the sixteenth century in wood materials. Both were later rebuilt in stone, in 1695 and 1713 respectively. These public spaces are simultaneously sacred to Florida's Spanish past and to St. Augustine's future. Because of their unique roles in today's built landscape in sustaining cultural and heritage tourism, their stories are included in part 3, to emphasize the importance of architectural preservation.

Florida's colonial Spanish architectural landscape is in need of more archaeology and translations of historic documents. One of the many interesting aspects about colonial Spanish architecture in Florida is that the British during 1763–84 converted many Spanish buildings for their own uses. British engineers measured and recorded the Spanish buildings before they renovated them—and the returning Spanish similarly measured the British buildings. Britain's most lasting architectural contribution may be the records of its governors, engineers, and craftsmen describing the Spanish buildings they converted. They are archived in the Public Records Office in Kew, England (fig. 10.2).

The prejudiced treatment of Indians and blacks in architectural activities, and the institution of slavery were colonial reality—just as slavery will be an American reality in part 3. A pious friar in Florida believed that Indians who died in the mission system were the king's *gifts to heaven;* and the British governor, James Grant, wrote a letter expressing the popular belief of his time: *this country can only be brought to that rich and plentiful state by the labor of slaves.*[12] In the American period discussed in part 3, we will see slavery institutionalized in church, military, and public architecture. Architectural landmarks associated with slavery and the demise of Indian cultures should not be ignored or forgotten. Indian and African contributions are huge in the colonial built landscape. It is our misfortune that they are too little known and undervalued. Like the white colonists, Indians and Africans labored on Florida's founding architectural landmarks that record many truths about the first successful European settlement in the United States. They so labored despite the threat of death that came with every sail on the horizon, and every freeze, hurricane, and epidemic. We are thriving off their labors.

9 ✛ The Nation's Oldest Town Plan

Our house was not unsentient matter—it had a heart and soul . . . it was of us and we were in its confidence and lived in its grace and in the peace of its benedictions. We never came home from an absence that its face did not light up and speak out to us in eloquent welcome—and we could not enter it unmoved.

MARK TWAIN

ST. AUGUSTINE is like Twain's house. It still has the heart and soul of the settlement that began very small at the edge of a very large new world in the sixteenth century. It still has the grace and benedictions of narrow streets, a central plaza, and a geography that sent most large commercial interests westward to U.S. Route 1. Stroll the city's diverse streetscape and be comforted by its agelessness, its intimacy and human scale.

Even after 450 years, too much is still unknown about the city's architecture in the sixteenth to eighteenth centuries. Can we ever satisfy the quest to know how the town looked and changed, how it endured and was rebuilt after endless enemy-set fires, unannounced hurricanes and floods? Maybe answers will begin and end with the town plan.

Spanish colonists founded St. Augustine in 1565, but laid out the town we know in about 1572–73, after they left Anastasia Island and relocated back to the mainland. It took shape in the area south of today's plaza (plate 6).[1] This was a good site. Its port was protected in the lee of Anastasia Island, and a fort to the north kept a defensive watch on the *arm of the sea* (*brazo de mar*), the ocean inlet that was its lifeline. About this same time, Spain's King Philip II published his Royal Ordinances for laying out new Spanish towns in the West Indies. The ordinances, however, were not new—many of their principles came from experience and earlier town plans in New Spain (Mexico) and Caribbean colonies.

They are thought to have been compiled in consultation with the learned men of the Crown's court: engineer-architects, churchmen, meteorologists, artists, and hygienists.[2] The ordinances were comprehensive and grounded in Classical ideals. They specified a rational grid around a central public space, the plaza, with specific ideas about the plaza's harmonious proportions and the locations of the parish church and public buildings. They addressed concerns for the public welfare in their rules for urban defenses, cleanliness, health, and aesthetics, and for the spiritual well-being of people isolated from the mother country. By contrast, Boston grew haphazardly; and it was not until 1638 and 1682 respectively that New Haven, Connecticut, and Philadelphia, Pennsylvania, were designed in a rational manner with grids and public spaces.

There is no document that states that St. Augustine was planned with the ordinances in hand—either in its initial layout in 1572 or when the town was rebuilt after English fires twice destroyed its wood buildings in 1586 and 1702. However, if we walk the historic section of the twenty-first-century city with a translation of some of the ordinances and copies of various colonial maps and documents, we discover that the principles of the ordinances were followed and that the essence of the sixteenth-century plan still exists today (fig. 2). In other words, we discover the nation's first comprehensive building codes. But something more than building codes happened here. Far from the world's cultural capitals and wealth, the sixteenth-century Spanish planners and builders were simultaneously expedient, original, and flexible. Lessons were learned from the sea, after it *had eaten a large part of the island where the fort and town were* in 1566–72 and after *flood-tides and water of the sea have been consuming a great part of the place.*[3] This chapter looks at the principles expressed in the ordinances, and how they might have influenced St. Augustine's town plan. It looks to understand why, after four centuries and four changes in government nationality, the sixteenth-century town plan and its kinship with place endured. Did the ordinances provide a Classical layout that was so rational, comprehensive, and environmentally logical that it enabled the colonial settlement to endure?

Below are a few specific ordinances quoted in italics and underlined (my emphasis) for clarity in the descriptions that follow of the historic and contemporary town of St. Augustine.

Ordinances numbered 110 and 112, as well as 113, 114 and 115, demonstrate the importance of laying out the plaza first and with specific town-planning principles.[4]

Ordinance *110*. . . . [*T*]*he plan of the place shall be determined . . . beginning* *with the main plaza.*

Ordinance *112. The main plaza whence a beginning is to be made, if the town* *is situated on the seacoast, should be made at the landing place of the port. . . .* *The plaza shall be of an oblong form, which shall have at the least a length* *equal to one and a half times the width, inasmuch as this size is the best for* *fiestas in which horses are used and for any other fiestas that shall be held.*

These rules clearly reveal that a plaza in a new town was to be the first priority. They specify that it was to be at the port's landing and that its size should be relative to the town's shipping, social, and religious life. The earliest-known visual image of St. Augustine is Baptista Boazio's "battle plan" of Francis Drake's raid in 1586 (text box). Boazio's depiction shows an open *oblong* space extending west from the Matanzas River *landing place* as specified in ordinance 112.[5] Its boundaries illustrated by Boazio are as follows: in the west by an architectural complex marked "12" and "13" (English edition: "M," "the towne house"; and "N," "the lookout"); in the north by cornfields, and in the south by the town buildings. The parish church occupies the southeast corner space according to ordinances 119, 120 and 121 quoted below (fig. 9.1; plate 6).

The map of St. Augustine that is attributed to Baptista Boazio depicts St. Augustine as of May 28–30, 1586, before it was set on fire by Francis Drake. Boazio drew the "battle plan" in England, and it was later engraved to accompany the first edition of Captain Walter Bigges's journal about Drake's Caribbean expedition of 1585–86. Boazio, an Italian artist living in London (1588–1606), drew five maps of the fleet's voyage from reports by participants and witnesses. Boazio's signature is only on the general map of the fleet's route, but his authorship of the five maps is noted in the second English edition of Walter Bigges's *A Summarie and True Discourse of Sir Frances Drakes West Indian Voyage*, printed in London by Roger Ward in 1589. There is no indication that Boazio accompanied Drake on the voyage. The engraver is tentatively suggested to have been Jodocus Hondius. The first editions of Bigges's journal were published in Latin and French in 1588. Boazio's four maps of the cities raided (Santiago, San Domingo, Cartagena, and St. Augustine) were issued to accompany the journal in two sizes. The larger size has Latin inscriptions and accompanied the first Latin edition of Bigges's *Summarie* under the title *Expeditio Francisci Draki Eqvitis Angli in Indias Occidentale* (1588). A copy of the large St. Augustine map from one of the 1589 English editions has an English key. The smaller maps have captions in Latin and French. There are slight differences in details of St. Augustine between the large Latin and English editions and the small Latin and French editions. However, the general layout of the town plan is substantially the same in the different editions.

Source: The British Library. *Sir Francis Drake: An Exhibition to Commemorate Francis Drake's Voyage around the World 1577–1580* (London: British Museum Publications, 1977), 107–10.

FIGURE 9.1. Detail, St. Augustine town plan of 1586, depicted by Baptista Boazio. Boazio's drawing was published in 1588. It represents the British view of the town the day before Drake burned it to the ground on May 30, 1586. Boazio depicts a plaza-like space near the landing place, a governor's house with a lookout at the west end of the plaza, a grid street plan, and the parish church in its own plaza-like space near the landing place where it could be "seen on leaving the sea" as specified in the Spanish ordinances. Photocopy courtesy of Florida State Archives.

Boazio's oblong plaza-like space on the "battle plan" suggests that Drake's men had identified a useful landing space. Presumably it was a place the Spanish had designated for unloading ships after they moved back to the mainland in 1572, and for the next fourteen years, for marketing goods as well as fiestas and church ceremonies. *"The towne house"* located on Boazio's map at the head of this plaza suggests it is the first Governor's House, the residence and office of Governor Pedro Menéndez Marqués, the official governor from 1577 to 1589. Its location and lookout provided him a view of plaza activities and port arrivals. Thus, today's plaza and Government House in principle predate 1586. However, Drake burned the town as he departed, and their locations relative to today's plaza and Government House are not precisely known.

Ordinance 113 proposes actual dimensions for the 1:1½ ratio (*length equal to one and a half times the width*) that was specified in Ordinance No. 112. No. 113 reads: *The choice of a plaza shall be made with reference to the growth that the town may have. It shall be not less than two hundred feet* [pies] *wide and three hundred feet long, not larger than eight hundred feet long and five hundred and thirty two feet wide. A moderate and good proportion is six hundred feet long and four hundred feet wide.* Ratios were an ancient canon of measure rooted in medieval and Renaissance architecture, when theology and arithmetic were closely related. In the writings of theologians like St. Augustine of Hippo, and in the practices of engineer-architects and church builders, harmonious ratios were symbolic of the order and harmony of God's universe. St. Augustine's town plaza dimensions changed over the centuries with new buildings and roads. Father Solana (1759) indicated it was about 200 varas square. Nevertheless, the original colonial plaza was probably established with spiritual undertones.[6]

After Drake burned the town in 1586, reconstruction began. A plaza beginning at the port would again be central to the town plan, and for the same reasons: ship landings, merchant sales and trades, religious and social activities. It is suggested therefore that a plaza may have been functioning for twenty-six years before 1598, when Governor Méndez de Canzo wrote the king: *Since I came* [on June 2, 1597] *I caused them to make a Plaza and all of them come to sell there, and a house for fish market and meat market where there is weight and measure which until now they had not had.* Méndez de Canzo took credit for *a Plaza* which in this instance means "marketplace." In other words, he formalized and regulated the selling of fish and meat in built structures and with a legitimate system of weights and measures, but did not "order the laying out of the town" in 1598 or in 1603 as written in the National Register of Historic Places Nomination Form (1986). Boazio's 1586 map shows the orderly town plan and oblong plaza space that was already functioning years before Méndez de Canzo arrived. Boazio's town depiction has validity in the archaeological excavations of Kathleen Deagan and Carl Halbirt south of today's plaza.[7] As for the 1598 marketplace, it became part of the town plan. Engineer Mariano de la Rocque noted *The Hall of the Market Place and Meat Market* at the east end of the plaza on his 1784 map. Even earlier, in 1772, the British had added a cupola to the market hall in which they hung a bell (fig. 9.3).[8]

Ordinance 114 specified that the plaza layout should consider the weather: *From the plaza shall run four main streets, one from the middle of each side of the plaza; and two streets at each corner of the plaza. The <u>four corners of the plaza shall face the four principal winds.</u> The <u>streets running thus from the plaza will not be exposed to the four principal winds which cause much inconvenience.</u>* A compass reading today indicates that the corners of St. Augustine's plaza face the local prevailing winds—northeast, southeast, southwest, northwest. The main pedestrian routes thus aligned with the cardinal directions do not face directly into these winds. It is tempting to think that today's plaza layout and street plan were planned with 1573 concerns for human convenience in the local climate.

Ordinance 115 expressed similar concerns for merchants: *The whole plaza round about . . . shall have arcades, for these are of considerable convenience to the merchants who generally gather there.* Protection from the sun and rain for merchants and buyers/traders and notaries was intended, a practice that was very old in Mediterranean countries.[9] If present in sixteenth-century St. Augustine, they might have been pole-and-thatch structures. The merchant story awaits more archaeology, maps, and documents.

Ordinances 119, 120, and 121 specified rules for building the parish church. Number 119 reads: *As for the temple of the cathedral, if the town is situated on the coast it shall be built in part so that it may be <u>seen on leaving the sea,</u> and in a place where its building may <u>serve as a means of defense for the port itself.</u>* Number 120 specifies its building lot *shall be assigned next <u>after</u> the plaza and streets, and shall be so completely isolated that no building shall be added there except one appertaining to its commodiousness and ornamentation.* Number 121 further explains that the *<u>church lot is to be near the port</u> and the government offices: After that a site and location shall be assigned for the royal council and cabildo house and for the <u>custom house and arsenal near the temple and port itself so that in times of need the one may aid the other.</u>*

The applications of these three ordinances are suggested in early drawings and maps. A large parish church was built soon after the town was laid out; it was known by its devotion to Nuestra Señora de los Remedios (Our Lady of Remedies), described in chapter 10. Boazio's 1586 drawing depicts it before Drake burned the town. He did not use a mapmaker's traditional church-with-spire symbol: he drew the basilica form, long and narrow, that was characteristic of Florida's colonial Spanish churches (plate 7; figs. 10.1, 10.3, 11.1). Hernando de Mestas's 1594 map depicts it rebuilt in similar form after Drake burned it (fig. 9.2). Its site at the harbor's edge on *both* maps points to ordinance 119, which specified that it be *seen on leaving the sea.* In addition, Mestas's drawing depicts it near the government's buildings as specified in ordinance 120. Governor Pedro Ybarra described the governor's house in 1603 as built *over the sea and is so cold and damp.*[10] It had replaced "the towne house" burned by Drake (see fig. 9.1).

In the report of the king's fort inspector, supplies that did not fit into the customs house or arsenal were stored in the church in 1578: *46 casks of wine; and outside, stowed against the church wall, under a roof of palmetto, 60 casks of flour all well placed on top of their planks; likewise 80 escaupiles* [cotton armor] *all hanging on their nails.*[11] Ordinance 121 had specified that these buildings be not only *near the port* but each other in order that *one may aid the other.* Thus, church and arsenal were near the port, and near each other. Historian Amy Bushnell discovered that the parish church of 1697 was still located so that "a person walking in the portico was near enough to the guardhouse to converse with the watch."[12] Mestas's map, like that of Boazio, suggests that the sixteenth-century drawings are more realistic representations than we thought—and that the king's ordinances had their effects on the town plan.

The parish church was burned by the English in 1702. One of its postmolds was recently found by the city archaeologist, Carl Halbirt, about where Boazio depicts it, and burials were found in the 1960s near today's Aviles Street.[13] Maps from 1730 to 1788 continued to note the location of the consecrated lot and cemetery where the destroyed church had stood near the port. The lots were closer to the riverbank in the sixteenth century—seawalls and fill material have since moved the waterfront eastward.

Ordinances 116, 122, and 133 were concerned with street widths, residential defenses, cleanliness, aesthetics, and health. Number 116 reads: *The streets in cold places shall be wide and in hot places narrow.* St. Augustine's narrow streets are now famous. Lined with stone house and garden walls, they shade pedestrians, a practice of ancient places in hot climates as far away and long ago as Mesopotamia, Rome, and Arabia, and their colonies.

Ordinance 133 makes clear that the narrow streets enclosed by fences and house walls that were built up to the street edges were also defensive. . . . *The buildings of the <u>whole town generally shall be so arranged that they shall serve as a defense and fort</u> against those who may try to disturb or invade the town. Each house in particular shall be so built that they may keep therein their horses and work animals, and shall have yards and corrals as large as possible for health and cleanliness.*

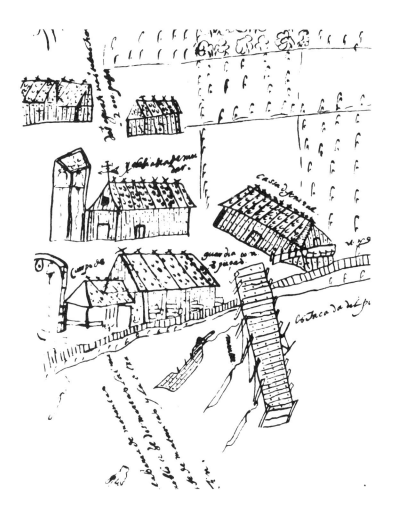

FIGURE 9.2. Parish church and principal government buildings, St. Augustine, depicted in 1594 by Hernando de Mestas. Mestas's drawing indicates that the post-1586 town plan also placed the church where it could be "seen on leaving the sea," and near the armory, and the custom and council house near the harbor and each other "so that in times of need the one may aid the other," as specified in the Spanish ordinances. Photocopy courtesy of Florida State Archives.

St. Augustine's historic residential lots were self-sustaining. They had wells, kitchen gardens, and domestic animals within their enclosures. Health, cleanliness, and fires in these residential compounds were issues of equal importance to their defensive characteristic. Detached kitchens helped to prevent the house fires that were a constant threat in the wood-and-thatch architecture. Preventive measures were the essence of many of the Spanish ordinances.

Ordinance 122 reads: *The site and building lots for slaughter houses, fisheries, tanneries and other things productive of filth shall be so placed that the filth can be easily disposed of.* Does this also suggest that Méndez de Canzo's *house for fish market and meat market* were erected on the plaza's river edge in 1598? Buildings designated for market activities were near the harbor in 1784 and the 1850s (fig. 9.3). The British public slaughtering pen was at the Barrier Gate (north of town) in 1767.[14]

The public welfare was also addressed in ordinance 121, discussed earlier: *The hospital for the poor and those sick of non-contagious diseases shall be built near the temple and its cloister.* In 1597, a hospital was built and attached to the shrine of Nuestra Señora de la Soledad west of the residential blocks (chapter 10) (plate 8). Bedding the sick near the altar was in keeping with Spanish beliefs about healing. La Soledad was the first hospital in the continental United States. Specific winds near the hospital and *the sick with contagious diseases* were also addressed in the ordinance as well as in ordinance 124.

Ordinances 117 and 134 addressed architectural aesthetics. Number 117 specified: *The streets shall run from the main plaza in such wise that although the town increases considerably in size, no inconvenience may arise which may cause what may be rebuilt to become ugly or be prejudicial to its defense and commodiousness.* Ordinance 134 specified: *They shall try so far as possible to have the buildings all of one form for the sake of the beauty of the town.* Both ordinances, like that of the plaza dimensions, imply that sixteenth-century builders valued symmetry and geometric order based on squares and rectangles.

During 1763–84, the British period, the street plan of the historic Spanish town (enclosed within the defensive Cubo and Rosario Lines) was kept more or less intact. Architectural infill occurred, and a number of Spanish buildings were converted by the British for their new uses, but the basic principles of the town plan were not changed as shown by comparing the town maps of Eligio de la Puente on the eve of Spain's departure (plate 12), and of Mariano de la Rocque after the Spanish returned in 1784. The most notable architectural addition concerning the plaza was the new parish church in 1797, today's Cathedral Basilica described in chapter 13 (fig. 13.3; plate 13). When Florida became an American territory in 1821, and when Henry Flagler's buildings were constructed in the 1880s, the essentials of the historic town plan remained unchanged. Flagler made significant changes to St. Augustine's built landscape, but his buildings were mostly beyond the boundaries of the historic town plan.

Flagler had quickly recognized that the town had a unique character: "Here was St. Augustine, the oldest city in the United States. How to build a hotel to meet the requirements of nineteenth-century America and have

FIGURE 9.3. View of St. Augustine plaza and major buildings, 1835. Standing around the plaza are Government House as renovated by Elias Wallen according to plans drawn by Robert Mills of Washington, D.C., in 1834; Trinity Church recently completed (1831) with pinnacles and as yet no steeple; the cathedral completed in 1797; and market buildings at the east end of the plaza. *View of Fort Marion and City of St. Augustine, Florida,* anonymous, courtesy of St. Augustine Historical Society.

it in keeping with the character of the place—that was my hardest problem."[15] His large hotel and church structures of the late 1880s not only preserved the integrity of the historic city layout, they validated and showcased St. Augustine's Spanish heritage by embracing the look of its tabby oyster-shell concrete and coquina walls—but with nineteenth-century technology (chapter 17; plates 26, 27, 29; fig. 17.1).

Today in historic St. Augustine, structures are repaired, restored, and added on to, and the debate continues about their use and the style of new construction in context with history. Of more concern is automobile traffic and parking. The spirit of the original town plan exists, and St. Augustine is still the oldest planned community in the United States. We cannot enter the city unmoved.

10 ✛ Living under Spanish Bells

> If the architect designed his sanctuary according to the laws of harmonious proportion, he did not only imitate the order of the visible world . . . but conveyed the perfection of the world to come.
>
> OTTO VON SIMSON

HARMONIOUS PROPORTIONS may have arrived in Spanish Florida with the ratios specified in the Royal Ordinances of 1573 and found at several Franciscan churches.[1] Spanish Florida also had a more common instrument dispensing a sense of order and spiritual harmony across the land—the voice of the church bells that pealed over marshes and rivers, across cultivated fields and artillery platforms, down the streets of St. Augustine, San Luis, and Pensacola, and into the far-flung wilderness missions to sound the hours of the day, to call the faithful to mass and evensong, to fetch Indian children to instruction and choir, and to celebrate the feasts of saints. They mourned each death. They set the watch on the ramparts of Spain's forts, and they sounded the early warnings of enemy sails on the Atlantic horizon.

Sonorous bells called out their messages at church entrances. In the sixteenth and seventeenth centuries, they were hung simply on ropes that were wrapped around wood beams supported by posts in the ground, and were rung by rope pulls (fig. 10.1; plate 7). By about the mid-1730s, wooden post-and-lintel *campanarios* were replaced by stone *espadaña* belfries in which bells were hung in openings in church walls like that of St. Augustine's Cathedral (fig. 13.3; plate 13). They moved Spanish colonists emotionally closer in spirit to their mother countries, Spain, New Spain, and Cuba.

FIGURE 10.1. Nuestra Señora de Los Remedios, sixteenth-century parish church, St. Augustine. "A," built ca. 1572, depicted by Baptista Boazio in 1586; "B," rebuilt ca. 1587 after Drake burned the city, depicted by Hernando de Mestas about 1594. Both are large structures of wood and thatch on an east-west axis, altars in the west. Dedicated to St. Augustine of Hippo, for whom the city was named, the church was soon known for its image and special devotion to the first Marian image brought to New Spain (Mexico), Our Lady of Remedies. Four bells, rung by rope pulls, announced religious events and warned of invading pirates and enemies. Drawings after Boazio and Mestas by the author.

As this chapter resurrects a few of the Spanish churches, imagine, if you will, an overture of melodious bell timbres echoing across Florida during the fragile years of settlement building—when the churches and their bells brought comfort and a sense of spiritual security much like the holy ratios.

A Church Not Found: September 8, 1565–May 1566

In its earliest and most humble form, the first Spanish church was a cross under the sun. It was erected simply, and soon after Pedro Menéndez de Avilés stepped ashore in 1565. Records show that catechism was obligatory and open-air masses were held before Menéndez and soldiers marched north and captured the French Fort Caroline.[2] But no details of a chapel built at the landing site have yet been found. Four clerics had arrived with Menéndez, and an inventory for the 1565 enterprise included *8 church bells and 4 ornaments for saying Mass.* When the French fort was secured and renamed Fort San Mateo, Menéndez wasted no time designating *a location for the erection of a church to be made from the lumber the heretics* [Huguenots, Lutherans] *had saved to build a ship.*[3] Solís de Merás, Menéndez's brother-in-law and chronicler of these 1565 events (written in 1567), wrote that Menéndez *marked out the site for a church where a wooden chapel was to be created immediately, so that mass might be said every day.*[4] Somewhere, in archive or archaeology, a similar chapel in St. Augustine exists.

Church of San Juan, 1566–1572

Eight months after the Spanish landed in 1565, their presidio was set on fire by Indians. The settlers moved to Anastasia Island, where in 1566 they built a new fort and the fort's *church of San Juan.* It was near *the well of Ensign Juan de Junco, which is next to the storehouse, which is joined with the church.* It had *four four-wick candles and 310 wax candles, all of Campeche* [Mexico] *wax.*[5] But the sea ate into the new fort and town, and *it was necessary to change it to the other side where it is now,* wrote Alonso de las Alas in 1600.[6] The church of San Juan, the fort, and the nascent town now lie under Salt Run on the east side of Anastasia Island—nature altered the landscape and the course of human history.

Parish Church, Nuestra Señora de los Remedios, 1572–1702

The settlers left the island about 1572 and built a new parish church and town on the mainland south of today's plaza.[7] They constructed their parish church and dedicated it to Saint Augustine of Hippo. It was depicted in 1586 by Baptista Boazio, and in 1594 by Ensign Hernando de Mesta, in what are now the oldest drawings of a European-style Christian sacred space in the United States.[8] As specified by the Spanish ordinances of 1573, both depictions place the church near the port and town landing where the plaza begins—*so that it may be seen on leaving the sea, and in a place where its building may serve as a means of defense for the port itself* (chap. 9; figs. 9.1, 9.2).[9] Its symbolism on many levels may have been an important element in town planning, and might explain why the sixteenth-century officials decided to build and rebuild the parish church from 1572 to 1702 on its precarious site on the banks of the Matanzas River, in the face of flood tides, storm surges, hurricane winds, and assaults by ship-borne pirates and British enemies (plate 6).

In 1576, the church was inventoried with a rich assortment of interior furnishings.[10] Saint Augustine of Hippo was the "Titular Saint of the church, and Patron Saint of the city," but the church took the name of Nuestra Señora de los Remedios (Our Lady of Remedies) after an image and its *advocación* were brought to the church. Nuestra Señora de los Remedios was the first Marian image brought to the New World—arriving in Mexico in the early years of Spanish colonization, where she became the symbol of the Spanish conversions of the natives. Sometimes she was associated with water (and prayed to for rain) because the original figure was found in a well by a shepherd in Spain. The cultivation of foodstuffs was important to the Florida settlers, and Paul Hoffman has noted that St. Augustine's "maize yields rose more or less with the rainfall."[11]

Remedios was set on fire twice, in 1586 by Francis Drake and 1702 by James Moore. We do not know who the architect (Maestro Alarife) was in 1572 or for the new structure post-1586. It was not rebuilt after 1702. The parish moved inland to a century-old hermitage, La Soledad, described below. The 1572 and post-1586 church dimensions were probably gauged by the eye or knotted cords, and if there were harmonious proportions (as noted later in the Franciscan churches in St. Augustine), it would have reflected medieval and Renaissance practices in which church architecture was like "frozen music," with ratios, patterns, and intervals thought to reflect the fundamental laws of nature and the universe. A proportioned church structure was believed to be the threshold to the Spiritual City of God. Simple 1:2 ratios called Solomonic ratios (from Solomon's Temple) characterized St. Peter's in Rome in A.D. 326 (400 feet long by 200 feet in breadth), and its planned enlargement in 1452 by Bramante (640 feet by 320 feet).[12] A more complicated ratio known as the "Golden Ratio" is suggested at the seventeenth-century Mission San Luis church (see below), perhaps reflecting the engineer's, or resident Franciscan friar's, education in arithmetic and religion. Robert A. Scott, in *The Gothic*

Enterprise, likened proportions to a "genetic code," with each building having its "own characteristic proportionality based on variations of a single length." He quotes Victor Hugo on the design of Notre Dame Cathedral in Paris: "To measure the toe is to measure the giant."[13]

Boazio's 1586 drawing of Remedios is a representation of a rectangular basilica church. He shows it extending the length of a town block, its entrance facing east, altar in the west. Mestas's 1594 drawing of Remedios is similar, with a double door and vertical plank walls joined by wrought-iron nails, and a detached post-and-beam belfry with four bells rung by ropes. Both drawings show palm-thatch roofs. Thus represented, Remedios had a long and narrow windowless nave, in which all eyes were drawn from the entrance through the darkness toward the light of the most sacred space, the candle-lighted chancel and sanctuary. The seventeenth-century church that has been re-created according to archaeological data at Mission San Luis in Tallahassee is very similar and suggests that the architecture of Remedios depicted by Boazio and Mestas (fig. 10.1) is more or less accurate.

Around 1598, Governor Méndez de Canzo boasted: *This city is at present with much public adornment of shrines of the principal church.* He also wrote that the church needed repairs: *Likewise the principal church of this city has the same necessity of being covered with a flat roof or tile and other very necessary repairs; Your Majesty being pleased to command to be given the proceeds of the tithes for three or four years it can be repaired . . . that which is done in the church has been at the cost of the soldiers and residents, who have done it from their poverty.*[14] Mestas had also noted the needed repairs on his 1594 drawing. In 1602, Méndez de Canzo praised the principal church as one of the *neatest and best finished of its kind in the Indies.*[15]

Robert Searle, alias the pirate John Davis, stripped the parish church of its ornaments in 1668.[16] In 1675, the visiting bishop of Cuba wrote the queen of Spain about the city of St. Augustine: *As regards its spiritual welfare, it has a parish church dedicated to St. Augustine.*[17] In 1697, a report indicates the church was still near the guardhouse/arsenal—a portico along its side wall allowed a person to talk to the guardhouse watch. Also in that year, Governor Quiroga built a new bell tower for the *iglesia mayor*, but no description follows.[18] Five years later, Carolina's Colonel James Moore laid siege to St. Augustine. In November 1702, the invaders were said to be *overwhelmed by the size of the church.*[19] The British were defeated, and on December 30, the departing enemy set fire to the church and most of St. Augustine's wooden buildings.[20]

Remedios was not rebuilt. This time its loss was too great a burden to bear. Its hallowed waterfront site, however, remained sanctified. An infant named María had been baptized there on June 25, 1594—recorded in what are now the nation's oldest church records.[21] A map in 1730 marks the site: *A cross where stood thereby Great Church destroyed 1706* [1702] *never since rebuilt.*[22] Mariano de la Rocque's 1788 map of the city shows two consecrated lots still set aside, one for the church and one for the cemetery. They were not built upon until Americans arrived in the nineteenth century.

Nuestra Señora de la Soledad

After Remedios was destroyed in 1702, the St. Augustine parish moved inland (fig. 2). They housed their church services in a century-old wood structure described in 1604 by Friar Pedro Bermejo as an *ermita o capilla* (shrine or chapel) that *belonged to the brothers of the cofradia* [brotherhood] of *Nuestra Señora de la Soledad* (Virgin Mary after the Crucifixion).[23] A *hospital for the soldiers* was attached to the shrine. In the words of Governor Ganzalo Méndez de Canzo:

> When I arrived at this city [1597] I found that they were beginning a hospital and gave the favor that it be made because it is the remedy of this Presidio, which if they had not had it this past summer many soldiers and Indian natives of Yours would have perished and died according to the great sickness of fevers that were here.[24]

This was our nation's first hospital. An old Royal slave, María Joije, served as cook, made beds, and kept the hospital clean.[25] In letters of February 1600 and April 1601, Méndez de Canzo reported:

> On March 14, 1599, there was a fire in this city which burned a number of houses, and the Franciscan convent the body of its church is covered with palm [south end of town], for which reason, to shelter the prior and certain religious it was necessary to put them into the Chapel of Our Lady of Solitude where the city hospital was and there was then no hospital nor any place to receive the sick, and so that the charitable work would not cease and because of the great need of the poor soldiers and the king's black slaves and native Indians, I set up at my own expense a commodius and decent hospital with a half dozen beds under the patronage of Santa Barbara.[26]

The records suggest he had extended the chapel hospital. In 1604, the friars moved out of Nuestra Señora de la Soledad and back into their newly rebuilt monastery at the south end of town.[27] Santa Barbara hospital continued to be maintained by soldiers' alms.[28] Some eighty years later, the visiting bishop of Cuba wrote Queen Mariana about an *ermita of Our Lady of Solitude* that had *a hospital contiguous to with six beds.*[29] Alonso de Leturiondo, the parish priest, described the *Hospital of Our Lady of Solitude* as

> *a room of the sick . . . juxtaposed with the main altar of the aforesaid hermitage or hospital and next to a kitchen where, since it is necessary to light a fire at all hours for the sick and for making the medicines as the buildings of the place are all of wood the church and the altars and images all receive much damage.*[30]

Between 1687 and 1693, Governor Quiroga y Losada *enlarged the shrine at the hospital of Soledad into a little church complete with a campanario.*[31] Such was the state of its architecture when Nuestra Señora de la Soledad became the parish church in 1702.

Forty-three years later, in 1735, the energetic bishop of Tricale, Francisco de San Buenaventura y Tejada, arrived in St. Augustine. He was a professor of theology, guardian of a Franciscan convent in Seville, and the first resident bishop in St. Augustine. In 1736, he was *bringing this Hermandad up to date* and making *the works of the said hermitage in stone.*[32] He called it the hermitage of *Santo Cristo de la Soledad and Our Lady of Aracelis;* in 1765, it was called the shrine of Our Lady of Aracelis. This *advocación* of Our Lady of Aracelis may have arrived at the parish church with the bishop of Tricale—it had been founded in Seville in the late sixteenth century and was closely associated with the Franciscans. His referring to the hermitage as Santo Cristo de la Soledad suggests he brought the Christ figure to the Virgin that was a solitary figure without Christ after the crucifixion. A Christ figure that went with La Soledad was referred to as *el Santo Cristo de la Soledad.*[33] Eligio de la Puente's city map in 1764 shows that the west entrance to the church property was through the defensive wall (Rosario Line) guarded by a redoubt called *Baluarte del Santo Cristo de la Soledad* (plate 12).

The bishop's improvements and expansions at La Soledad were described by Father Juan José Solana, the parish priest in 1759:

> *With regard to the material of the church, it is reduced to a small construction of stone, with its sacristy, and a small room above for the assistant curate and another room more narrow (austere) for the acolytes;* [the church] *is 20 varas long* [55.5 feet], *the presbytery/chancel 5 varas* [13.9 feet] *and 11½ varas wide* [31.9 feet] *. . . in place of the ancient and damaged wood it had, a new front was erected with three stone arches, and above them a wall which serves as the tower in which the bells are rung. The roof is wood boards (tablas) . . . a new choir was built.*[34]

Solana's letter is a complaint and a revelation. He complains that La Sole-dad is so small and narrow that the faithful have to hear mass in the street, where they suffer in the sun and rain. This was a fund-raising tactic aimed at the king's royal purse. Solana wanted the Crown to build a bigger and better church. That the roof leaked on the altars was probably true. However, La Soledad in other reports was known to have had an organ and an organist, and a bell-ringer—and a retablo gilded and painted for the great altar and new ornaments made in St. Augustine in 1754.[35] Eligio de la Puente in 1764 described it as: *Igesia de Piedra que servía de Parroquial* (parish church of stone), and when the British arrived in 1764, they found it acceptable to be converted into their Anglican church.

Solana's letter reveals La Soledad's front elevation had *three entrance arches*, above which was the *stone wall which serves as the tower in which the bells are rung* (plate 8). One bell was inscribed "St. Joseph."[36] La Soledad's stone belfry was one of three espadaña-style belfries built in St. Augustine in the mid-1730s: one at the church of the Convento de San Francisco, described by John Bartram as having *5 arches in 4 of which perhaps hanged a bell by a cros bar that was fixed under ye crown of ye arch;*[37] another was at the church of Nuestra Señora de La Leche at the mission Nombre de Dios (chapter 11). This dramatic change in architecture occurred when coquina stone in the king's quarries was made available during and after the construction of Castillo de San Marcos. The belfry was reminiscent of those in Spain and Cuba.

St. Peter's Anglican Church, 1764–1784

Spain ceded Florida to the British in 1763. Engineer James Moncrief was charged with measuring the Spanish church, La Soledad, for its conversion into St. Peter's Church. Similarly, when Florida was retroceded to Spain in 1783, the Spanish engineer Mariano de la Rocque would measure the building formerly used by the British. Their measurements indicate the structure was larger than implied in Father Solana's letter quoted above. It was at least 120 feet long and 48–53 feet wide, about the same size as the parish church that would be built in 1797, now the Cathedral Basilica (chapter 13).[38]

La Soledad had fronted on St. George Street, and its altar was in the west. The British reversed this plan. St. Peter's altar was in the east, opposite a newly built entrance and bell tower in the west (plate 8). The tower base served as the vestibule, had two arched entrances, south and west, and supported a tall, slender spire. According to the Anglican liturgy and canon law at that time, a wooden altar was to be placed within a railed chancel at the east end.[39] Excavations by archaeologist Kathleen Deagan confirm the reversal. Spanish shroud burials in the church floor had their heads in the east (facing the west altar if they were to stand up), and English coffin burials in the churchyard had their heads in the west in order to "face" east upon arising.[40]

John Hewitt was the contractor for St. Peter's. He owned one of the earliest water-powered sawmills in Florida (south of St. Augustine on Pellicer Creek), the wood from which was probably used to build the iconic English spire and box pews. St. Peter's steeple was the tallest feature on the city skyline, a 70–80 foot staged bell tower topped with a graceful broach spire and weathervane. It was a point of pride for Lieutenant Governor John Moultrie:

> Government has most bountifully given a Clock and Bell to that Church … and I also thought that your Lordship would not be displeased that I expended a little on the Church when not only real use was intended by decency in the appearance of the House of God for publick worship … an ornament to this young province.[41]

Hewitt was paid £319 on June 25, 1773, according to his voucher: *being in full for building a spire to the Church of St. Peter in St. Augustine, agreeable to Plan and elevation of the same delivered to me.*[42] (It is conjectured that the tower was stone, but a wood tower scored to look like stone was possible). Additional amounts were paid for the installation of sheet lead, the board fence with gates around the church yard, a glazed window, and locks and bolts on the church door. Hewitt also built pews, each with a step and a back, painted with three coats of oil paint in imitation "stone" and numbered. Two were more elaborate and closer to the high pulpit and reading desk—they were reserved for the high-ranking.[43]

A drawing of the steeple (tower and spire) was forwarded in 1773 by Moultrie (acting governor 1771–74) to the Board of Trade, and it is conserved today at the Public Records Office, England's national archives (fig. 10.2). It is very English in feeling, styled after the Georgian-Palladian churches of Christopher Wren and James Gibbs in London, embellished with classical quoins, a classical surround, Ionic columns, a town clock, an oculus, and an Adamesque swag. It appears to have been inspired by Gibbs's *Book of Architecture* (1728), which was widely used as a pattern book to design churches in the Anglo-American colonies; it contained eighty plates of drawings of steeples (including a large fold-out) he had designed for St. Martin's-in-the-Fields in London. The drawing is not signed, but circumstantial evidence suggests Moultrie might have had a

FIGURE 10.2. Drawing of English steeple added in 1773 to the Spanish parish church Nuestra Señora de la Soledad, St. Augustine. The British converted the Spanish church into their Anglican St. Peter's Church. They added an entrance and tall steeple with town clock at the west end and reversed the altar from west to east. They also built box pews with backs, numbered them, and painted them a "stone" color: two were more elaborate and closer to the altar. Photograph courtesy of Public Record Office, PRO: CO 5/554, f.3.

hand in the design. St. Michael's Church in Charleston (1751–61) was built by Samuel Cardy (d. 1774), who used Gibbs's book,[44] and Moultrie was a plantation owner from a well-connected family in Charleston—his father was a vestryman at St. Michael's.[45] Did Moultrie ask Cardy to draw St. Augustine's steeple?

In 1784, the English took leave of Florida, traveling with their pews, bells, and clock to the Bahamas. Moultrie lost most of his fortune and lived out his life in England, where he is buried near his wife's family estate in Shropshire. (One of his daughters married Captain William Bligh of *Mutiny on the Bounty* fame.) La Soledad–St. Peter's was dismantled by the Spanish, and its coquina stone was recycled in 1793 into the stone walls of the new parish church completed in 1797, today's Cathedral Basilica. La Soledad–St. Peter's site is now owned and preserved by the Sisters of St. Joseph. This hallowed ground is one of the oldest cemeteries in the United States. Beneath its surface are some of the city's first burials, as well as the footings of La Soledad church and first hospital, and the first Anglican church.[46]

Mission San Luis Church, 1656–1704

In the seventeenth century, cattle ranches and wheat haciendas followed the Franciscan missions westward to one of the most fertile regions of Florida—between the Ochlockonee and Aucilla Rivers. It was the homeland of the Apalachee Indians. Agricultural products were shipped from a landing at the confluence of the St. Marks and Wakulla Rivers to St. Augustine, the Yucatan, and Cuba. As these enterprises expanded and grew in importance and fed St. Augustine, they gave rise to a Spanish community beginning in 1656 that grew with administrators and their families, a landed aristocracy, a garrisoned fort, and a mission village with a large church and some 1,500 Christian Apalachee Indians (fig. 10.3). Mission San Luis (Tallahassee) became the western capital of Spanish Florida. Gabriel Díaz Vara Calderón, bishop of Cuba, inspected the missions in 1674–75 and wrote Queen Mariana of Spain that Mission San Luis de Talimali is *the largest of them all.* He indicates the church may have been built by the Apalachee: he described Florida's Indians as being *quick to learn any art they see done, and great carpenters as is evidenced in the construction of their wooden churches which are large and painstakingly wrought.*[47] Similarly, Fray Alonso de Jesús had written in 1630 about Indian skills: *for the construction of our temples and houses we no longer have need of nails and iron tools.*[48]

Mission San Luis was destroyed in 1704 in advance of an assault led by the same James Moore of Carolina who had torched St. Augustine in 1702. Officials in St. Augustine ordered the people of San Luis to withdraw in 1704 and burn all buildings in advance of the enemy.[49] A year later, during a survey by Admiral Antonio de Landeche, a drawing was made of the church, its *campanario*, a circular plaza, and fort, all of which are

FIGURE 10.3. Seventeenth-century church, Mission San Luis, Tallahassee. Leon County. The enormous size of this church—re-created in situ with wood timbers, plank walls, and palm thatch roof according to the archaeological data—makes one think again about colonial Spanish architecture and the skills of the Apalachee Indians who constructed it. In advance of an attack by the English and allied Indians, the Spanish burned all the mission's buildings including the church in 1704. Up to nine hundred Christian Indians are buried in the nave's earth floor. Photograph 2003 by the author.

re-created in situ based on documents translated by historian John Hann and many years of archaeological excavations and data collected by Gary Shapiro, Richard Vernon, and Bonnie McEwan.[50]

Entering the enormous twentieth-century re-created church is a breathtaking nostalgic experience. Centuries melt away in the dim nave with the pungent smell of the earth floor and of the massive pine and cypress posts, and the palm thatch that roofs the structure. Long ago, baptismal processions might have formed in the circular plaza outside and proceeded to the baptismal font at the left of the entrance, the Gospel side. From a choir loft over the entrance, Indian voices would have filled the processional nave and carried out the door, past the post-and-beam *campanario*, and the whitewashed wattle-and-daub friary, and across the plaza. San Luis's single-nave mendicant church was long and narrow—some 100 feet long, 50 feet wide, and 50 feet high. It had planked walls, a steeply pitched thatch roof, a sanctuary, and an altar oriented westward. It was similar to St. Augustine's first parish church, Los Remedios, and to the sixteenth-century thatched church at Nombre de Dios, both of which are depicted in the drawing of 1594 by Ensign Hernando de Mestas seen in figures 9.2 and 11.1.

The architect and his methods for designing and siting the church and conveying the design particulars to the Indian artisans are unknown. Its final appearance met the liturgical requirements of the Catholic church, and reflected the skills and methods of the Indians who worked the native materials. A proportional system might have been employed, with numerical modules diminishing or increasing to the Golden Ratio (in which the smaller part relates to the larger part as the larger part relates to the whole).[51] If the Golden Ratio was intended, the church designer might have had religious beliefs about church architecture and sacred geometry.[52]

We may never know, however, what the Apalachee builders of the church believed. They preferred their own building traditions and its ancient beliefs as demonstrated in their council house, described in chapter 6. However, up to nine hundred Christian Indians lie buried in Spanish tradition under the church's consecrated earth floor.[53]

Spanish Panzacola, 1698, 1723, 1757

Tristán de Luna attempted to establish a large settlement in August 1559 in what is now Pensacola. The expedition met a tragic end during a fierce

September hurricane—the remains of two ships were discovered in 1992 and 2006, now known as the Emanuel Point Shipwreck Site. After 139 years, the Spanish returned to the deepwater bay to attempt another settlement. Presidio Santa María de Galve was founded in 1698 by Governor Andrés de Arriola, from Veracruz, leading colonists from Mexico, many from its jails. They settled high on the mainland bluff (Barranca de Santo Tomé) on the west side of the bay overlooking the harbor entrance near today's Pensacola Naval Air Station and built Fort San Carlos, described in chapter 20. A church with a long, narrow nave, a post-and-lintel *campanario*, a cemetery, and a *casa de padres* appears outside the fort walls on engineer Jayme Franck's map of the presidio in 1699. It may have served as the presidio's parish as well as an Indian mission. It did not last a year, burning in 1699.

A second church was built by 1702, its location unknown. It likely had board walls and a board roof like the rest of the presidio buildings. It burned in 1704 when a kitchen fire was left unattended by the friars' cook, Pedro Gonzáles. A third church was built inside the fort and lasted from 1706 until 1719, when the fort was captured by the French. Documents and its partial excavation suggest to archaeologists that it may have been 80 by 30 feet (2,400 square feet) with board walls, a masonry chimney, and a glass window that came from French Mobile. Some one hundred pieces of aqua or light-green window glass have been found. In 1706, paint supplies were requested from Veracruz: orange, indigo, green, purple, vermilion, gold, and white pigments, a grinding stone, glue sizing, oil, brushes and red ochre for the drawing.[54] Had some creative artist painted the whitewashed walls or an altar retablo?

An end came in 1719, when church and presidio were burned and the settlement surrendered to France. When the site was returned to Spain in 1722, all that remained of earlier architectural activities were a wreck of a cabin, a bake oven, and a lidless cistern. In 1723, the presidio moved across the harbor to Santa Rosa Island. A young French artist on a Spanish merchant ship in the bay depicted the new church in 1743 (engraved and published in 1763). It resembles an octagon with a lantern reminiscent of early Christian baptistries (fig. 10.4). The artist, Dominic Serres (1722–1793), had an unusual biography. He was born in Gascony but ran away to Spain, where he became master of a trading vessel to Havana until he was captured by the British in 1752. In London, he became a talented painter known for his paintings of the siege of Havana in 1762, and by 1768 he was a founding member of the prestigious Royal Academy of Art. A decade later, he was the most successful English painter of marine events during

FIGURE 10.4. Drawing of Spanish presidio and church, Santa Rosa Island, Pensacola. Santa Rosa County. A drawing made in 1743 by Dominic Serres depicts an atypical church structure in Spanish Florida, an octagon with a lantern. It would have been built sometime between 1723 and 1752, when it was destroyed by a November hurricane. Photocopy courtesy of Florida State Archives.

the American Revolution and was appointed maritime painter to King George III in 1780. His paintings are noted for their historical accuracy and can be seen today at the Greenwich Maritime Museum.[55]

The Santa Rosa presidio and church were doomed by their location, a barrier island at the mercy of the hurricane in November 1752 that delivered the mortal blow. On orders from Mexico, the presidio was relocated back on the mainland and named San Miguel de Panzacola after its patron saint, San Miguel Arcangel, and the native Panzacola Indians. A church erected about 1757 was inside the stockade due to frequent Indian attacks. It is thought to be a timber-frame structure walled with planks and roofed with palmetto or "bark" (the British term for Pensacola roofs, meaning slabs cut from the outermost side of timbers). It served a colony of seven hundred, including 184 women and children, and 180 Christian Indians from nearby villages, as well as soldiers and some criminals released from Mexico's prisons and sentenced to hard labor in the new colony.[56]

Very soon after the move to the mainland, all the buildings newly built inside the stockade lost their roofs in a hurricane. In 1761, a new commandant-governor, Colonel Diego Ortíz Parrilla, an experienced Indian fighter, arrived and was so appalled at the condition of the buildings that he ordered them rebuilt during 1762. Presumably the church was one of the first. A year later, Florida was ceded to England, and Spanish Panzacola became Great Britain's Pensacola, capital of British West Florida (1763–83). English engineers measured and drew the floor plan of the Spanish parish church, revealing that it had a gallery (loggia) and post-and-lintel *campanario*. A choir and a sacristy are left to our imagination.[57] Details of a British church building, however, are missing. Could they have converted the Spanish structure into their own church as they did in St. Augustine? Details of a "Second Spanish Period" church (1783–1821) await discovery.[58]

In addition to the above-described churches, many more were built in the far-flung Indian missions along the east coast and across to the Panhandle. Today's San Luis church provides us a perspective on a tumultuous period in Florida history when the church structure was the most important nonmilitary architectural activity.

11 ✛ Nombre de Dios

The First Spanish Mission

Ye indian or milk church half a mile out of town is ye compleatest piece of architecture about ye town....
It is strange ye spaniards should bestow ten times more labour & charge on this indian church then any
of thair own in ye town.

JOHN BARTRAM

FEW AMERICANS KNOW that the nation's earliest and longest-lived Spanish mission was in Florida. It was founded in an Indian village called Nombre de Dios north of St. Augustine (fig. 11.1). Its eventful two centuries of architectural history began ca. 1580—decades before the colonization of Roanoke, Santa Fe, Jamestown, and Plymouth—and its final church, known as Nuestra Señora de la Leche (Our Lady of the Milk), stood for two decades after the Declaration of Independence. A stone's throw to the east of the mission's founding site is the ocean inlet through which Pedro Menéndez de Avilés brought his eight hundred colonists to St. Augustine in 1565 (fig. 8.1).[1]

The mission's architecture in its first century was pole and thatch, its humble simplicity perpetuated by a saga of cataclysmic events. Its last church was stone, the intricately carved *compleatest piece of architecture* described by John Bartram in 1766.[2] This two-century-long construction history is conjectured in this chapter through eyewitness accounts, official documents, ancient maps, and archaeology. A more complete story, however, is still in the ground and archives, but for the moment this mission deserves a more prominent place in American history. Its builders and buildings are no longer above ground, but their spirit of place blankets a large hallowed area conserved today by the Fountain of Youth Park and the adjacent Catholic Diocese's nineteenth-century Mission Nombre de Dios.

The Prologue, 1565–1580

Sixteenth-century accounts vividly describe why missions to the Indians were not successfully established until about fifteen years after the Spanish landed in 1565. They enumerate the problems of the settlement's landing place, food shortages, mutinies, Indian hostilities, and language and cultural barriers. Officials, priests, and soldiers were preoccupied with a governing system, eliminating the French enemy at Fort Caroline, confronting the settlement problems, relocating to Anastasia Island in 1566 and back to the mainland in 1572, and building the town that is today's St. Augustine.[3]

Menéndez as early as 1565 had pressed Francisco de Borja (later St. Francis of Borgia), vicar-general of the Jesuit Order, to send Jesuit missionaries to Florida (plate 30).[4] By 1572, a number of Jesuits had come and gone, their missions unsuccessful. Three Franciscans arrived in 1573 and were assigned to Santa Elena (now South Carolina), then the intended capital of La Florida, but they left in 1574 upon the death of Pedro Menéndez. From the beginning of his enterprise in Florida in 1565, he had intended to bring the Gospel to the Indians, but by his life's end he was so distraught by the *failure of his Indian policies,* he wrote in anguish that it was *fitting they be declared slaves.* The dates and numbers of the Franciscans who arrived before 1587 are not clear, according to the Franciscan historian Rev. Maynard Geiger, O.F.M. In 1575, Acting Governor Diego de Velasco had asked that *two priests be sought for these forts* (Santa Elena and St. Augustine). In 1577, Pedro Menéndez Marqués was appointed royal governor, and the next year he reported: *I have here two very estimable friars, and one is a most excellent and learned theologian of the order of St. Francis, by name Fray Alonso Caveças.* Caveças was from Jerez de la Frontera, Spain, and in 1578 he was listed as chaplain at the St. Augustine fort. Geiger, however, found no record of him doing missionary work. At this time, St. Augustine was redirected as the capital, and the governor became preoccupied with holding the capital and northern provinces together against divisive powers, poor economics, low morale, and continuing Indian hostilities.[5]

By mid-1578, Governor Marquéz was able to report to the king that the Indians around St. Augustine were more peaceful. He expressed hope this would lead someday to their becoming Christians, but indicated that at the present time, there was no discussing that with them. In 1579, he wrote that they showed no interest in abandoning their ancestral religion.[6] By 1580, however, the governor must have felt there was a measure of Indian willingness to coexist with the Spanish. Royal Accountant Lázaro Sánchez de Mercado, and Royal Treasurer Juan Cebadilla (new officials sent by the king in 1579 to keep an eye on the governor) informed the king about the governor's policy as to the *best means of the settlement and pacification. . . . We have only seen that the soldiers have gone half a league from here to a savannah of his and have built some houses and huts in which they say Indians are to come to live here. We do not know what effect it may have, although, since the governor has done it, it will therefore be advantageous to your Majesty's service.*[7]

Governor Marquez might have had in mind Indians working communal cornfields, supporting themselves and their chief, and supplying corn to the garrison that was reconstructing the rotting wood fort north of town. In 1583, he reported baptisms, including that of the chief who was *cacica* [woman chief] *of this land bordering the presidio . . . the nearest cacica to this presidio of St. Augustine and the first to become Christian.*[8] In exchange for the village built on her land, she might have received gifts, Spanish protection, religious instruction, and baptism in the parish church or a *visita* chapel in her village.[9] She remained loyal to the Spanish governor through Francis Drake's raid in May 1586. Her village may have been that described by Juan de Posada in September 1586 as a village of Christian Indians a cannon shot from the fort that was spared by the English.[10] It is to this village that a trained resident Franciscan was assigned in 1587. He was Alonso Gregorio de Escobedo –one of twelve Franciscans who arrived in October 1587. With his arrival, the mission with the name Nombre de Dios is formally established.[11] Its site is north of the fort in the vicinity of today's Fountain of Youth Park.

Nombre de Dios Architecture, 1594

In October 1594, Ensign Hernando de Mestas delivered a map of St. Augustine to the king showing *pueblo de yndios nombre de dios* (village of nombre de dios Indians) with a notation that it was a thousand paces from the fort (or *two shots of a musket,* according to Governor Méndez de Canzo during his tenure, 1597–1603). In this centuries-old drawing, we see a village with both Indian and European architectural traditions built with wood and thatch (fig. 11.1a). The Indian structures represented are the sacred/secular council house (see chapter 6), the chief's residence, and the granaries raised off the ground. European buildings are the church and a possible *convento* (friary) and *cocina* (kitchen) (fig. 11.1b). Raised granaries (*hórreos*) were a tradition in both cultures; examples still stand in northern Spain. Mestas's council house was that of *cacica* Doña María (Christian daughter of the first *cacica*), who was married to a Spaniard. Her council house is described by Governor Méndez de Canzo as a *hotel for the caciques and Indians that come here.* At one meeting she organized for the governor about agricultural and labor matters, *twenty-two caciques* were overnighted. Her council house also likely served spiritual needs, including ceremonial dances, feasts, and the ritual drinking of the *cacina* tea brewed from Yaupon leaves, *Ilex vomitoria,* in ceremonial purification rites. Near her residence and council house were the Indian-style granaries, raised high off the ground, but topped with a cross like those on the *hórreos* built to hold corn in Asturias and Galicia, Spain. Governor Avendaño in 1594 imposed an annual tribute of maize and required mission villages to maintain granaries under the chief's control. Nombre de Dios's *cacica* was to collect 48 arrobas, equivalent to 1,200 pounds.[12]

Mestas's drawing matches the 1674 council-house description by Gabriel

Díaz Vara Calderón, bishop of Cuba, who visited Florida's missions: *Each village has a council house called the great bujio, constructed of wood and covered with straw, round, and with a very large opening in the top. Most of them can accommodate from 2000 to 3000 persons. They are furnished all around the interior with niches called barbacôas which serve as beds and as seats for the caciques and chiefs and as lodgings for the soldiers and transients.* Jonathan Dickinson overnighted in a council house in 1696 at Tolomato then about two leagues north of St. Augustine, and described the roof opening as a 15-foot square (see fig. 11.1b).[13]

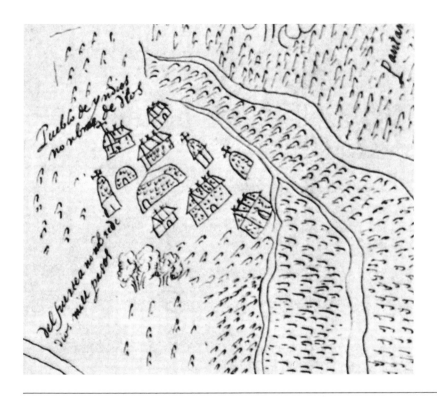

FIGURE 11.1. *Pueblo de yndios Nombre de Dios,* by Hernando de Mestas, about 1594. Mestas depicts the Indian village of Nombre de Dios that was officially designated a mission in 1587 with a resident friar. The drawing is the earliest view of a Spanish mission in the United States. Fig. 11.1a (*facing*) is Mestas's map of St. Augustine and its environs showing the location of the Indian village of Nombre de Dios. Fig. 11.1b (*above*) is a detail illustrating the village, showing the European-style Franciscan church, the Indian chief's council house, the chief's residence, two granaries (for the corn that the Indian village was required to give the Spanish presidio), and various other buildings, which might be the friar's convent and kitchen, and houses for Indian, Spanish, and mestizo families. Mestas indicates that the mission village was a thousand paces from the fort. Photocopy courtesy of Florida State Archives.

Mestas's drawing of the European church shows in 1594 that it resembles the parish church in St. Augustine (Nuestra Señora de los Remedios) and the late 1600s church at Mission San Luis (replicated *in situ* in 2000 in Tallahassee) with the exception that its walls may have been thatch (figs. 10.1, 10.3). No named architect/engineer, Indian craftsman, or published pattern has been found. In 1595, Fray Pedro Bermejo (Vermejo) was Nombre de Dios's resident friar, and as vicar in 1602, he made the mission his headquarters. He described the church as *adorned with statues of the saints.* On March 26, 1606 (Easter), it was the scene of 216 confirmations by Father Romero and visiting Bishop Juan de las Cabezas de Altamirano of Spain. Casica Doña María, her mestizo children, twenty Spaniards from her village, and Indians from other pueblos were included. Two gabled rectangular buildings drawn near the church might be the friary and kitchen. Indian parishioners stood and kneeled in the nave without pews to celebrate and receive blessings—the packed earth floor was traditionally reserved for burials of Christian Indians in Spanish Florida. In 1603, Governor Pedro de Ybarra reported burials in the church at Nombre de Dios (fig. 11.2).[14]

Four groups of Christian Indian burials have been discovered at the Fountain of Youth Park since the 1930s. Unfortunately, excavations in the 1930s and 1950s were not well documented. However, immediately west of these burials, a place of intensive seventeenth-century Indian occupation was investigated in 2000 and 2001 and conjectured by archaeologist Kathleen Deagan to be part of the mission.[15] Smallpox epidemics in 1654–55 virtually wiped out the population of the village. New Indian arrivals are thought to have settled southward, closer to the fort. A hurricane in 1674 flooded the area. In 1675, Bishop Calderón reported to Queen Mariana in Spain: *Going out of the city, at half a league to the north there is a small village of scarcely more than 30 Indian inhabitants, called Nombre de Dios, the mission of which is served from the convent.*[16] Is the bishop telling us the mission no longer had a resident friar? Or a church in decent shape? With the mission eighty-some years old and in disrepair after the depopulation and hurricane, Nombre de Dios Indians might have been served in 1675 from the Franciscan monastery headquarters in St. Augustine.

The First Stone Church Is Built

Historian Amy Bushnell writes that on January 1, 1678, Governor Pablo Hita y Salazar (in office 1675–80) was elected steward of the *cofradía* (confraternity, brotherhood) of Nuestra Señora de la Leche. It was established at Nombre de Dios earlier in the seventeenth century when an image of Our

FIGURE 11.2. Christian Indian burials discovered in the 1930s at the Fountain of Youth Park, St. Augustine. They most likely were buried in the floor of the church of Mission Nombre de Dios. The mission was founded by 1587, and was the nation's first and longest-lasting mission, but the excavations in the 1930s were not well documented and took place before today's scientific practices. Photograph by Frances Benjamin Johnston, 1936, who was funded by the Carnegie Corporation to document architecture in the southern states, courtesy of St. Augustine Historical Society.

Lady of the Milk was brought to the mission. Treasury officials were put into all the *cofradía* offices. Following tradition, the governor made a generous contribution: he "built a church for Our Lady out of mortar and masonry, and boasted it was the only one like it in the provinces."[17] Its construction in stone was made possible by the opening of coquina quarries on Anastasia Island for the new fort in 1672. Another event at this same time might shed light on the construction of the new church. "The building of Castillo de San Marcos came to a complete halt on December 31, 1677," when funds had dried up, according to fort historian Luis Arana. "After twenty months of idleness, construction at the Castillo resumed August 29, 1679."[18] Thus, the 1678 stone church may have been built by the skilled stonecutters and masons and lime burners idled at the fort, among them Indians and slaves. It was southward of the founding mission site and the earlier church(es) of wood and thatch. Its foundation stones may have been located sixty years ago by Father Charles Spellman, and rediscovered in his notes in 2011 by Diocese archivist Cathy Blitzer, and in a recent excavation by archaeologists Kathleen Deagan and Gifford Waters.

Church Destroyed, Rebuilt, and Destroyed

Juan Solana, government scribe, wrote on November 14, 1702: *in the pueblo nombre de Dios . . . the enemy garrison has taken over the stone church.*[19] War had erupted in Europe between France, Spain, and England over the succession to the Spanish throne (in English America called "Queen Anne's War," 1702–14), spurring James Moore, governor of Carolina, to move on St. Augustine before it was strengthened by an alliance with France. His son, Colonel James Moore, occupied the city from November 8 to December 30 with a large force of Carolinians and allied Indians. The mission Indians and some 1,500 townspeople fled into the Castillo with their animals and lived behind its walls for fifty-two days. Moore was headquartered in the Franciscan monastery at the south end of town, and he signaled John Martin, headquartered at Nombre de Dios at the north end, by flying an English banner *from the stone church*. When Moore abandoned the unsuccessful siege, he torched the stone church's wood timbers and thatched roof, other wood mission buildings, and most of St. Augustine.[20]

The church was rebuilt, but the details are not clear. However, a convent (monastery) and a *doctrinero* (resident friar) appear in post-1702 documents describing Nombre de Dios baptisms. Governor Antonio de Benavides Vazan y Molina (1718–34) visited the mission in 1726 and reported: *Church of stone and convent.*[21] In 1728, Fray Joseph de Bullones, Florida's Franciscan provincial, describes the church and convent:

> *Macariz, alias Nombre de Dios, was about two rifle-shots distant from the presidio. . . . The church was always the best one for the reason that the statue of Our Lady de la Leche was placed in it and with the alms from the devout its walls were made of stone and mortar. Although the roof was of palm, it was decorated with every decency and the convent also was of lime and stone and roofed with palm.*[22]

"Macariz" was the name of the creek close by. Palm roofs were the practice because board roofs were *very expensive* owing to their scarcity due to *enemies who have plagued this presidio.*[23] In 1728, tragedy struck again. Like the church that was set on fire by the English in 1702, the new church was destroyed as the result of an English raid:

> During this present year [1728] on the twentieth of March, on the enemy's entering (whose army was composed of two hundred Englishmen and a like number of Indians) into the village of Nombre de Dios in Macariz and into this place alone, after setting fire to it, he [Col. John Palmer] robbed the church and the little convent and did some nasty damage to the statues and they killed the docile Indians who were fleeing and carried off others as prisoners. . . . After the enemy had withdrawn, the governor of the presidio ordered the blowing up of the church and convent, of which nothing more is left than the ruins.[24]

Third and Last Stone Church

A new stone church was built shortly after 1728. This one was even farther south, across Macariz Creek, and inside the city's outer entrenchment barrier (an early 1700s earth bulwark, forerunner of the *Hornabecque*) that was north of the fort, running from Macariz Creek west to San Sebastian River. Nombre de Dios Indians had been planting their corn in the area for some time.[25] This new church was commonly called by its devotion, Nuestra Señora de la Leche, and was described by the parish priest, Father Solana, in whose care the church rested after the Crown formally dissolved the Franciscan missions.[26]

> The Church of our Lady of La Leche is newly erected with the alms of the faithful and devotees of this Supreme Señora; its length 18 varas, its width 9 varas, its height [of walls] 4½ varas. Its walls were stone, its roof of shingles, and its front wall was the belfry in which were hung the bells. It had a gallery (corridor or comedor) off which was a room that was used as a sacristy in which the religious lived, and an adjoining room to the north for those who made a pilgrimage to the miraculous image of the virgin Mary as nursing mother. It stood a stone's throw from the edge of the sea, and it faced east with a view over the harbor and its entrance through the sand bar, and was 850 paces from the city. The doctrinero lived in the Sacristy with 6 monks, including one who was the Guardian [Franciscan Superior].[27]

Among the priest's revelations about the east-west axis, sacristy-friary, and pilgrimage space is the espadaña belfry (fig. 11.3). In the mid-1730s, the same style belfry would be erected at La Soledad (plate 8), and the church newly rebuilt at the Franciscan monastery headquarters (both in the style of the 1797 cathedral, plate 13).[28] Father Solana estimated the nave dimensions of the church of La Leche at width one-half the length. No matter how simple the ratio, a belief in spatial symbolism may have still captured his imagination. John Bartram of Philadelphia saw its Classical-style facade in 1765, which he described as: *ye gable end according to ye spanish taste, y collums is fluted, hath ye capital & base & frize near ye dorick order to ye quare, above which is A prodigious sight of carved stone according to thair fancy."* Bartram was amazed that the coquina shell stone could *stand ye chisel without flying to pieces or breaking farther then was desighned.*[29]

La Leche's sanctuary was darkened in 1763 when Spain ceded Florida to England and the Spanish left. They took the image of Our Lady of Milk with them. In Havana, a street was named "Calle de la Leche" and also "Calle de la Floridana." Many of the Indians who left with the Spanish died within a year and were buried as paupers in Guanabacoa.[30] La Leche was sold to John Gordon, a Catholic resident of St. Augustine, for three hundred dollars, a nominal amount that, according to Michael Gannon, was to guard against seizure of the church property. However, the incoming British governor, James Grant, *declared all the churches to be the King's.*[31] The British bedded their sick in La Leche's nave, and a sketch of the church was made and marked "Hospital" by Sam Roworth, surveyor (fig. 11.3). It is the only known visual image of the church. Thereafter, Macariz Creek just north of the church was called Hospital Creek. A number of British maps as well as Spanish maps mark the new church site. One signed by Juan Joseph Eligio de la Puente in 1769 also marks the general site of the earlier destroyed churches of 1702 and 1728 north of the creek.[32]

In 1783, after Florida was retroceded to the Spanish, title to the church was held by the Spanish government for "military defense of the place." Minorcan families cultivated the land and used the church. In 1793, La Yglecia Nuestra Señora de la Leche was dismantled, and its stones were used in the construction of the new parish church of 1797 (fig. 13.3), today's Cathedral Basilica (plate 13).[33]

Epilogue: The Twentieth-Century La Leche Shrine

In 1868, Bishop Augustin Verot bought an acre of ground to, in his own words, *perpetuate the memory of the martyrdom of a missionary which*

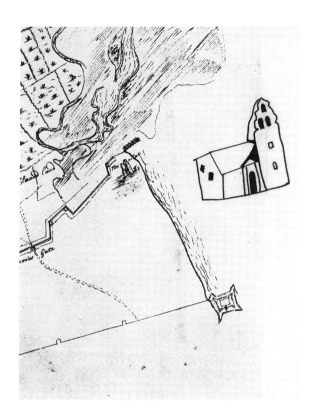

FIGURE 11.3. 1760s drawing, stone church Nuestra Señora de la Leche, built about 1730. The church served Mission Nombre de Dios, which had then moved closer to the protection of St. Augustine's fort. The drawing by the English surveyor, Sam Roworth, is the only view of the stone church described by John Bartram in 1765 as highly ornamented, and having a Classical entrance surround with Doric columns, and a front wall with bells. According to Father Solana in 1759, it faced east and had resident friars and an adjoining room for pilgrimage visits to the shrine of Our Lady of the Milk. It was dismantled in 1793, and its stones were used to build today's cathedral. Roworth's drawing courtesy of St. Augustine Historical Society; enlargement of church sketch by the author.

occurred there. His warranty deed read: *a certain tract of land having been formerly the seat of a Catholic Chapel having been beside the spot on which a missionary of the Catholic Church was formerly killed and made a martyr of the Indians.*[34] This information about a sixteenth-century martyr was in error, a mistaken identity published in George Fairbanks's 1858 history of St. Augustine.[35] On his acre, Verot built a chapel in 1875 and placed in it a statue of the Virgin of the Milk. The ground surrounding his acre and chapel was bought by Bishop John Moore in 1879.[36] Verot's chapel did not survive the hurricane of 1894.[37] However, a new chapel with a devotion to *María Santissima de la Leche* was built by Bishop Michael Curley during 1918–25 with funds donated in the name of Union General Martin D. Hardin. Today it is a vine-covered chapel standing on a quiet knoll on the Catholic Diocese property known as Mission Nombre de Dios (fig. 11.4).[38] Nearby is the stunning 208-foot-tall stainless-steel cross that overlooks the inlet through which the Spanish first arrived those many centuries ago (fig. 8.1).

FIGURE 11.4. Shrine of Our Lady of La Leche, 1918, St. Augustine. St. Johns County. A shrine was built in 1918 on the Catholic Diocese's property that is the site of the earlier Spanish Mission Nombre de Dios. It commemorates the long history of the devotion to Our Lady of the Milk, whose image was brought to Mission Nombre de Dios early in the seventeenth century. Photograph 2011 by Kenneth M. Barrett Jr.

12 ✢ Fort Mose

Slave Sanctuary

Fort Mose—or Gracia Real de Santa Teresa de Mose—was the first legally sanctioned free black town in the United States, built near St. Augustine in 1738 by once-enslaved Africans and their Spanish allies.

KATHLEEN DEAGAN

MOSE'S BUILDERS trudged through swamps, a breath ahead of snarling dogs and the cracking whips of Carolina slavers, to escape enslavement. They found safety in Spanish Florida in a small fort with walls of mud and cactus three-quarters of a league (2 miles) north of the St. Augustine presidio. Mose is actually a story of two small forts, two brief, unconventional architectural moments in mid-eighteenth-century history. It is also a story of how archaeology and historical documents come together to discover a lost cultural landmark and sacred site. It had slipped away beneath rising waters and a tidal marsh, and its rediscovery in excavations and documents in the twentieth century reveals that Mose was simple in material things, but large in things of the spirit.

There is a prologue. Documents from 1602 to 1727 reveal there was a missionized Indian *village of Mose* about 2 miles north of St. Augustine. But the seventeenth century was one of turmoil and epidemics, and of movements of refugee Indians, whole villages, and missions. Little precise information about the Indian *village of Mose* is available. In 1602, it was subject to the region's paramount *cacica,* the woman Indian chief named Doña María who, with her mother, was instrumental in the founding and development of Mission Nombre de Dios (chapter 11). Fray Bullones's report on the missions in 1728 included the village: *Mose was about three-quarters of a league distant from the presidio. . . . And in a plague that oc-curred during the past year of twenty-seven* [1727] *no more than three Indians survived and a like number of women.*[1] After 1728, the Indian village of Mose disappeared from population lists.

Ten years later, a village with a fort took shape in the same area north of St. Augustine. Gracia Real de Santa Teresa de Mose was named after the Indian *village of Mose* and Saint Teresa of Ávila—a runaway at age seven who established convents across Spain beginning in 1562 for her order, the Bare-foot Carmelites.[2] Mose, like St. Teresa's convents, sheltered runaways—the escaped slaves from English plantations. Mose, however, also had a small fort. As former slaves guarded their lives and freedom, they also guarded the northern entrance to Spanish St. Augustine.

Architecturally, Mose is the story of two fort villages: one built in 1738 and destroyed two years later, and the second built in 1752 and occupied for eleven years until 1763, when Spain ceded Florida to England. The first fort begins in 1738 after some one hundred fugitives had arrived in St. Augustine following a Spanish decree of 1693 that gave sanctuary to fleeing slaves if they converted to Catholicism.[3] Some had been sold again to new masters even as far away as Cuba, but on March 15, 1738, Governor Manuel de Montiano granted freedom to refugee slaves who were Catholic. They were formed into a free black company and were moved with their families to the Mose site to build a fort, their own houses, and a chapel. They planted the fields that were then high and dry and surrounded by woods. A royal official, Captain Sebastián Sánchez, supervised the construction of the fort. He and a young Franciscan, José de León, were appointed to instruct the thirty-eight families in the Roman Catholic religion. Governor Montiano "loaned" them food from the king's storeroom.[4]

Their success led to their fort's destruction. Word spread about the Span-ish sanctuary. Slaves near Charleston joined together, armed themselves, and headed for Florida and freedom. Their revolt was crushed by militia and blamed on the Spanish. It was the year that England and Spain had declared war (the War of Jenkins's Ear), and fearing both a Spanish attack and another slave uprising, the English marched on St. Augustine in 1740 led by General James Oglethorpe of Georgia. Fort Mose was St. Augustine's first line of defense facing Oglethorpe's eight hundred troops attacking by land. It was evacuated, briefly occupied by the English, who torched the wood structures and abandoned it, then reoccupied it with a smaller enemy force. A Span-ish force of 340 and twenty of the freedmen counterattacked and defeated the English. But Mose was so badly damaged that it was abandoned. Pedro Ruiz de Olano, who had come from Venezuela to supervise the continuing construction of the Castillo, drew a map on August 8, 1740, that reported the "Plan of the Siege of Florida" and recorded the *small fort of tunas* [prickly pear cactus] *and sod that the Negro fugitives from Carolina occupied named Mose.*[5]

Fort Moosa, as the English described it, was *four Square* [i.e., square] *with a Flanker at each Corner, banked round with Earth, having a Ditch without on all Sides lined round with prickly Palmeto Royal and had a Well and House within, and a Look Out.*[6] The "House" most likely was the guardhouse and munitions storage. This first slave sanctuary was located in cultivated fields on Eligio de la Puente's map of 1769. It is submerged today.[7]

By December 1752, the second Fort Mose was constructed. It was near the first fort, but this time it was a three-sided structure on the bank of Mose Creek that flowed eastward to Tolomato River, and southward toward St. Augustine, where it was known as Macariz Creek.[8] The freedmen and -women had not been eager to return to a northern outpost to defend against attacks on St. Augustine. They feared its exposure to the English and Indian allies who would kill or enslave them and did not want to leave the protection of the Castillo, their urban community, their occupations and society. But the new governor, Fulgencio García de Solís (1752–55), punished resisters and sweetened their situation with daily wages, three to four cannon, a guard of four cavalrymen, and an officer in charge of the fort.[9]

This second Fort Mose is described in 1759 by St. Augustine's parish priest, Juan José Solana: *the side facing the river* [east side] *had no protection or defenses, and is formed of two small bastions that face the land on which are mounted two cannons and six swivel guns divided between them, and a curtain wall between them about 30 tuesas long* [250 feet], *the terreplein covered with prickly cactus, and a moat three pies wide and two deep.* Solana also gives us a short view of the buildings: *The houses are of palm* [bojíos de guano], *and the chapel is ten varas long and six varas wide* [roughly 28 × 17 feet], *erected in part with board walls, and a sacristy which is completed and in which the friars live, and a very small room that serves chapel services.*[10] Depicted in 1763 by engineer Pablo Castello on a map prepared for turning Florida over to the English, and on Eligio de la Puente's map of 1769, it was located on the "river" cited by Solana (fig. 12.1). Eligio de la Puente's map key reads: *Fort of sod and thorny hedges with the corresponding fossa* [ditch] *which in the time of the spanish surrounded the town of the free Morenos.* Both maps reveal the fort was the terminus of a newly built defensive line running westward to the San Sebastian River. Again the freed slaves were to defend St. Augustine.[11]

A Franciscan, Father Andrés de Vilches, was stationed at Mose during its first year (1752) and wrote that he helped build the church. He was succeeded

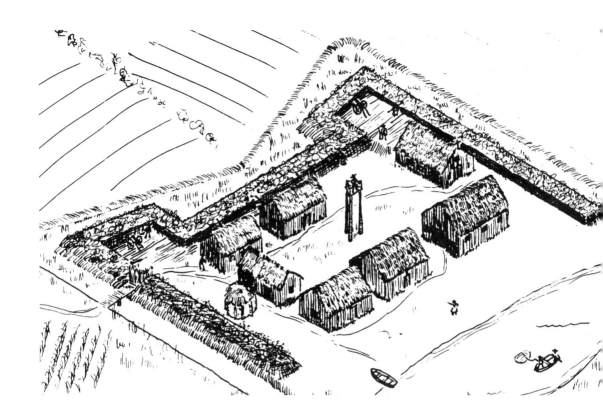

FIGURE 12.1. Fort Mose, slave sanctuary, conjectured layout 1752–63. St. Augustine, St. Johns County. Fort Mose was the first legally sanctioned free black village in the United States. The first structures were built in 1738, but were destroyed during an English raid. The second fort-village was constructed in 1752. It was located and excavated in 1986–88. A drawing by Albert Manucy in 1989 conjectured its layout based on Spanish maps and various English and Spanish descriptions. Photocopy courtesy of St. Augustine Historical Society.

by Father Juan de la Vía in 1753, who in turn was succeeded by Ginés Sánchez in 1757. A number of Mose families lived in houses outside the fort near their farm fields. At one point, according to a census in 1759, there had been eighty-four individuals and twenty-two houses. Some residents may have only recently survived the slave ships to South Carolina; others had lived among the Yamasee Indians; and a few had wives and children who were still slaves in St. Augustine. It was not a perfect picture. But historian Jane Landers has gone beyond the bookkeepers' lists of nameless people, and has applied her research talents to learn some of their names, marriages, births of children, and locations of their houses in St. Augustine. One name in particular stands out: Francisco Menéndez. He was enslaved more than once, by the English and the Spanish, but while in St. Augustine, he was appointed commander of a slave militia, and participated in defending and maintaining both Fort Mose structures.[12]

In 1759, Father Agustín Gerónimo Resio was the resident priest, but by then many of the Mose residents, except a few freedmen employed to garrison the fort, were leaving and buying houses in St. Augustine.[13] They were weary of the constant dangers of slave raids, enemy threats from the north, and loss of liberties that they were subjected to in their lonely defense of the city to the south. When Spain ceded Florida to England in 1763, twenty-three freedmen of Mose and their families sailed to Cuba with the Spanish.[14]

During Florida's British years, a small garrison was kept at Mose. They fixed the fort gates and dug a new well. Their correspondence supports the earlier views of its architecture: *a redoubt of turf two miles from St. Augustine . . . all the runaway Negroes from our colonies were protected and had lands assigned them about the fort.*[15] John Bartram the botanist and his son, William, both explorer-naturalists, walked to the *ould fort* in 1765 and collected plants.[16] Mose's agricultural fields that were once tilled by freed slaves had become part of Governor Grant's farm in 1764 and were tilled by slaves—men and women he purchased within days of arriving in St. Augustine. He wrote the Earl of Egmont (John James Perceval, First Lord of the Admiralty): *this country can only be brought to that rich and plentiful state by the labor of slaves.*[17] Nearby Indians were sequestering runaways, but Grant put a stop to this. Lieutenant Governor Moultrie wrote:

> I dare say that this transaction will soon put a stop to run away Slaves flying into their towns, for they will not seek shelter there when they see that the Indians assist in bringing them back. I have paid two pounds Sterling per head for eight that they have brought and assisted in bringing in, which was provided as a reward by Governor Grant.[18]

On August 31, 1775, Governor Tonyn dismantled Fort Mose and sent the ordinance and munitions to St. Augustine.[19] When the Spanish returned to Florida in 1784, engineer Mariano de la Rocque observed that Fort Mose was in bad condition and recommended reconstruction of the earthwork. In the summer of 1797, engineer Pedro Díaz Berrio (who was then finalizing the construction of the new cathedral) created embrasures (openings) through which cannon could be fired. Between then and 1812, a battery was maintained by the Spanish for cannon, and stakes and chains were placed across

Mose Creek to close it to armed schooners and launches from the Tolomato River. But on April 11, 1812, "Moosa Old Fort" changed hands. It became an American campsite and was occupied briefly during the Patriot War by American rebels in preparation for an attack on St. Augustine.[20]

When Florida became an American territory in 1821, the small defensive outpost's walls had eroded. The fort was no longer necessary or visible. During 1986–88, archaeologist Kathleen Deagan and historian Jane Landers brought Fort Mose back to life. Excavations revealed the size of the walls and the *fossa* (ditch, moat). "The moat was 6 feet wide and two feet deep," larger than estimated in the documents. The walls were each about "65 meters to a side" and constructed with "packed earth and faced with clay and sod and were planted with cactus," similar to the first fort that Pedro Ruiz de Olano described in 1740. One of the structures represented on engineer Castello's 1763 map likely served as the guardhouse that housed the two large gunpowder chests listed on a military inventory.[21] Deagan's excavations and research were funded by the State of Florida and carried out by the Florida Museum of Natural History at the University of Florida. In an interview for a University of Florida publication, Deagan revealed the difficulties encountered in her excavations, how she had to await years of research and contend with the logistical problems of the wet marsh, the local politics—and people who disagreed about its very existence to the point of accusing her of making up documents and planting artifacts to do revisionist history.

The unique and priceless story of Fort Mose's rediscovery in the marsh was taken to the public and to schools in a traveling exhibit that was designed by the Florida Museum of Natural History and that breathed life into the sanctuary's buried past.[22] Both of the Mose forts, along with the churches and houses, are gone, but the site was designated a National Historic Landmark in 1994 to honor its significance as the place of the "first legally sanctioned free black town in the United States." The spirit of the place and its builders can be viewed from the Fort Mose Historic State Park boardwalk.

Architecture takes one directly to the truth in history. Slavery in nineteenth-century Florida is made visible in preserved architectural landmarks like the slave galleries in antebellum houses of worship (chapter 15). Human enslavement is also made real by the tabby slave cabins at Kingsley Plantation on Fort George Island, north of Jacksonville (Duval County). The plantation was begun around 1795, and by the early 1800s, thirty-two slave houses had been erected in an unusual semi-circular layout in sight of the manor house

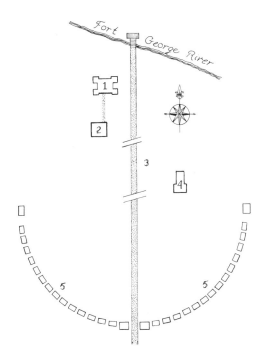

FIGURE 12.2. Site plan, Kingsley Plantation, ca. 1820s, Fort George Island. Duval County. Thirty-two tabby houses were built in a semi-circle (5), thirteen to each side of a north-south shell road (3) that led past the barn (4) to the wharf on the Fort George River. This unusual arrangement enabled a clear view of all the slave houses from the main houses (1, 2). All the houses were slave-constructed with oyster-shell tabby cement, a labor-intensive practice requiring the burning of oyster shells to make lime. One house has been restored (Herschel Shepard, preservation architect). Drawing by the author after Daniel W. Stowell and Henry A. Baker.

(fig. 12.2). They were built by the resident slaves themselves, who made the thick tabby walls by mixing oyster shells, sand, water, and shell lime made from burning (calcining) oyster shells. They tamped the mixture into board lifts, and raised the walls layer upon layer. The houses' ruins are open to the public, and one can walk into one cabin that has been fully restored (plate 14). Also standing at Kingsley Plantation is the home of Anta Majigeen Ndiaye (Anna Jai Kingsley), a former slave who married Zephaniah Kingsley. She often managed the plantation while Zephaniah was away.[23]

Today, the Kingsley Plantation, its main house, slave cabins, and Anna's house are a National Historic Landmark and part of the Timucuan Ecological and Historic Preserve, as is Fort Caroline (described in chapter 14), protected and maintained by the National Park Service. The Preserve ensures that the larger story is told about natural Florida, the native Indians, the French fort, its capture by the Spanish, and the Spanish mission, San Juan del Puerto, that had existed on the island since about 1587, long before Kingsley Plantation.

13 ✠ Voices in the Spanish Cathedral

In April, 1793, the present Roman Catholic church was commenced. . . . The cost of the church was $16,650, of which about $6,000 was received from the proceeds of the materials and ornaments of the old churches, about $1,000 from the contributions of the inhabitants, and the remaining $10,000 furnished by the government. One of its four bells has the following inscription, showing it to be probably the oldest bell in this country . . . Sancte Joseph Ora Pro Nobis D 1682.

GEORGE R. FAIRBANKS, 1858

AMONG THE $1,000 of citizen contributions estimated in George Fairbanks's quote above were chickens, corn, lime, wood, and labor. Other materials on Mariano de la Rocque's 1792 list that were needed to begin the church's construction included: picks, hoes, splitting axes, dirt scrapers, hide sieves to sift lime, sisal rope, hemp cloth and *twenty heads of Majagua* [cordage made from the Cuban linden tree] *with bindings to garnish the apparatus for lifting stone and arm the scaffolding.*[1] These eighteenth-century tools—primitive in comparison to today's bulldozers, cranes, and power tools—gave us the Cathedral Basilica in St. Augustine.

It was constructed during 1793–97 while George Washington was serving as the first American president and before Lewis and Clark saw the Pacific Ocean. Florida history wells up in its cool coquina walls layered with stones recycled from older mission and the parish churches. Candlelight softened these walls and the realities outside during the Seminole Indian Wars and the Civil War. The walls were restored and added onto before World War I by James Renwick, one of America's leading nineteenth-century architects. But the cathedral is also a story for today—its 1965 alterations demonstrate how historic churches across the nation are meeting the challenges of their city locations, modern necessities, and growing or declining congregations while maintaining the fabric of a National Historic

Landmark. Florida's only extant colonial period Spanish parish church is an extraordinary place to believe in, comforting and reassuring in its survival and agelessness (plate 13).

The cathedral's stone construction history begins in 1784, the year the British left Florida and the Spanish returned. They set up their temporary house of worship on the second floor of the British Statehouse, in the rooms where the debates of the English general assembly had been loudly heard. Royal engineer Mariano de la Rocque had cleverly adapted the English-style cupola or belfry into a *campanario* and hung three bells. The statehouse was formerly the Spanish Bishop's House (*palacio episcopal*), expanded by the British with stone wings, a portico and loggia facing the plaza, and the second story that would be the parish church for thirteen years (fig. 13.1). Its footings are under today's Trinity Episcopal Church (figs. 15.1, 15.2).[2] Letters between Father Thomas Hassett (parish priest), Governor Manuel de Zéspedes, and Cyrilio de Barcelona, bishop of Tricale and auxiliary bishop of Santiago de Cuba, reveal that a sacristy was lacking, and that the bells hung in the cupola were about to fall because the hemp rope was exposed to weather. Worse, a Spanish guardhouse and armory of the night guard had been ensconced on the first floor directly under the main altar of the church above. Loud talking of the guards interrupted the Holy Sacrifice of the Mass, and the prisoners held in the guardhouse were claiming ecclesiastical immunity. Royal approval to construct a new parish church arrived in 1786.[3]

Engineer Mariano de la Rocque sketched the first set of plans. They were rejected in October 1788 as too expensive. Redrawn on July 31, 1789, they were approved by His Majesty on March 1, 1790, and modified by local officials on April 11, 1791 (fig. 13.2). But in late March 1793, after the dimensions of the church were cordoned off and the footings were demarcated, parishioners were still concerned that the church would be too small for services, holy days, and festivals. Three militia captains (Miguel Ysnardy, Bernardo Seguí, and Jorge Fleming) petitioned the governor; on March 26, the governor's council of royal officials decided to increase the length by 19½ feet and the width by 5 feet. Rocque accommodated the change: *its length at present being 124 feet and 41 in width from outside to outside instead of 108 long and 36 wide, without interior arches and pilasters, all the rest remaining in the same terms as were those of the plans and profile approved by his majesty in Royal order of March 1 of the year '90.*[4]

The first stone was placed on April 8, 1793 (the deed was recorded April 12). Rocque's letters reveal he planned for the church to hold 547 people as

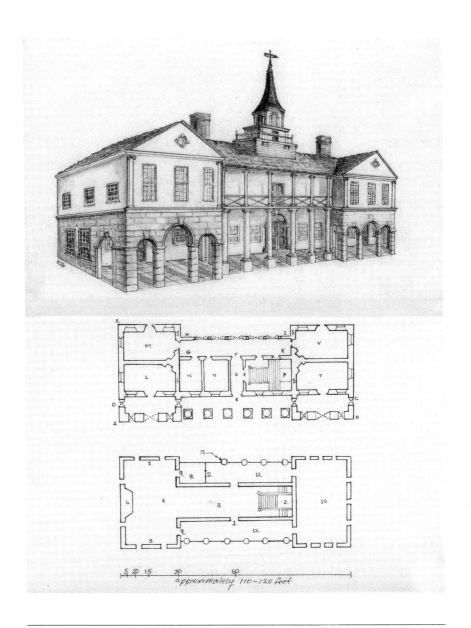

FIGURE 13.1. Temporary Spanish parish church, St. Augustine, 1783–97. After England retroceded Florida to Spain in 1783, the Spanish set up their provisional church on the second floor of the British Statehouse and hung their bells in the cupola. The armory and guardhouse were on the first floor. Fifty years earlier, the first floor was the Spanish bishop's house (1735). In 1763, the British converted the house into barracks, then into their statehouse, adding a second floor and wings. Engineer Mariano de la Rocque's conversion plan reveals the details. After the new cathedral was built in 1797, the statehouse was dismantled. Some of its stones went into the plaza obelisk commemorating Spain's constitution, and some may be in the foundation of today's Trinity Episcopal Church built on the site in 1831. Drawing by the author conjectured from Rocque's plans and descriptions.

follows: *2190 square feet* [nave 73 × 30 feet] *divided by 4 square feet which is what a man occupies in front and depth, that is 2 feet by 2 are 4 and consequently it will contain 547 persons.*[5]

Royal engineer Pedro Díaz Berrio replaced Rocque on June 6, 1793, and oversaw the construction of the church until its completion in 1797 (fig. 13.3).[6] Changes were made to Rocque's facade: paired columns at the entrance instead of single columns, and a belfry raised higher with an additional curve and step. Berrio enhanced its scale and proportions, but he was nevertheless faithful to the spirit of Rocque's Neoclassical facade, shaped pediment, and espadaña belfry. HABS's detailed drawings of the cathedral in 1934 reveal Rocque's 1789 changes to the interior plan and Berrio's changes to the exterior. HABS also reveals that the scale in "pies" equaled the 12-inch English foot (fig. 14.5).[7]

Rocque had gathered the construction materials before he left Florida. To cut costs, he dismantled older churches to recycle their coquina stone blocks into the new structure. Taken down were: La Soledad–St. Peter's (see chapter 10) and the ornate Nuestra Señora de la Leche that John Bartram praised in 1765 as having *A prodigious sight of carved stone* and a *dorick order* (see chapter 11). La Leche's Classical Doric entrance and bell wall had been much admired, even to the point of a proposal by Spanish officials to move the *frontispiece . . . to locate it in the plaza by the proposed Church and in such a manner it will be saved.*[8] It was not moved. A clue as to why is found in Rocque's own words: *The materials . . . from the two buildings* [La Soledad–St. Peter's and La Leche] did *not give all the stone that was expected and consequently it is necessary to bring the lacking stone from the King's quarries.* And again: *the two buildings torn down not having yielded the stone that was expected. Because of its being full of conchas* [oyster shells] *and soft in quality much was shattered.*[9] But La Leche's architectural spirit is embedded in the new church in the Doric entrance surround, fluted columns, and espadaña belfry.

The story of Florida's only surviving Spanish colonial church cannot be told without mention of the people who played major roles in its construction. Father Thomas Hassett was the parish priest; his assistant and successor was Father Michael O'Reilly. They were age thirty-three and thirty-two respectively and had recently completed their studies at the Irish College, El Real Colegio de Noblese Irlandese, in Salamanca, Spain (founded in 1593). Hassett was consulted in liturgical matters during the formation of the plans, and O'Reilly would bring them to a conclusion and become the first pastor, 1797–1812. Father O'Reilly died in 1812; his tabby-and-coquina house is now a museum.[10] Mariano de la Rocque was the royal engineer-architect responsible for all buildings from 1784 to 1793. He was born in 1736 in the

FIGURE 13.2. Architectural plans, Cathedral of St. Augustine, 1789, elevation by Mariano de la Rocque. When conditions in the provisional church in the state-house grew unbearable with the loud talking of the armory guards under the altar, Rocque was asked to draw up plans for a new church. His design reflects his Classical training and adaptation of the shaped parapet with bell niches that was a characteristic of Spanish architecture. Photocopy courtesy of St. Augustine Historical Society.

FIGURE 13.3. Cathedral of St. Augustine, 1797. The first stone was laid April 8, 1793. The new church building was constructed of coquina and completed in December 1797 with a covering of white oyster shell lime plaster. Its construction was supervised by engineer Pedro Díaz Berrio, who might have heightened the front facade and added paired columns. Photocopy courtesy Florida State Archives.

province of Tarragona, Spain, and arrived in St. Augustine in 1784, leaving his post in Havana at age forty-eight to assume his chief-engineer duties in East Florida. Shortly after arriving, he reported on the condition of major buildings, designed the Classical entrance to the Castillo de San Marcos chapel (plate 10), converted the British Statehouse into the temporary Spanish parish church (fig. 13.1), drew a fine map of St. Augustine and environs, and drafted the plans for the new parish church (fig. 13.2). He saw the cathedral's cornerstone placed in April but turned over the church construction two months later to royal engineer Pedro Díaz Berrio and left Florida. He died in 1795 at age fifty-nine and is buried in Havana. Pedro Díaz Berrio oversaw the church's construction from 1793 to its completion in 1797. Miguel Lorenzo Ysnardy (Isnardy), a captain in the militia, was the cathedral's contractor. He was born in Seville, Spain, in 1727, a former frigate captain who became a wealthy merchant-entrepreneur and owner of a sloop, two schooners, some fifteen houses, and a number of slaves. His own residence was one of the city's largest—it fronted the Matanzas River and formerly belonged to Don Juan Joseph Eligio de la Puente, a Treasury official, and to William Drayton of Charleston during the British period. As a former frigate captain, Ysnardy was versed in mathematics and experienced in measuring vertical angles using triangulation and the quadrant. Before he died in 1803, he asked to be buried in the new church.[11] Keeping watch over the plans, estimates, and construction costs were three governors in succession: Manuel de Zéspedes from 1784 to 1790; Juan Nepomuceno de Quesada from 1790 to 1796, who watched the progress from his balcony at Government House; and Enrique White from 1796 to 1811, who saw its completion.

The construction contract specified that doors and windows were to be painted, the windows glazed, and the wood floor planed (flat, leveled). The choir was a mezzanine supported by two Tuscan columns and accessed by a winding wood staircase. On March 20, 1795, engineer Berrio wrote the governor that there was a shortage of residents of the city of St. Augustine to be employed as quarrymen to acquire more stone for the church. He assigned six *forzados* ("forced laborers," unpaid hard-labor convicts) to cut stone.[12] The original roof was slate, but it leaked because of faulty installation and was replaced in 1801 with wood shingles at Don Miguel Ysnardy's own expense, *from his private purse.*[13]

An order for church furnishings was sent to Duran, Llanza & Gasco in Barcelona, Spain. The bill of lading, dated October 1, 1794, shows that eleven crates were shipped on the brigantine *The Sweet Name of Mary,* captained by Don Pablo José Español. They contained altar pieces gilded and tapestried, canvas paintings of Jesus, crucifixes, gilded crowns, many vestments of linen and silk, bells, chalices, brass lamps, missals, an altarpiece of the Doric order, and many more items. Three statues were also made in Barcelona, *well designed and finished.* They were about 4–5 feet tall and shipped in their own crate on *The Sweet Name of Mary:* one each of Saint John Nepomuceno, Saint Augustine, and Our Lady of the Conception. But *The Sweet Name of Mary* was captured by French pirates and brought into Wilmington and sold, with its contents offered to the Spanish governor for 2,500 pesos plus a 14 percent commission by one Don Juan Bautista Villanueve, a factor in Charleston. A number of letters later, no ransom was paid. Moreover, the crate containing Our Lady went astray. It ended up in Cadiz and was shipped to Havana on the brigantine *Holy Trinity* late in 1795. An end to this story has not yet been found.[14]

Father O'Reilly wrote on December 8, 1797, *the ciborium* [holding the reserve sacrament] *was transferred* [from the temporary church in the British Statehouse] *to the new parish church although it is not yet finished.*[15] It was, however, resplendent with thick coquina walls covered in the soft-white oyster-shell lime plaster, buttressed with engaged pilasters. Its stepped and curved Moro-Christian espadaña belfry soared high and was topped with a gilt cross. Four bells hung in the belfry niches, rung by boys standing behind it on a covered wood platform using mallets or ropes tied to the clappers. A coquina stone wall enclosed the churchyard. The architecture recalled that of the mother countries, Cuba and Spain (fig. 13.3).[16]

The Doric frontispiece announces that this is a very important sacred space. Like the Classical Greek temples, it has paired fluted columns, an entablature and frieze of channeled triglyphs alternating with plain metopes. Above is a Renaissance dentilled "broken" pediment. Rocque's church embraced the harmony and symmetry of Classical architecture, and the chaste planes of the *herreriano desornamentado* style of Juan de Herrera, Renaissance-inspired but devoid of excessive ornamentation. Herrera had designed El Escorial (1563–84), the palace-monastery of King Philip II, who reigned when St. Augustine was founded. Rocque consistently employed references to the circle, the symbol of perfection (see chapter 6): round-headed bell niches, round-headed window to light the passage to the bell-ringer's platform, two round vents, and a half-round wood doorhead over the entrance doors. There were small nineteenth-century additions: a clock before 1862, and two round-headed windows that flanked the entrance. These additions did not violate Rocque's colonial-period architectural scheme.

Photographs reveal that Berrio extended the exterior Classicism into the interior with the 1794 Doric altar screen ordered from Barcelona that complemented the Doric exterior. Also pictured are three round-headed niches holding sculptures, a wood chancel rail, moveable Ionic side altars, and a plain wood ceiling (fig. 13.4).

In 1853, a drawing was made of a schoolhouse built on the east side of the church. In the schoolhouse was the apartment in which Father Felix Varela, beloved for his labors for Cuban independence, died that year. The drawing was made at the request of José Ignacio Rodríguez, one of the people supporting Varela during his final illness. A copy of the drawing was found by Charles Tingley at the St. Augustine Historical Society research library.[17]

Noted June 8, 1867, in the *St. Augustine Examiner*: *In the Catholic Church a new gallery has been erected for the use of colored people. The funds raised at the colored fair, last winter, were used for this purpose. The gallery supplies a want which has been long felt.*[18] An engraving in the *Daily Graphic* (1876) shows it

FIGURE 13.4. Interior, Cathedral of St. Augustine, 1797 until 1887 fire. The colonial period cathedral's original interior reflected its Classical-style entrance—like the exterior entrance surround, it had a Doric altar screen. The ceiling was wood and flat. The altar screen and other furnishings were made in Barcelona, Spain. The interior was destroyed during a fire in 1887 that sent the roof crashing into the nave. Photocopy courtesy of Florida State Archives.

was a second rear gallery built above the choir. About the same time, two stone side chapels were added; they were still in existence in 1884 when noted on the Sanborn Map. In 1870, when a Bishopric of Florida was established and Bishop Verot made St. Augustine his residence, the parish church was designated a Cathedral.

On April 12, 1887, sparks flew from a hotel fire next door and ignited the cathedral's sheet-metal and wood roof. Ysnardy in 1801 had removed the slate roof originally installed in 1797, and replaced it with wood shingles *from his personal purse* because he had installed the roof poorly. The burning roof catapulted into the church nave and incinerated the interior, including a most unusual painting, *Devil of the Wicked*. The Doric frontispiece, entrance facade, belfry, and the thick stone nave walls (some 2–3 feet thick) stood intact.[19] Coquina saved the century-old church.

When the cathedral caught fire, Henry Flagler was readying his Hotel Ponce de Leon (completed in May, now Flagler College) for its grand opening in January 1888—it was to be the keystone of his "American Riviera" and "Newport of the South." A blackened Cathedral on the plaza within sight of the hotel would not win tourists' hearts. James Renwick (1818–1895), designer of the Smithsonian Institution in Washington, D.C., and the magnificent St. Patrick's Cathedral in New York City, and a winter resident in St. Augustine, planned the Cathedral restoration. Flagler may have provided financial assistance and labor to hasten the restoration.[20]

By April 23, within two weeks after the fire, Bishop John Moore was able to present the plans to the public with the hope that contributions would be forthcoming immediately. Renwick's plan included lengthening the nave, enlarging the sanctuary, and adding *new chimes,* an oak pulpit and new choir loft. J. K. Smith of Waterbury, Connecticut (tile contractor for the Ponce de Leon roof), was hired to tile the church roof.[21] William T. Cotter, of Sanford, Florida, was hired as the general contractor. His business letterhead identified him as "Architect and Builder" with "The 'Gate City' Planing Mills," specializing in "Mouldings, Brackets, Lumber Dressed to order, Balusters, Rails, Newel Posts, Church Furniture, Interior Finish, Architects Designs Executed, Woodwork, Store Fronts, Doors and Blinds to order."[22]

Renwick's and Cotter's exterior restoration remained faithful to the eighteenth-century facade, even to a Neoclassical wood-paneled door, which can be seen on the HABS drawing (fig. 14.5). The small round-headed window was transformed into a niche with a cherub support for a statue of St. Augustine of Hippo, the city's patron saint. To the body of the church, Renwick added east and west transepts in a cruciform plan and lengthened the sanctuary northward 12 feet. In the interior, he designed a pulpit placed at the crossing—it was crafted with oak by Florida craftsmen. He moved the high altar into the new addition north of the bishop's chair and former sanctuary, and built confessionals where the colonial side doors had been. He flanked the high altar with Chapels of Our Lord (east) and of St. Anthony (west) and their respective altars of Saint Joseph and the Blessed Virgin. The high altar was adorned with figures of Pope Pius V and St. Francis of Borgia sculpted by J. Massey Rhind of New York City in Carrera marble ca. 1894 (plate 30). The ceiling was intricately coffered, a detail captured in the 1934 HABS survey and measured drawing, sheet 2. To enclose the churchyard and rectory, Renwick added a cast concrete wall with tracery.[23]

Renwick also added a Neoclassical-style 120-foot-tall campanile (the *new chimes*) (fig. 13.5). It stands today connected to the church by a passageway and a new baptistry. The bell tower was cast in place with the concrete layers that were the hallmark of Flagler's hotels in St. Augustine, derived from the city's colonial tabby-making method and the modern technique using Portland cement and crushed coquina pioneered by Franklin W. Smith for his Moorish style house, the "Villa Zorayda" (1883–85) named after one of the princesses in Washington Irving's *The Alhambra*. Renwick's campanile cost $15,000. The church restoration and enlargement cost $35,000–$40,000, according to Cotter. Many extras (tile floor, sewer, sidewalk, lightning rods, water closet and plumbing, oak pews, wainscoting, confessionals, cedar cases, baptistry, vestibule, organ gallery, pulpit, and enclosure railing) brought the total cost to $70,000.[24] Renwick did not rebuild the gallery for "colored people." In 1909, stained-glass windows created by Mayer and Company of Munich, Germany, were installed in the Renwick Cathedral.[25]

The Cathedral was remodeled in 1965. The exterior was somewhat changed, and the interior was greatly altered. Its exterior lost the colonial circular windows, and the round-headed windows flanking the entrance, which were enlarged and squared, and covered with grilles. The iconic colonial paneled entrance door was replaced with a door with vertical planks and strap hinges. Both church and campanile were painted with a modern material called Kenatex.[26] It was a protective covering, but it homogenized their architectural

---

FIGURE 13.5. Cathedral restored after 1887 fire with "new chimes" added. James Renwick, architect. Renwick preserved the colonial exterior and extended the church body to the north and in east and west transepts. His high altar included Carrera marble statues of Pope Pius V and St. Francis of Borgia. Renwick, one of America's leading architects, designed St. Patrick's Cathedral in New York City and the Smithsonian in Washington, D.C. His lasting contribution to Florida's built landscape is the 120-foot-tall campanile, the "new chimes" connected to the cathedral through the baptistry, and constructed with the same cast-in-place concrete method employed by Carrère and Hastings at the Flagler hotels and churches. William T. Cotter of Sanford, Florida, was the contractor. Photocopy courtesy of Florida State Archives.

history. The public will little know the difference between the eighteenth-century colonial coquina church and the nineteenth-century poured co-quina concrete tower that was characteristic of the Flagler era. Additionally, the two-story nineteenth-century rectory with mansard roof to the west of the tower was torn down, as well as the Renwick stone wall. Where the rectory stood, there is now a courtyard with a statue to the Minorcans and their

FIGURE 13.6. Renovated interior, Cathedral Basilica of St. Augustine, 1965–present. George Wesley Stickle of Cleveland, architect. Stickle removed Renwick's coffered ceiling, exposed the roof beams, and stenciled them with the coat of arms of St. Augustine's bishops. The sanctuary was enlarged; a new choir and organ loft were built behind the new altar reredos; the floor was tiled with hydraulic cement tiles made by Cuban refugees in Miami; and new shrines, oil paintings, murals, and entrance door were added. With its colonial exterior, Renwick chimes, and 1960s interior, the Cathedral Basilica embraces place, history, and change. Photograph by Kenneth M. Barrett Jr.

beloved priest, Father Pedro Camps. They had settled in St. Augustine in 1777 after much suffering on a failed plantation in New Smyrna. Father Camps is buried in the Cathedral.[27]

With good intentions to meet modern conditions and a growing congregation, the Renwick interior was extended, heightened, and ornamentally altered. Commissioned by Archbishop Joseph P. Hurley, the Cleveland architect George Wesley Stickle removed the wood ceiling, exposed the truss beams, and stenciled them in a Mediterranean Revival style with the coats of arms of the bishops of St. Augustine on the cross beams (fig. 13.6). The sanctuary was extended 12 feet (this time the material was concrete block). With the enlargement of the sanctuary, part of the Renwick Classical marble altar superstructure was incorporated into the reredos (altar screen) behind the Renwick marble altar table, and behind the reredos, a new choir and organ loft was built. In effect, the main altar was moved forward to reflect the Vatican II directive that encourages the priest to interact with the congregation. The Blessed Sacrament Chapel was added to the west of the sanctuary Renwick's confessionals were turned into shrines to St. Patrick and St. Joseph, with their images carved in wood by Richardo Moroder in Ortisci, Italy. Their tile surrounds were created by the Lee Burnam Studio of Hawthorne, Florida. Fourteen new oil paintings of the Stations of the Cross were added to the church as well as murals painted by Hugo Ohlms that depict the church's history and historical religious events and people in Europe and Florida. The large 1909 stained-glass window honoring Saint Cecilia was moved to the front entrance. Hydraulic cement tiles in a striking pattern were laid on the nave floor, made by Cuban refugees in Miami following a centuries-old process.[28]

The Carrera marble statues of Pope Pius V and St. Francis that were removed from the Renwick altar were buried in an undisclosed location, salvaged later, and placed in St. Augustine's San Lorenzo cemetery. They have recently been retrieved and are now conserved inside the new museum at Mission Nombre de Dios (plate 30).

These interior changes were spatial and stylistic decisions. They illustrate choices confronting many historic churches today that have a growing (or declining) parish and an important historic fabric to maintain. In St. Augustine, the Catholic Diocese has preserved an architectural landmark with more than two centuries of Spanish and American history. The church was designated a National Historic Landmark (1972) and a Minor Basilica (1976) by Pope Paul VI in recognition of its historic significance. It has a profound spirit of place, and gives to the visitor "that understanding, that solace, and that peace we find so hard to come by with ordinary resources."[29]

PART 3

American Florida

1821 to 1950

14 ✣ The Magic of Architecture

Unlike a painting, a building is stuck in normality, as real as a mountain or a meadow. A boring building is just a hole in the landscape.

JONATHAN HALE

FLORIDA'S SHORT BUT fast-paced American period, 1821–1950, produced many outstanding religious and public buildings that make up a substantial part of today's built landscape. They are the choices of generations of people, and their choices reflect them and their time and place in Florida. Their buildings tell us about the local geography, climate, national and local tastes and trends, and about each community and its economy, society, and achievements. They compose the biography of Florida.

This chapter points the way to the architectural discoveries in part 3. It begins in 1821, when Anglo-Americans began rolling across the Georgia border into the new Florida Territory, granted United States sovereignty in 1821.[1] Discovery begins in the agricultural northern regions, and continues with arrivals of peoples on the many Florida frontiers, north to the south. The trail stops about 1950, except for a few notable preservation activities, additions, and reconfigurations to pre-1950 historic buildings and styles.

Anglo-American pioneers in the 1820s left worn-out farm fields in northern states to take up virgin land and Spanish and Indian old fields in Florida. As they transplanted their families and their agricultural traditions, they transplanted their traditional Protestant and Classical ideas about church and government buildings. A map of 1832 Florida shows twelve counties in the north with six towns of consequence, and the rest of the state marked: "Seminole Indians, Mosquito, and Monroe."[2] The new U.S. territory's population was then 34,730 (18,385 white, 16,345 black). Thirty years later, the population had quadrupled to 140,423 (77,746 white, 62,677 black), but most of it was still in the agricultural belt of north Florida. In the cotton counties, blacks outnumbered whites.[3] Between statehood (1845) and the Civil War, houses of worship and courthouses became the prominent features of new village greens and town centers, and Florida became a microcosm of the American states to the north with churches and courthouses on "Church Streets" and "Main Streets"—in places named Mount Pleasant, New Hope, Hard Labor, and Alligator. They were built with Florida materials, carpenters' handbooks, and local talent, white and black.

When France sent Alexis de Tocqueville to the United States in 1831 to study its social and political institutions, he was struck by the *religious aspect of the country*.[4] In the newly acquired territory, just as in the newly independent United States, the house of worship stood central to history. At first it was an expedient log cabin that also served as a blockhouse because of the "Indian problem" (Seminoles). Vintage drawings and photographs of the first churches do not show the muslin covering the windows, or the gun slots to take care of the Indians, or the holes made in the floorboards for spitting tobacco. Log cabins were replaced with small wood braced-frame structures fastened with wood pegs, or balloon-framed clapboard structures roofed with cypress or cedar shakes. They were planned by committee in family parlors, and built on donated land with donated local lumber—southern yellow pine and cypress.

Local carpenters and masons designed and supervised the construction of Florida's first churches, using builders' handbooks and memories of church structures they had left behind in the North. In the cotton belt, men of the congregation and their slaves were both the labor and the craftsmen of the details. Pews and bells were often donated. Ladies' guilds raised money for the furnishings with their teas, bake sales, and church suppers. Churches were air-cooled by cross-ventilating windows that had louvered wood shutters to protect the windows from hurricanes. Some frontier churches heated with wood stoves; others did not have heat, or plumbing. Some were never painted or electrified. Planks from dry-goods boxes, rum barrels, and nail kegs were the first benches, and at least one pulpit on the east coast was fashioned from driftwood washed ashore from a wrecked sailing vessel. This was a time in Florida when choirs generally sang unaccompanied by instruments, and baptism was mostly by immersion in Florida's then-pristine ponds, lakes, and rivers. Baptisms by immersion have continued into the twenty-first century, including that of Billy Graham in Silver Lake in December 1938 near Peniel Baptist Church (erected 1883–85, Putnam County), where he was ordained in 1939.[5]

A few frontier churches still stand unaltered on their original sites, in their original fabric to tell the story of pioneer Florida, as described in chapter 15. They are raised off the ground on piers—cypress, brick, limestone, or cabbage palm to circulate air underneath and protect them from rot or floods. But the devil was in that detail. Pigs and dogs found their own heaven in the shade underneath. As they slept, their fleas multiplied and viciously attacked the worshipers above through cracks in the floorboards. Under urban St. Augustine's Olivet Methodist Church, the tides of Maria Sanchez Creek ebbed and flowed with crabs that stole the attention of bored children peeking through the floor cracks.[6]

Unlike the preserved frontier churches, the earliest public buildings have not been saved. Their stories are lost under larger replacement buildings. Church buildings may have lived on because they were the centers and glue of frontier Florida families and their social and religious life. Congregations came from outlying farms by boat, oxcart, foot, and horseback to attend Sunday services, and brought wild hog, venison, turkey, mullet, heart of palm, sea-grape preserves, and sweet potato pies for church suppers.

With agricultural prosperity (cotton, tobacco, timber), image and symbolism became defining architectural principles. Antebellum churches and public buildings were enhanced by white Classical temple-fronts. Monumental porticoes with colossal columns lent an air of the noble ideals of democracy and the American republic, and of order and logic and community aspirations, and were the community's most intellectual facades. They drew from New England's Georgian-Palladian and Greek Revival architecture, and from Thomas Jefferson's Roman-based Palladian style, the latter a favorite of the landed gentry for plantation houses. White columns were emblematic of their society, economy, and politics (fig. 14.1).

Classical temple-fronts were attached to boxlike wood or brick structures and were patterned after those in handbooks that had instructional drawings for Classical Orders—Greek, Roman, and Tuscan (figs. 15.4, 19.1). In rural settings, the Classicism was greatly simplified, reduced to abbreviated cornice returns at the gable end to suggest a Greek pediment. Examples exist at Old Pisgah (1858) in Leon County and at Old Philadelphia Presbyterian Church in Gadsden County (1859). The institutions of slavery and of class and gender hierarchy did not number among the noble ideas of democracy

FIGURE 14.1. "Verdura" plantation house ruins, Tallahassee, 1830s. Leon County. Tall Classical columns are all that remain of Benjamin Chaires's stately and massive three-story plantation manor house that was built on 500 acres 10 miles east of Tallahassee. On the east and west ends of the house, the columns reached three stories high, supporting two stories of verandas above the ground floor. These columns, like the house, were constructed with bricks made by slaves from clay deposits on the plantation. The house burned in the 1880s, leaving these iconic symbols of Florida's antebellum architecture. Photograph 2009 courtesy of Roy Hunt.

and were built into the church structures, in the form of slave galleries, separate slave entrances, separate entrances and seating for women, and front pews reserved for the rich and powerful. These characteristics of the antebellum churches record real-time history.

Florida withdrew from the American Union of States on January 10, 1861. At the end of the Civil War, war-weary church builders embraced change. They "Gothicised" their impoverished Neoclassical church structures, or built new picturesque churches in the Gothic Revival style. Richard Upjohn in 1852 had published a book of plans for erecting small wood churches patterned after England's small twelfth- and thirteenth-century rural stone Gothic churches that were perceived to be more churchly, more ritually and emotionally symbolic (fig. 14.2; plate 22). At first they were painted in accordance with Upjohn's instructions in soft hues of browns and grays that did not clash with nature's earth and greenery. It was not until later that white paint covered them and became the popular church color.

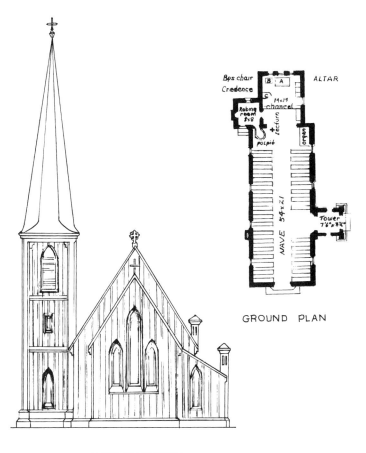

GROUND PLAN

EAST ELEVATION

FIGURE 14.2. Carpenter Gothic church plans, by Richard Upjohn, 1852. Upjohn was America's foremost designer of Gothic Revival church buildings when he published (1852) a book with church plans patterned after England's small rural stone Gothic churches, but in wood, America's plentiful material. The book emphasized Gothic verticality with steeply pitched roofs, board-and-battens, pointed windows, and tall steeples. His plans were used to erect small chapels in Florida's new rural communities after the Civil War. Drawing by the author after plans in *Upjohn's Rural Architecture: Designs, Working Drawings, and Specifications for a Wooden Church, and Other Rural Structures* (1852).

Variations of Carpenter Gothic churches were built in the 1870s to early 1900s in new communities along rivers and inland in budding orange groves and vegetable farms. With skill and grace, homesteaders and their carpenters built their own small churches in the spirit of Gothic verticality, with pointed windows, boards-and-battens, bell cotes or bell towers, and tall, slender spires—in wood, Florida's most plentiful material (figs. 14.3, 16.3). Passionate Goths donated stained-glass windows, artful altars, and red pew cushions, and said their prayers under open-beam ceilings and under the towers and bells that lifted their eyes and hearts toward heaven. Slave galleries and gender and class privileges were abolished.

It was not long after the Civil War that Florida's real estate became a hot commodity. Wealthy entrepreneurs and developers chased railroads and orange blossoms, and the dollars of health-seeking winter residents, tourists, and settlers down both the east and west coasts. Henry Flagler, Henry Plant, Carl Fisher, D. P. Davis, Barron Collier, Addison Mizner, George Merrick, and Hamilton Disston were among those who dreamed big. They moved earth and water and created new shorelines and building lots from wetlands and mangroves with canals that writhed through themed suburbs. Flagler ran his railroad and hotels down the east coast to Palm Beach (1894), to Miami (1896), and to Key West (1913), and Henry Plant in the 1880s ran his across Florida and down the west coast. Disston drained the Everglades. Carl Fisher, automobile maverick and wizard of promotion, built bulkheads around mangrove islands and pumped up bay bottom to turn them into building lots and create Miami Beach (1915). He laid out polo fields, golf courses, yacht basins, the Flamingo Hotel for prospective buyers—which he promoted with bathing beauties on billboards and an elephant carrying President-Elect Warren Harding's golf clubs at his hotel (1921). For the not-so-rich to get to Miami, he created the Dixie Highway, a 4,000-mile brick road from Chicago to Miami. By 1924, he had made a fortune. Around the corner from Fisher, George Merrick developed Coral Gables in only four years, 1921–25, with the look of "castles in Spain" and a Venetian Pool (plate 46). D. P. Davis turned a Tampa sandbar into Davis Island, and Barron Collier's Tamiami Trail in 1924 turned the ooze of a primeval swamp into an automobile highway from Miami to the Gulf coast. There were 1,681 permanent residents in Miami in 1900, 111,000 in 1925, and 2.5 million on their way—until a hurricane in 1926, and the Great Depression in the 1929–30s stalled everyone's dreams.[7] But not before they had their effects on architecture.

In Florida, by the late nineteenth century, religious and public buildings were being designed in the Romanesque Revival style, with dominant masonry half-round arches that exhibited strength and importance (plates 31,

FIGURE 14.3. The Christian Church of McIntosh, 1904. Marion County. Florida's earliest Carpenter Gothic chapels were small and had board-and-batten siding, lancet windows, and bell cotes, but a half century later, the style was updated with larger spaces, larger windows, clapboard siding, and towers with open belfries. Some became highly ornamented. Their many variations are what make them so special in Florida's built landscape. Photograph by the author.

32; fig. 17.1). In the early twentieth century courthouses and city halls with Beaux-Arts Classicism demonstrated importance with temple-fronts, Classical ornamentation, and towers with the town clocks (plates 38, 42). Still others looked to the Italian Renaissance, Italianate villas, and Spanish Colonial Revival styles with arcades, shaped pediments, overhanging eaves, and flanking tower (plate 41). Or they and their designers combined these styles into eclectic compositions that spoke to many tastes and encouraged winter residents, tourism, and the growth of new communities. In subtropical Florida, developers were unfettered by architectural tradition. They hired professional architects who had studied at the famous École des Beaux-Arts in Paris to create architecture that alluded to the many architectural periods of the Mediterranean world and colonial Spain. Florida's late nineteenth- and early twentieth-century churches and public buildings thus began to reflect more than the magnificent Florida climate and luxurious landscape. They were influenced as well by the clients' and architects' own travels to Europe, the Romanesque Revival style of H. H. Richardson, the Beaux-Arts Classical training of architects, the popularity of the 1893 World's Columbian Exposition, Chicago, and the national architectural trend in academic eclecticism. California's nostalgic Mission Revival movement that was promoted at the Panama-California Exposition at San Diego's World's Fair in 1915 would also have an effect.[8] Old World and New World styles were cobbled together in Florida's religious and civic architecture, but because it is often confusing as to where overlapping styles begin and end, the stylistic label "Mediterranean Revival" has become useful and popular.

Cool masonry walls, shaded arcades, loggias, ornate towers, and shaped parapets rose out of south Florida's tropical thickets. Tall, La Giralda–style towers added an exotic synthesis of Islamic and Catholic Renaissance traditions in Miami (plate 47; fig. 14.4). La Giralda is the twelfth-century Islamic minaret that became the bell tower of Seville's Late Gothic Catholic cathedral (begun 1401). The name refers to the tall pinnacle sculpture with a weathervane that was added in 1568 with a new Renaissance-style belfry. The tower's imagery may have been introduced in American architecture by McKim, Mead and White on Madison Square Garden in New York (1891).[9]

Some of the more exotic and romantic architectural combinations were designed by Addison Mizner in Boca Raton and Palm Beach during 1918–32. While creating his flamboyant Old World–style architecture, he was also creating an industry of manufactured architectural items for the new eclectic age: prefabricated cast-stone elements, window and door surrounds, arches, and columns, and ornamental ironwork and glass, a practice that is still popular. His architecture was so exotic that a former ambassador to Spain

---

FIGURE 14.4. La Giralda–style tower, Miami Biltmore, Coral Gables, 1926. Dade County. Schultze and Weaver, architects. The Biltmore's Spanish Renaissance–style tower was one of three in the Greater Miami area during the 1920s that were inspired by the Cathedral of Seville's bell tower, a twelfth-century Islamic minaret with a fifteenth-century Renaissance belfry. The fight to save the Biltmore dates to 1942, when the U.S. government acquired the hotel. After decades of ups and downs, the Biltmore's illustrious architecture and social history are now preserved, and designated a National Historic Landmark. Photocopy courtesy of Florida State Archives.

was described by Beth Dunlop as saying it was "more Spanish than anything I saw in Spain."[10] Mizner's one church, Riverside Baptist in Jacksonville, lives up to his reputation (fig. 17.9)

Historical eclecticism in Florida had actually been introduced in St. Augustine in the 1880s by Henry Flagler's architects, Carrère and Hastings.

Their hotels, the Ponce de Leon and Alcazar, and their two churches, Grace United Methodist Church (1888) and the Flagler Memorial Presbyterian Church (1890), were brilliant syntheses of Old World architecture (plates 26–30). John Mervin Carrère and Thomas Hastings (known by their firm's name, Carrère and Hastings) were then young and eager to create buildings that Flagler wanted to make the city "more Spanish" to attract the wealthy to his "Riviera of the South." They created a fantasy of Spanish architecture by combining elements from Spain and other Mediterranean countries in large fireproof elegance. Their École des Beaux-Arts academic eclecticism in chapter 17 begins the story of Florida's Mediterranean Revival buildings.

With the stock market collapse in 1929 and the Great Depression of the 1930s, President Franklin Roosevelt's New Deal programs (Public Works Administration [PWA], Civil Works Administration [CWA], Works Progress Administration [WPA], and Civilian Conservation Corps [CCC]) brought designers, craftsmen, contractors, artists, and building industries together to construct some of Florida's outstanding public buildings. Architects and contractors were encouraged to use local materials, hire local craftsmen, and create buildings in a style suited to Florida's climate. Under the New Deal's Treasury Section of Fine Arts, a number of post offices and courthouses from the period were ornamented with murals, paintings, and artistic lights and furnishings (plates 50, 52). In addition, the Historic American Buildings Survey (HABS) was created in 1933; it is now the nation's oldest historic preservation program, under which architects, writers, and photographers research, photograph, and draw the elevations, floor plans, and details of historic buildings (fig. 14.5). HABS is archived in the Library of Congress and is a vital tool for restorers, renovators, preservationists, and historians (see appendix 2).[11]

Reviving old styles and antiquing walls to look old became old in itself when Florida came out of the Great Depression. Architects who were freed from site, space, and climate restraints by air-conditioning and new structural materials like laminated and steel beams were inspired to look for a new architectural vocabulary. Frank Lloyd Wright's Annie Pfeiffer Chapel (1938–41) (plate 55) and William H. Danforth Chapel (1955) illustrate a regional modernist architecture on the campus of Florida Southern College. Victor Lundy's St. Paul's Church in Sarasota also departs from the traditional and the Mediterranean Revival pasts in Florida (plate 57). Lundy was a member of the Sarasota School of architects (1941–66), who formulated a philosophy of regional modernism with a focus on the coastal environment and light-filled spaces.[12]

FIGURE 14.5. HABS Survey, Cathedral of St. Augustine, 1934. The Historic American Buildings Survey (HABS) was established in 1933 as a Depression-era program to document America's architectural heritage. It is the nation's first federal preservation program and is national in scope. Since 1933, thousands of buildings have been documented, photographed, and measured. The comprehensive documentary record of the American builders' arts is permanently archived at the Library of Congress. The measured drawing of St. Augustine's Renwick-restored cathedral before the 1965 renovations exemplifies HABS's value as a tool for building restorations, renovations, and historical research. Photocopy courtesy of St. Augustine Historical Society.

Florida's shores have continuously welcomed new residents. Their ethnic and cultural diversity is showcased in their religious architectural activities. Cassadaga, founded in 1895 (Volusia County) as a religious community (the Southern Cassadaga Spiritualist Camp Meeting Association) is today a 75-acre campus of tranquil parks and numerous frame vernacular buildings that make up the living community of practicing Spiritualists and healers.[13] Tarpon Springs (Pinellas County) has St. Nicholas Greek Orthodox Cathedral (1943), which is an architectural landmark capturing the spirit of people who came from the Greek Islands in the 1880s to work as sponge divers in

Figure 14.6. Cambodian Buddhist temple Wat Khmer Savy Rattanaram. Florida's welcoming shores have continuously beckoned people from other places and cultures. From the spiritualists arriving at Cassadaga in 1895 in Volusia County, to the utopian community established at Koreshan Unity in 1894 south of Ft. Myers, to the more recent arrivals of Cambodian monks at the temple in Jacksonville, the diverse cultural ways of the newcomers are recorded in their architecture. Photograph courtesy of Charles Tingley.

Florida's once-thriving sponge industry (plate 56).[14] Polish immigrants arriving in 1914 built St. Mary's Church in Korona (Flagler County). The trend continues to this day, as exemplified by "La Ermita," the Cuban Shrine of La Caridad del Cobre built by Cuban refugees in 1966 in Miami with architectural symbolism and a large mural honoring the patroness of Cuba and the six provinces of Cuba; the Hindu Temple Shiva Mandir in Oakland Park; and the recently built Cambodian Buddhist temple Wat Khmer Savy Rattanaram on 3 acres in Jacksonville (Duval County) (fig. 14.6). These are the sacred places of devotion and meditation of more recent arrivals of people with older religious architectural traditions.

A number of historic houses of worship have become megachurches with additional buildings serving outreach programs (plate 37). Some are leaving city centers, rebuilding their sanctuaries on large megachurch campuses. These campuses have huge sanctuaries holding thousands of people, and outbuildings that are restaurants, theaters, schools, sports complexes, stores, and administrative offices. A December 2005 *Florida Trend* article told of the plans of Calvary Chapel in Fort Lauderdale: a 75-acre campus, a sanctuary holding 3,500 people with plans for a 6,500-seat sanctuary by 2009, a $40 million annual budget and 550 employees, with an average weekly attendance of 18,000 people, and a long list of outreach social programs.[15] This is an architectural story that is still evolving.

Florida's historic landmark buildings are as diverse, pragmatic, and inspirational as the people who created them. The religious architectural landmarks described in chapters 15–17, and the public buildings that form the subject of chapters 18–20, demonstrate why these cultural landmarks should never be allowed to slide into obscurity—and with them the truths in today's story of the state.

15 ✠ Frontier Forerunners

Antebellum Houses of Worship

On my arrival in the United States the religious aspect of the country was the first thing that struck my attention.

ALEXIS DE TOCQUEVILLE

SOON AFTER FLORIDA BECAME a U.S. territory (1821), circuit-riding "gentlemen of the cloth" followed the tree-stump trails blazed by the pioneers in the forests of north Florida. These Protestant missionaries traversed the region with the same evangelical fervor as the friars on the Spanish mission trail. Where there had been some one hundred Catholic Franciscan missions in seventeenth-century Florida, the nineteenth-century landscape had only their ashes, postmolds, or a name in old documents. In the early 1800s, Anglo-American Protestant families packed up their belongings and slaves in wagons, crossed into Florida, and began filling the landscape once more with Christian houses of worship. Florida was no longer wholly Catholic.

In the 1820s, congregations formed, and pioneers felled trees and built expedient log-cabin churches with the munificence of Florida's piney woods and cypress stands. In remote areas, the churches doubled as blockhouses to defend pioneers against the "Seminoles."[1] This was not unlike the first Spanish parish church in St. Augustine, which was built to *serve as a means of defense* (chapter 9). Small graveyards today record how the pioneers met their tomorrows.

In the 1830s, with increased populations and capitalistic prosperity, milled planks and bricks began to replace notched logs, and glass replaced muslin. Vernacular and Classical ideas prevailed, with the general notion that the latter was appropriate for the new American territory.

Church builders arriving from the North were familiar with the Classical Wren, Georgian-Palladian, and Greek Revival architecture where they came from, but without specific scholarship or trained professional architects, they depended on builders' guides, pattern books, and their memories to create Florida's churches with frontal or gable bell towers, classical columns and pilasters, cornices and pediments.[2] Meanwhile, a very good Doric Order was ornamenting the Spanish-built Cathedral in St. Augustine since 1797 (fig. 14.5).

A limited number of Florida's antebellum houses of worship stand as built on their original sites. In chronological order, vignettes of a few of them are presented below as priceless windows into frontier Florida, its culture, builders, and architectural tastes before the Civil War.

Trinity Episcopal Church, St. Augustine

In 1830, Trinity Church in St. Augustine and Christ Church in Pensacola were under construction by the Domestic and Foreign Missionary Society of the Episcopal Church. They were completed in 1831 and 1832 respectively, and are the oldest standing Protestant church structures in Florida.[3]

Trinity's walls rose with locally quarried coquina stone, and those of Christ Church with locally made bricks and mortar. Both fronted on important central town spaces, a historic plaza and square. Both were simple rectangular structures with pitched roofs: Trinity was then 36 feet wide by 50 feet long; Christ Church was 40 feet by 80 feet.[4] Their entrances are the frontal towers at the opposite ends from their chancels. But beyond that, their architecture was drafted from very different traditions.

Trinity's lot was officially deeded to the church in February 1827. On March 18, 1830, notice was published in the *St. Augustine Herald* accepting bids for its construction.[5] Trinity was completed in June 1831 and was described in November as *built of hewn stone in the Gothic or pointed style*.[6] It was the first church in Florida in the Gothic Revival idiom. Since its completion, 180 years have passed, and today the 1831 church is preserved as the north transept of the enlarged cruciform church (plate 15).

Trinity's Gothic inspiration at such an early date in Florida is remarkable. It was built during the first major period of Gothic Revival churches in America, an example of which was Trinity Church in New York City (1790–1839, architect unknown), a Georgian-Gothic in the "castellated style" having a tower or roof that was "crenellated" or "battlemented," with merlins or "crenels" and embrasures. The ancestry of the early American Gothic Revival style was the ecclesiastical movement in England. It began in the late eighteenth century to advocate that the architecture of Anglican churches be designed with liturgy and ritual symbolism in mind, like that of Catholic cathedrals.[7] Incredibly, St. Augustine's church was erected *before* the ecclesiological reform movement had seriously kicked off at Oxford in 1833, and *before* the influential Gothic Revival designs and writings of A. W. Pugin were published (late 1830s–40s), and *before* the Cambridge Camden Society's publication of the *Ecclesiologist* in 1841, and *before* the New York Ecclesiological Society was founded in 1848. St. Augustine's Trinity, a vernacular Gothic Revival, was a forerunner on a frontier.[8]

Trinity's design is attributed to Peter Mitchel, a land speculator and developer who was elected a vestryman of Trinity Church in 1827.[9] A drawing was published in the *Episcopal Recorder* in November 1831 with the following appraisal: *the chasteness of the design and the harmony of its parts, a happy combination of the useful and the agreeable* (fig. 15.1).[10] This drawing shows us a simple rectangular building made to look Gothic with vertical "pointed" elements: front buttresses rising above the roof ridge to form the extension of the tower; roof and tower crenels; corner pinnacles pointing skyward; pointed entrance, and pointed windows. It measured 43 feet from the ground to the pinnacles.[11] With the completion of Trinity's tower in 1831, two crenellated towers stood in sight of each other on the plaza: that of Trinity (1831) and that of Government House (chapter 18).

Trinity's pinnacles are very visible in the 1835 harbor-view drawing shown in figure 9.3. The spire was added later. Not all early American Gothic Revival churches could afford them at the start. Trinity's octagonal cedar-shake spire was in place by 1843, when a notice in the newspaper called for its leading. Francis Huger Rutledge was rector, 1840–45 (see below, St. John's Church, Tallahassee). The north-facing narthex (enclosed entrance porch or vestibule) and small vestry might have been added shortly after, during John Freeman Young's ministry of 1845–48, or with the arrivals of Isaac Bronson and George Fairbanks in 1842. They were both vestrymen and both from Watertown, New York, where Gothic Revival churches had been built. Trinity's pinnacles and crenels were removed after 1867—perhaps in 1889, when the old choir loft and outside stairway were taken down.[12] It is said that the Ten Commandments were painted on the walls on either side of the chancel.[13]

The Civil War had left Trinity an "almost defunct and vacant parish" and a "decrepit church" that was kept alive by northern clergymen and winter residents.[14] When times improved, stained-glass windows were added, including one by Louis Comfort Tiffany, *Cornelius and the Angel*, and one depicting Fairbanks's deceased wife. In 1902, the congregation had outgrown

FIGURE 15.1. Drawing, Trinity Church, St. Augustine, 1831. St. Johns County. Trinity is the oldest Protestant church building in Florida. It was completed in June 1831 to the design of Peter Mitchel, which was published November 21, 1831, in the *Episcopal Recorder* with the description: *built of hewn stone in the Gothic or pointed style*. Its early American Gothic Revival elements included pointed windows and entrance, buttresses, a crenellated tower with pinnacles and crenellation along the roof edges. The spire would be added by 1843. Photocopy courtesy of St. Augustine Historical Society.

the historic space, and Trinity was enlarged with a cruciform plan, a new east-west nave, a sanctuary at the east end and a new entrance at the west end (fig. 15.2). The addition was designed by Edward Potter (Snelling & Potter, New York), who at the same time was designing St. John's Episcopal Cathedral in Jacksonville, "one of the gems of Jacksonville's downtown architecture."[15] Potter (1831–1904) specialized in High Victorian Gothic churches and colleges, and is known for his design of Mark Twain's house in Hartford, Connecticut.

Old Trinity is preserved today as the north transept, known as the Chapel of St. Peter in memory of the British church of 1764–84 described in chapter 10. During recent maintenance (and in 1939), Trinity's exterior stucco was removed and the original 1830 coquina church walls were revealed. The stones are thought to have once been part of the British Statehouse foundation (1775–84), and before that of the Spanish Bishop's House (1735–63) (fig. 13.1).[16]

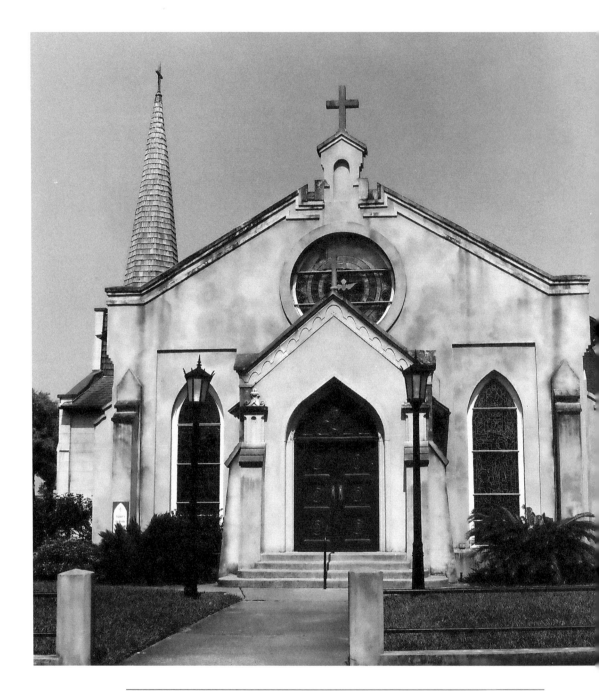

FIGURE 15.2. Trinity Church, addition, St. Augustine, 1902. St. Johns County. Edward Potter, architect. When Trinity was enlarged to meet the needs of a growing membership, the 1831 church was preserved as St. Peter's Chapel and the north transept. Its 1843 shingled steeple is seen peeking up on the north side of the church in this photograph. Potter specialized in Gothic churches—he designed St. John's Episcopal Cathedral in Jacksonville. He also designed Mark Twain's house in Hartford, Connecticut. Photograph 1995 by Kenneth M. Barrett Jr.

Old Christ Church, Pensacola

When Christ Church (now Old Christ Church) was completed in 1832 in Pensacola, it was not "Norman Gothic" as is written in church histories. Christ Church's red-brick building was modeled after American colonial churches in the states to the north that had favored England's Christopher Wren churches. Wren's most illustrious American influence is found at "Old North" Christ Church in Boston (1723, William Price architect), famous for its lighted belfry that sent Paul Revere on the ride that ignited the Revolution. Pensacola's Christ Church in 1832 was characterized by a simple rectangular box with square frontal bell tower, round-headed arches, and a fanlight over the entrance. A staged wood belfry surmounting the tower shows up in a photograph in 1889.[17] If its nave had the column-supported gallery typical of the time, it was removed in 1878 by Charles Haight as he adapted the church to the newer Gothic Revival style.[18]

Pensacola's church was a financial struggle from the beginning. Little money could be raised locally, and eventually two thousand dollars in relief came from "friends in the East" (Connecticut and Philadelphia) to pay for its completion in 1832. During the Civil War, it suffered severe damage when the congregation fled to Montgomery, Alabama, and the vacant building was used (abused) by Union troops as a jail, barracks, and hospital.[19]

In 1878, Charles Coolidge Haight, with Joseph Areson, a local contractor, renovated Christ Church. Haight's office in New York was in the same building as Richard Upjohn's, who was by then the foremost designer and promoter of American Gothic Revival churches.[20] In 1878, Haight was also designing the Upjohn-style St. Mary's Church in Green Cove Springs, Florida (fig. 16.3). Haight extended Christ Church's nave 20 feet to the west, added a sacristy and Gothic Revival–style side entrance porch, and replaced the flat pre–Civil War ceiling with the dramatic exposed Gothic Revival arch-braced beam ceiling. A pointed Gothic Revival stained-glass window was placed over the altar (plate 16). By 1884, more stained glass had replaced the earlier clear glass, but all the round-headed windows were retained. In the 1889 photograph, Christ Church has corner pinnacles and crenellation (like that of Trinity Church in St. Augustine), but later they were removed and the brick tower was extended upward and topped with the pyramidal roof we see today. Not long ago, research revealed that the church had been whitewashed prior to 1878. Accordingly, the red brick has recently been painted white (fig. 15.3).

By 1903, membership growth necessitated a new Christ Church. It was splendidly built in 1903 in the new Spanish Revival style (plate 36). Old

FIGURE 15.3. Old Christ Church, Pensacola, 1832/1878/2000. The second-oldest Protestant church building in Florida began as a red-brick building in the manner of colonial America's Wren-style churches with round-headed windows and a square frontal tower that eventually supported a staged wood belfry. In 1878, after the church had been abused by Union troops, Charles Haight of New York added several popular Gothic Revival elements. When the wood belfry was removed, the red-brick tower was extended upward and given a conical roof. The church is now part of Historic Pensacola Village; the white paint and fence are recent additions. Photograph courtesy of West Florida Historic Preservation, Inc.

Christ Church was not torn down. While it was vacant, windows were broken and pews stolen, and in 1936 it was deconsecrated and deeded to the City of Pensacola for its first public library. Deeded back to the vestry of Christ Church in 1959, "Old Christ Church" was leased to the Historic Pensacola Preservation Board for a community center and restored to its Gothic Revival period. It won a 2000 Statewide Preservation Award, and is a centerpiece of the city's cultural history.[21]

First Presbyterian Church, Tallahassee

Florida's next two oldest standing churches were constructed in 1838. First Presbyterian Church in Tallahassee and Trinity Episcopal in Apalachicola introduce the Classical temple-front church portico with variations in column arrangement. One was built in Tallahassee with a prostyle portico (columns in front of the building); the other was prefabricated in New York and reassembled in 1839 in Apalachicola with a *portico-in-antis* (recessed columns).

Tallahassee was the capital of the Florida Territory, the seat of government and the center of an affluent, slave-based economy. It attracted the scions of the Old South planters from Virginia, the Carolinas, and Georgia as well as their bankers, lawyers, and entrepreneurial factors. They brought substantial resources, and an established southern culture with conservative values and ideas about architecture: the Classical style with which they were familiar. As their cotton and shipping interests prospered, so did the architecture of their churches, banks, plantation manor houses, and their Capitol, newly built in 1845 (figs. 14.1, 19.1) Temple-fronts with monumental white columns were perceived to express principles of harmony, logic, and democracy and were seen as the right image for the young American territory.

First Presbyterian Church has a temple-type portico. Its construction was financed in advance by the sale of forty pews at three hundred dollars each. Designed during the national craze for all things Greek (1820–50), it is, however, more Roman and Jeffersonian than Greek (fig. 15.4). The local craftsmen were dependent on the carpenters' handbooks that were available, most of which came out of English Roman-Palladian traditions, with few drawings of correct Greek Orders.[22] The Tallahassee church has tall, unfluted Doric columns, a Tuscan entablature, and a triangular pediment with an unusually steep pitch (a half-round window was added later). Typical of the time, its front facade was plastered, scored, and painted white to look like stone architecture. Photographs after 1870 and before its twentieth-century restoration reveal that pointed Gothic Revival elements were added after the Civil War. They were removed in restoration. The church stands today as originally

FIGURE 15.4. First Presbyterian Church, Tallahassee, 1838. Leon County. Architect unknown. First Presbyterian was financed before construction started by its wealthier members who bought pews at three hundred dollars each. Like many colonial American churches influenced by the designs of England's James Gibbs, it has a Classical-style temple-front and a staged wood tower rising from the gable roof. The bricks were locally made at Captain Richard A. Shine's brickyard; the front facade was plastered and scored to look like stone. After the Civil War, First Presbyterian was Gothicized with the pointed door and tower window in this older photograph, later removed during its restoration. Photocopy courtesy of Florida State Archives.

designed: a rectangular brick block with a classical temple-front, a staged wood tower and belfry rising from the gable, and a round-headed entrance door. The bricks were locally made at Captain Richard A. Shine's brickyard. It is said to have been used as a place of refuge for women and children during the Seminole Indian wars.[23]

First Presbyterian's interior is the popular ground plan of the time, with two east-west longitudinal aisles, three pew sections, and balconies on three sides supported by wood Doric columns that still show the hand-adze marks. The balconies are an efficient use of the interior space. Slaves sat in the north slave gallery. Another distinctive element is the style of window sash with multiple small, clear glass lights. The box pews that were once reserved for the wealthy parishioners are mahogany, mortised and tenoned, showing great pride in craftsmanship.[24]

Trinity Episcopal Church, Apalachicola

In 1838, Apalachicola was the third-largest cotton port on the Gulf and the largest east of Mobile. Cotton came down the Apalachicola River from plantations in Georgia, Alabama, and Florida and was stored in forty-three warehouses lining the river's edge before it was shipped through the Florida Straits to factors in New York. The Apalachicola Land Company donated a lot for the church, and the decision was made to have the building prefabricated in white pine in New York in the Greek Revival style that was popular in New York and New England in the 1830s, particularly in the work of the architectural firm of Ithiel Town and Alexander J. Davis. This decision might have been guided by Rev. Charles Jones, the missionary who arrived in 1838 from the Diocese of New York. Trinity was shipped south in sections and reassembled with wood-peg fasteners.[25]

Trinity has meetinghouse proportions (41 × 61 feet) and is entered through the temple-front *portico-in-antis*. There are two columns (*distyle*) of the Ionic Order positioned in the center of the entrance, with the two walls on either side of them framed by pilasters: sometimes called *distyle-in-antis* or *distyle-in-muris* (plate 17). This arrangement provided more space for two interior open staircases (with turned rail and balusters) that led to the slave balcony at the rear of the nave supported by Ionic columns.[26] Above the portico columns is a plain entablature of Roman Doric or Tuscan Order, a pediment, and a small square belfry on the gable. Sash windows have twenty-four lights and louvered wood shutters. Interior details were locally made, including its original cypress altar (now in nearby Carrabelle), cove ceiling, beadboard walls, and pews that originally had to be bought or rented—the doors are now removed. The ceiling is stenciled with floral patterns, vines, biblical passages, and the twenty-seven stars added for the twenty-seven states in the Union when Florida became a state in 1845. A painting by George Washington Sully in the 1830s suggests that the church had a picket fence and cypress-board walk.

During the Civil War, Trinity's pew cushions and nave carpets were given to the Confederate Army for bedding, and the bell was donated to make armament. Like many of Florida's early Classical churches, Trinity fell under the Gothic Revival spell after the Civil War, and a "pointed" window and pyramidal roof thereafter ornamented the bell tower. But no colored glass rebuked the chasteness of the classical design until 1922. Today, one sees additions like the gas chandelier, and small expansion in the sanctuary that recessed the altar, and the 1922 middle aisle, but they do not intrude upon the originality of this sacred space that preserves its special story about Florida.[27]

St. John's Episcopal Church, Tallahassee

St. John's architecture today is brick and Gothic Revival, an 1881 building that rose from the ashes of its 1838 wooden temple-fronted Classical building. St. John's 1838 plan had been drawn by a Mr. Lockerman "in the Grecian order." Its monumental portico had four two-story-tall Ionic columns. The preconstruction costs were defrayed by selling subscriptions to its affluent churchmen and women. When completed in May 1838, it was the most important church in the Episcopalian diocese and by far the most valuable piece of ecclesiastical real estate in the state, valued at ten thousand dollars. Known as the gentleman's path to heaven, its pew holders included Catherine Murat, a great-niece to George Washington; Richard Keith Call, former territorial governor; Francis Eppes, grandson of Thomas Jefferson; and most of the area's planter elite.

Francis Huger Rutledge, the rector in 1845, was soon to be the first bishop of the Episcopal Diocese of Florida and at the forefront of Florida's secession movement. He was born into a wealthy Charleston family, graduated from Yale and Hobart in Geneva, New York, and was rector of Trinity, St. Augustine, from 1840 to 1845. He was comfortable in Tallahassee society's "large concentration of comparative wealth, intelligence, refinement, and of consequence, a high social life."[28]

On the other hand, there was George Proctor, a "free Negro" and building contractor who was married in St. John's Church in 1839 to Nancy Chandler, "a slave whom he purchased for $1,300, paying $450 cash and mortgaging

Nancy as security on his note to the plantation owner for the remaining $850." The church recorded his marriage as: "A free black who purchased his wife." A widespread depression caused him financial difficulties, and in 1854, his wife and six children were sold at auction to satisfy the plantation owner's lien.[29]

After the Civil War, St. John's sanctuary was remodeled with Gothic symbolism financed by people from the northern states who considered it to be more emotionally expressive. When Reverend C. F. Knight came from Massachusetts to serve the congregation during his winter vacations, he erected a new Gothic Revival–style altar and sedilla (seats in the chancel for officiating clergy). Shortly thereafter, in 1879, the belfry was struck by lightning. Several months later, a chimney fire destroyed the church, including its organ and the rectory.[30] When it was rebuilt during 1880–81, again free of debt, its builders decided it should be fireproof and more expressive in ceremony and architecture—in short, Gothic Revival. Today St. John's has richly decorated fenestration, pointed windows with tracery, and stained glass as well as a rose window. There are pinnacles and crockets, and a tall tower and a twelve-bell carillon. Its open ceiling has exposed hammer-beams and king post trusses, and the carved wood furniture is rich with trefoil arches and quatrefoil medallions. St. John's is brick—lightning will not destroy this church twice.[31]

Black Creek; Moss Hill; Pisgah; and Old Philadelphia

Outside city centers, pre–Civil War churches were less ornate, and less about the niceties of planter-class privilege.[32] Many of the first plain Protestant churches are gone, but a few survivors pick up the past and move the story of Florida forward. They continue the antebellum separation of the sexes and slaves, and references to Classicism, but in simple ways.

Black Creek (now Middleburg) Methodist-Episcopal Church (1847) in Clay County was originally named for a tributary of the St. Johns River. It is a small church building that was constructed in 1847 by the slaves of Josiah Buddington and George M. and Osia Branning, holders of large Spanish land grants. The design by Charles F. Barthlow alludes to Classicism, with cornice returns and a small portico, and square-edged heart pine boards (10 inches wide) set edge to edge and painted to imitate white stone (plate 20). Drop siding covers the rest of the structure. It is raised off the ground above flood level on piers, and was built with local lumber donated by Branning and wrought nails donated by the local blacksmith. There are six-over-six window sashes, and wood pews hand-drawn and fastened with wood pegs by slaves—the marks of their draw knives are still visible. Two pews in the back were reserved for the slaves. A wide aisle separated white men and women. Above was a flat tongue-and-groove ceiling.

In 1852, a bell for the church was cast in New York, a gift of George Branning. The congregation immediately set to work on a wood bell tower at the front entrance. It was centered over the entrance and on the top of the small portico supported with chamfered square columns. The bell was hung in the open belfry and rung with a simple rope pulled from the portico. Tragically, it tolled for the first time on February 29, 1860, for Branning's twenty-year-old son, who had died from swamp fever. He is buried in the little churchyard.[33]

Moss Hill United Methodist (1857) in Washington County is a very rare unaltered frame church, never electrified, never plumbed, never painted or added on to. The congregation formed in 1825 and met in a log blockhouse until 1857. That year, Igdaliah (Eagle Eye) Wood gave a gift of land on a hill under large oaks dripping with Spanish moss. He had considerable land and thirteen slaves. Four miles away was Vernon, a turpentine and sawmill town near the St. Augustine to Pensacola trail, then a dirt road. Chipley, Bonifay, and Marianna did not yet exist—not until there was a railroad. An upright, water-driven saw at Davis Hill on Hard Labor Creek was fed the virgin pine that is the substance of the exterior siding and interior walls and ceiling of the small church. Planks were knot-free and up to 20 inches wide, hand-planed and hand tongue-and-grooved.

Lamp Powell, the head carpenter, with his assistant Green Worthington and members of the congregation and their slaves, erected the church and fastened it with square wrought nails and wooden pegs. Still visible are footprints of the boys who stood on the rosin-impregnated heart pine boards to hold them down for men starting nail holes. Moss Hill is raised off the ground on piers, and was the second structure in the county to have glass windows. Its meetinghouse arrangement has no stained glass, no bell cote or tower. The preaching table and bench seats are finely crafted. Cornice returns that allude to a Classical pediment are the only exterior embellishments. Two entry doors at the gable end opposite the preacher's desk lead to separate seating for women and men. Moss Hill was a social as well as religious center for Holmes Valley pioneers, a place where camp meetings were set up in tents on the hill under the oak trees with Spanish moss, within hearing of the choir's spiritual hymns.[34]

Unlike Moss Hill, Pisgah United Methodist Church (1858) and Old Philadelphia Presbyterian Church (1859) were painted white, the color that is symbolic of Classical temples. Pisgah United Methodist Church (Leon County), formed in 1823, was a log structure in 1830. In December 1858, Jacob and Rose

FIGURE 15.5. LaGrange Community Church, Titusville, 1869. Brevard County. Titusville was a thinly populated frontier when the nondenominational LaGrange log-cabin church was built. When a larger space was needed, the tall upright logs were cut shorter and covered with clapboards. Today it is a church with a log cabin inside. Photograph 2011 courtesy of Charles Tingley.

Anne Felkel deeded 7 acres to the trustees for $125, and five months later the church building was completed at a cost of $5,200. It is a braced-frame rectangular box that is raised above grade and does not have a belfry. Where Moss Hill and Old Philadelphia have simple cornice returns, Pisgah wants to be more Classical. It has a full-blown cornice defining the closed triangle that is basic to ancient Greek and Roman pediments. There are supporting corner pilasters with recessed panels that are local interpretations of engaged columns. Pisgah's unknown carpenter-designer was familiar with the spirit of American architecture in the 1840s–50s in the South, but he probably used a builders' handbook to achieve his ideas. In the interior, there are longitudinal processional aisles, and on three sides there are galleries carried on simple rounded Doric columns, a typical plan in early American houses of worship. Pisgah's hand-hewn box pews, tall sash windows, slave gallery, and three entrance doors separating gender and race were also typical of its time.[35]

Four miles north of Quincy, in Gadsden County, stands Old Philadelphia Presbyterian Church, erected in 1859. Presbyterians from the Carolinas and Georgia settled in the area in 1822 and founded their church in a log cabin about 1826–28. It was destroyed by fire. Their 1859 frame-and-clapboard structure has the cornice returns and white paint that was typical of Florida Classicism in rural settlements. As at Pisgah, slaves, women, and white men were separated. Two longitudinal aisles and a partition down the middle of the box pew section separated men and women; slaves sat in the rear gallery. The Endowment Association has restored Old Philadelphia (1936–45) and installed unobtrusive electrical lighting.[36]

In 1852, a family from Mississippi arrived in what is now Titusville in Brevard County. It was then a frontier with scattered Seminole Indian residents and a little settlement activity that was dependent on water travel. It grew with the arrival of more families, and soon the community built a log cabin church. When the time came for a larger church, instead of tearing down the log cabin, the members of the LaGrange nondenominational church removed the second story of their vertical log cabin and placed horizontal boards over the logs. Today, the vernacular church with a pointed widow and twin entries is a church with a log cabin inside (fig. 15.5).[37]

Along Florida's country roads, there are more antebellum and old new-frontier churches to be discovered that have stood the test of time, and that are now monuments to their builders who stood the test of hardships and dangers in building Florida's first communities. In the next chapter, post–Civil War Florida welcomes a new church architecture for a new era.

16 ✛ Post Civil War

Gothic Passions and Carpenters

The masters of the Gothic revival stand revealed as the prophets of modern architecture.

WAYNE ANDREWS

WITH THE END OF THE CIVIL WAR, tourists, health seek-ers, winter residents, entrepreneurs, and settlers flowed into Florida looking for opportunities in the state's vast acreage and sunshine. Many came from New York, Pennsylvania, and New England, and they brought new money and ideas about church architecture. Well-to-do winter residents and clergy financed the construction of churches in the Gothic Revival style. It was considered to be more churchly and to have a spiritual and emotional richness in ceremony and structure. Postwar Florida was in need of new beginnings, and it was not long before Classical temple-fronts, white columns, symmetry, and slave galleries gave way to Gothic Revival irregularity, artistic ornamentation, ritual symbol-ism, and pew equality.[1] Small, picturesque wood Carpenter Gothic churches appeared along the St. Johns River with Gothic verticality symbolized in their pointed windows and board-and-batten siding (plate 22; fig. 16.3). Soon afterward the jigsaw unleashed carpenters' imaginations, and their ornamental poetry in wood soared with passion and lifted spirits.

American Gothic Revival architecture began with an An-glican movement in England. Its greatest nineteenth-cen-tury advocate was A. W. N. (Augustus Welby Northmore) Pugin (1812–1852), who equated the English Gothic style with Catholic architecture in the Middle Ages: *Everything glorious about the English church is Catholic,* he wrote, its *spires, chancels, screens, stained windows, brasses and vestments.* His *True Principles of Pointed and Christian Architecture* (1841) and the Cambridge Camden Society's journal the *Ecclesiologist* (1841) promoted a Gothic Revival architecture that pointed toward heaven and had ritual-emphasizing elements and religious art similar to that of the great medieval cathedrals and Anglican churches.[2]

Richard Upjohn, however, was largely responsible for the new style in Florida. Upjohn (1802–1878) was born in England and trained as a carpenter-draftsman-cabinet maker. He emigrated to America at age twenty-seven in 1829, and by the time he retired in 1872, he had become one of America's most esteemed church architects, and a cofounder and president of the American Institute of Architects (AIA). He was the most prominent Gothic Revival church designer in the United States. His book *Upjohn's Rural Architecture: Designs, Working Drawings, and Specifications for a Wooden Church, and Other Rural Structures* (1852) made known that no matter how small or vernacular a church building, it could embody the requisite Gothic principles of the medieval Catholic cathedrals (fig. 14.2).[3] He stripped away the interior plainness thought to be symbolic of devoutness, and even went so far as to have "approved of good crimson damask for seats and cushions, which he fancied would form the proper contrast to the black walnut pews."[4] His Carpenter Gothic style flourished as a national adaptation of the Gothic Revival, and to the delight of many new communities in wood-rich Florida, his published plans were not only small and intimate, they were affordable. Frontier settlers and carpenters could build their own "pointed style" buildings. What began as an Episcopalian movement soon turned other denominations into passionate Goths. New church buildings rose with Upjohn's published plans, and antebellum Classical churches were recast with pointed windows, doors, and pinnacles, and flat ceilings were opened to expose trusses with vertical symbolism (plate 16).

When the Gothic Revival movement was firmly established in Florida in the 1870s (after its introduction at St. Augustine's Trinity in 1831 and Palatka's St. Mark's in 1854), church architecture was handsomely ornamented with steeples, crenellated towers, pinnacles, open ceiling beams, altars glowing with candles, and sanctuaries and naves illuminated by light streaming through richly colored stained-glass and traceried windows. These architectural arts variously appear in the different Gothic Revival phases: Early Gothic, Carpenter Gothic, High (Victorian) Gothic, and Tudor Gothic. Protestant plainness, however, had only been an interlude: Spanish Florida's early Catholic churches had a similar emotional richness in the altar rituals dramatized with candlelight, and interiors adorned with statues of the saints and paintings.

One man in particular, John Freeman Young, saw to it that Upjohn's Carpenter Gothic–style churches were constructed down Florida's east coast. Elected Episcopal bishop of Florida from 1867 to 1885, he rowed and sailed the St. Johns and Indian Rivers in the 1870s and 1880s, sleeping in a leaking sailboat and dreaming of establishing twelve river missions with Gothic Revival churches built according to Upjohn's principles if not his published plans, a style that he believed was crucial to the service.[5] From 1886 to 1924, Edwin Gardner Weed (Episcopal bishop from 1886 to 1924) took up Young's dream along the Indian River and into Florida's central lake country, promoting Gothic Revival architecture in the heartland of the citrus and vegetable growers.

Even if local carpenters did not fully understand ecclesiological correctness, or never saw a medieval cathedral or twelfth-century Anglican church, they understood the imagery of the vertical thrust of the "pointed" style. They created their own pointed windows and tall spires, and vertical rhythms with vertical boards and 3-inch-deep triangular battens that cast shadows in Florida's crisp light (fig. 16.4). So what if inventive local carpenters oriented their churches to community practicalities instead of to the symbolic East? They intentionally fronted their buildings to main streets for parishioners arriving by horseback or carriage, or to the prevailing winds for ventilation, or to the boat landings, where their worshipers and circuit-riding ministers arrived on the river tides, sometimes seasonally, sometimes monthly, and only sometimes on time.

Only one Florida Carpenter Gothic church was designed by the hand of Upjohn: St. Mark's in Palatka. Others were designed by Charles C. Haight and Robert S. Schuyler using Upjohn's book or other published plans, or "as built" churches for models. Haight's name is on the church plans for Pensacola, Green Cove Springs, and Maitland. Schuyler moved from New York to Fernandina, Florida, and designed several Upjohn-style Carpenter Gothic churches (some without charging a fee). He also designed the brick (and black mortar) St. Andrew's Episcopal Church (1887) in Jacksonville that has a 120-foot-tall steeple and was once the city's tallest landmark and largest church. In the 1970s, it stood vacant and in disrepair, just like its vacated neighborhood, but today "Old St. Andrew's" is beautifully restored and the headquarters of the Jacksonville Historical Society. It was rescued in part by the arrival of the NFL Jaguars team and Alltel Stadium. Schuyler also designed the stone St. Peter's Church in Fernandina Beach (1884) with a crenellated tower; the church was rebuilt to his plans in 1893 after a fire.

Wood Carpenter Gothic gems still stand at the bend of a river or road away from life in the fast lane. Their architecture looks back to England, Europe, and Richard Upjohn for its inspiration, but in their time it looked forward to Florida's new tourist and winter resident economy, population growth, and social reform.

A number of Gothic Revival church histories read "designed by Upjohn," but in reality, only St. Mark's Episcopal Church in Palatka (Putnam County) had plans hand-drawn by Richard Upjohn. He drafted the plans in 1854, two years after the publication of his book (fig. 16.1). St. Mark's is also the only pre–Civil War Carpenter Gothic church in Florida. Palatka in 1854 was becoming an important port on the St. Johns River for cotton, citrus, tourism, and agricultural trade with inland Florida. Thirty years later (1888), Henry Flagler would build the first wooden bridge across the river at the foot of Main Street. St. Mark's founders were prominent players in this growth. One was federal judge Isaac Bronson, from Watertown, New York, who was appointed to the U.S. Congress in 1837 and who introduced the act by which Florida eventually became a state in 1845. Appointed Florida's federal territorial judge and circuit judge after statehood in 1845, he made his headquarters in St. Augustine, where he was a member of Trinity Episcopal Church, the first church of the American Gothic Revival trend in Florida. In 1852, he built a large home in Palatka, Sunny Point, now a house museum. Another founder was William Moseley, a planter from North Carolina who built a plantation in Jefferson County and was the first governor of Florida after statehood. He moved to Palatka in 1851.[6]

St. Mark's board-and-batten hand-drawn design and accompanying letters were sent by Richard Upjohn to the church fathers between May 23, 1853, and March 14, 1854.[7] Its core "pointed" space proceeded from Upjohn's 1846 design for St. John's in the Wilderness, a small rural community church in Copake Falls, New York. Upjohn published its design and working drawings in 1852 in his book *Upjohn's Rural Architecture.* Palatka's church has most of the Upjohn vertical hallmarks on display in *Rural Architecture:* a steeply pitched roof, board-and-batten cladding, exposed ceiling rafters, and lancet windows. A large hexagonal window is over the entrance. His plans enabled carpenters to create simplified pointed Gothic windows and doors using straight lines that meet to form a point at the top.

A locally written history of St. Mark's concludes: "Our original little Church has been expanded and added on to many times and much more can be said about its history." An 1870 photograph reveals there was originally

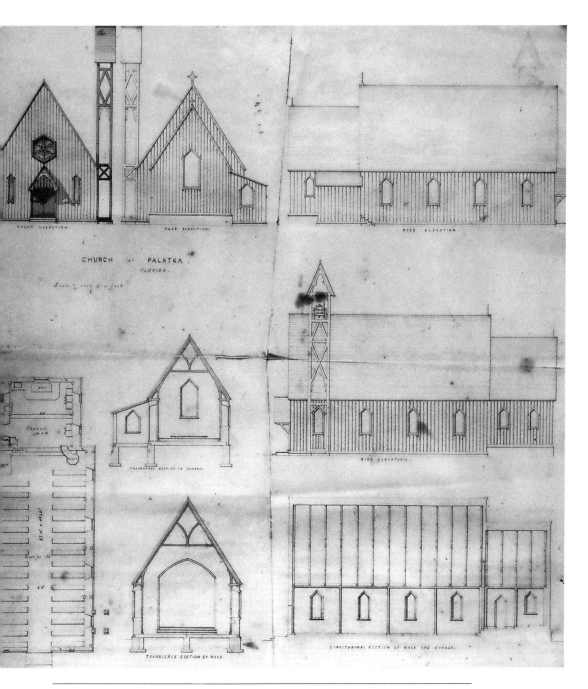

FIGURE 16.1. Richard Upjohn's plans, St. Mark's Church, Palatka, 1854. Putnam County. St. Mark's is the only church in Florida for which Upjohn personally drew plans. Old photographs show that it was built true to these plans with the Upjohn vertical hallmarks (pitched roof, board-and-batten siding, lancet windows, exposed ceiling beams), and a large hexagonal rose window. After the Civil War, a bell tower was added, ornamented in the Victorian period taste. Photocopy courtesy of Florida State Archives.

a small exposed post-and-beam belfry west of the entrance. However, St. Mark's suffered during the Civil War and from postwar neglect, and "the rotting belfry made the church unsafe." Its current Victorian period picturesque bell tower was built on the east side of the church after 1870. In 1886, iron braces had to be installed to prevent the church roof from spreading, paid for with funds raised in a concert. White paint has replaced Upjohn's gray paint, and the entrance door has been painted a martyr's red (plate 21). The Palatka community suffered a devastating, landscape-altering, downtown fire (1884) and economic downturn, but the members of St. Mark's believe in protecting their historic Upjohn church.[8]

Along the darkly beautiful, north-flowing St. Johns River, small board-and-batten Carpenter Gothic churches illustrate the story of the many post–Civil War Episcopal river missions. St. Margaret's (1875) at Hibernia (Latin for Ireland); Grace Church (1880) at Orange Park (now shingled); St. George's (1882) on Fort George Island; St. Paul's (1882) at Federal Point, and St. Mary's in Palatka (1883). They were Upjohn plans adapted to their sites and budgets by Bishop Young and architect Robert Schuyler.

St. Margaret's at Hibernia (Fleming Island) is the smallest, seating fifty people. It was financed and built by Margaret Seton Fleming on the western shore of the St. Johns River, on what was a Spanish land grant plantation (1790). Shaded under spreading oaks, it stands beside the Fleming family cemetery. Margaret Fleming's son, Francis Philip Fleming, was Florida's fifteenth governor. Her tiny chapel was built solidly and slowly beginning in 1875, with a raised chancel, heart-pine floors, slate roof, and shadow-casting boards-and-battens. The first service held was her funeral in April 1878, before the additions of a memorial window in the chancel (1880), or the leaded stained-glass windows, pews, organ, and interior wainscoting and paneling of 1884 (plate 22).[9]

Fort George Island was predominantly the Kingsley Plantation before the Civil War, and before that, it was the Spanish Franciscan mission San Juan del Puerto (1587–1702). After the war, it was a popular winter resort and residence of wealthy New England families. Returning annually, Mrs. Ellen Ward was urged by Bishop Young to donate money to build St. George's Church (1882–83). She was a daughter-in-law of Robert Stuart, John Jacob Astor's business partner.[10] St. George's, like the churches at Hibernia, Federal Point, Orange Park, and Palatka's St. Mary's, has a gable bell cote instead of a spire. Federal Point's St. Paul's (painted tan originally, now white) was built with lumber that arrived on the river "highway." It was built for one thousand

FIGURE 16.2. St. Paul's by the Sea Episcopal mission, Pablo Beach, 1887. Duval County. Robert Schuyler, architect. One of the early Upjohn-style Carpenter Gothic river mission chapels, this little church has struggled over the years: at one time it was vacant, filled with sand, and its windows were broken. It has been moved five times, and when its congregation grew in the 1950s, it was enlarged by cutting it in two and adding a 24-foot section in between. Photocopy courtesy of Episcopal Diocese of Florida.

dollars by J. C. Janley of Jacksonville after he exacted promises that the congregants would haul the wood up to the site from the dock. St. Mary's was built by black Episcopalians, John Henry Purcell and his sons.[11]

Schuyler also designed the board-and-batten St. Paul's by the Sea at Pablo Beach (1887). It has been moved five times and cut in half and enlarged (fig. 16.2).

Upjohn-style Carpenter Gothic churches were also built inland in the small communities of Waldo, Fairbanks, and Earleton in the 1880s, financed by George Rainsford Fairbanks, a founder of the University of the South in Sewanee, Tennessee, who was from Watertown, New York, and a friend of Judge Bronson, the founder of St. Mark's in Palatka. Fairbanks had moved to St. Augustine in 1842, where he became a vestryman and warden of Trinity Church (chapter 15).[12] His last house, a large Italianate house (1885) in Fernandina (now a bed-and-breakfast), was designed by Robert Schuyler. Fairbanks's elderly granddaughter revealed in 1980 that she had stood with her grandfather in the house tower and could see Jacksonville burning in 1901. Waldo's and Earleton's churches have passed on, like their worshipers whose graves in the church cemeteries mark the church sites. All Saints Church in Fairbanks was moved to Starke, where a relocated World War II military chapel from the U.S. Army's Camp Blanding became its parish house. Trinity Church in Melrose is also an Upjohn-style church designed by Schuyler, built in 1886 by Elson L. Judd of Naugatuck, Connecticut.[13]

These historic churches are raised off the ground on piers and share many of the traditional exterior and interior design elements illustrated by Upjohn in his 1852 book of plans: the vertical board-and-battens, lancet windows, long narrow naves, central processional aisles, chancel rails, a rose window, and stained glass. If they followed Upjohn's specifications, their walls are either plastered white or paneled, and the ceiling beams are exposed and painted a warm color, or are well oiled and rubbed. Their stained-glass and rose windows are crucial to their Gothic Revival scheme and its love of illumination, a defining element of the medieval Gothic style.[14]

Upjohn's specifications in his *Rural Architecture* also called for the wood churches to be painted a "warm brown color," or muted, soft, cool or warm tones, like the stone churches of Anglican England. Upjohn's book and Andrew Jackson Downing's *Victorian Cottage Residences* advocated picturesque colors "in exquisite keeping with the surrounding objects." Color was important to increasing the building's emotional appeal. They saw the glaring white in contrast with soft green foliage as unpleasant to the eye.[15] It was not long, however, before the muted Upjohn-style churches were painted white, Classical white. Tradition prevailed. A few doors are now painted red, a symbol of martyrdom (plate 21).

There is a striking exception to the white paint. Christ Episcopal Church in Monticello (Jefferson County) is a Carpenter Gothic church built in 1885 that has been returned to its original exterior yellow color with brown trim, and a warm soft rose color on interior walls (plate 25). A tour of this eye-stopping church with Patricia Patterson, the church organist, revealed that the original colors were painstakingly found under brass fixtures and clapboards. Its ceiling is tongue-and-groove oak and its exposed beams are beveled and outlined in red. Pews are fastened with wood pegs. T. M. Ferguson of Georgia designed this church, and among its prized architectural elements are the double-lancet windows inlaid with stained glass from England that are being restored by the Sisters of St. Joseph in St. Augustine. There is a hand-pumped English organ and Communion Table that were original to the first (1843) church building, and the original Credence Table and Prayer Desk carved from local woods by Joseph Trummer.[16]

Green Cove Springs (Clay County) has two landmark Carpenter Gothic structures: St. Mary's Episcopal Church (1878) and First Presbyterian Church (1898). Green Cove Springs was a popular St. Johns River boat stop, known for the sulphur-spring baths at the Clarendon Hotel and the homes of well-to-do winter residents from Boston, New York, and Philadelphia.

St. Mary's is larger than the small Episcopal river missions (fig. 16.3). A winter resident from New York, Thaddeus Davids, donated the church lot at Bishop Young's urging, and an initial subscription of one thousand dollars by Lawrence Lewis of Philadelphia began the building. Mrs. Lewis later donated the bishop's chair, altar cross, and chancel rail. Young furnished the plans in 1878. They were drawn by Charles Haight. Upjohn had recently passed away (1878), and Haight was working on the Gothic-style renovations of Christ Church in Pensacola (plate 16). His St. Mary's design was similar to that published in Upjohn's book in 1852, with the steeply pitched gable, slender pointed windows, vertical triangular-battens, and tall, tapering, octagonal broached spire (fig. 14.2). Rising twice the height of the nave, the steeple was a visible beacon on the St. Johns River to members arriving by boat (plate 23). The exposed hammer-beam ceiling is composed of curved struts (carried on wall brackets) meeting at the center apex in pointed arches. A concession to practicality, paneled doors under the lancet windows open to cross-ventilate the nave and provide hasty exits if the resin-impregnated heart-pine church caught fire, or if fidgeting children needed to escape long-winded sermons (fig. 16.4).[17]

Bishop Young "kept his initial little wooden board-and-batten churches chaste and free of ostentatious Victorian bric-a-brac."[18] But, inevitably, not all carpenters or contractors could resist the lure of the jigsaw and the Victorian period's love for ornamentation. First Presbyterian Church (1898), down the road from St. Mary's in Green Cove Springs, demonstrates a carpenter's remarkable legacy. In Victorian and wedding-cake exuberance, the tower, gable, eaves, doors, and particularly the portico are festooned with a profusion of brackets, spindles, moldings, casings, raised paneling, drop pendants, applied trefoils, and diamonds. No surface escapes the carpenter's enthusiasm (fig. 16.5). First Presbyterian's architectural plans were drawn by the prominent New York City architect J. A. Wood, who had designed buildings for Vassar College. Wood also designed the Hillsborough County Courthouse in Tampa, and the magnificent Moorish-style Tampa Bay Hotel for Henry Plant in Tampa in 1889, now the University of Tampa, known for its Moorish architecture, minarets, and onion domes (plate 34; figs. 18.15, 18.17).[19]

FIGURE 16.3. St. Mary's Episcopal Church, Green Cove Springs, 1878. Clay County. Charles Haight, architect. Green Cove Springs was a popular St. Johns River stop and winter-resident community known for the sulphur-spring baths at the Clarendon Hotel. St. Mary's picturesque tall, octagonal, broached spire was a river beacon for those arriving by boat to attend services. The church was built on a lot donated by Thaddeus Davids of New York, and with a thousand-dollar subscription by Lawrence Lewis of Philadelphia. Photograph 2002 by M. Gordon.

FIGURE 16.4. Detail, triangular battens and trap doors, St. Mary's Episcopal Church, Green Cove Springs. The 2–3-inch-thick battens cast shadows in a rhythmic pattern that emphasizes Gothic verticality. If the heart-pine structure caught fire, one could escape through the trap doors under the lancet windows. They might also have been "escape hatches" for fidgety children during long sermons. Photograph 2002 by the author.

FIGURE 16.5. Carpenter Gothic portico, First Presbyterian Church, Green Cove Springs, 1898. Clay County. J. A. Wood, architect. In the 1870s and 1880s, Bishop Young saw that the Upjohn-style Carpenter Gothic Episcopal river mission chapels were kept chaste and free of ostentatious Victorian bric-a-brac. St. Mary's in 1898, however, is one of the many later Carpenter Gothic churches that is festooned with brackets, spindles, drop-pendants, applied trefoils, moldings, and diamonds. The designer, J. A. Wood, had recently applied equal Victorian exuberance on his exotic Tampa Bay Hotel designed for Henry B. Plant. Photograph by the author.

At Sanford, on Lake Monroe (formerly Mellonville and Fort Mellon) at the head of the St. Johns River navigation, two Holy Cross Church structures (1873 and 1882) were "designed by Upjohn," according to Bishop Young's convention address of 1874. However, Upjohn had retired in 1872 and the Sanford church is not in the list of Upjohn works published by his grandson, Everard Upjohn. Old photographs suggest that Upjohn's plans in his *Rural Architecture* were the source for the design, with Bishop Young and an unknown carpenter. Holy Cross's 1874 consecration was attended by many church members and the curious, who ascended the St. Johns River from St. Augustine, Jacksonville, and Fernandina Beach to see the first of the picturesque slender-spire churches. Holy Cross's parish grew with the bright future of the citrus industry until 1880, when the church, the groves, and the town were swept away in a hurricane. After the second church was destroyed by fire, the decision was made to rebuild the third church in the Mediterranean Revival style that was masonry and fireproof.[20]

Narcoossee's St. Peter's (1893) and Chetwynd's Holy Trinity (1888) are the landmarks of the English families who were brought to Florida to develop the citrus industry. In 1881, Hamilton Disston had sold 2 million acres to Sir Edward Reed, acting on behalf of the Florida Land and Mortgage Company with offices in London that sold land and encouraged its development by English people. St. Peter's Church in Narcoossee was designed by F. J. Kinnard, and its construction was begun by English settlers in 1892. Within two years, the freezes of 1894–95 destroyed the fruit crops and English communities across central Florida. Bank failures and a depression followed. But St. Peter's English church builders clung to their dreams and finished their small wood house of worship in 1898; they said their prayers for Queen Victoria of the United Kingdom of Great Britain and Ireland and the Royal Family. St. Peter's steeple resembled those of St. Mary's in Green Cove Springs and Holy Cross in Sanford and was one of the tallest in the state. Shortly after their triumph of spirit, however, conditions were such that a mass British exodus occurred. St. Peter's was left vacant between 1910 and 1930. In 1930, it was moved piece by piece 7 miles to St. Cloud and reconstructed in its original form as the Church of St. Luke and St. Peter. Population growth eventually resumed and led to a new church building. The Narcoossee Carpenter Gothic church, however, was not torn down but was saved, with its beautiful wood details, and used for a day-care center. As of this writing, however, the century-old church is for sale and in need of restoration.[21]

In Chetwynd (now Fruitland Park, Lake County), the story of Holy Trinity Episcopal Church begins in 1881, when a twenty-three-year-old

Englishman, Granville Chetwynd Stapylton, bought an orange grove and planned a community he called Chetwynd. Many English settlers arrived, and church services began in a barn until their Holy Trinity Church could be built in 1888 (J. J. Nevitt, architect). Holy Trinity declined during the disastrous freezes, but a few of the English settlers hung on, kept the church open, and refused to move it. It is now the only English-built Carpenter Gothic church still standing where it was constructed. Oil lamps once lighted the pews, and its hitching posts were once lined with horses. Its original lych-gate—a roofed gateway where clergy and the bier begin the burial procession into the churchyard—is maintained, and may be the only one in Florida.[22]

Far to the west, St. Mary's Episcopal Church (1874) in Milton (Santa Rosa County) is a Carpenter Gothic with local variations. When it was consecrated in April 1894, a change had occurred that was so pronounced that Bishop Edwin Gardner Weed had this to say: *It is impossible to describe the improvements which have been made in this church; suffice it to say, what a few years ago looked much like a barn, and very little like a church, a house of God has been transformed that the people and the rector can justly boast of having one of the most perfectly finished and most artistically decorated churches in the Diocese.*[23] He also noted the iron fence about it. St. Mary's exterior is vertically boarded-and-battened and elaborated with bargeboards and jigsawn quatrefoil and trefoil ornamentation, and Gothic-arch windows with hood molds. It has no bell tower or bell cote. Oral tradition has it that a ship's carpenter crafted the interior of applied foliate and tracery details and the ceiling's exposed chamfered (beveled) scissor trusses, purlins, and carved pendants. Muslin covered the first windows: brass kerosene lamps lighted the pews and aisles—and still do, only they are now electrified. Frank Lloyd Wright is said to have mentioned St. Mary's in his book *The Aesthetics of American Architecture:* "Saint Mary's is a jewel created in the purest tradition of the Gothic revival. It survives today with its pure lines intact, its muted colors untouched. Purity, it is without a blemish."[24] The muted colors were later painted over with white (fig. 16.6).

Locally created variations and details are what made Florida's Carpenter Gothic churches so special. The ceiling at Emmanuel at Welaka (1880) was painted sky-blue with stars. Towers placed at the intersection of two gabled wings distinguish a number of Carpenter Gothic churches, including Starke's First Presbyterian Church (1886) in Bradford County, and Citra's Baptist Church (1880) in Marion County (plate 24). Their symmetry

FIGURE 16.6. St. Mary's Episcopal Church, Milton, 1874. Santa Rosa County. A variation on the board-and-batten Gothic Revival churches was one erected by the rector of St. Mary's, Charles E. McDougall, who was also a physician. Milton was a center of a lumber industry, with many shipbuilding businesses and mills, which is reflected in this church's abundance of beautiful woodwork, from decorative bargeboards to window hood molds to jigsawn quatrefoil and trefoil ornamentation. Photograph courtesy of Charles Tingley.

is uncharacteristic of the Gothic Revival style, but their Victorian period ornamented central towers bring their compositions together, and pull the profiles upward in allusions to Gothic height and thrust. Citra's jubilant bell tower is the entrance into an Akron Plan assembly room where the baptism pool is under a platform.[25]

By the end of the nineteenth century, change was in the air. Bishop Weed seemed to welcome it in his speech on December 28, 1894, when he consecrated All Saints Church in South Jacksonville. He thanked Mrs. Alexander Mitchell (Martha Reed Mitchell), H. M. Flagler, and Mrs. W. L. Crawford for their contributions to the erection of *this beautiful church— different in style from any other in the Diocese. It seems to me that the architect has made a most happy combination and has given us some relief from the faint imitation of gothic architecture.* All Saints was a Queen Anne Shingle style. Mrs. Mitchell was the sister of Governor Harrison Reed, and she was one of three founders of the Mount Vernon Ladies' Association that saved George Washington's home from destruction and eventually led to the National Trust for Historic Preservation. Her own home in Jacksonville, Villa Alexandria (1870s), and its 140 acres with elaborate exotic gardens did not survive: it is now San Marco, Jacksonville's first residential development in the Mediterranean Revival style, a style discussed in the next chapter.[26]

Lake Helen's 1894 Blake Memorial Church (Volusia County) was also shingled, "cypress shingles sawn, not shakes" and painted gray according to the architect's instructions. It has an oversized, round-headed window recalling the Romanesque style instead of the recently popular pointed Carpenter Gothic windows. John Porter Mace was both architect and builder. The solid double framing and flooring is heart pine, and pews of white oak are curved and covered in red damask. Wainscoting is inset with panels of curly pine saved from the veneers of fruit boxes. Originally it was heated with a wood stove. A concrete pool under a platform opens on tracts for the baptistry. The large stained-glass window depicts a six-point star set inside a circle, with a dove descending on a beam of light (fig. 16.7).[27]

There was once another shingled chapel, this one in Mandarin (Duval County), that was ornamented with fish-scale shingles and a Queen Anne belvedere. It had been an important biographical landmark. Harriet Beecher Stowe worshiped here after the Civil War until 1884, during which time she wrote *Palmetto Leaves.* Her book was a travel guide with descriptions so wondrous of natural and built Florida that it enticed many to move to the state in the 1880s. Her church was destroyed by Hurricane Dora in 1964 and not rebuilt.[28]

Churchyards and picket fences have given way to sidewalks, roads, and parking lots, and a few bell towers and spires have been stripped away. Carpenter Gothic churches that stand on their original site in their original fabric are numbered. The little artistic wooden churches, always

FIGURE 16.7. Shingle-style Blake Memorial Church, Lake Helen, 1894. Volusia County. John Porter Mace, architect and builder. By the end of the nineteenth century, the Carpenter Gothic style was losing favor. A change was in the air, as illustrated at Blake Memorial, a shingle-style church with large round-headed windows. It was seen as a "relief from the faint imitation of gothic architecture," said Bishop Weed when he consecrated another church that was Queen Anne Shingle–styled. Blake's wainscoting is inset with panels of curly pine saved from the veneers on fruit boxes. In the large stained-glass window, a dove descends on a beam of light. Photograph by Kenneth M. Barrett Jr.

endangered by hurricanes and fires, changing popular tastes, and growing parishes, are more than old religious artifacts. Where preserved, they mark where the wealthy wintered and the sick renewed their health, where land was parceled out under the Homestead Act, and where large commercial orange groves were planted by an investment company of London that promoted a second wave of English immigration.[29] They also mark the big freezes of 1894–95 and the end of central Florida as the citrus capital. They are reminders of a time when Florida's rivers were main transportation routes, and when northeast and central counties were the state's main vegetable and fruit baskets, and railroads ran down the centers of towns. One small Carpenter Gothic church marks the arrival of Jewish families in Ocala and may be the oldest standing synagogue structure in Florida. The United Hebrews of Ocala Synagogue is an 1888 building, now used as a Christian Bible Chapel.[30] These small wood architectural treasures are the state's history books.

A number of historic wood churches in Florida have been moved, in various ways and sometimes more than once. In addition to the examples of St. Paul's by the Sea, which was cut in half and moved five times (fig. 16.2), and Narcoosee's St. Peter's, which was moved piece-by-piece, one of the most ingenious moves of any wood church was depicted in a drawing by a Kiowa Indian named Bear's Heart. In 1877, he drew a diagram showing how he and Plains Indian prisoners at Fort Marion (Castillo de San Marcos) moved a wood chapel for the Presbyterian Sunday School in St. Augustine. They moved it some 1,100 yards, over land submerged at high tide, and reversed its orientation from east to west. A teacher of the Indians named Miss Sarah Mather was in charge of raising funds for this maneuver, but she lacked enough money to pay regular movers. She hired the Indians. They made their own windlass, and a track with rollers, by renting timbers and the lifting screws and borrowing heavy ropes and blocks from a naval vessel. Indians worked the windlass and were paid from the balance in the fund. On the drawing are the church measurements: it was 28 × 48 feet with a tower 54 feet high.[31] Bear's Heart's drawing in graphite, colored pencil, and ink on paper tells the whole story. It is archived at the Beinecke Rare Book and Manuscript Library at Yale University.[32]

17 ✦ Changing Directions on New Frontiers

History is not only relevant, it is essential to creation of the new. . . . I strongly believe that history is a continuum and architecture needs to flow with it.

I. M. Pei

HAVING LOOKED AT north Florida's frontier antebellum religious landmarks (mostly vernacular and Classical in spirit), and at the post–Civil War small wood picturesque chapels (mostly Carpenter Gothic), we turn in this chapter to new designs in the first half of the twentieth century that will revive elements of the best architectural traditions of the Mediterranean world and colonial Spain. Discovery begins in the Flagler era in St. Augustine. It gains momentum on newly laid rails and roads heading south in the wake of arriving tourists, winter residents, entrepreneurial developers, and style-making professional architects. In Florida's subtropical balmy climate and vast tracts of undeveloped land, the new way of designing created an artfully diverse built landscape. Houses of worship would no longer be wood or small, or symbolize agricultural interests. They would be large and masonry and fireproof, and they would be intellectual and resonate with the aspirations inspired by Florida's new economic opportunities.

The making of a Florida style on new frontiers and in newly established towns and counties was affected by the geography and climate, materials and building techniques, personal travels to Europe, a national trend toward academic eclecticism, and a nostalgia for California's Spanish mission heritage. (Florida's own Spanish heritage was little known or appreciated at that time within the state.) Houses of worship rose in south Florida on newly cleared lots because of American ingenuity in turning wetlands and swamps into building sites. They rose with expectations for Florida's future, and like the public buildings described in chapter 18, they were often a new community's best and most intellectual architecture. They tell us a story of Florida's growth and development, and of decisions about artistic directions that still characterize a large part of today's built landscape.

Henry Flagler's two churches in St. Augustine—Grace United Methodist Church (1888) and the Flagler Memorial Presbyterian Church (1889–90)—begin the story of Florida's Mediterranean Revival architecture. They were both designed by the firm Carrère and Hastings (John Mervin Carrère, Thomas Hastings, and, briefly, Bernard Maybeck) to replace smaller churches. Flagler had hired these young architects in 1885 to design his hotels, the Ponce de Leon and the Alcazar, in a "Spanish Renaissance" style that would be grand enough to attract the wealthy to St. Augustine, the city he called the "Newport of the South" and the "American Riviera" (plates 26, 27). Carrère, Hastings, and Maybeck were recent graduates of the École des Beaux-Arts in Paris, at that time the world's most influential school of architecture. After a short stint with the prestigious McKim, Mead and White firm in New York, Carrère and Hastings formed their own firm, and Flagler became their first big client. Bernard Maybeck joined them; he had been Hastings's roommate at the École. In St. Augustine, their method of design was a brilliant synthesis of the best of historic Spanish and Italian architectural traditions. The two churches would follow in the same eclectic style (plates 28, 29).[1]

Both churches owe something of their design to the Romanesque Revival architecture popularized in America by H. H. Richardson. Richardson was an 1865 graduate of the École des Beaux-Arts. His Trinity Church in Boston (1877) won the most prestigious architectural competition of the time and "set the tone for larger more aggressive" rusticated stone architecture for churches, county courthouses and federal buildings, universities, railroad stations, and large residences (fig. 17.3). The first reference to Romanesque Revival architecture in Florida, however, was an elegant small church in Palatka, the First Presbyterian Church (1881), with a tower and semi-circular porch in smooth-faced monochromatic brick. It is notable for its architect, Richard Morris Hunt. He was the first American to attend the École des Beaux-Arts in Paris, and is best known for his sumptuous Vanderbilt mansions: the Breakers for Cornelius Vanderbilt (1893), in Newport, Rhode Island; and the

Biltmore, for George Vanderbilt (1895), in Asheville, North Carolina. Palatka's Presbyterian Church replaced the log-cabin powder magazine that had served as a church structure since 1856. In 1880, Palatka was known as the "Gem City of the St. Johns River"; its wharves bustled with river commerce, railroad produce, and arriving wealthy winter residents, one of whom was Robert Lenox Kennedy of New York. He donated twelve thousand dollars and hired Hunt.[2]

Carrère and Hastings's first church, Grace United Methodist, has a more characteristic Romanesque facade with an entrance arcade of three half-round arches supported on short, square brick columns (fig. 17.1). Grace hints of the architects' attraction to Spain's early Christian, Romanesque, Moorish, and Renaissance aesthetics. Facade ornamentation is limited to the arcade and tower crown (plate 28). The single tower with conical helmet reflects Andalusian practices. It hints of the Cathedral of Seville, where a minaret was converted into a highly ornamented Renaissance bell tower. Grace's concrete walls were cast in the same novel concrete technique (Portland cement and crushed coquina) that was pioneered by Franklin W. Smith in St. Augustine at his Villa Zorayda and used to build the Flagler hotels. Walls were poured in place in wood molds.[3] The red-brick and terra-cotta ornamentation sets up a striking contrast with the muted tones of the wall surface, and accentuates the arches and belfry.

Construction on Flagler's Memorial Presbyterian Church was completed in 1890. Construction began in 1889, immediately after the unexpected news was received of the death of Jennie Louise Flagler Benedict, Flagler's daughter, who died on the ship that was bringing her to St. Augustine. She died shortly after her baby daughter, who died at birth in New York. The Neoclassical mausoleum added at the west side of the church in 1906 holds the remains of Henry Flagler, his first wife, Mary Harkness, their daughter, Jennie, and her baby.

Memorial, like Grace Methodist, is cast coquina concrete. It is a complex composition reflecting the Beaux-Arts Classicism and academic eclecticism of its time. Characteristic of the Romanesque Revival are the heavy masonry massing, wide stairway approach, arcade entrance, gable facade flanked by twin towers, and a large traceried rose window set in a large round-headed ornamental brick arch. But Carrère and Hastings added a Renaissance-style pendentive dome and drum (tambour) over the crossing of a Latin-cross plan, and ornamental details from Spain's Moorish, Gothic, Renaissance, and Baroque periods, adapted so as to make their precise sources unknown (plate 29; fig. 17.2). The effect is such that a traveled visitor to St. Augustine might

FIGURE 17.1. Grace United Methodist Church, St. Augustine, 1888. Carrère and Hastings, architects. Grace United Methodist was inspired by Henry Flagler's charge to his young architects to make St. Augustine look more "Spanish" for the wealthy tourists wintering in his hotels. It was their first church, and the first example of a religious building in Florida that would romantically allude to Spain. Moreover, it was the first church to be constructed with poured concrete. Photograph 2012 by Kenneth M. Barrett Jr.

imagine the cathedrals and churches of Salamanca and León and in Andalusia (particularly Seville), from where Carrère and Hastings borrowed motifs for the Flagler hotels, or one might imagine churches along the pilgrimage route from France to Santiago de Compostela in Spain as well as in Tuscan Italy. That is the magic of architectural storytelling.

A newspaper reporter at the dedication in 1890 described the style of Memorial Presbyterian as *Transitional Renaissance and somewhat in the character of Venetian Renaissance*. Other writers followed suit and have written that it was patterned after St. Mark's Cathedral in Venice. However, Memorial Presbyterian is not patterned after St. Mark's. The Venice church is a Greek cross inscribed within a square under five domes that are not raised on drums. It may be that the decorative ogee arches applied above Memorial's south entrance arcade and various windows conjured up the image of the Venice cathedral (fig. 17.2). Ogee arches, however, are also found in Spain (known as Spanish Flamboyant Gothic arches): examples exist at the entrance to the New Cathedral of Salamanca (1512) designed by Juan Gil de Hontanon, and in Seville at the church of Santa María (1578) and at the Gothic Palace of Jabalquinto, Baeza (in the Isabelline style).[4] Closer to home, decorative ogee arches have been prominent in New York City at Richard Upjohn's Trinity Church since 1846.

Memorial's dome was the first pendentive dome on a Florida church. Hemispherical domes (a Roman invention) have long been believed to have spiritual qualities symbolizing Heaven's sacred dome. Memorial's dome reaches an impressive height, some 120 feet from the floor, and is topped with a cross 14 feet high. The dome is raised on a column (a drum or tambour) that is a basic feature of the Renaissance. It is supported by four piers and pendentives (curved walls between the piers). Pendentives (and sometimes squinches) form the transition from the circle of the dome to the square of the four piers at the crossing. Renaissance drums were a sixteenth-century innovation that added impressive height to the dome and church exterior, and brightened the interior with natural light falling on the crossing. St. Peter's Basilica in Rome, the Florence Cathedral, and the Cathedral of Salamanca in Spain have pendentive domes.

Cornice returns suggest a classical pediment; and the color scheme is Renaissance influenced, as are the round-headed arches on tall, slender, garlanded columns. The eclectic flanking stair towers reflect Spain's Romanesque, Islamic, and Renaissance architecture. La Giralda, the Cathedral of Seville's bell tower, might have influenced their design. While Carrère and Hastings were drafting plans for Flagler's Presbyterian church, McKim,

Mead & White were designing Madison Square Garden (completed in 1891) with the imagery of La Giralda.[5] A number of the architectural elements described above can be recognized in the twentieth-century houses of worship discussed below.

It is very significant that the Ponce de Leon Hotel has been preserved and is now Flagler College, that the Alcazar now houses city offices and the Lightner Museum, and that both buildings continue to be magnificently maintained. They are important to the history of Florida architecture and the state's cultural heritage, and allow us to think about these young architects making their start in the Flagler buildings in St. Augustine. One can almost feel their excitement in the challenge to create Florida's first large concrete resort hotels and churches with grand and romantic allusions to other times and places. Carrère and Hastings's visionary work in St. Augustine, however, has been eclipsed by their renowned academic-specialized Beaux-Arts reputation in Washington, D.C., and New York. Their place in Florida's architectural history has been overlooked because eclectic combinations of Spanish and Italian architecture arrived in south Florida on a vast scale with fanfare two decades later. One writer posits that Richard Kiehnel was "the first of Florida's Mediterranean Revival architects" and that he designed the "earliest known, full-fledged Mediterranean Revival work."[6] Carrère died young in 1911, but Hastings (1860–1929) continued to practice under the firm's name, and was awarded the gold medal of the Royal Institute of British Architects in 1922. Maybeck moved on to California, where his award-winning designs continued to express his love for eclectic architecture: he combined climate-responsive and indigenous elements with his moody mixtures of Romanesque, Gothic, Renaissance, and Moorish traditions. His role in the St. Augustine designs is not fully known.[7]

FIGURE 17.2. South facade, Flagler Memorial Presbyterian Church, St. Augustine, 1889. Carrère and Hastings, architects. Current with the national trend toward diversity and academic eclecticism, and in keeping with their Beaux-Arts training, the architects blended together Romanesque and Renaissance elements from France, Spain, and Italy: Romanesque in the massing, the large half-round applied arch with rose window, and flanking towers; Renaissance in its dome and the many ornamental details. The applied brick pointed ogee arches are known in Spain as Spanish Flamboyant Gothic, and in Venice as Venetian Gothic. Under "In Memoriam," the door surround hints of Greek Revival, from the Erechtheion in Athens. Photograph 2012 by Kenneth M. Barrett Jr.

FIGURE 17.3. H. H. Richardson's award-winning Trinity Church in Boston, 1873, commemorated in the U.S. postage stamp on the right. Henry Hobson Richardson is said to have initiated the Romanesque Revival style in the United States with his personal style (known as Richardsonian Romanesque) that was influenced by the stone Romanesque and Gothic churches in France and Spain. Richardson's style influenced many church and government buildings, railroad depots, university campuses, and residential designs across the United States. U.S. postage stamp in author's collection.

Proceeding southward from St. Augustine in the 1880s, a Richardsonian Romanesque church in Jacksonville illustrates the architectural style named after Henry Hobson Richardson. He is said to have initiated the Romanesque Revival in the United States with his personal style, which was an adaptation of eleventh-century stone churches in Spain and France that synthesized the best of Romanesque and Gothic architecture (fig. 17.3).[8] Jacksonville's First Baptist Church (1903) shows Richardson's signature rough-cut rugged rock walls, and semi-circular arches supported on short columns that emphasize its heavy stone construction (fig. 17.4). Henry John Klutho was primarily responsible for its final "as built" design, which was based on Rev. W. A. Hobson's choice of architectural style and the Akron Plan. Klutho, the son of German immigrants, taught himself architecture by sketching Gothic cathedrals and Renaissance buildings in Europe. He would become known in Florida for his Prairie School style and city skyscrapers. Akron Plans were popularized by pattern books in the late nineteenth and early twentieth centuries to promote a close relationship between congregants, worship, and Sunday

FIGURE 17.4. First Baptist Church, Jacksonville, 1903. Duval County. Henry John Klutho, architect. Klutho's church design typifies the Richardsonian Romanesque signature characteristics: large half-round arch, rough-cut stone, and stout columns supporting round-headed arches, all of which emphasize the heavy massing and stone construction. Photograph 2012 by Kenneth M. Barrett Jr.

school. It first appeared in Akron, Ohio, in 1872 at the First Methodist Episcopal Church, where several congregations (Congregationalists, Baptists, and Presbyterians) adopted a plan typified by an auditorium worship space ("rotunda") surrounded by Sunday school classrooms.[9]

In Tampa (Hillsborough County), Sacred Heart Catholic Church (1905) is also a Richardsonian Romanesque Revival structure, characterized by heavy massing and rusticated stone (plate 40). There is a wide stairway leading to a three-arch arcade flanked by paired towers, and a huge half-round Romanesque arch on the front gable facade in which is set a large rose window, the same elements (different details) used by Carrère and Hastings fifteen years earlier at Memorial Presbyterian. Sacred Heart also has a Renaissance-style dome and lantern, and alternating colors and textures in the flanking towers. Today, when a shaft of sunlight escapes between surrounding skyscrapers to strike Sacred Heart's granite and marble facade, the illuminated structure offers a stunning contrast to its towering modern plate-glass and shining-steel neighbors. Seventy stained-glass windows pour light into the nave and sanctuary. They were created by the Franz Mayer Company of Munich, Germany, the same company that created windows in 1909 for the Spanish Cathedral in St. Augustine and Jacksonville's Late Gothic Immaculate Conception Catholic Church (1910)(fig.17.15).[10]

Variations on the Romanesque Revival theme appear at St. Ann's Roman Catholic Church (West Palm Beach, 1913) and Trinity Episcopal Cathedral (Miami, 1923). They replicate some of the same neo-Romanesque elements described above, and introduce the blind arcades characteristic of northern Spain, and of Italy's medieval Lombardic architecture. Trinity (Harold Hastings Mundy, architect) has a large cross set in the rose window, and paired buttresses (fig. 17.5). St. Ann's first church (1896) was an enormous wood church of Gothic Revival style built on land described as broiling and mosquito-infested. The land was donated by Henry Flagler, who had run his railroad to the Lake Worth area (1894), created West Palm Beach, and built his Royal Poinciana Hotel. St. Ann's in particular shows its indebtedness to H. H. Richardson's award-winning Boston church. It is notable as the church attended by President John F. Kennedy and his mother, Rose.[11]

In Miami, there is an *original* twelfth-century Spanish Romanesque-Gothic monastery. (Gothic architecture slowly evolved from Romanesque, and elements of both are often seen in medieval European churches.) William Randolph Hearst went to Europe in 1925 and bought a Cistercian monastery in Sacramenia (province of Segovia), Spain, as a chapel for his San Simeon estate in California. It was dismantled, and its 35,871 massive stone blocks

FIGURE 17.5. Trinity Episcopal Cathedral, Miami, 1923. Dade County. Harold Hastings Mundy, architect. Trinity's Romanesque Revival facade is dramatized in a nighttime photograph that emphasizes the cross set in the rose window and the Lombardic-style blind arcade in the gable. The entrance portico has the characteristic round arches. Photograph by Evelyn Hemp.

were numbered and packed in 10,761 crates, for which he had to buy a small forest, a sawmill, and fields of packing hay, and build a narrow-gauge railway and a road to transport them to the nearest port. After arriving in New York, the stones were unpacked and the hay set on fire to kill hoof-and-mouth disease, as a result of which the assembly numbers were lost and the stones were repacked in the wrong boxes. History and Hearst's death (1951) intervened.

FIGURE 17.6. Twelfth-century Cistercian monastery of St. Bernard brought from Spain and reassembled in Miami. Dade County. William Randolph Hearst bought a monastery in Spain and sent it to New York stone by stone. The stones were packed in hay, and because of the dangers of hoof-and-mouth disease, the hay was set on fire. The boxes and their reassembly numbers were lost. In the 1950s, the stones were bought, shipped to Miami, and the puzzling reassembly of elements like the ribbed vaulting began. It is telling that one photograph shows a pile of leftover stones. Photograph 1998 by Roger Blackburn.

Developers bought the stones, shipped them to Miami, and reconstructed the monastery's massive walls, arcaded cloister, and ribbed vaulting in 1953 (fig. 17.6). A pile of leftover stones in one photograph adds intrigue to the story. The re-created structure is called the Monastery of St. Bernard after a monk of the Cistercian Order who was abbot of the Monastery of Clairvaux (France) and who had established many monasteries, of which Sacramenia was one.[12] The Episcopal Diocese of South Florida bought the monastery in 1965. Today it is a cultural center.

From Lake Worth, Flagler ran his railroad south to Miami in 1896 and Key West in 1912, enabling the vast development and rapid growth of Miami, Coral Gables, and Coconut Grove. Henry Plant and Hamilton Disston similarly opened the west coast and inland areas south of Orlando in the 1880s: Plant with his rail-steamship lines, and Disston by draining some 6,000 square miles of swamp and overflow land.[13] Expansive southern frontiers attracted people like them, who were able to leverage huge tracts of land and create building lots, some with mud pulled from swamp and bay bottoms.[14]

The year that Miami was incorporated, 1896, the Gesu Catholic Church parish was founded. The parishioners built a church in 1922 that is now one of Miami's oldest churches. It is four stories high and combines Romanesque and Classical elements in what is today called a Spanish Colonial Revival style. When Cubans began arriving in Miami in 1959, the church became responsible for their needs, religious and humanitarian, and it was the place where mass was celebrated for the soldiers who were about to embark on the Bay of Pigs invasion in 1961 (fig. 17.7).[15]

The Rev. Solomon Merrick caught the Florida frontier fever in 1898. He was a winter-weary Congregational minister from Massachusetts who became determined to go south to the subtropics to establish a home for his family and create a retirement community for other clergymen. His dream led his son George to a bigger dream. He hired architects Phineas Paist and Harold Steward, and artist Denman Fink as artistic advisor, and created Coral Gables. They laid out a business center, recreational areas, educational facilities, and spaces for religious and community activities, a rational plan like the one laid down four hundred years earlier in St. Augustine (chapter 9). In twentieth-century Coral Gables, however, architectural style was emphasized. It was a fiction of Romanesque and Gothic traditions freely combined with Moorish, Renaissance, and Spanish Colonial Baroque ornamentation that now is often called Mediterranean Revival. Like Carrère and Hastings's

19 The Gesu Church, N. E. First Av. & Second Street, Miami, Florida

FIGURE 17.7. Gesu Catholic Church, 1922, Miami. Dade County. Architect unknown. One of Miami's oldest churches, it is a four-story combination of Romanesque Revival and Classical elements in what is sometimes called a Spanish Colonial Revival style. Thousands attended a mass here before soldiers embarked for the Bay of Pigs. Photograph from the 1940s courtesy of Florida State Archives.

architectural style for Flagler's St. Augustine, Coral Gables' architectural allusion to the Mediterranean lent itself to Florida's subtropical climate and the aspirations of the many who dreamed of palaces in Spain and Italy. Venetian gondoliers were hired for the man-made canals to add romance to the allusion, and a quarry pit was turned into a popular swimming pool with Venetian features. The Venetian Pool of Coral Gables (1924) was substantially restored in 1989 (plate 46).[16]

Richard Kiehnel designed in the Spanish Renaissance, or Mediterranean Revival, style. In 1924, Kiehnel and his partner, John Elliott, designed the Coral Gables Congregational Church with the sculptured entrance surround and the bell tower that reminds one of Spanish Colonial Baroque architecture (fig. 17.8). Across the street from it was the soon-to-be-completed Miami Biltmore Hotel (1926), with its tower inspired by that of the Cathedral of Seville's Islamic and Spanish Renaissance tower (fig. 14.4). Coral Gables Congregational Church was the first in the Gables, and it is commonly believed to have been commissioned by George Merrick in honor of his minister father.[17]

FIGURE 17.8. Coral Gables Congregational Church, 1924, Coral Gables. Dade County. Kiehnel and Elliott, architects. First church in the Gables, this Spanish Colonial Baroque building was commissioned by George Merrick to honor his father, who preceded him with development dreams in South Florida. George dreamed even bigger: he was the creator and developer of Coral Gables. Across the street in 1924 the Biltmore was under construction. Photocopy courtesy of Florida State Archives.

The flamboyant Addison Mizner is better known for his large exotic mansions in Palm Beach and Boca Raton during the 1920s and 1930s than for the Riverside Baptist Church he designed in Jacksonville in 1924–25 (Duval County). His evocative, unconventional compositions of Old World forms were said to be more Spanish than anything in Spain.[18] Mizner was both architect and entrepreneur. He invented an industry of manufactured architectural materials that fed his eclectic designs: cast-stone door and window surrounds, terra-cotta details, colored glass, and wrought-iron grilles. In his Jacksonville church, he created an allusion to Spain's early eleventh-century

Romanesque architecture that is striking for its distinctive volumes: rectangles, squares, and octagonal domed central cores. His design comes out of Roman and Byzantine architecture, and particularly Justinian's Basilica di San Vitale (A.D. 526–547) in Ravenna, Italy, which was on everyone's Grand Tour of Europe must-see list (fig. 17.9).

Wayne Wood's *Jacksonville's Architectural Heritage* reveals that Mizner anticipated the movement of light inside his church. He designed the large central octagonal nave to be filled with light tinted by blue glass, and the altar to be illuminated by a golden glow from amber windows. His eaves have projecting stringcourses of blind arcades or corbel tables, and he had the walls of the church sprayed with buttermilk and rubbed with umber to create the centuries-old look. His design provoked strong reactions from the Baptist congregation. Some complained that the church design related more to the high-church ritual of his Episcopal upbringing, rather than the sermon-oriented Baptists, and that the baptismal pool was cramped. Others felt that Mizner mocked them with his humorous sculptured faces of a nun and a monk on transept walls, and they resigned.[19]

Octagonal schemes occurred elsewhere in Florida. In St. Petersburg, St. Mary Our Lady of Grace (1925) is a variation on the theme constructed in red brick. Henry L. Taylor, St. Mary's architect, also designed a small red-brick octagonal Romanesque Revival "Public Comfort Station" in St. Petersburg. His Mediterranean Revival Vinoy Park Hotel (1925), one of St. Petersburg's earliest and largest luxury resort hotels, continues to be a destination today. The William Jennings Bryan Memorial Church (1926) in Coconut Grove is another variation—this one stark white—on the octagonal theme.[20] Much earlier, in 1743, the Spanish church on Santa Rosa Island (Pensacola) was octagonal (fig. 10.4), but details are missing.

Two of Florida's early religion-associated colleges have campus chapels in the Spanish Revival theme: the Knowles Memorial Chapel at Rollins College, and St. Leo's Church of the Holy Cross at St. Leo College (now University). Rollins was founded by New England Congregationalists in Winter Park, Orange County, in 1885, and St. Leo's was founded by Benedictine monks in 1889 at St. Leo Abbey in Pasco County. Rollins College hired the Miami firm of Kiehnel and Elliott to design the Mediterranean Revival campus buildings, and hired Ralph Adams Cram of New York to design its Knowles Memorial Chapel in 1926, the year he was on the cover of *Time* magazine. He was the supervising architect of Princeton University and one of the most prolific and

FIGURE 17.9. Riverside Baptist Church, 1924–25, Jacksonville. Duval County. Addison Mizner, architect. Mizner designed some of Florida's most exotic and romantic Mediterranean-inspired residential and commercial architecture, mostly in Boca Raton and Palm Beach. Riverside Baptist is his only church. He looked to Roman and Byzantine traditions for his church model, and rubbed the church walls with buttermilk and umber to create a centuries-old look. Not all of its congregants were pleased with his architecture: some complained that the baptismal pool was cramped and that the Romanesque sculptured faces of nuns and monks mocked them. Photograph 2011 by Kenneth M. Barrett Jr.

best designers of churches in the United States. His Gothic St. John the Divine (1913–39) in New York City is larger than Renwick's St. Patrick's. Cram was thought of as an impassioned Gothist who influenced church design to move away from the Richardsonian Romanesque toward the Gothic Revival. At Rollins College, however, he designed the chapel in keeping with the campus architecture in the Spanish Renaissance style (fig. 17.10). He may have felt it was predetermined by history, tradition, and architectural style in Florida, a view he had expressed when he designed Sweet Briar College, Virginia, in a neo-Georgian theme. Cram was devoutly religious, and might have seen a connection between his Gothic architecture and Spanish-style Catholic churches and towers.[21] Later, in Winter Park, Cram designed All Saints Episcopal Church (1940) in an understated Gothic Revival style (fig. 17.11).

FIGURE 17.10. Knowles Memorial Chapel, Rollins College, 1926, Winter Park. Orange County. Ralph Adams Cram, architect. The year that Cram was on the cover of *Time* magazine honoring his Gothic-style architecture, he was commissioned to design a chapel for Rollins College. He was a well-known designer of Gothic Revival churches. For the Rollins campus, however, he designed the memorial chapel in the Mediterranean Revival style of the campus buildings planned by Kiehnel and Elliott. Photograph 2011 by Kenneth M. Barrett Jr.

FIGURE 17.11. All Saints Episcopal Church, 1940, Winter Park. Orange County. Ralph Adams Cram, architect. Fourteen years after designing the Knowles Chapel for Rollins College, Cram, who is well known for his large Gothic St. John the Divine design (1913–39) in New York City, designed this small, restrained Gothic Revival church in Winter Park. Photograph 2011 by Kenneth M. Barrett Jr.

Saint Leo Abbey was built on 100 acres owned since 1889 by a small party of monks of the Order of St. Benedict in the hill-studded central region of San Antonio in Pasco County. The monks established a monastery, a Catholic high school, the town of St. Leo, and large orange groves. A number of German Catholic immigrants arrived, and the Catholic colony became known for its strawberries. St. Leo's monastery and convent were elevated to abbey status and were completed before the end of World War I. An article in *Tampa Bay History*, a journal of the University of South Florida, discloses that during the Great War, "Florida was convulsed with an unprecedented wave of anti-German feeling combined with a strong anti-Catholic movement led by the state's governor, Sidney J. Catts [1917–21]. Governor Catts was widely quoted (and widely believed) to the effect that the German monks at St. Leo had an arsenal and were planning to arm the Negroes for an insurrection in favor of Kaiser Wilhelm II, after which the Pope would take over Florida and move the Vatican to San Antonio."[22]

Today's Church of the Holy Cross was built in 1935 and now serves St. Leo University students and the St. Leo Community. It was designed by Brother Anthony Poiger in the Romanesque tradition of northern Spain and Lombardic Italy. It is characterized by a dramatic round-headed entrance portal, a large rose window, and an 86-foot-tall bell tower topped with a belvedere and tile roof (plate 53). It is known as "the church that orange juice built" because St. Leo Abbey supplied Saint Meinrad Archabbey in Indiana with oranges for years in exchange for many of the carved-oak interior furnishings and the deep-yellow Indiana limestone, cut and polished for the exterior and interior trim and side altars. An 11-ton crucifix above the main altar was sculpted in 1947 of Tennessee rose marble and framed in a mosaic from Italy. The stained-glass windows artistically depicting saints in antique glass were designed and made locally by Karl Mueller of Zephyrhills.[23]

Coconut Grove's Plymouth Congregational Church (1917) and Daytona Beach's Seabreeze Church (1929) illustrate Florida's twentieth-century taste for the Spanish Colonial and Mission Revival styles. They were not the first in Florida, however. In 1903, when Pensacola's Gothicized Christ Church of 1832 was outgrown, the parish took a new direction. Bishop Weed's report of 1904 reads: *The parish of Christ Church has departed from the well-worn path of American Gothic and has adopted the Spanish style in building the new church. The design is perfect in all its details. . . . It seemed to me to be a venture. However, the venture was a wise one and has amply rewarded all who undertook the construction* (plate 36).[24] The inspiration for Florida's early Spanish Colonial revival styles might have been California's nostalgia for its Spanish Franciscan mission heritage. It was popularized in the 1890s. Helen Hunt Jackson's influential book *Ramona* (1884) had romanticized the missions, even in ruins, as the grandest architecture in America. Additionally, California's building in the World's Columbian Exposition in Chicago in 1893 was of the "Mission and Moorish type." In 1896, the *American Church Review* promoted the beauty and harmony of the picturesque forms of California's missions as architecture of "a superior order."[25]

Plymouth Church and Seabreeze are both constructed with Florida limestone and are characterized by their shaped mission parapets and belfries. Florida's own mission architectural history was little known at this time. Plymouth's plan is said to have been designed by Clinton McKenzie of New York after an old Spanish mission church in Mexico (California's missions were still mostly in ruins). Its native limestone was laid by a single mason,

FIGURE 17.12. Plymouth Congregational Church, 1917, Coconut Grove. Dade County. Clinton McKenzie, architect. Plymouth Congregational was built with Florida limestone and is South Florida's first church to revive the look of a Spanish mission church. California's historic missions had recently been described as having architecture of "a superior order" in the *American Church Review*. McKenzie of New York, however, is said to have looked to Mexico for his details—California's missions were not yet restored, and Florida's Spanish mission architecture was unknown. Photograph 2000 by the author.

a Spaniard named Félix Rebón. Plymouth's door is 375 years old and from a monastery in the Pyrenees Mountains (fig. 17.12). Like many of Florida's historic churches trying to meet the needs of growing congregations and tourist and wedding destinations, Plymouth's original basilica-style nave has been expanded into a cross-shaped floor plan with two transepts. Daytona Beach's Seabreeze is known as "the Tourist Church" because it welcomed all denominations (fig. 17.13). Its Mission-style building and artistic details were designed by architect Harry M. Griffin, who also designed Daytona Beach's band shell (plate 54) and the keystone-clad U.S. post office under the WPA program described below.[26]

The Basilica of St. Paul (1927) in Daytona Beach (Volusia County) illustrates another form of Spanish Colonial– and Mission–style buildings. It has neither the typical curved mission parapet nor flanking towers, but its entrance surround has the characteristic ornamentation that sets it apart as the most important element of the building. Its design by Gerald A. Barry of Chicago reflects the missions in colonial Mexico and Texas, where entrance facades were elaborated with Baroque sculptural treatment. St. Paul's is ornamented with Solomonic (twisted or spiral) columns, a motif brought to Texas by Franciscans from Mexico that may have been patterned after the Bernini columns at the Baldacchino of the Altar of the Confessional in the Basilica of St. Peter, Vatican City. Bernini is thought to have patterned his twisted columns after one salvaged from Constantine's fourth-century basilica, which had come from the Temple of Solomon. Daytona's Basilica of St. Paul was designated Florida's second basilica (after the St. Augustine Cathedral), honoring its 1881 founding and the area's first Catholic family, who had arrived from Germany.[27]

Not everyone in the newness of the twentieth century was enamored of things Spanish, Italian, or neo-Mediterranean. Gothic imagery and all its glorious historical churchly symbolism has continuously tugged at the heartstrings of many parishes and builders of Florida's houses of worship since its first appearance at St. Augustine's Trinity Episcopal Church. Palm Beach's Bethesda-by-the-Sea (1926) is a Gothic Revival building in a spacious landscape reminiscent of England's fifteenth-century castellated designs. It has a tower with crenels, corner finials, pointed arches, and a cloister of foliated arches enclosing a quadrangle in the style of medieval convents. Bethesda-by-the-Sea's architecture recalls the sense of peace and serenity one associates with monastic beliefs and scholarship. The architects were Hiss and Weekes, commissioned to replace a smaller structure of 1895 on the eastern

FIGURE 17.13. Seabreeze United Church, "The Tourist Church," 1929, Daytona Beach. Volusia County. Harry M. Griffin, architect. Griffin's Mission Revival church was nondenominational and served Daytona Beach's tourists. Its rustic-looking native limestone probably appealed to the tourists' imagination of Spanish Florida. During the next several years, Griffin would also artistically use Florida native materials in his other Daytona Beach structures: keystone in his post office and coquina in the band shell (plates 51 and 54). Photograph 2011 by Kenneth M. Barrett Jr.

shore of Lake Worth that was accessed only by boat or a bicycle path along the shore. The 1895 structure (John H. Lee, architect) was deconsecrated in 1925 and is now a stunning private residence (fig. 17.14). Its conversion retained its original Shingle-style Richardsonian Romanesque arches at the entrance porch and the octagonal picturesque Victorian-period tower, reminding one of a windmill. The historic interior design focused on a single room with a massive hammer-beam ceiling.[28]

A splendid early twentieth-century Late Gothic Revival church building was erected in 1910 in Jacksonville (Duval County). Immaculate Conception Catholic Church (designed by M. H. Hubbard of New York County)

FIGURE 17.14. Bethesda-by-the-Sea, 1895, Palm Beach. John H. Lee, architect. Deconsecrated in 1925, this church building on the shore of Lake Worth has been converted into a private residence and rejuvenated as one of Florida's most unusual houses. The owners have preserved its shingled Romanesque-style porch and picturesque octagonal tower, which recalls a windmill. As a church, it was accessed only by boat or path and was replaced in 1926 by today's Bethesda-by-the Sea, a much larger Gothic Revival church building in a spacious landscape. The newer church is reminiscent of England's fifteenth-century churches and convents with its pinnacled and castellated tower, pointed arch entrance, and cloisters recalling monastic serenity. Photocopy courtesy of Florida State Archives.

is distinguished by its traditional vaulted interior spaces, cruciform floor plans, buttresses, pinnacles, crockets and spires, pointed arches and traceried windows (fig. 17.15). It was solemnly dedicated in 1979, and cannot be purposefully torn down or used for anything other than a church.[29] St. Paul's in Key West (G. L. Pfeifer, architect) is a 1914 Gothic Revival design with English Tudor–style elements (fig. 17.16). It was the fourth church building. The (1839) coral rock building was destroyed in the 1846 hurricane; the second was wood (1848), which burned in 1886; the third (1887), also wood, was destroyed in the 1909 hurricane. Today's building is concrete. It had to be restored during 1991–93 because the original concrete had been made with seawater and beach sand, and the steel reinforcement had rusted and expanded.[30]

After the Civil War, black Americans designed and built their own churches. Many took up the Gothic Revival style. The congregation of Mount Zion AME Church in Ocala (Marion County) built today's masonry structure in 1891 according to the Gothic Revival plan of its black architect, Levi Alexander Sr. In Key West (Monroe County), a former slave from Maryland, Sandy Cornish (1793–1869), organized the first black congregation in 1864, and in 1903, the Cornish Memorial AME Zion Church was built in his honor. Its white frame structure is a simplified American Gothic design. In 2009, Key West appropriated $417,000 to begin its multiphase renovation and replace the tin roof. Also in Key West is the Gothic Revival St. Peter's Episcopal Church, designed and built by Joseph Hannibal, son of Shadrack Hannibal, a runaway slave.[31]

Bethel Baptist Institutional Church (1904) in Jacksonville was begun after its black members withdrew in 1868 from a mixed-race Baptist congregation to build their own church. Their first structure burned in Jacksonville's Great Fire of 1901 that destroyed the city. After the catastrophe, they chose a masonry building distinguished by an eclectic combination of roof styles and heights inspired by Romanesque and Gothic Revival, Neoclassical, and Queen Anne architecture. The church is dominated by a large and tall frontal tower with a conical roof sheathed in Victorian-era pressed-metal shingles. It was designed by M. H. Hubbard of New York a year after the firm designed Jacksonville's Late Gothic Revival Immaculate Conception Church (fig. 17.15). Bethel Baptist today is a "megachurch" (two thousand or more attending) with many additions for educational and outreach services (plate 37).[32]

Prince W. Spears, a local black mason and architect, built St. James AME Church in 1913 in Sanford (Seminole County). His brick Gothic Revival

FIGURE 17.15. Late Gothic Immaculate Conception Catholic Church, 1910, Jacksonville. Duval County. M. H. Hubbard, architect. In contrast to the early Gothic Revival Trinity Church in St. Augustine (1831) and the nineteenth-century Carpenter Gothic churches that followed it after the Civil War, Jacksonville's Immaculate Conception is known as Late Gothic Revival, distinguished by its vaulted spaces, cruciform plan, buttresses, pinnacles, crockets and spires, pointed arches, and traceried windows. Photograph 2012 by the author.

FIGURE 17.16. St. Paul's Episcopal Church, fourth structure, 1914, Key West. Monroe County. Architect unknown. Three church buildings preceded this one, destroyed one by one by hurricanes and fire. Today's St. Paul's is concrete and is Gothic Revival with English Tudor features. Its 1914 concrete material had to be repaired: the original mixture had been made with seawater and beach sand, and the steel reinforcement rusted and expanded and cracked the cement. Photocopy courtesy of Florida State Archives.

design includes two large Tudor-style windows and a castellated tower with a pyramidal roof. In Miami, in 1940, a black congregation hired the black architectural firm of McKissack and McKissack of Nashville, Tennessee, to design their St. John's Baptist Church (now St. John's Institutional Baptist). Its Gothic Revival massing is overpowered by its stunning buff-colored Art Moderne facade. The angular and geometric machine-age image was current with the Moderne architectural trend of its time, and today is a listed landmark in the Overtown neighborhood.[33]

An exception to the Gothic Revival trend among black congregations is the temple-fronted Mount Olive AME Church, built in Jacksonville in 1922 by that city's first black architect, Richard Lewis Brown. Brown (1854–1948) was born in poverty in South Carolina and moved to Florida at the end of the Civil War. Frugal, hardworking, and talented, he served two terms in Florida's House of Representatives, and taught himself the arts of architecture. He was also the contractor for the Centennial Hall at Edward Waters College (1916).[34] His unusual church design is characterized by a first floor of roughed-up concrete blocks set in brown mortar to simulate a rusticated podium (a Roman and Palladian motif) for the three massive Doric columns forming the second-story entrance temple-front portico (fig. 17.17). Flanking balustraded staircases lead to the portico and sanctuary on the second story, which is constructed with rough-cut cement blocks to look like quarry stone.

Not to be caught in the lethargy of the Great Depression and the tradition of reviving Old World–style buildings, Florida's 1930s and 1940s designers began stripping down and streamlining their buildings with Industrial Age images, hard edges, metal, glass blocks, flagpoles, and neon. It was Moderne or Art Deco, sometimes nautical, sometimes sleek, and sometimes tropically colorful—and known as "Florida Art Deco." Miami architect Henry Hohauser (1895–1963) was one of the leading architects in this style that made Miami Beach famous.[35] When the original 1928 Beth Jacob Synagogue (H. Frasser Rose, architect) in Miami Beach became too small, Hohauser designed the Congregation Beth Jacob's second synagogue (1936) with Art Deco elements. The Hohauser-designed building was restored by Ira Giller in 1995 and today is the Sanford L. Ziff Jewish Museum of Florida: Home of MOSAIC. It is known for its Art Deco chandeliers and sconces, eighty stained-glass windows, a Moorish copper dome, and a marble bimah, the platform or table from which the Torah scrolls are read.[36]

Florida's 1930s–40s Art Deco architecture is known for its tropical motifs and Maya imagery. Maya Art Deco motifs inspired Jules Andre Smith's Open-Air Chapel in Maitland (Orange County). Smith, who had a master's degree in architecture from Cornell University, established an art studio in Maitland that was expanded in 1937 into the nonprofit Maitland Art Center supported by Mary Curtis Bok (see Bok Tower below). It provided room and board for Bok Fellows and artists devoted to modern art. Well-known artists lived there, exchanging ideas in the courtyards, garden, and refectory. In 1940, it was opened to the public, and the roofless open-air Art Deco chapel was added. Its Maya-style bas-reliefs carved in cement depict events in the life of Christ, viewed with eyes transfixed heavenward toward Florida's blue sky.[37]

Frank Lloyd Wright's legendary Annie Pfeiffer Chapel (1941) is another

FIGURE 17.17. Mount Olive AME Church, 1922, Jacksonville. Duval County. Richard Lewis Brown, architect. Brown was Jacksonville's first black architect. Born in poverty in South Carolina, he moved to Florida at the end of the Civil War. He served two terms in Florida's House of Representatives and taught himself the arts of architecture. His unusual church design has rough-cut concrete blocks that look like stone. He created the effect of a rusticated podium on the first floor for his second-story temple-front distinguished by massive Doric columns. Photograph 2011 by Kenneth M. Barrett Jr.

landmark of new architectural directions in Florida's built landscape as the state eased past the Depression. It is characterized by Wright's ideas about innovative structural systems and expressions of regional modernism. The chapel was his first completed building of the master plan he designed for Florida Southern College in Lakeland (Polk County) in 1938. He had recently finished his famous Fallingwater, the Kaufmann House in Pennsylvania (1935–38), and *Time* magazine had featured his face on the 1938 cover, identifying the seventy-year-old Wright as the greatest architect of the twentieth century.[38] New York's Solomon R. Guggenheim Museum was soon to follow in 1943; it was completed in 1959, the year Wright turned ninety-two. Florida Southern College had been founded in 1885 in Leesburg as a Methodist seminary, and had acquired its permanent campus in 1921 in Lakeland and an architectural plan with neo-Georgian red-brick buildings, as well as a white Hindu temple with a reflection pool and meditative garden.[39]

Wright was hired by the college president, Dr. Ludd Spivey, to plan the new west campus buildings in keeping with his vision of the college as a "modernist institution" with an ideal education program that equally blended religious, cultural, and scientific knowledge. For Wright, it was an opportunity to advance his ideals of a modernist architecture not only for Florida, but for the United States as well. Wright was known for seeking "fresh forms" that would change the nature of architectural space and elevate American society through architecture. He wanted to emphasize structural innovation with a regional authenticity that would be distinct from the current International style of European modern architecture. It would not be a traditional college campus in Colonial, Classical, Romanesque or Gothic Revival (Collegiate Gothic or Tudor), or, as of late in Florida, Mediterranean Revival. He told a Lakeland audience when he agreed to design the new campus:

> No real Florida form has yet been produced. Most of you here have simply built as you built back home. We do not need a French château for a firehouse nor a Greek temple for a bank. . . . I believe we are now ready for a culture of our own, something indigenous to America . . . something we in America could call our own.[40]

Student labor built the chapel. Its signature structural system was the cantilever and pairs of triangles that emphasized its spatial form rather than its material elements. The material was cement "textile" blocks (9 × 36 inches) cast by the students in wood molds (forty-six different molds) with a sand made from crushed coquina stone, an indigenous material of Florida's Atlantic coast in keeping with Wright's ideal of an organic regional architecture. (Carrère and Hastings had used crushed coquina in the concrete Flagler hotels and churches to convey the essence of an earlier regional architecture, that of the coquina and tabby buildings of Spanish Florida.) Blocks were laid dry with grooved edges holding steel reinforcement rods; two thicknesses and an airspace were in between. Wright's central lantern tower was composed of three tiers of concrete "bow ties," designed with chimes (modeled on Japanese temple gongs) and flowers and vines hanging from intricate wrought-iron trellises atop colored-glass skylights. The natural light was planned to constantly change as it passed down through the tower to illuminate the sanctuary. (Hanging plants proved to be unworkable.) Students dubbed its wrought-iron imagery "the bicycle rack in the sky." To others, it might recall the essence of a Gothic tower illuminated by stained glass. Wright also designed the balconies, the pulpit, and the 90-foot ornamental choir screen (plate 55).[41]

His second chapel for the campus, the William H. Danforth Chapel (1955), is smaller than the Annie Pfeiffer Chapel. It has a prow-like front of red cypress and glass, based on an idea about triangulated forms and spaces that he had expressed at an earlier church, the Unitarian Church (1947) in Madison (Shorewood Hills), Wisconsin. A number of religious (and public) designs in Florida thereafter took up triangulated forms and prow-like imagery. Among them are St. Paul's Lutheran Church in Sarasota, designed by Victor Lundy (plate 57). Wright's ideas about regional modernism are reflected in the designs of the Sarasota School of architecture (1941–66), of which Lundy was a member. At the end of World War II, Sarasota did not have pricey megamansions and high-rise condos hugging the bayfronts and downtown as it does today. The city's natural beach frontage and a postwar optimism brought together a number of architects who were excited about the contemporary designs of Frank Lloyd Wright and Ludwig Mies van der Rohe. They forged a style of architecture for the Florida landscape just after World War II that was meant to respect the land and climate, use local materials, and show honesty in "organic" structural design. "We didn't have air-conditioning," said Tim Seibert, one of the architects of the Sarasota School, as the group is now called. "I always thought architecture was a lot more fun when we worked with nature instead of against it."[42]

During the 1940s and 1950s, the members of the group experimented with structural innovations, new materials, and ideas about shapes, space, and light. They used precast concrete and long-span laminated beams, steel-cable catenary roofs, umbrella roofs and broad overhangs, and glass walls that merged the indoors and outdoors.[43] As Gene Leedy described it: "I guess what we really did was humanize the Bauhaus. We threw in a little Frank Lloyd Wright and used local materials. It was hot as hell."[44]

Victor Lundy's St. Paul's Lutheran Church (1958) is a unique play on the prow-like Wright element and the Gothic principle of a vertical thrust toward heaven (plate 57). It received the FA/AIA Award for Excellence in 1959, and the American Institute of Architects' National Design Award in 1960. Its upward-swooping roof is supported by curved laminated wood beams. It is now the Fellowship Hall, and the newer sanctuary beside it reinterprets the theme (fig. 17.18). Window slits in roof edges create unusual natural lighting effects in the interiors. Lundy's first church project was a "Drive-in Garden Sanctuary" in 1954 for Venice-Nokomis Presbyterian Church in Venice, Florida, that was a glass-enclosed elevated platform set in the midst of pine trees. It was intended to be surrounded by parishioners in their cars. The idea of a drive-in auto-audience church received national recognition in *Life* magazine. It is now only a memory.[45] The Sarasota School buildings of the 1950s and 1960s are now a half century

FIGURE 17.18. St. Paul's Lutheran Church, 1958/1970, Sarasota. Sarasota County. Victor Lundy, architect. Lundy, a member of the Sarasota School of architecture (1941–66), became interested in new materials and a modernist style of architecture for the local environment. St. Paul's is a complex of buildings, the first of which is the award-winning former sanctuary, now Fellowship Hall (plate 57), inspired by Frank Lloyd Wright's triangulated spaces and prow-like imagery at the Danforth Chapel (1955) at Florida Southern and his Unitarian Church (1947) in Wisconsin. This second church building reinterprets the triangulated form of Lundy's Fellowship Hall, including an unusual interior natural lighting system. Photograph 2011 by the author.

old and are eligible to be nominated for listing in the National Register of Historic Places.

Among the many historic Gothic Revival structures, there is one that stands out, not as a church building, but as a sanctuary that combines a glorious Gothic-inspired work of architecture with nature, gardens, music, and the visual arts. Bok Tower, or Bok Sanctuary, as it is commonly called, is a "singing tower" built on peninsular Florida's highest point, the Lake Wales Ridge in Polk County. "Singing towers" (the name for carillons in the Netherlands) became fashionable in America in the early twentieth century after the end of World War I. They were inspired by Europe's traditional campaniles, carillons, and watchtowers that rang out in celebration of American troops liberating European towns. By 1925, following a widely circulated *National Geographic* article on the singing towers of the Netherlands, France, and Belgium, eleven carillons were dedicated in the United States.[46] Bok Tower was under way in 1923 and dedicated in 1929 (plate 49).

This singing tower was gifted to Florida by Edward Bok. He originally called it "Mountain Lake Sanctuary and Singing Tower." Bok arrived in America from the Netherlands when he was six years old, and by age thirteen, he was a school dropout. He made his fortune in the publishing world as the editor of *Ladies' Home Journal*. Escaping Philadelphia's winters, he purchased the sand hill called "Iron Mountain" (324 feet above sea level) and hired Frederick Law Olmsted Jr. to create his dream garden of 250 acres. Olmsted was the son of the famous landscape architect who designed hundreds of American parks, including New York's Central Park. Where only pine and scrub palmetto grew naturally, thousands of plants and trees were brought in and rooted and watered in transplanted topsoil. As the plants and trees grew, so did his gift of architecture.

Today's magnificent carillon tower (205 feet tall) is a Modern Gothic framework for an Art Deco masterpiece. It was designed by Milton B. Medary of Philadelphia and built with coquina ashlar and 2,000 tons of pink Etowah Georgia marble. Some twenty-six stone craftsmen intricately carved bands of encircling herons, pelicans, and flamingoes, and pinnacles resembling herons and eagles that symbolized Florida and the nation. Among the artists was New York sculptor Lee Lawrie, who added bas-reliefs of mythical figures, flora, and fauna. Then came Samuel Yellin, the master ironsmith who worked red-hot iron into a stairway up the tower equal to twenty stories with delicate images of plants. He also fabricated the great entrance doors of brass depicting the creation of all forms of life with images inspired by the Book of Genesis. (Yellin also designed the metalwork at Vizcaya, the Italian palacio in Miami, and Sarasota's Spanish Renaissance–style courthouse). These artists turned the tower into a majestic fairy tale that was soon "singing" with the sounds of sixty-one bronze bells (forty-eight tones, four octaves), the smallest weighing 17 pounds, the largest 11 tons (23,400 pounds). They are located in the bell chamber behind eight window grilles—35 feet high—made of colorful ceramics depicting undersea life. The weight of the tower and its bells required 160 reinforced concrete pilings 13–24 feet underground. The bells sounded when a carillonneur struck wooden keys with his fists or feet on a keyboard (clavier) that would make the clappers strike the bells.[47]

Florida's built landscape moves in new directions even as it reconfigures styles from Florida's past. One example takes us back some 130 years to the arrival of the small Carpenter Gothic river mission chapels in the 1870s and 1880s that were built along the St. Johns and Indian Rivers during the healing years after the Civil War with pointed architectural elements that were symbolically meant to lift the human spirit. Their architectural principles return with a modern feel at the Baughman Chapel and Meditative Center (2000) overlooking Lake Alice on the campus of the University of Florida (plate 58). John Zona, the designer of the Baughman Chapel, might not have known about Florida's small river missions, because he was creating a modern form of Carpenter Gothic after the style of Fay Jones's Mildred B. Cooper Memorial Chapel (1988) at Bella Vista, Arkansas. Jones, a former student-apprentice of Frank Lloyd Wright, was the architect of the award-winning Thorncrown Chapel (1980) in the Ozark Mountains near Eureka Springs.[48] The Baughman Chapel building brings back to Florida the principles of Richard Upjohn's Carpenter Gothics (chapter 16) as updated by Fay Jones's Ozark Gothic designs. Like the Bok Sanctuary, the Baughman Chapel is a gift to Florida that intentionally brings together the Gothic arts in a meditative sanctuary that weds art, music, nature, and people. The small nondenominational chapel is the gift of George F. and Hazel Baughman, designed for private contemplation, weddings, memorials, and musical events.[49] Its architectural style mimics, is a part of, and is enhanced by nature. In its light-filled space, as one looks through the large window oriented to the east, the lake water and surrounding trees become extensions of the clear glass and Gothic-inspired tracery (plate 59).

Architecture is not created in a vacuum. Connections and continuities in historic Gothic Revival sensibilities and symbolism in Florida, some more subtle than others, can be found, for example, in the recently built Ave Maria Oratory (2003) in Collier County (Cannon Design, New York). In this striking design, the pointed Gothic arch is the substance and the spirit of the church building. It is the entrance, the whole of the facade and the massing, as well as the nave's exposed-beam structural system (plate 60). The pointed Gothic arch since medieval times has characterized the principle of verticality and strength. It arrived in Florida in the pointed windows of Trinity Church, St. Augustine, and in the small lancet windows of the Upjohn-style board-and-batten chapels. At the 1920s Temple Israel in Miami, however, we see it in a large, modern format (fig. 17.19). Orlando's Cathedral Church of Saint Luke (designed by Frohman, Robb, and Little of Boston, the architects of the Washington Cathedral) is also entered through a large, contemporary pointed Gothic Revival arch.

The Ave Maria Oratory hints of Louis I. Kahn's 1943 sketch of a structural system of Gothic arches and his article that "prophesied that light tubular steel members could form the basis of an updated Gothic architecture."[50] In the breathtaking Oratory nave, the effect of the repetitive interlacing Gothic arches recalls not only medieval English and French traditions, but the modern simplicity of the pointed steel arches in Fay Jones's twentieth-century Mildred B. Cooper Memorial Chapel, which in turn inspired Florida's Baughman Chapel. The $25 million Ave Maria Oratory is the architectural centerpiece of the campus of Ave Maria University and its planned community and college town near Naples. It was founded as a joint venture between Thomas S. Monaghan, founder of Domino's Pizza, and the Barron Collier Companies.[51]

Reconfiguring new architecture to relate to earlier historic practices is illustrated in Flagler's late nineteenth-century churches and hotels in St. Augustine, where Carrère and Hastings not only created an allusion to Spain, but their choice of coquina aggregate recalled Spanish colonial tabby and coquina practices in the city. Spanish heritage is also recalled a century later at the Good Shepherd Catholic Church (1996) designed for Miami by Duany Plater-Zyberk and Company (DPZ). DPZ might have been looking more to Cuba for its architectural model, and to the traditions of Florida's Cuban population, but this Spanish Mission-style church connects to Florida's colonial roots as well as Florida's Mission–style churches of the early twentieth century (figs. 17.12, 17.13). Good Shepherd, according to a project description, was intentionally designed with numerological and spatial symbolism. Similar symbolic thinking also is

FIGURE 17.19. Temple Israel, 1928, Miami. Dade County. Architect unknown. A contemporary Gothic-influenced pointed arch forms the entrance and dominates the facade in this 1935 photograph. The temple is now part of a larger complex, with the addition of the Nathan and Sophie Gumenick Chapel in 1969, an abstract design of sculptured concrete and colored glass designed by Kenneth Treister, and a garden with plants mentioned in the Bible. Photocopy courtesy of Florida State Archives.

evidenced in Florida's Franciscan mission churches. Good Shepherd has a long passageway leading to a sacred ritual at the baptismal font—a similar plan existed in Florida's Spanish mission churches but with a focus on the ritual at the altar. Good Shepherd, however, transforms the chancel and altar space into a circular space reflecting the modern post–Vatican II approach that encourages parish-priest participation around the altar. In addition, Good Shepherd has a plaza space that recalls the plan of the parish church Los Remedios in St. Augustine as specified by the Royal Spanish Ordinances of 1573 described in chapter 9.[52] History is a continuum, and architecture flows with it.[53]

PLATE 1. Before there were enclosed sanctuaries and altars. About 8,000 to 6,000 years ago, there were people living in Florida who buried their dead in water in a ritual that had meaning to them. At one pond it has been discovered that succeeding generations continued the practice, suggesting that the ritual, if not the water or water sources, had spiritual meaning. *Morning in Guana,* by permission of the artist, © 2003 J. E. Fitzpatrick.

PLATE 2. The Miami Circle, Miami, ca. 100 B.C.–A.D. 100. Dade County. An ancient circle was carved into the bedrock limestone, where a freshwater river met the salt water of Biscayne Bay, now Brickell Point. The motives of its carvers remain a mystery, but the act of creating the circle may have had meaning beyond its geometric figure. Rescued by archaeologists from a developer's backhoe in 1998, and after years of scientific studies, it is covered and preserved for the public that cherishes its own "Stonehenge." Photograph 2011 by Robert McCammon, by permission of HistoryMiami Archives and Research Center Collection.

PLATE 3. Crystal River burial mound, 2,000–1,500 years ago. Citrus County. Florida Indians left us no writing or oral histories about the ancient burial mounds. They are Florida's oldest sacred public monuments, and may be the oldest in the United States. Archaeological discoveries in Florida's burial mounds suggest that symbolism permeates the architectural activities and that the mounds should be thought of as much more than cemeteries. Photograph 2001 by the author.

PLATE 4. *Early-Mid Pineland Bounty*, 2,000–1,700 years ago. Lee County. Archaeologists excavating Pineland's wet midden conjecture that people lived in houses on pilings at the water's edge. Long before maize became a food staple in Florida, Pineland's inhabitants built sedentary villages along shifting shorelines to harvest the aquatic species that were their primary sources of protein. If maize and its agricultural myths and beliefs were not venerated in their burial mounds, what was? Painting by Merald Clark, courtesy of the Florida Museum of Natural History.

PLATE 5. Mount Royal burial mound, Welaka, ca. A.D. 800–1300. Putnam County. Constructed over some five hundred years by villagers living along the St. Johns River drainage, the mound entombs many generations of deceased Indians who did not cultivate maize but subsisted primarily by harvesting aquatic species. When the last burial ritual ended, the mound was thickly covered with red-dyed sand. It was named "Mount Royal" by the British Governor James Grant in 1764, who chose the mound for a house site for the Earl of Egmont. *Mount Royal* by permission of the artist, © 2000 J. E. Fitzpatrick.

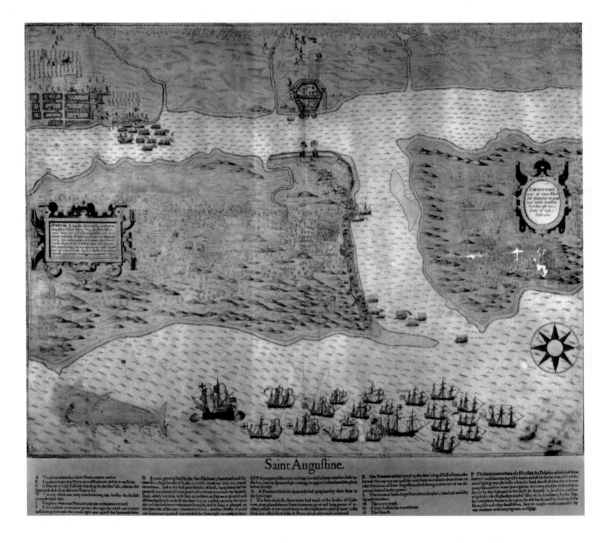

Saint Augustine.

PLATE 6. Town plan, St. Augustine, 1586 depiction, by Baptista Boazio. Francis Drake burned the wood town of St. Augustine on May 30, 1586. It had been laid out on this site since about 1572. Boazio's drawing was made to illustrate Drake's "battle plan," and it represents the town before it was set on fire. His drawing was published in 1588 in Latin and French, and in 1589 in English, and is the earliest depiction of any European settlement in the United States. Photocopy courtesy of Florida State Archives.

PLATE 7. Conjectured colonial Spanish church architecture, 1572–1704. The first Spanish parish and mission church buildings in Florida were constructed with wood; floors were packed earth; and the roofs were timber-framed and covered with palm thatch. Long, narrow naves focused eyes on the candle-lighted rituals at the altar end in the west. Bells were hung from post-and-lintels and were rung by rope pulls. Painting, 2011, conjectured from sixteenth- and seventeenth-century depictions and archaeology, by F. Blair Reeves, FAIA.

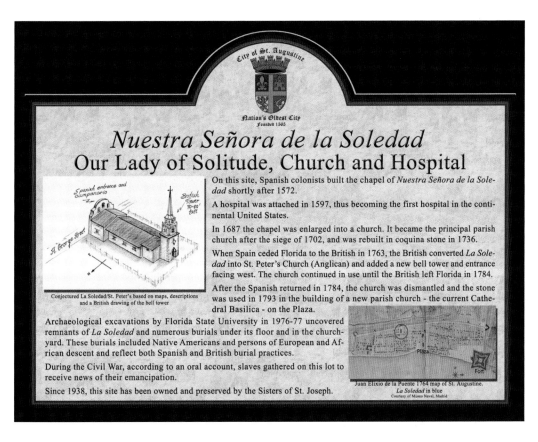

City of St. Augustine

Nation's Oldest City
Founded 1565

Nuestra Señora de la Soledad
Our Lady of Solitude, Church and Hospital

Conjectured La Soledad/St. Peter's based on maps, descriptions and a British drawing of the bell tower

On this site, Spanish colonists built the chapel of *Nuestra Señora de la Soledad* shortly after 1572.

A hospital was attached in 1597, thus becoming the first hospital in the continental United States.

In 1687 the chapel was enlarged into a church. It became the principal parish church after the siege of 1702, and was rebuilt in coquina stone in 1736.

When Spain ceded Florida to the British in 1763, the British converted *La Soledad* into St. Peter's Church (Anglican) and added a new bell tower and entrance facing west. The church continued in use until the British left Florida in 1784.

After the Spanish returned in 1784, the church was dismantled and the stone was used in 1793 in the building of a new parish church - the current Cathedral Basilica - on the Plaza.

Archaeological excavations by Florida State University in 1976-77 uncovered remnants of *La Soledad* and numerous burials under its floor and in the churchyard. These burials included Native Americans and persons of European and African descent and reflect both Spanish and British burial practices.

During the Civil War, according to an oral account, slaves gathered on this lot to receive news of their emancipation.

Since 1938, this site has been owned and preserved by the Sisters of St. Joseph.

Juan Elixio de la Puente 1764 map of St. Augustine.
La Soledad in blue
Courtesy of Museo Naval, Madrid

PLATE 8. La Soledad, St. Augustine, 1570s–1793. St. Johns County. In 2012, the St. Augustine Archaeological Association developed signage to show the public where a 1570s wood shrine stood and how it became the nation's first public hospital in 1597. In 1702, the shrine of Nuestra Señora de la Soledad and the attached hospital of Santa Barbara became the parish church, and eventually was partially rebuilt with stone and had a stone belfry. In 1763, the English made the Spanish church their Anglican St. Peter's by reversing the altar; in 1773, they added a steeple. Dismantled in 1793, the stones of La Soledad are in the walls of today's Cathedral Basilica. Conjectured church architecture by E. Gordon. Photograph 2011 courtesy of SAAA and Nick McAuliffe.

PLATE 9. Bastion, Castillo de San Marcos, St. Augustine, begun 1672. St. Johns County. Ignacio Daza, architect. Built of coquina stone quarried on Anastasia Island, the fort was completed in 1695 with continuing additions until 1763, including a covering of white lime plaster made from oyster shell lime. The turrets and the cordon were painted red. White and red were the colors of Spain's flag and symbolized Spanish dominion. Today the stucco and Spanish symbolism have weathered away. Photograph 2011 by the author.

PLATE 10. North wall and chapel entrance, Castillo de San Marcos, St. Augustine. The fort's 1688 chapel was enhanced with a Neoclassical entrance surround by Mariano de la Rocque in 1784 (reconstructed in 1915), the same engineer who a decade later would design the cathedral's Classical Doric entrance. In 1702, the townspeople and Indians from the surrounding missions crowded into the Castillo's vaulted rooms and central court with their animals and possessions, and lived in the fort for the fifty-two days of a British siege. Photograph 2011 by the author.

PLATE 11. Governor's House, St. Augustine, 1764 depiction. Architect unknown. The anonymous painting *View of the Governor's House at St. Augustine, in E. Florida, Nov. 1764* is the earliest depiction of the house (now called Government House) built with coquina stone. The painting shows a five-story battlemented tower, an elaborate wood balcony hanging over "governor's street," and a two-story courtyard wall with a Classical Doric entrance. The wall, entrance, tower, and balcony were removed in 1834 when Government House was converted into an American courthouse. Photocopy courtesy of the British Library, Maps K. Top. 122.86.-2-a.

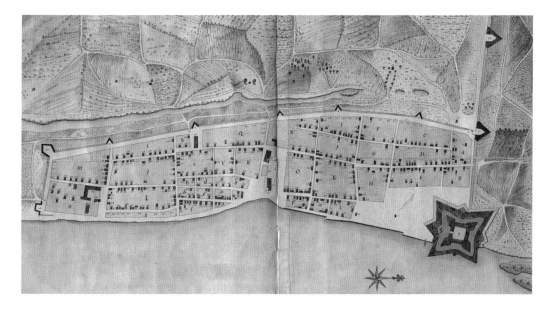

PLATE 12. Town plan, St. Augustine, 1764. Signed by Eligio de la Puente, the plan (shown here without its surrounding key) shows how the layout of the sixteenth-century town was still more or less in place two hundred years after it was laid down in the 1570s. The grid street plan grew with Classical symmetry, radiating outward from the central plaza. A vacant lot at the harbor's edge to the southeast of the plaza is the consecrated ground of Nuestra Señora de los Remedios, the first parish church and its cemetery, that existed from ca. 1572 until its destruction in 1702. Plan scanned 2010 courtesy of the Museo Naval, Madrid.

PLATE 13. Cathedral of St. Augustine, 1797/1888/1965. Mariano de la Rocque, architect. The cathedral was designed by Mariano de la Rocque during 1788–93, and was constructed with changes made on-site by Pedro Díaz Berrio during 1793–97. The 1797 walls are coquina and include stones from earlier dismantled churches. In 1887, its roof caught fire and crashed into the nave. James Renwick (who designed St. Patrick's Cathedral in New York City) supervised its restoration and additions, including the new 120-foot-tall bell tower. Photograph 2011 by the author.

PLATE 14. Tabby slave house, Kingsley Plantation, Fort George Island, ca. 1820s, restored 1980s. Duval County. The slaves of Zephaniah Kingsley and his wife, Anna Jai Kingsley, a former slave, built their own cabins with tabby concrete. It was laborious work, tamping a mixture of oyster shells, sand, water, and shell lime (made by burning oyster shells) into a board lift. When it hardened, the board frame was lifted and the process repeated. Today there are thirty-one house ruins and one restored house. Herschel Shepard, restoration architect. Photograph 2002 by M. Gordon.

Trinity Episcopal Church, St. Augustine, Fla.

PLATE 15. Trinity Church, St. Augustine, 1831. Peter Mitchel, architect. Trinity is the oldest Protestant church building in Florida, and the first with Gothic Revival imagery. This postcard view ca. 1910 shows the pointed windows and buttresses, and the addition of the spire by 1843 and a vestry. The 1831 merlons, crenels, and pinnacles, and the outside choir loft stairway have been removed. Trinity was enlarged in 1903, and the original Trinity structure is now the north transept and Chapel of St. Peter's, named after the 1763 British-period St. Peter's Anglican Church in St. Augustine. Collection of the author.

PLATE 16. Interior, Old Christ Church, Pensacola, 1832/1878. Escambia County. 1832 architect unknown; Charles Haight, Gothic Revival renovation architect. Old Christ Church was completed in 1832 with frontal tower and round-headed windows. It is Florida's second-oldest Protestant church building. During the Civil War, Union troops used it as a jail, barracks, and hospital. In 1878, Charles Haight of New York added Gothic Revival elements: a braced-arch open-beam ceiling and a stained-glass window over the altar. Gothic Revival architecture became popular in war-weary Florida after the Civil War. It was considered more picturesque and churchly. In 1936, the church was deconsecrated and today is preserved as part of Historic Pensacola Village. Photocopy by permission of West Florida Historic Preservation, Inc.

PLATE 17. Trinity Episcopal Church, Apalachicola, 1838. Franklin County. Architect unknown. Apalachicola was the third-largest cotton port on the Gulf of Mexico when the Classical temple-front Greek Revival–style Trinity Church was built. It was prefabricated in white pine in New York and was sailed to Apalachicola in sections and reassembled with wood pegs. It has a *portico-in-antis* (recessed) and a stenciled ceiling. The former slave gallery is in the rear, supported on Ionic columns. Photograph 2003 by the author.

PLATE 18. Florida State Capitol, Tallahassee, 1845/1902. Leon County. Architect Cary Butt, 1845; Frank Pierce Milburn, 1902; Herschel Shepard, 1982 restoration. Despite a governmental vote in 1971 to demolish the Capitol, public opposition saved it, leading to the restoration of its 1902 architecture. Built with locally made bricks, it was completed in time to celebrate Florida's admittance to the Union on March 3, 1845; the election of Florida's first elected governor; and the seating of the first General Assembly. In 1970, a new Capitol was built, and the "Old" Capitol was restored and now houses the Florida Center of Political History and Governance. Photocopy courtesy of Florida State Archives.

PLATE 19. Fort Jefferson, Garden Key, Dry Tortugas, begun 1846. Monroe County. Architect: military engineers. Aerial view of the largest coastal fort in North America. Its walls, 8 feet thick and 50 feet high, built by slaves and Union deserters, are anchored to a coral reef 70 miles west of Key West. Dr. Samuel Mudd, wrongly convicted of complicity in President Lincoln's assassination, was imprisoned here. Captured deserters were also imprisoned here and were deterred from escaping by shark-infested waters. It can be visited by seaplane or boat. Photocopy courtesy of Florida State Archives.

PLATE 20. Black Creek Methodist Episcopal Church, Middleburg, 1847. Clay County. Charles F. Barthlow, architect. This small wood vernacular church was built by slaves. Its designer had Classical architecture in mind: there are cornice returns, a portico, and square-edged, 10-inch pine boards set edge to edge on the front facade and painted white to look like stone. The bell was donated by George Branning and cast in New York; it arrived February 29, 1860, the day his twenty-year-old son died of swamp fever and was buried in the little churchyard. Photograph 1998 by the author.

PLATE 21. St. Mark's Church, Palatka, 1854. Putnam County. Richard Upjohn, architect. St. Mark's is the only church in Florida built to plans drawn by the hand of Richard Upjohn, at the time America's most esteemed Gothic Revival church architect. Palatka was then a bustling port on the St. Johns River for Florida's agricultural and timber products. The small wood church has Upjohn's Carpenter Gothic characteristics: steeply pitched roof, vertical board-and-battens, pointed lancet windows, and a rose window. The tower was added later, as were the white paint and red door. Painting by F. Blair Reeves, FAIA.

PLATE 22. St. Margaret's Church, Hibernia (Fleming Island), 1875. Clay County. Robert S. Schuyler, architect. The smallest of the Episcopal board-and-batten Carpenter Gothic mission churches along the St. Johns River, St. Margaret's seats fifty, and has a bell cote astride the gable and its original soft muted color. It was financed by Margaret Seton Fleming and built on her property that had once been the Spanish land grant plantation of George Fleming, the father of her husband, Lewis. Her son Francis Philip Fleming was Florida's fifteenth governor (1889–1893). The first service held was for her funeral and burial next to the church in the Fleming family cemetery under spreading oak trees. Photograph 2001 by the author.

PLATE 23. St. Mary's Church, Green Cove Springs, 1878. Clay County. Charles Haight, architect. Haight's office in New York City was in the same building as Richard Upjohn's. St. Mary's is typical of Upjohn-style Carpenter Gothic designs: vertical board-and-batten siding, pointed windows, open-beam ceiling, and tall, slender steeple, all designed to lift eyes and hearts heavenward. The church was constructed close to the St. Johns River, and some of its parishioners and ministers arrived on the wind and tide. *St. Mary's on the River,* by permission of the artist, © 2003 J. E. Fitzpatrick.

PLATE 24. Citra Baptist Church, Citra, 1880. Marion County. Architect unknown. Citra's Victorian Carpenter Gothic church has more elaborate ornamentation, including a distinctive gridded window, stick-like details, and a central open bell tower placed at the intersection of two matching gables. The tower is the entrance into the church, which has an Akron Plan–style assembly room, at the far end of which is the baptism pool under a lifting platform. The church reflects the growth of the citrus industry and the region's new railroads. Photograph 2004 by the author.

PLATE 25. Christ Episcopal Church, Monticello, 1885. Jefferson County. T. M. Ferguson, architect. Wood Carpenter Gothic churches were typically painted tans or grays or colors compatible with the picturesque landscape. Later, many were repainted Classical white. Christ Church is the rare church building restored to its original colors, inside and out. The colors were painstakingly discovered under exterior siding and interior brass lamps. The interior ceiling is tongue-and-groove oak, with exposed beams that are beveled and outlined in red. The prized double-lancet stained-glass windows are being restored by the Sisters of St. Joseph in St. Augustine. Photograph courtesy of Leslie Jane Spencer.

PLATE 26. Ponce de Leon Hotel, now Flagler College, St. Augustine, completed in May 1887, and opened January 1888. St. Johns County. Carrère and Hastings, architects. Flagler hired the young architects to design a grand hotel in a Spanish Renaissance style that would attract the wealthy to his "Newport of the South." They brilliantly synthesized the best of Spanish and Italian architectural traditions and created an allusion to romantic Spain. Their hotel was the first large concrete building in Florida, the first luxurious resort, and the first in the style now called Mediterranean Revival. Photograph 2011 by the author.

PLATE 27. Alcazar Hotel, now Lightner Museum and city offices, St. Augustine, 1888. Carrère and Hastings, architects. This second hotel designed for Henry Flagler was also Spanish Renaissance–inspired. Like the Ponce de Leon, it is a landmark of a new concrete construction technology, and of the large-scale, culturally themed resort hotels that promoted tourism. The exotic theatrical Alcazar was designed with a courtyard garden, Turkish and Russian steambaths, a gymnasium, tennis courts, a ballroom, and an indoor swimming pool large enough for water polo, races, and other events. Photograph 2011 by the author.

PLATE 28. Terra-cotta detail, Grace United Methodist Church, St. Augustine, 1888. Carrère and Hastings, architects. Their first church design for St. Augustine reveals the young architects' attraction to Andalusia, Spain, and its Moorish, Romanesque and Renaissance architecture. Red brick and terra-cotta elements, in contrast with the poured coquina-concrete walls, define the Romanesque Revival entrance arcade and the striking Renaissance-inspired belfry under a conical helmet. Photograph 2011 courtesy of Kenneth M. Barrett Jr.

PLATE 29. Flagler Memorial Presbyterian Church, St. Augustine, 1889–90. Carrère and Hastings, architects. The Presbyterian Church building had already been designed when the tragic news came that Flagler's daughter, Jennie, had died onboard the ship bringing her to St. Augustine. A mausoleum was added to the west side in 1906 and holds the remains of Jennie and baby and Henry Flagler and his first wife, Mary Harkness. The church is often said to be "patterned after St. Mark's Cathedral in Venice," but a closer look reveals that it is Romanesque Revival and has a Renaissance-style dome at the crossing, the first such dome to be built in Florida. Photograph 2009 by the author.

Plate 30. Detail, James Renwick's marble altarpiece, Cathedral of St. Augustine, ca. 1889–90s. After a fire destroyed the Spanish cathedral interior in 1887, James Renwick of New York City designed its restoration and additions, including two Carrera marble statues sculpted by J. Massey Rhind for the high altar, one of Pope Pius V and this statue of St. Francis of Borgia, vicar-general of the Jesuit order in 1565, the year Menéndez founded St. Augustine. When the cathedral was renovated in 1965, the statues were removed and forgotten, until they were discovered and placed in St. Augustine's San Lorenzo Cemetery. Recently rescued from the outdoor conditions, they are now housed in a new museum at Mission Nombre de Dios. Photograph 2003 by the author.

PLATE 31. Osceola County Courthouse, Kissimmee, 1890. F. C. Johnson, architect; George H. Frost, contractor. Osceola County's courthouse is the oldest courthouse in continuous use in Florida and in its original architecture. It was dedicated on July Fourth 1890 with a large public celebration. The three-story building is Romanesque Revival, characterized by the wide stairway leading into the portico of three round-headed arches on stout piers. The locally made red bricks, the symmetry, and the tall tower still express authority and county pride. Photocopy courtesy of Florida State Archives.

PLATE 32. Key West Custom House and Courthouse, 1891. Monroe County. William Kerr, architect. Now known as the "Old Customs House," it is considered to be Florida's finest Richardsonian Romanesque building. Large, red-brick Romanesque arches form its entrance portico. Its second floor was the site of the 1898 court inquiry into the sinking of the battleship *Maine* in Havana Harbor, which led to the Spanish-American War in 1898. Thomas Edison perfected his torpedo inventions on the third floor. Photocopy courtesy of Florida State Archives.

PLATE 33. Nassau County Courthouse, Fernandina Beach, 1891. Architect unknown. Nassau County's courthouse is the second-oldest still-serving courthouse building in Florida. Its downtown Center Street Victorian-period architecture is an eclectic combination of styles and elements, Corinthian cast-iron columns, Renaissance-inspired loggia, and a frontal brick tower with a staged wood belfry and town clock. A few blocks away is the small railroad depot that brought prosperity to the town, if not the mass-produced cast-iron columns; farther still down the street is the harbor that was once filled with the shrimp boats that also were central to Fernandina's livelihood, which is now better known for its restaurants and yachts. Photograph 2003 by the author.

PLATE 34. Tampa Bay Hotel, now University of Tampa, and Henry B. Plant Museum, Tampa, 1891. Hillsborough County. J. A. Wood, architect. Plant's building is now considered to be the finest example of Moorish Revival architecture in the United States. The huge, luxurious brick and wood hotel was designed and built for his system of railroads and hotels that crossed Florida and ran down the Gulf coast in the 1880s, spurring the Tampa region's growth: the village of Itchepucksassa became Plant City, and Vincente Martinez Ybor brought his cigar business to what became Ybor City. Photocopy courtesy of Florida Department of State/Division of Historical Resources.

PLATE 35. Bradford County Courthouse, Starke, 1902. Smith and Blackburn and F. Dobson, architect builders. Like a number of Florida's early county courthouses, Bradford County's is Romanesque Revival, influenced by the style of Henry Hobson Richardson. The entrance is dominated by a large brick half-round arch; its red-brick massing in 1902 conveyed an image of strength and permanence. The tower was the tallest in the county, which at the time included what is now Union County, and reflected the prosperity brought by lumber, cotton, and oranges, which lasted until the boll weevil and the 1895 freeze arrived. Today this renovated "old" courthouse is a regional center of Santa Fe College. Photograph 2011 by the author.

PLATE 36. Christ Church, Pensacola, 1903. Escambia County. Architect unknown. When the original 1832 red-brick Christ Church was outgrown (see fig. 15.3), the parish decided on a new church building and a new architectural direction (or "venture," as the bishop described it): Spanish Colonial, with shaped parapet, Baroque entrance, and espadaña belfry. It might have been influenced by an article in the *American Church Review* in 1896 that promoted the picturesque forms of California's missions as an architecture of a "superior order." Photocopy courtesy of Florida State Archives.

PLATE 37. Bethel Baptist Institutional Church, Jacksonville, 1904. Duval County. M. H. Hubbard, architect. Bethel Baptist's first church burned in Jacksonville's Great Fire of 1901. The black congregation hired M. H. Hubbard of New York to design a larger masonry building. It has an eclectic combination of roof shapes and architectural revival styles, and a large, tall dominating frontal tower. Behind the tower is a Classical-style cupola atop a mansard roof that covers the interior domed ceiling. Today it is a megachurch with a very large attendance and outreach programs. Photograph by the author, 2012.

Plate 38. Suwannee County Courthouse, Live Oak, 1904. Benjamin B. Smith and the Hugger Brothers, architects. While other north Florida county officials were deciding to build their courthouses in the Romanesque Revival style, or with white Classical-style temple-fronts, the decision makers in Suwannee County selected a different architectural image. With Beaux-Arts aesthetics, the yellow brick courthouse has contrasting white ornamenting elements. Live Oak became the county seat in 1868 because it was at the intersection of several rail lines linking Jacksonville and Pensacola and points north and south and the Suwannee River, carrying the county's lumber, turpentine, and other wood products and cotton. Photograph 2011 by the author.

PLATE 39. Columbia County Courthouse, Lake City, 1905. Frank Pierce Milburn, architect. Lake City was formerly an Indian village named Alligator Town until growth came with a railroad, and prosperity came with cotton, tobacco, lumber, naval stores, and citrus (until the big freeze of 1895), and the name was changed and dignified. The historic courthouse is still in government use. It was built three years after Milburn completed the Beaux-Arts renovation of the State Capitol and is distinguished by its yellow brick, Beaux-Arts ornamentation, and second-story temple-front on a rusticated first floor podium (a Roman tradition popularized in Renaissance Italy by the sixteenth-century architect Andrea Palladio). The dome has recently been restored. Photograph 2011 by the author.

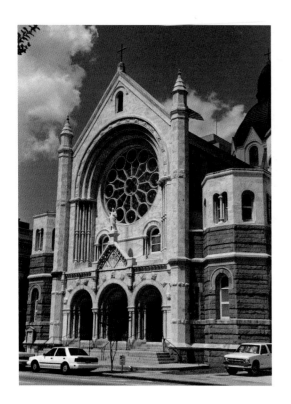

PLATE 40. Sacred Heart Church, Tampa, 1905. Hillsborough County. Architect unknown. After Henry Hobson Richardson's Trinity Church in Boston won awards in the 1870s, his style of architecture synthesizing Romanesque and Gothic elements became the model for many religious and public buildings across the United States. Sacred Heart has the style's characteristic heavy rusticated massing, symmetry, wide stairway, entrance arcade, large rose window, and flanking towers. Surrounded today by tall steel-and-glass skyscrapers, the marble and granite Romanesque Revival Sacred Heart Church presents a contrast that is a signpost of Tampa's roots. Photograph 2010 by the author.

PLATE 41. Pensacola City Hall, now T. T. Wentworth, Jr. Museum, Pensacola, 1907. Escambia County. Frederick Ausfield, architect. Looking somewhat like a robust Italian Renaissance villa, with a hint of Romanesque Revival and colonial Spain, this historic city hall is striking for its symmetry, flanking towers with wide bracketed eaves, arcade entrance, and curved parapets. It was built when Pensacola was Florida's third-largest city, with a railroad serving its waterfront piers, terminals, and warehouses. Photocopy courtesy of Florida Department of State/Division of Historical Resources.

PLATE 42. Jefferson County Courthouse, Monticello, 1909. Edward C. Hosford, architect. Jefferson County was named for Thomas Jefferson, and the county seat, Monticello, was named after the former president's home in Virginia. In 1906, the first courthouse of 1841 on Courthouse Square was torn down, "its many memories of the good and bad, heroes and rascals, consigned to oblivion," according to one local historian. A building committee comprising D. A. Finlayson and Josiah T. Budd saw that a new building rose on the same site, but with paired Corinthian columns, a dome, and a clock. Cotton had been replaced by pecans, tobacco, lumber, and the railroads that brought a more diverse economy, as well as an opera house in 1890 and the first telephones in 1901. Photograph 2011 by the author.

Plate 43. U.S. courthouse and post office, now Hippodrome State Theatre, Gainesville, 1909. Alachua County. James Knox Taylor, architect. Considered Florida's finest Beaux-Arts Classical building, the yellow-brick structure has a colossal portico of six two-story-tall Corinthian columns. After it was restored and renovated, leaving in place many original post office and courthouse fixtures, the Hippodrome became a State Theatre in 1981. The "Old Post Office" became the center of a lively downtown scene, surrounded by restaurants, art studios, urban apartments, art shows, and a weekly farmers' market. Photograph courtesy of Roslyn Levy.

PLATE 44. St. Petersburg's "open-air" post office, 1917. Pinellas County. George W. Stuart, architect. Innovative climate-friendly Italian Renaissance–style loggias with outdoor mailboxes were designed to serve and shelter foot traffic from rain and sun. Its elegant arcades, bracketed eaves, terra-cotta and marble ornamentation, and the Italian mosaic tile mural of a Venetian canal have been restored. Photograph courtesy of Florida Department of State/Division of Historical Resources.

PLATE 45. Palatka Post Office, now City Hall, 1917. Putnam County. Architect unknown. A decision by some unknown public official gave the small town of Palatka an elegant Italian Renaissance–style post office building a stone's throw from the St. Johns River. Its yellow-brick and cream-colored Classical arcade has fluted Corinthian columns and full-length windows. Viewed from the main thoroughfare, it is an uplifting sight in a city that has seen better times. Photograph 2011 by the author.

PLATE 46. Venetian Pool, Coral Gables, 1924. Dade County. Denman Fink and Phineas Paist, architects. It began as the quarry pit for the oolite limestone material used to build Coral Gables, but with the imagination and talents of many people it became a natural-looking pool with underwater caves, rock outcropping cliffs, green lagoons, shady loggias, Venetian-looking lamps and bridge, changing rooms, lush tropical plants, a Spanish fountain, a dance floor, and places to eat. It was, and is, an icon of exotic, romantic, boomtime Florida, and is now restored with a newer water system installed. Photocopy courtesy of Florida Department of State/ Division of Historical Resources.

PLATE 47. Freedom Tower (Miami Daily News Building), Miami, 1925. Dade County. Schultze and Weaver, architects. What was once the very expensive commercial space of the nation's fifth-largest newspaper has become the symbolic Statue of Liberty and Ellis Island for the Cuban arrivals who fled a dictator. Its 225-foot-tall tower was one of three in Miami that recalled the tower at Seville's cathedral, known as La Giralda, a twelfth-century minaret with a sixteenth-century Renaissance belfry. The meaning of the two Temple of Hathor pillars in this ca. 1926 postcard is unknown, but they reflect the eclectic nature of 1926 Miami. Public voices in 2005 protested the tower's development, and the developer donated it to Miami Dade College. Today it is part of the Wolfson Campus center dedicated to the study of architecture, education, and culture. Author's collection.

PLATE 48. Walton County Courthouse, DeFuniak Springs, 1926. Architect unknown. Walton County's courthouse has a rare example of a more correct Greek Revival portico, in which the monumental Doric columns are fluted and sit directly on the porch floor, supporting an entablature with triglyphs, metopes, and mutules. What inspired Walton officials and their architect remains to be discovered. Many nineteenth- and early twentieth-century Classical-style temple-fronts in Florida are Roman or Tuscan derived. Photocopy courtesy of Florida Department of State/ Division of Historical Resources.

PLATE 49. Bok Singing Tower, Lake Wales, 1929. Polk County. Milton B. Medary, architect. Bok Tower was one of a number of carillons in the United States that were inspired by the singing towers of Europe that rang out in celebration of American troops liberating European towns at the end of World War I. Florida's tower was a gift of Edward Bok, who emigrated from the Netherlands and made a fortune as the editor of *Ladies' Home Journal*. It is 205 feet tall, a Modern Gothic framework for an Art Deco masterpiece that is the work of many artists. Reliefs of flora and fauna, mythological figures, and sculptured bird pinnacles ornament the tower. Bok Tower is a sanctuary, a place to meditate in a landscape designed by Frederick Law Olmsted Jr. that combines music, nature, and art. Photograph 2003 by the author.

PLATE 50. WPA mural, Madison Post Office, 1930. Madison County. During the Great Depression, under the New Deal's Treasury Section of Fine Arts, artists could compete for commissions to paint murals and canvas paintings to brighten Florida's public buildings. Among the artists who won a competitive commission was George Snow Hill, whose *Long Staple Cotton* adorns the Madison Post Office. Photocopy courtesy of Florida Department of State/Division of Historical Resources.

PLATE 51. (*left*) Daytona Beach Post Office, WPA, 1932. Volusia County. Harry M. Griffin, architect. Using Florida's native keystone, Griffin designed one of Florida's more unique post offices, with elements from the Beaux-Arts and Arts and Crafts traditions. Full-length windows on the ground floor are set in cast-iron surrounds with bird imagery and framed in stone arches supported by small Classical columns. The fossilized marine life in the weathered keystone has a lace-like appearance. Cast-iron lights at each side of the stairway are supported by mythological birds and dolphins.

PLATE 52. (*right*) Light fixture detail, Daytona Beach Post Office, WPA, 1932. Harry M. Griffin's artistic cast-iron light illustrates how exceptional arts that enhance civic structures create a reverence for place. Griffin's lights, created with commissions awarded under the New Deal programs, inspired designs for public lighting elsewhere in Daytona Beach. Photographs 2011 by Kenneth M. Barrett Jr.

PLATE 53. St. Leo Abbey Church, St. Leo University, 1935. Pasco County. Brother Anthony Poiger, architect. St. Leo Abbey monastery was founded by Benedictine monks in 1889. Despite a wave of anti-Catholic propaganda led by Florida's own governor, Sidney J. Catts, during World War I, St. Leo's orange groves prospered, and the Church of the Holy Cross was built and a college was established. It is now a university with a sizable campus. The Abbey Church is known as the "church that orange juice built," and its architecture is in the Romanesque tradition of northern Spain and Lombardic Italy, but ornamented with yellow Indiana limestone that was traded for oranges. Photograph 2011 by the author.

PLATE 54. Coquina band shell, Daytona Beach, WPA, 1939. Volusia County. Harry M. Griffin, architect. Long before families were entertained by television and Disney World, this band shell at the beach was a major local attraction and popular with tourists. WPA projects promoted the use of Florida's native material. The band shell was built with the local coquina shell stone quarried along Florida's Atlantic coast. Photograph 2011 by Kenneth M. Barrett Jr.

PLATE 55. Annie Pfeiffer Chapel, Florida Southern College, Lakeland, 1941. Polk County. Frank Lloyd Wright, architect. Few Americans know that Wright, identified by *Time* magazine as the greatest architect of the twentieth century, designed twelve of the university's buildings between 1938 and 1950. The Annie Pfeiffer Chapel is the signature building, and is in keeping with his ideas at the time about advancing a modernist and organic regional architecture. Students molded the concrete blocks (forty-six different molds) using crushed coquina from Atlantic coast quarries. The central tower (described by students as a "bicycle rack in the sky") was designed to have natural light streaming down through vines and flowers, iron trellises, and colored glass. Photocopy courtesy of Florida Department of State/Division of Historical Resources.

PLATE 56. St. Nicholas Greek Orthodox Church, Tarpon Springs, 1943. Pinellas County. Architect unknown. The church is the cultural landmark of the unique community of sponge divers who came to Florida from the Greek Islands in the 1880s. The sponge industry thrived in Florida until killed by a red tide and foreign competition. This church building replaced an earlier one built by the first Greek settlers and is a reflection of St. Sophia in Constantinople, with beautiful icons and stained glass. Tarpon Springs today is known for its Epiphany Celebration on January 6, a celebration of life, the highlight of which is the dive by Greek American youths into the cold waters of Spring Bayou to retrieve the Epiphany cross. Photocopy courtesy of Florida Department of State/Division of Historical Resources.

PLATE 57. St. Paul's Lutheran Church, Sarasota, 1958. Sarasota County. Victor Lundy, architect. Lundy was a member of the Sarasota School of architecture, 1941–1966. Inspired by Frank Lloyd Wright's contemporary designs and ideas about regional modernism, Lundy reinterpreted Wright's triangulated and prow-like forms that had been expressed at Florida Southern College in Lakeland. Lundy and other Sarasota School architects experimented with new machine-made and natural materials to forge a style of architecture for Sarasota's climate and Gulf Coast environment. His upward-swooping roof is supported by laminated beams and draped steel cables. Photograph 2011 by the author.

PLATE 58. Baughman Meditative Chapel, University of Florida, Gainesville, 2000. Alachua County. John Zona, architect. This small Carpenter Gothic–influenced chapel overlooking Lake Alice is a modern version of the Carpenter Gothic river mission chapels built in Florida from the 1870s through the 1890s. Its contemporary style was inspired by Fay Jones's award-winning Ozark Gothic chapels in Arkansas. The Baughman Chapel is a gift to Florida that is designed to bring people together with architecture, music, performing artists, the lake, and nature. Photograph 2012 by the author.

PLATE 59. Interior, Baughman Meditative Chapel, University of Florida, Gainesville, 2000. Alachua County. Looking through the large Gothic-style window toward Lake Alice, the architecture and the viewer in this small nondenominational chapel building become one with nature and the serenity of the lake. This light-filled sacred space is aligned with a sunrise-sunset axis at the summer solstice. People come here to meditate, celebrate life, get married, or hear a concert. Photograph courtesy of University of Florida Performing Arts through gift from Evelyn Hemp, photographer, Gainesville.

PLATE 60. Ave Maria Oratory, Ave Maria University, Ave Maria, 2003. Collier County. Cannon Design, architect. The Oratory is the architectural centerpiece of the new campus and college town of Ave Maria University near Naples, founded as a joint venture between Barron Collier Companies and Thomas S. Monaghan, founder of Domino's Pizza. Its architectural form and style are derived from the pointed Gothic arch of Europe's medieval cathedrals. Gothic-inspired architecture arrived in Florida in 1831 at Trinity Episcopal Church in St. Augustine. Trinity was followed by Carpenter Gothic chapels built in wood, from the 1870s through the 1890s. The American Gothic Revival taste was transplanted to Florida after the Civil War by new arrivals of families from the North, as well as from England. The more churchly Gothic architecture and its ritual symbolism lifted war-weary spirits. Ave Maria Oratory is a spectacular example of, in I. M. Pei's words, how history is not only relevant, but is also essential to the creation of the new. Photograph courtesy of Ave Maria Development LLLP.

18 ✛ Civic Adornment

This sense of time, the awareness that countless others have come before and that others will follow in endless generations, distinguishes man from other animals. With this discovery of the meaning of death—that man's own life is limited—the life of architecture begins.

DANIEL BOORSTIN

IN THE PRECEDING CHAPTERS, generations of Floridians reveal themselves in the architecture of their houses of worship. In the three chapters to come they reveal themselves in their civic buildings designed for the betterment of the community. Their architectural stories, told in this chapter, are selected from the period 1890 to 1940, a time rich in the arrivals of style-making architects, national trends, new architectural needs, and changing tastes. It is also a period of rapid growth as new frontiers are opened with the railroads and automobiles, and many new Florida towns are established and in need of public architecture. Its storytelling begins in the north and moves southward into Florida's fabled Keys. Civic buildings like the houses of worship described in chapter 17 resonate with the economic changes that rolled over the land with waves of arriving peoples. Today they are the landmarks of state history and community identity.

As this manuscript is being written, rural Evinston residents in Alachua County are pleading for their small historic post office to stay open in the face of the U.S. Postal Service's plans to shut it to reduce the service's budget. The old heart-pine post-office structure was built in 1884, and named after the Captain W. D. Evins family, who gave the right-of-way for the narrow-gauge Florida Southern Railroad and a depot in 1882, the year the Evinston Post Office was established to serve the local community of orange growers. Inside the historic little post-office building are the original rows of metal mailboxes, and a country store added in 1896 that to this day sells cold drinks and homemade jams. It is a cultural landmark, a tangible living-history experience, and an oasis from today's quickening pace. Evinston's fight for its historic post office raises the question, "How many buildings still stand that can be counted as recording the state's, or a community's, first civic landmarks?"

Many of Florida's first nineteenth-century Anglo-American public buildings were expedient Florida-vernacular designs, built to house under one roof multiple government and community functions. They housed the tax collector, land surveyor, fire marshal, police, mailman, custom official, judge, and jury. They were usually situated in the center of parklike village greens or courthouse squares, with hitching rails, water troughs, saddled horses, wagons, and the jail. Under the one roof were the records of births, marriages, and deaths, land deeds, taxes owed and paid—as well as the town clock and bell, and posted public announcements, weather and market reports.[1] In them America's birthday celebrations were held, as well as chess championship matches and farmers' markets. They were wood, like Florida's first State Capitol. They have been replaced by the larger masonry structures illustrated in this chapter.[2]

Their masonry replacements reflect the lessons learned about wood architecture in Florida's moist, termite- and hurricane-prone environment, and many more painful lessons learned from the raging fires that flattened many a heart-pine Florida city. The larger masonry architecture also reflects the exuberance of the diverse arrivals of people eager to start new lives and invest in growing cities. Their public architecture would express messages about aspirations and success. In the context of their time and place, the city, county, and federal buildings were expected to be the biggest, tallest, and most prestigious. Like the houses of worship described in chapter 17, the civic buildings were inspired by the best of Europe's and America's architectural traditions. Now they are milestones, marking each community's rites of passage, and the soul and heart of the state. The historic-building vignettes presented below demonstrate why history and art are priceless architectural attributes that profit the state and the public—which is us.

At the end of the nineteenth century, some county officials looked to the Romanesque Revival architectural style for their local government building—it made a strong public statement and exhibited authority. Osceola County's courthouse in Kissimmee is Romanesque Revival and is Florida's oldest courthouse in continuous use. Its dedication July 4, 1890, was a large public celebration. F. C. Johnson's design is expressed in locally made red bricks (George H. Frost, contractor). We recognize some of the same elements in the Romanesque Revival church designs in chapter 17: symmetry, heavy masonry massing, dominant entrance arcade with large half-round arches on stout piers, and a wide staircase approach. A tower and belvedere established it as the county's tallest building. Osceola's courthouse symbolized county pride and future in canals and land sales, citrus, cattle, and sugarcane (plate 31).[3]

Key West's 1891 U.S. courthouse, post office, and custom house—now affectionately called the "Old Custom House"—is considered to be Florida's finest Richardsonian Romanesque building (plate 32). Its design by William Kerr is in the style of Henry Hobson Richardson's Romanesque Revival designs of the 1870s and 1880s that influenced many civic and religious buildings across the United States (fig. 17.3). Key West's building emphasizes the style's symmetry and imposing entrance arcade with exaggerated round-headed arches on short columns. Fine brick and terra-cotta ornamentation enhances its public appeal. The building's second floor was the site of the 1898 court inquiry into the sinking of the battleship *Maine* in Havana Harbor, the event that precipitated the Spanish-American War (1898). On the third floor, Thomas Edison perfected his torpedo inventions. The Custom House was abandoned in 1974 by the U.S. Navy and federal government, was purchased in 1987 by a developer, and was rescued in 1991 by the Resolution Trust Corporation and Florida's CARL Program (appendix 2). It was leased in 1992 to the Key West Historical Society to raise money, supervise its restoration, and operate it as the Museum of Art and History. Had this building been erased from the landscape, how would Americans or international visitors visualize the history and sense of place of Key West, which was once the largest and wealthiest city in Florida?[4]

Bradford County's courthouse (1902) in its county seat, Starke, and Calhoun County's courthouse (1904) in Blountstown are very similarly designed in red brick, characterized by symmetry and a large round-headed arch entrance. Starke's building, designed by Smith and Blackburn, additionally has a tall tower displaying the town clock (plate 35). Frank Lockwood and Benjamin Smith of Montgomery, Alabama, no doubt designed the Blountstown building to express that town's prosperity—which had arrived on the Apalachicola River when it was the stopover from cotton plantations to the north before the Civil War.[5] In 1969 and 1972, respectively, Bradford and Calhoun planners built new courthouses with similar tastes—they chose contemporary designs that expressed the historic values of Classical white columns (fig. 18.1). Both "old" courthouses have been saved and restored: Bradford

FIGURE 18.1. Bradford County Courthouse, 1969, Starke. Architect unknown. Bradford County's public officials, like those in Calhoun County, replaced their Romanesque Revival courthouses (plate 35) with a white modern building with hints of Classical columns. The old courthouse has been restored and rejuvenated for new uses by Santa Fe College. Changes in taste are one way of looking at Florida's built landscape. Photocopy courtesy of Florida State Archives.

County's "Old Courthouse" serves as the regional center of Santa Fe College, and Calhoun's "Old County Courthouse" is a multipurpose public structure.

Hamilton County's jail, built in Jasper in 1893, is Florida's oldest functioning jail. Its red-brick Romanesque Revival building was considered escape-proof. The designer-builder was the Peter and John Pauly & Brothers Building & Mfg. Co. of St. Louis, Missouri, which had also built a similar jail in 1891 in St. Augustine that was St. Johns County's jail. Their Romanesque designs have three-story towers (sometimes called "hanging" towers but without an explanation) dressed with pyramidal roofs and corbeling along the eaves. The entrepreneurial Pauly brothers emigrated from Germany to St. Louis, where they took up manufacturing hardware for paddle-wheel steamboats. When steamboat traffic declined, they changed to repairing and constructing jails, and filed for patents for steel-clad fireproof jail cells. St. Augustine's jail housed the sheriff and his family, and a kitchen where the sheriff's wife prepared the inmates' meals and sent them up by dumbwaiter. Since 1953 it has been a tourist attraction.[6]

Preferences for the principles of Classical architecture were expressed in many ways in Florida's civic structures in the late 1890s and early years of the twentieth century. Classicism in America was firmly reestablished with the Columbian Exposition of 1893 in Chicago, and with McKim, Mead and White's influence in reviving a Classicism cut from many pieces: Roman, Italian Renaissance, Palladian, French eighteenth century, English Georgian, and American Colonial.[7] In 1905, Henry J. Klutho called it "Modern Classic."[8] It is also called "Beaux-Arts" and "Academic Eclecticism." "Beaux-Arts" refers to the aesthetics of the École des Beaux-Arts in Paris, where a number of American architects were trained and influenced by its emphasis on the Classical architecture of Greece and Rome and its principles of symmetry. It is generally characterized by ashlar stone bases, Classical columns, grand stairways, monumental attics, and ornamentation of balustrades, modillion cornices, decorative swags, medallions, and sculptured figures.[9] In Florida, Spanish Colonial elements were sometimes added to the mix.

Nassau County's courthouse was built in 1891 in Fernandina Beach and is Florida's second-oldest still-serving courthouse. It reflects the Victorian era, when eclecticism was made possible by advances in industrialization, mass production, and railroads transporting materials. This downtown brick courthouse, near a small railroad depot, has slender cast-iron Renaissance-style Corinthian columns supporting an entrance arcade, above which is a second-story loggia, round-headed arches and window heads, and bracketed eaves. It has a frontal tower with a staged wood belfry in the earlier American-Georgian tradition, topped with a small dome and lantern, and exhibiting the town clock (plate 33).

Across the street, at the U.S. courthouse and post office designed by James Knox Taylor in 1910, there is an Italian Renaissance–style facade characterized by three floors articulated by different window traditions (fig. 18.2). This is a hallmark of the Italian Renaissance architect Andrea Palladio (1508–1580), the most influential architect of the last five hundred years. His drawings in *I quattro libri dell'architettura* (*Four Books of Architecture*), published in 1570, have influenced many American buildings.[10] Another example of this Palladian facade is in Miami, in the conversion of the city's first major U.S. post office and courthouse, which was designed in 1912 by Oscar Wenderoth. Conversion photographs in 1937 show how Kiehnel and Elliott dramatically reduced the size of the original building and converted it into the First

FIGURE 18.2. U.S. courthouse and post office, Fernandina Beach, 1910. Nassau County. James Knox Taylor, architect. This Renaissance Revival courthouse and post office is notable for its facade with three floors articulated by different window traditions under bracketed eaves. Facades with alternating window treatments were a hallmark of the sixteenth-century Italian architect Andrea Palladio, the most influential architect of the past five hundred years. The Palladian effect in Fernandina gives the public building an elegance and historical link to Renaissance Europe. Photocopy courtesy of Florida State Archives.

Federal Savings and Loan Association with a Palladian window scheme similar to that of the Fernandina building. Its alternating window treatments are clad in Indiana limestone, and Ionic pilasters divide the bays under bracketed roof overhangs.[11]

Italian Renaissance was also the choice in Live Oak for the 1909 city hall and police department, its design resembling the Italian farm villa illustrated in plate 48 of Andrea Palladio's *I quattro libri dell'architettura*. This "Old City Hall" (designed by Walker, Paul, Peavy and Jones) is now the Suwannee County Chamber of Commerce, recently restored and gleaming white, with a tall Italianate tower on Main Street in sight of the Suwannee County Courthouse and the Union Depot of the Atlantic Coast Railroad (fig. 18.3). Was this Palladian-style city hall a reference to the county's agricultural prosperity?

Suwannee County's restored courthouse in Live Oak is still in use. It was built in 1904 by Benjamin B. Smith and the Hugger Brothers with a combination of Renaissance Revival and Beaux-Arts Classicism, a creamy confection of yellow brick and white ornamenting details (plate 38). Symmetry is

FIGURE 18.3. Live Oak City Hall and Police Department, 1909. Suwannee County. Walker, Paul, Peavy and Jones, architects. Recently restored, this Italianate–style building is now the Suwannee County Chamber of Commerce. Its stunning white tower with wide, bracketed eaves is a highly visible landmark on the landscape. The building resembles that of plate 48 of Andrea Palladio's Renaissance Veneto farmhouse design in his *I Quattro Libri dell'Architettura* (*Four Books of Architecture*), published in 1570. Published in English in 1715, it widely influenced architecture in England and America. Photograph 2001 by the author.

central to its design. The entrance arcade is flanked by pedimented pavilions and topped with a clock tower with a ribbed metal dome. The white balustrade and modillion cornices, quoins, and window hoods are emphasized by their contrasting color with the yellow brick. An elegant courtroom has paired Corinthian columns and a broken pediment and swag.

A preference for things Italian and Renaissance (Mediterranean Revival) gave the small town of Palatka (Putnam County) in 1917 its one story villa-like cream-colored U.S. post office, now the city hall (plate 45). Pensacola's striking 1907 city hall (Escambia County) was designed by Frederick Ausfield with Classical Italian Renaissance symmetry and color, yellow brick under red-tile roofs. Ausfield combined a Richardsonian Romanesque entrance arcade with shaped parapets and flanking towers shaded under wide bracketed eaves. Now the "old" city hall is the T. T. Wentworth, Jr. Museum, exhibiting Pensacola's and the state's history (plate 41).[12]

In St. Petersburg (Pinellas County), the 1917 U.S. post office also reflects the trend in Italian Renaissance architecture (plate 44). However, its uniqueness lies in the indoor-outdoor mailbox spaces designed by George W. Stuart to accommodate foot, bicycle, and baby-carriage traffic. There are three loggias at the "open-air" post office that protect the visiting public from sun, heat, and rain. The award-winning restoration of this civic building preserved its elegant arcades, and the bracketed eaves, terra-cotta and marble ornamentation, as well as the Italian mosaic tile mural of Venice's Grand Canal.

A number of Florida's Classical-style temple-fronted courthouses have been restored and serve their original purpose, or have been adapted for new public uses. They preserve the spirit of Florida's early twentieth-century public architecture. A few might have been inspired by the enhancement of the Florida State Capitol in 1902 with Beaux-Arts Classical ornamentation and the addition of a dome and lantern by the well-known architect Frank P. Milburn (fig. 19.2). Several courthouses have white column temple-fronts combined with stylistic elements drawn from Italianate, Prairie School, and Spanish Colonial practices. Their columns vary in number, arrangements, as well as in their Classical Orders.

Jefferson County's courthouse in Monticello (fig. 18.4) and Polk County's courthouse in Bartow (both 1909) were designed by Edward C. Hosford of Georgia. They are two-storied symmetrical structures that are topped with central domes, lanterns, and town clocks, and are entered through two-story-tall tetrastyle (four-column) porticoes (plate 42). Their domes and temple-

FIGURE 18.4. Jefferson County Courthouse, 1909, Monticello. Edward C. Hosford, architect. A 1930s photograph shows schoolchildren lined up in front of their county courthouse. Forty years after the large Fourth of July celebration that drew crowds for the dedication of the Osceola Courthouse in 1890, courthouses were still at the center of community activities. Jefferson County's courthouse shows three columnar porticoes in this photograph, and the symmetry typical of its Beaux-Arts influenced Classicism. The ribbed metal dome and cupola suggest it might have been inspired by the 1902 Beaux-Arts enhancement of the State Capitol in nearby Tallahassee. Photocopy courtesy of Florida State Archives.

fronts express governing authority through democratic principles. A dome might also be a subliminal religious symbol of the heavenly dome. Citrus County's courthouse (1912) in Inverness (J. R. MacEachron and Willis R. Biggs, architects) has paired columns and a copper dome, and in the eclectic trend of the time, the building evokes Italian Renaissance, Spanish Mission, and Prairie School styles in addition to Classical (fig. 18.5). Paired columns at the Pasco County Courthouse (1914) support a Classical pediment. Madison County's courthouse (1913) has a *portico-in-antis,* as does the Lafayette County Courthouse in Mayo (1908), the 1905 U.S. courthouse in Tampa (fig. 18.6), and the Pinellas County Courthouse in Clearwater (1917).[13]

Lake City was formerly a Seminole village called Alligator Town (Alpata Telophka). It is the county seat and location of the Columbia County Courthouse, still in use since it was designed in 1905 by Frank Pierce Milburn, architect of the Beaux-Arts additions to the Capitol. Milburn's Beaux-Arts Classical design in Lake City introduces in Florida the temple-front portico on the second story. Its white Ionic columns stand out in contrast against the yellow brick of the second story, and the buff-colored brick of the first-story podium that is the entrance, a motif of Roman and Palladian Renaissance architecture (plate 39). Charles Bulfinch in Massachusetts used this plan for the State House in Boston (1795). It came from the English Palladian style

FIGURE 18.5. Citrus County Courthouse, Inverness, 1912. J. R. MacEachron and Willis R. Biggs, architects. Like the Jefferson County Courthouse in figure 18.4, the Citrus County Courthouse has the same symmetry, and metal dome and cupola, but it also has an eclectic reference to Italian Renaissance and Prairie School designs. Eclectic combinations were popular nationally at this time. Photocopy of 1950s photograph courtesy of Florida State Archives.

FIGURE 18.6. U.S. courthouse and post office, 1905, Tampa. Hillsborough County. James Knox Taylor, architect. Constructed with granite and marble, this Beaux-Arts Classical public building has a *portico-in-antis* (recessed) with fluted Corinthian columns and with the words "United States of America" blazoned proudly over the entrance. Photograph 1998 by the author.

made famous by William Chambers's Somerset House in London in 1786, then a new government building celebrated all over Europe.[14] The Columbia County building is recently restored, and the dome has been reinstalled.

Gainesville's former U.S. post office/courthouse (Alachua County) is considered one of the finest Beaux-Arts Classical buildings in Florida. The 1909 design by James Knox Taylor has a colossal portico of six two-story-tall Corinthian columns. The building's materials are yellow brick, granite, and carved limestone. Above the portico is a richly detailed entablature and a second story with a balustrade, and above that is the attic story with elaborate eave ornamentation. This building in the city center was renovated in 1980 for the home and stage of today's Hippodrome State Theater (plate 43).

Walton County's 1926 courthouse in DeFuniak Springs (A. C. Stanford, builder) has a portico that is more true to Classical Greece's Doric architecture: its monumental columns are fluted and have simple abacus capitals; they sit directly on the porch floor as do the Greek Parthenon's columns—with no base, plinth, or pedestal. Its entablature has Greek Revival triglyphs, metopes, and mutules (plate 48). Also in DeFuniak Springs is the wood-frame

Chautauqua Auditorium (1910), with a domed Hall of Brotherhood that has long been a center of educational and cultural programs. It has five porticoes, each designed in the two-tiered Palladian style. The forty columns are said to have represented the forty states at the time of its construction. It suffered damage in a 1975 hurricane, but has been repaired with state grants.[15]

Two county courthouses (Sumter and Sarasota Counties) and the Coral Gables City Hall are examples of Florida's public buildings with one-of-a-kind designs. Sumter County's courthouse (1914) in Bushnell revives colonial Spanish architecture, characterized by a Mission-style shaped parapet and identical flanking bell towers. The central two-story arcade is composed of tall, slender columns supporting round-headed arches, above which is the parapet topped with a Baroque broken-pediment element (fig. 18.7). The two end wings, however, hint of the Prairie School style. The designing architect was William A. Edwards, of the firm Edwards & Walter of Columbia, South Carolina, who designed most of the historic buildings from 1906 to 1925 at the University of Florida in the Collegiate or Tudor-Gothic style (fig. 18.11). Edwards also designed the Carnegie Library at Florida A&M University in Tallahassee, described below.[16]

Sarasota County's courthouse, like that of Sumter County, is also a unique expression of Spanish colonial architectural practices, and noted for its elegant tall tower that pierces the city skyline (fig. 18.8). Rising from a central courtyard and flanked by identical judicial buildings, the design is a synthesis of Spanish Colonial, Renaissance, and Baroque traditions. This attractive complex is the 1926 work of Dwight James Baum, whose other well-known architectural masterpiece is the extravagant Moorish and Venetian–styled Sarasota Bay waterfront residence, Ca' d'Zan, built for John Ringling and his wife, Mable, one of America's great mansions. Ringling's house and the county's courthouse are landmarks of Sarasota's 1920s boomtime development. More restrained than Ca' d'Zan, the courthouse is ornamented with cast-stone elements, blue-glazed tiles, and the wrought-iron artistry of Samuel Yellon, whose work is also seen at Bok Tower (chapter 17) and Vizcaya, the magnificent Italian Renaissance villa created for James Deering in 1914 in Miami. Before the courthouse was renovated, judicial functions and the jailer and sheriff were housed in the east wing, where the jail cells, witness rooms, and restrooms were labeled "colored" and "white"—a piece of history that has been removed in this still-functioning courthouse in the center of Sarasota's downtown.[17]

FIGURE 18.7. Sumter County Courthouse, Bushnell, 1914. William A. Edwards, architect; James Naim, builder. Sumter County's courthouse is a Spanish Colonial Revival design centered on a shaped parapet above an eye-catching portico. The yellow-brick parapet ends in a Baroque broken pediment. The two-story-tall white Ionic columns support round-headed arches. These central features are flanked by twin bell towers. In addition, there are identical wings that have Italianate or Prairie School wide eaves. Edwards also designed the Tudor Gothic buildings of the University of Florida and the Classical Carnegie Library now part of FAMU's campus. Photograph 1998 by the author.

The year after Sarasota's courthouse opened, another unique civic design rose, this one in Coral Gables. Very different in inspiration, the Coral Gables City Hall (1927) is the Classical Revival design of architects Phineas Paist and Harold Steward, with Denman Fink as artistic advisor, and is said to be the most imposing of the notable public buildings in the Gables (fig. 18.9). Its monumental semi-circular facade closely resembles and appears to have been inspired by William Strickland's Philadelphia Exchange (Merchants Exchange), Strickland's most successful work of urban architecture, occupying a difficult site at a triangular intersection. The Coral Gables building differs from Strickland's in a few details: it was built with Florida materials,

FIGURE 18.8. Sarasota County Courthouse, Sarasota, 1926. Dwight James Baum, architect. Sarasota's elegant Spanish Colonial Revival courthouse has been in continuous use since it was built in 1926. The domed tower soars high into the sky from its courtyard base and flanking judicial buildings, each with an entrance ornamented with blue-glazed tiles and cast-stone ornamentation. The tree canopy in this 1949 photograph has been stripped away, as well as the "colored" and "white" signs on the interior witness rooms and restrooms. Dwight James Baum also designed the exotic Moorish and Venetian waterfront residence of the circus baron, John Ringling and his wife, Mable, now a house museum open to the public. Photocopy courtesy of Florida State Archives.

Key limestone, and pecky cypress, and it has a square stepped clock tower (Strickland's was circular). Twelve Corinthian columns compose the Gables semi-circular colonnade elevated on a rusticated ashlar ground floor. Below it, on the sidewalk level, is a fountain; above it is a balustrade and a large Baroque shield designed by Fink and embellished with the coat of arms of Coral Gables: a crocodile, a fish, and a lion, and figures symbolizing art and labor. On the back of the shield the Venetian Pool (plate 46) is portrayed.[18]

FIGURE 18.9. Coral Gables City Hall, 1927. Dade County. Phineas Paist and Harold
Steward, architects, with Denman Fink as artistic advisor. The monumental semi-
circular facade appears to have been inspired by William Strickland's Philadelphia
Exchange (Merchants Exchange) designed a century earlier. The Florida building,
however, is constructed with Key limestone (keystone) and pecky cypress, and has
a fountain on the street level and a shield surmounting the whole with the Coral
Gables coat of arms, featuring images of a crocodile, a fish, and the Venetian Pool.
Photograph 1998 by Roger Blackburn.

During the early twentieth century, free public libraries were built in Florida with funds donated by the Andrew Carnegie Foundation. They are known as Carnegie Libraries, and most are Classical-style buildings. If one drives across the United States, one discovers many Carnegie Libraries in the heart of small downtowns that are still functioning as free public libraries. Among those in Florida is DeLand's Carnegie Library (1906) built at Stetson University and now Sampson Hall. Its Beaux-Arts Classical temple-front portico was designed by Henry J. Klutho. In Tallahassee, a Carnegie Library (William A. Edwards, architect) was built in 1906 on the former site of Governor William P. Duval's house, now a part of the college campus of Florida A&M University. Today it houses the Southeastern Regional Black Archives Research Center and Museum. Its Beaux-Arts Classical temple-front portico is centered on a white rectangular brick building, a style recalling Florida's State Capitol.[19] Another Carnegie Library was built in Bradenton (1905, T. W. Hullinger, architect). St. Petersburg's first library was its Carnegie Library (1915, Henry Whitefield, architect); it has been restored and still serves as a public library.[20]

Henry J. Klutho built the largest Carnegie Library in Florida (fig. 18.10). When it was completed in 1905 in Jacksonville (Duval County), it was one of the first public buildings constructed after the disastrous 1901 fire that leveled most of the city. Klutho called its style "Modern Classic." Inspired by the Greek Revival style, he "modernized" his "free public library" in the "Beaux-Arts" tradition. Over the entrance are the words "Open to All." There are a basement, two stories, a roof balustrade, modillion cornices, and a skylight of "art glass." The basement housed a fumigation plant to purify books from infectious diseases like yellow fever. Its entrance facade is dominated by a three-bay colossal portico of four fluted columns that have capitals composed of the sculpted heads of great men of knowledge, including Plato and Shakespeare. Still in fine condition, it is now privately owned.

FIGURE 18.10. Carnegie Free Public Library, Jacksonville, 1905. Duval County. Henry John Klutho, architect. Klutho's Carnegie Library is one of a number of libraries gifted to Florida communities. It was built with Carnegie financing. Klutho called the style of his library's design "Modern Classic." In the basement, books were fumigated to purify them of infectious diseases. On his front Corinthian columns, Klutho inserted the heads of Plato, Shakespeare, and other men of knowledge. Photograph 2011 by Kenneth M. Barrett Jr.

FIGURE 18.11. Tudor (Collegiate) Gothic University Auditorium, 1922, University of Florida, Gainesville. Alachua County. William A. Edwards, architect. The preservation of the earliest buildings of the historic campus (1906–25), along with their sense of history and tradition, is a priority of the university. Its Tudor (or Collegiate) Gothic style is rooted in the architectural ideals of English medieval universities. A number of the earliest academic and residential buildings have been restored with private and state financing. On many of their facades are sculptures representing Florida history and academic areas of study. Photocopy courtesy of Florida Department of State/Division of Historical Resources.

In that same year, 1905, Klutho was one of two architects who submitted competitive drawings to design the campus plan and first buildings for the University of Florida. He lost to William A. Edwards of Edwards & Walter. If he had won, the university would look very different today: Classical and domed instead of the Collegiate Tudor-Gothic look that is rooted in the ideals of English medieval universities (fig. 18.11). The multitalented Klutho, however, went on to other "Modern Classic" designs, including two in Tallahassee, the first governor's mansion in 1906, and the wings for Florida's State Capitol in 1923. These wings were removed in the Capitol restoration (1982), and Klutho's governor's mansion was replaced in 1957 with the larger Classical-style mansion of today, designed by the Palm Beach architect Marion Sims Wyeth. Klutho also designed Palatka's Art Deco Larimer Library (1929), donated by James R. Mellon and named for his wife, Rachel Huey Larimer, and now an arts center. Klutho today is better known for his Prairie School architecture and Jacksonville's first commercial skyscrapers.[21]

As the population in Florida's urban centers grew in the early decades of the twentieth century, land became costly and space in the sky became the new frontier. The Tampa City Hall (1915), the Miami Beach City Hall (1927), and Dade County's courthouse in Miami (1928) illustrate the newer trend in which buildings reached new heights with tripartite schemes—base, shaft, and crown. The scheme might have been influenced by the Chicago School of commercial architecture. Ornamentation was still Classical, with Beaux-Arts aesthetics. These first tripartite public buildings rose higher than other buildings in their respective cities, but they are now dwarfed by more modern skyscrapers. Their smaller heights, however, are the preserved high-water marks of their time.

The Tampa City Hall has been in continuous use since 1915. Bonfoey and Elliot, architects, designed the main base block with three stories and multiple Doric columns, above which rises the multistoried midsection (the shaft), and above it is the clock tower with metal dome (the crown). The traditional modillion cornices, balustrades, terra-cotta medallions and figures ornament the building (fig. 18.12). A three-part plan similarly defines the Miami Beach City Hall of 1927 designed by Martin Luther Hampton (known for his Art Deco works), and restored in 1987 by preservation architects Stuart Grant and Randall Sender. Now known as the "Old City Hall," the restored building still reveals its two-story 1927 horizontal base, nine-story shaft, and pavilion crown. Its Beaux-Arts Classicism includes urn finials, small garlanded Corinthian columns, round-headed arches, blind arches, and sculptural details articulated in bright yellow to contrast with the white walls and terra-cotta roofs. It was replaced by a newer Miami Beach City Hall (1977), a Late Modern horizontal concrete building recalling the 1920s International style and Le Corbusier's taste for geometric order (Grove and Hack, and Bouterse Borelli and Albaisa, then Bouterse Perez and Fabregas, architects).[22]

Miami's Dade County Courthouse is a 1925–28 building designed by A. Ten Eyck Brown and August Geiger. It, too, has a three-part plan: base, shaft and crown, and Beaux-Arts Classical detailing. When built, it was the tallest and first multistory skyscraper in Miami. (The crown is shown under construction in figure 18.13.) Among its distinguishing details are: cut-out and chamfered corners, Stone Mountain granite facing, and Doric half columns. Embellishments include balustrades, modillion cornices, Corinthian pilasters, and a stepped pyramidal roof. The jail was on the top nine floors and was thought to be escape-proof—until a prisoner picked a window lock and fled down a fire hose. At the main entrance, in the shadows of the tall fluted

FIGURE 18.12. Tampa City Hall, Tampa, 1915. Hillsborough County. Bonfoey and M. Leo Elliot, architects. When urban space becomes scarce and costly, buildings grow upward, and Tampa's city hall was one of the first public buildings in Tampa to reach skyward for new space. It has a tripartite scheme of base, shaft, and crown, and a Beaux-Arts aesthetics characterized by the Doric columns, modillion cornices, balustrades, terra-cotta medallions, and sculptured figures. This historic city hall is a high-water mark of Florida's growth in 1905, demonstrated by the steel-and-glass buildings surrounding it. Photograph 2000 by the author.

FIGURE 18.13. Dade County Courthouse, under construction, 1928, Miami. A. Ten Eyck Brown and August Geiger, architects. The Dade County courthouse, like that in Tampa, was built with a tripartite plan of base, shaft, and crown. In this 1927 photograph, the crown is under construction. When finished, the public building will be faced with Stone Mountain granite, and ornamented with Beaux-Arts balustrades and modillion cornices, and a stepped pyramidal roof. One of the first tall structures in Miami's skyline, it started sinking before it was learned that the cement pilings had to go much deeper. The jail—on the top nine floors—proved not to be escape-proof. Photocopy courtesy of Florida State Archives.

Classical columns, photographs reveal that a lively Miami Arts Series was held in the 1970s. Another photograph, that of the smaller Classical Revival courthouse of 1904 that the skyscraper replaced in 1928, reveals how quickly the built landscape changed in twenty-four years (fig. 18.14).[23]

Equally revealing is a photograph of the demolished Hillsborough County Courthouse in Tampa, built in 1892 with an onion dome and horseshoe arches (fig. 18.15). Henry Plant had brought his railroad to Tampa in 1884, and Vincent Martinez Ybor had founded his cigar industry in what is

FIGURE 18.14. Dade County Courthouse, 1904, demolished, Miami. Architect unknown. The built landscape in Miami changed rapidly in the 1920s, demonstrated by this photo of the small, elegant, Classical-style Dade County Courthouse that was demolished to accommodate the larger and taller 1928 county courthouse. The story of Florida's first county courthouses will have to be found in Florida's more rural communities. Photocopy courtesy of Florida State Archives.

FIGURE 18.15. Hillsborough County Courthouse, 1892, demolished, Tampa. J. A. Wood, architect. A victim of Tampa's growth, particularly after the arrival of Henry B. Plant's railroad and Tampa Bay Hotel (1891), the onion-dome courthouse with Moorish horseshoe arches was soon left behind in the ever-rising-higher Tampa skyline and expanding population. The irony is that it, too, was designed by Plant's personal architect, the designer of his 500-room Tampa Bay Hotel that accelerated the city's development. Archived photographs are important to Florida's story. Photocopy courtesy of Florida State Archives.

now Ybor City in 1886, both events accelerating Tampa's growth so that the courthouse soon became too small. Several more followed it, including the 1955 structure that suggests a contemporary Classical style (fig. 18.16). The 1892 onion-dome courthouse was designed by Henry Plant's architect, J. A. Wood, a year after he designed Plant's luxurious 500-bed Tampa Bay Hotel (1891) in the Moorish Revival style. The latter is now the University of Tampa and the Henry B. Plant Museum, considered to be the finest Moorish Revival architecture in the United States. Its minarets and onion domes add excitement and diversity to the skyline (plate 34; fig. 18.17). Rapid development can result in tearing down even the most history-laden public buildings in urban centers in order to quickly facilitate the population growth. Restored courthouses in smaller and rural communities are therefore left to become the keepers of Florida's early government history and architectural heritage. They are also a part of the "old is the new green" movement.[24]

Miami's Freedom Tower is a former commercial building that in the 1960s became the symbol of the Cuban exodus to the United States. When it opened in July 1925, it was the headquarters of the *Miami Daily News*, the fifth-largest newspaper in the country. It was designed by Schultze and Weaver (of New York) at the height of south Florida's boomtime. Its owner, James M. Cox Sr., former governor of Ohio, spent a fortune to build the multistory building that became a Miami icon (plate 47). Like the Dade County Courthouse in Miami begun the same year, it is a tripartite base-shaft-crown structure, but

FIGURE 18.16. Hillsborough County Courthouse, 1955, Tampa. Architect unknown. Several courthouses after the Moorish Revival onion-domed courthouse in figure 18.15, Tampa officials might have decided on this contemporary style courthouse as a product of its time like the one before. It thus might reflect a 1950s Florida trend in retro-Classicism with a temple-front updated. Change can promise a redefinition and a vibrant new beginning. Photograph courtesy of Florida State Archives.

FIGURE 18.17. Tampa Bay Hotel, now the University of Tampa and the Henry B. Plant Museum, Tampa, 1891. Pinellas County. J. A. Wood, architect. Plant's huge hotel, like Flagler's Ponce de Leon Hotel in St. Augustine, is rejuvenated as a university and a museum. The Plant Museum showcases the Victorian era, the Gilded Age, that is the architectural story beneath the onion domes. In addition to stylistic history, there is a room dedicated to the story of the officers and troops during the Spanish-American War in 1898. Tampa was the embarkation site for Cuba. Photocopy courtesy of Florida Department of State/Division of Historical Resources.

with a taller shaft and a crown ornamented in the Spanish Renaissance style, inspired by the Giralda Tower of the Cathedral of Seville, the twelfth-century minaret with a sixteenth-century Renaissance belfry. Schultze and Weaver had also designed the Miami Biltmore Hotel in Coral Gables (opened January 1926) with the La Giralda motif (named for its weathervane) (fig. 14.4). This style tower had become popular after McKim, Mead & White's version of it on New York's Madison Square Garden (1891).[25] In 1957, the *Miami News* vacated the building. From 1962 to 1974, it was leased by the federal government as a refugee center to process, document, and provide medical and dental services, food and resettling help for some four hundred thousand Cuban arrivals. During this time, it was renamed the Freedom Tower and was thought of as Florida's Statue of Liberty and Ellis Island, the symbolic beacon to more than a half million Cubans who fled a dictator (fig. 5).

After 1974, the Freedom Tower's future wended along an arduous path. It passed through the hands of different owners, was listed on the National Register of Historic Places in 1979, and was restored in 1988, winning a 1989 Florida Preservation Award (J. Heisenbottle Architects). But in 1993, legal and financial troubles closed the tower, and it was abandoned. It was bought in 1997 by the family of Jorge Mas Canosa, a leader of the exile community. Its planned restoration and conversion into a monument and meeting place for Cuban refugees and offices for the Cuban American National Foundation was not completed. In 2004, it was sold to a developer, Pedro Martin, chairman and CEO of Terra Group. After a thorough analysis of the historic building and its site, he planned to build a sixty-two-story condo beside the tower and preserve the tower except for a rear portion. Public objection was such that he donated the building in 2005 to Miami Dade College. Today it is part of the Wolfson Campus and is a center dedicated to architecture, education, and culture. In 2008, it received National Historic Landmark status for its role in welcoming the Cuban community.[26]

While South Florida's spectacular and innovative skyline was moving upward and was replacing the first-built public spaces, there is a different story of expansion and a dramatic rescue in Palm Beach County. The 1916 Palm Beach Courthouse (in West Palm Beach) was about to be unknowingly demolished because it had been absorbed and entombed inside a mammoth 1968 "wraparound" addition that had bought more space for the dollar. In 1995, the "ugly" building was about to be torn down when a discovery was made. County Commissioner Karen Marcus, who knew about the original Beaux-Arts Classical building, and Rick Gonzalez, preservation architect, conducted a grassroots investigation, and from the twelfth-story of a neighboring building, they discovered the courthouse's historic pediment poking up though the 1960s wraparound. When the addition was carefully removed, the 1916 Beaux-Arts Classical building was found intact—with the exception of twelve Corinthian portico columns. They were discovered by Rick Gonzalez lying in the cemetery grass. Restoration was completed in November 2007, and today the restored 1916 courthouse houses the County Attorney's Office, the Public Affairs Department, the Richard and Pat Johnson Palm Beach County History Museum, and the County Historical Society.[27]

The Great Depression of the 1930s brought about a special chapter in the making of Florida's built landscape. Under the New Deal WPA (Works Progress Administration) and CCC (Civilian Conservation Corps), engineers, architects, builders, artists, and laborers were hired to design and build courthouses, post offices, city halls, libraries, hospitals, jails, bridges, parks, and roads, including Florida's extraordinary Overseas Highway to Key West. Few Floridians know that Washington, D.C.'s Reagan Airport was a WPA Depression-era building. In Florida, the WPA financed architects, local craftsmen, artists, and builders, and promoted Florida materials and designs and local industries (fig. 18.18). Aesthetically pleasing civic structures were designed and built. In addition, HABS (Historic American Buildings Survey) was established (see appendix 2), and hundreds of historic structures in Florida have since been measured, photographed, and researched (fig. 14.5). HABS drawings, photographs, and building histories are important tools for today's architects, archaeologists, restorers, renovators, preservationists, and architectural historians.[28] Between 1936 and 1942, murals and canvas paintings were commissioned by the New Deal's Treasury Section of Fine Art to be placed in Florida's older or newly constructed government buildings. These commissions were awarded based on national and regional art competitions, and only the best were selected. New Deal fine arts projects depicting local Florida history and industries still brighten the lobbies of public buildings, including *Loading Pulpwood* by George Snow Hill at the Perry Post Office; *Harvest Time* by Denman Fink at the Lake Wales Post Office; and *Long Staple Cotton* by George Snow Hill at the Madison Post Office (plate 50).

In the main lobby of the historic U.S. courthouse in Tallahassee, there is a WPA mural with eight scenes illustrating Florida history. It was painted in 1939 by the Hungarian-born American artist Edward "Buk" Ulreich (1889–1966). The Tallahassee Courthouse itself was WPA-financed, designed in 1937

FIGURE 18.18. Stage entrance, coquina band shell, Daytona Beach, WPA, 1939. Volusia County. Harry M. Griffin, architect. WPA projects promoted the use of native materials and a style related to Florida. The stage door to the Daytona Beach band shell does both with the Spanish-style door and the coquina stone. The band shell still looks good all these years later (see plate 54). One can walk on coquina rocks at places like Washington Oaks in Flagler County and see the native stone that the ocean gave to Florida's earlier builders. Photograph 2012 by Kenneth M. Barrett Jr.

FIGURE 18.19. U.S. courthouse, Tallahassee, WPA, 1937. Leon County. Eric Kebbon, architect. Kebbon's design, like the Columbia County Courthouse in Lake City (plate 39), has a second-story portico supported by the first-floor rusticated podium, a Roman feature and Palladio leitmotif. In the main lobby is a WPA Treasury Section mural, painted in 1939 by Edward "Buk" Ulreich, who won the competitive commission. Its eight scenes depict Florida history. This historic courthouse today is the U.S. Bankruptcy Court for the Northern District. Its award-winning restoration in 2003–5 was designed by Akin & Associates Architects, with Peter R. Brown Construction. Photocopy courtesy of Florida State Archives.

by architect Eric Kebbon of New York (fig. 18.19). It has a second-story portico on a rusticated podium that resembles the plan of the Columbia County Courthouse designed by Frank Pierce Milburn in 1905 (plate 39), which had precedents in London and Massachusetts as noted earlier in this chapter. The Tallahassee courthouse interior is exceptional for its original brass doors, the curved stairway, and many marble details. Today this WPA building is still in use as the U.S. Bankruptcy Court for the Northern District. It was restored during 2003–5 (Akin & Associates Architects, and Peter R. Brown Construction) and won an outstanding achievement award from the Tallahassee Trust for Historic Preservation.

Another WPA courthouse of note is Franklin County's courthouse in Apalachicola. It is a rare combination of Classical and Art Deco elements, chosen to replace an earlier brick Romanesque Revival courthouse building. The design is by Warren, Knight, and Davis, with A. James Honeycott, builder, in 1939.[29] One wonders if its *portico-in-antis* was a reference to Apalachicola's historic Trinity Church, a Greek Revival built in 1838 with a *portico-in-antis,* the first of its kind in Florida (plate 17).

Lake City's post office (Columbia County), designed by James A. Wetmore, and Clearwater's Cleveland Street post office (Pinellas County), designed by Theodore H. Skinner, are both WPA buildings that emphasize Florida's Mediterranean-inspired tradition. Also locally inspired, the Miami Beach Post Office (1939, Howard L. Cheney, architect) is in keeping with the Miami Beach Art Deco neighborhood. It is a streamlined Art Deco design (sometimes known as "Moderne," "Depression Moderne," or "Deco Federal") that is a rotunda at the apex of two wings (fig. 18.20) and lighted by a lantern skylight. The rotunda walls and ceiling are painted by Charles Hardman, who won the Treasury Department's fine art commission (1941). His large tripartite wall mural depicts Florida Indian history, and the ceiling is a giant sunburst in the cerulean sky with forty-eight stars edged in silver and bronze. Suspended from the sunburst is an Art Deco skylight made of bronze and opaque glass.[30]

WPA architectural projects in Florida made particular efforts to use Florida's native materials. Florida's Key limestone ("keystone" or "coral stone") is the substance of the Daytona Beach Post Office and the building that was the Miami Beach Public Library and is now the Bass Museum of Art. As it weathers, Florida's keystone reveals its marine fossils. The Miami Beach Library was designed by Russell T. Pancoast (1930), the grandson of one of the pioneer developers, John Collins, who laid out Collins Park and its formal gardens in the 1920s. Pancoast's Florida-style Art Deco has Maya influences: carved seagulls flying off at the corners, reminiscent of the corners on Maya architecture at Uxmal, in the Yucatan, and bas-reliefs like those of the lintels in Maya temples. They are by the sculptor Gustav Bohland, and in addition to a stylized pelican and fish, he depicts colonial Spanish sailing ships, and modern planes and cruise ships bringing people to Miami Beach (fig. 18.21). A new wing was added in 2001, designed by Arata Isozaki, combining Japanese and Western modernism sensibilities. Isozaki has an international reputation: he designed the Olympic Stadium in Barcelona and the Museum of Contemporary Art in Los Angeles, as well as the Team Disney Building in Orlando.[31]

FIGURE 18.20. Miami Beach Post Office, WPA, 1939. Dade County. Howard L. Cheney, architect. Cheney's streamlined Art Deco (Moderne) post office is a rotunda at the apex of two wings, lighted by a lantern skylight. The lobby has a large tripartite wall mural depicting Indian history known at the time, and a ceiling depicted as a giant sunburst in a cerulean sky, with forty-eight stars edged in silver. The murals were painted by Charles Hardman, who won the competition in 1941. Photocopy courtesy of Florida State Archives.

FIGURE 18.21. Miami Beach Library, WPA, 1930, now Bass Museum of Art. Dade County. Russell T. Pancoast, architect. Pancoast was the grandson of John Collins, who laid out Collins Park. The library is faced with keystone, weathered to reveal its marine fossils. Its Art Deco style has classic-period Maya-influenced elements carved by Gustav Bohland. Now the Bass Museum of Art, it has a new wing added in 2001 designed by Arata Isozaki, who also designed the Team Disney Building in Orlando. Photograph 1991 by the author.

At Daytona Beach in 1932, Harry M. Griffin designed one of the most unusual and artistically eclectic WPA post offices in Florida. It is faced with the coral stone quarried in the Florida Keys and sawed in slabs, and its surfaces have weathered a soft gray that accentuates the continuous lace-like quality of its fossilized marine life. Griffin synthesizes Beaux-Arts Classicism with American Arts and Crafts sensibilities, and creates a facade that feels right for Florida (plate 51). He set full-length windows on the first floor in cast-iron surrounds with bird imagery, which in turn are set within paired arches supported on slender small and elegant Corinthian columns. On the second floor are iron balconies and a decorative drip over the main entrance to divert water. The clay roof tiles were imported from Cuba. Two cast-iron lights at each side of the curved entrance stairway are an artistic highlight. They represent imaginative horned heads of mythological birds supporting four dolphins with their flipper tails supporting round globes (plate 52).[32] Griffin also designed the Daytona Beach coquina band shell (plate 54) and the limestone Seabreeze Church (fig. 17.13).

Florida's oldest government building is the Governor's House, now called Government House, in St. Augustine. It is an architectural landmark of extraordinary significance to Florida's Spanish, English, and American periods. What we see today is an enduring building that has been improved and culturally altered multiple times during the last three centuries. A major renovation in 1936 restored it in part to its colonial appearance depicted in a 1764 watercolor painting that is currently in the British Library collection in London (plate 11). Two of its iconic colonial features were not rebuilt: the crenellated tower and the two-story courtyard wall with the Classical entrance. They had been torn down in 1834.

The importance of this building, its architectural history and lasting symbolic presence at the head of St. Augustine's Plaza, is a rich architectural story. It was the residence, social center, and administrative office of the governors of Spanish and English Florida. Within its walls, Spanish and English governors graciously and copiously wined and dined many guests, officials, and overnight visitors, and in so doing added to the building their personal touches, improvements, and paint colors, which are forthcoming in documents and structural reports. In addition, its architectural story includes the 1833 plan for its renovation that came from the hand of Robert Mills, one of America's best-known architects. Government House deserves its own book-length biography.

Its history begins with a wood structure about 1572. In 1586, it was depicted standing at the west end of the plaza in a drawing by Baptista Boazio illustrating Drake's battle plan (published in 1588; see text box in chapter 9). In Boazio's drawing, in English tradition, it is called the "towne house" and is a gabled structure with a nearby watchtower (plate 6; fig. 9.1). It was burned by Drake's English troops on May 30, 1586. The governor's house was rebuilt closer to the harbor, labeled *casa de general* on a map drawn by Lt. Hernando de Mestas in 1594. Around 1598, its history restarts at the west end of the plaza. Burned again by the English in 1702, it was rebuilt by

1713 with coquina stone (first floor) in the same location at the west end of the plaza. It was two-storied (the second story might have been wood), and it had a balcony facing east, toward the plaza and harbor, from where the governor addressed the people gathered in the plaza. During the colonial period that lasted until 1821, it was the administrative and social center of the Spanish and English governors. Eligio de la Puente's map of January 1764 describes it as the *stone house of the King where the governors live* (plate 12). The 1764 watercolor painting in plate 11 and the 1776 carving on a powder horn (fig. 18.22) depict its castellated (crenellated) tower and the two-story courtyard wall, as well as the balcony facing the plaza. The architect and construction dates of the stone tower and Classical entrance have not been found. The delicate watercolor painted in 1764 by an anonymous English artist (shortly after Spain ceded Florida to England) reveals an eggshell-blue balcony ceiling. English documents describe the house's

FIGURE 18.22. Powder horn detail, Governor's House, ca. 1776, St. Augustine. Carved on this powder horn, Government House (as it is called today) is depicted with the five-story tower, the balcony, and the grand two-story balustraded Doric entrance that appear in a 1764 painting (plate 11). Eligio de la Puente's map of January 1764, made as the Spanish left Florida and the British arrived, describes the building as the "stone house of the King where the governors live." Collection of the Museum of Florida History.

extensive garden with legumes and fruits, and its flowing wine cellar, as well as glazed windows, new chimneys, additional courtyards, improved kitchen, and new stables.[33] Indian and black slaves were no doubt among the quarrymen, lime burners, masons, and carpenters whose labors constructed this important building.

When Spain ceded Florida to the United States in 1821, the building was used as a federal courthouse and post office. Thomas Douglas, the first U.S. attorney for the Eastern District, lived in its tower in 1827, which he described as five stories, 70 feet high, with excellent views of the city and comfortable during the summer heat.[34] In 1834, Government House was modified to better serve the functions of the court and postal service. This was done according to a plan by Robert Mills in 1833, then of Washington, D.C., who was a draftsman with the land office and architectural advisor to the secretary of the Treasury. In 1836, Mills was promoted to architect of public buildings. He is better known as the designer of the Washington Monument, and many other American landmark buildings. Mills was a brilliant architect, but his sympathies did not lie with St. Augustine's Spanish past or its architectural traditions. Government House's iconic tower and Doric courtyard entrance and balustrade were removed. Also removed was the elaborate wood Spanish balcony when the east gable facade was remade into a style popularized by Benjamin Latrobe and characterized by corner pavilions, a parapet, hipped roof, and a symmetrical arrangement of six windows and two doors (fig. 18.23). Some exterior and interior walls were moved and rebuilt at this time, but a copy of the construction contract with John Rodman and Elias Wallen archived at the St. Augustine Historical Society Research Library called for reusing the original coquina stone. The contract also called for a "belfry to correspond with Mr. Mill's of wood and blinds," which shows up on a drawing from around 1835 (fig. 9.3).[35] The story of some of these renovations and courthouse rooms may be forthcoming in a historic structures report recently undertaken by the University of Florida.

In 1936, under the New Deal WPA program, the structure was partially restored and greatly rebuilt for U.S. Postal functions (figs. 18.24, 18.25). As a result, seventy-six years later, today's east gable facade re-creates the colonial appearance that was depicted in the 1764 painting, which includes the elaborate roofed balcony. Melvin Clark Greeley of Jacksonville was the lead architect, and Clyde E. Harris was the head draftsman. A letter from Mr. Greeley indicates that the second-floor coquina walls were removed "probably down to the level of the second story floor joists." Embedded

FIGURE 18.23. Government House remodeled in 1834, St. Augustine. St. Johns County. Robert Mills, architect. Mills in 1833 was the architectural advisor to the secretary of the Treasury in Washington, D.C. He was charged with renovating the former Spanish Governor's House for use as a U.S. courthouse and post office. His design resulted in the demolition of the five-story tower and the two-story wall and grand entrance. He moved and rebuilt some interior and exterior walls, changed the east facade design, and removed its iconic balcony. After the renovation, it no longer looked Spanish. Photocopy courtesy of Florida State Archives.

in the removed coquina walls were wood posts and beams that suggest that sometime in the colonial period the second story was wood. His letter also indicates that something of the colonial east façade coquina wall remains, and that other walls were demolished and rebuilt.[36]

Government House today currently serves multiple public uses, and has a bright future with community events as well as with heritage and cultural

tourism. Plans are under way as directed by the University of Florida for expanding exhibit spaces, classrooms, reception rooms, and outdoor uses of the courtyard. Its historic site at the west end of the plaza, with a view of plaza activities and the harbor where tall ships once anchored, is a basic element of the city's sixteenth-century town plan.[37] The south entrance was created in 1936 with a Renaissance Revival surround that restores a sense of the building's colonial grace and its very long and distinguished cultural role under the Spanish, English, and American governments (fig. 18.25).[38] Its symbolism is like that of the graceful 1927 Bridge of Lions, which has recently been restored to renew the sense of a grand entrance into Florida's centuries-old and oldest city. Government House architecture today is a twenty-first-century story that revolves around the critical issues of its preservation, renovations, uses, maintenance, interpretation, and public/private fund-raising. Perhaps somewhere in its future, a Classical entrance will again welcome people into the courtyard that was once paved with ballast stones from the colonial sailing ships in St. Augustine's harbor.

At Islamorada (Monroe County) on November 14, 1937, a public memorial was dedicated to an extraordinary architectural and engineering feat in Florida and to the builders who died during its construction. This story begins in 1904, when, stringing the Keys together like a pearl necklace, a railway was built (1904–12) to connect Key West to Miami. Following the rail bed, a road was built during 1935–38. They were known as the "Overseas Railroad" and the "Overseas Highway" and were described as the "impossible dream" and the "Eighth Wonder of the World."

Henry Flagler's Florida Overseas Railroad was completed a century ago, in January 1912, costing $27 million. It had overcome setbacks in four hurricanes, suffered the loss of three hundred lives, and went bankrupt

FIGURE 18.24. Government House today, St. Augustine. St. Johns County. In 1936, with WPA financing, architects Melvin Clark Greeley and Clyde E. Harris of Jacksonville re-created the look of the eighteenth-century Spanish east facade in the painting of 1764 (plate 11). They re-created the wood balcony, eliminated Mills's added windows and doors, exposed some of the original coquina for the public to see, and rebuilt the south porch. Photograph 2011 by Kenneth M. Barrett Jr.

in 1932, as did Key West in 1934. It had been built by Cubans, Spaniards, and blacks from the Cayman Islands recruited for the job. Its Seven Mile Bridge spanned 9 miles between Knight Key to Bahia Honda, with a swinging span 253 feet long for shipping, and 210 concrete arches at the last span approaching Bahia Honda. It was a stunning achievement.[39] But the era of the automobile demanded change. Following the tracks laid by Flagler, many war veterans under FERA (Florida's Emergency Relief Administration) arrived and built the Overseas Highway that would bring tourists to Key West and cure its insolvency. A small road already existed between Miami and Lower Matecumbe Key, where cars had to take a four-hour ferry across a 35-mile gap to pick up another road at No Name Key to Key West. Work camps were built, a keystone quarry was opened on Plantation Key, and construction began in 1935. On September 1 and 2, the work camps, the road, and the East Coast Railway from Lower Matecumbe Key northward up to Plantation Key took an unexpected direct hit by a category-5 hurricane. The wreckage was complete; the bodies of 405 veterans and civilians were difficult to find. Work camps were rebuilt by the WPA, and on March 29, 1938, the construction of the highway to Key West was completed and opened to automobiles.[40] It is today's U.S. Highway 1.

Islamorada's WPA memorial is a crypt, dug down to keystone bedrock. It holds the remains of the 405 who were trapped in the Labor Day hurricane of 1935 with no way to get off the Keys. Most of them were World War I down-and-out veterans trying to earn a living on a dollar a day. An Art Deco–style relief of hurricane-blown waves and bent palms is carved on the 18-foot-tall keystone obelisk designed by Harold Lawson.[41] This historic memorial artfully records the extraordinary architectural and engineering achievements, the human efforts, risks and lives lost, financial investments, and the development that followed the road across an ocean.

FIGURE 18.25. South entrance, Government House, St. Augustine. Restoration architects Melvin Clark Greeley and Clyde E. Harris in 1936 created the south portal when they renovated and partially rebuilt Mills's Government House. With imagination, artistic license, and perhaps the Castillo de San Marcos's chapel entrance as one of their models (see plate 10), they reintroduced a sense of the Classical grandness of this residence that had existed when it was the residence of Florida's Spanish and English governors, but was lost with its conversion to an American courthouse and post office in 1834. Photograph 2011 by Kenneth M. Barrett Jr.

In 1979, with the establishment of the Art in State Buildings Program, the Florida Legislature recognized the power that the arts of architecture have on public pride. Earlier, individual cities and counties had established their own Art in Public Places programs. These programs require that a percentage of the original construction cost be appropriated for acquiring exterior or interior permanent artwork that makes public spaces more attractive and user-friendly.

19 ✦ Rescuing the Old State Capitol

> Either a building is part of a place or it is not. Once that kinship is there, time will make it stronger.
>
> WILLA CATHER

FLORIDA'S CAPITOL, the building that was dedicated with statehood, was almost lost forever. Its historical significance to the state and to its capital, Tallahassee, was not served well by a political process that in 1971 recommended demolition. Public opposition saved the building. When architects proved that the structure was sound, safe, and visually important to the state's historical identity and the capital's built environment, the demolition votes changed.[1] The Old Capitol was restored in 1978–82. Its preservation has given the state a giant of an architectural landmark that is sacred to Florida with its spirit and reverence of place. It takes you to Florida's beginnings, its pioneers, flourishing moments in democracy and statehood. Architecturally it recaptures the early Classical temple-front style that was transplanted to Florida with the state's agricultural beginnings. Today it is also a testimony to the voices of citizens that were heard in the 1970s.

The Capitol's architectural story begins shortly after Florida became a U.S. territory in 1821, and Tallahassee was selected as the permanent capital in 1824. The first building that housed the territorial legislative council was a log cabin—like the many first houses, churches, and commercial establishments—constructed in April 1824 by Judge Jonathan Robinson and Sherod McCall. One approached it by dirt "roads" that still had tree stumps in them. Tallahassee was then a "place" halfway between Pensacola and St. Augustine, the only established centers of population at that time (with the exception of the island Key West). The "place" had formerly been known to the sixteenth-century Apalachee as Anhaica, and had been the winter camp of Hernando de Soto in 1539–40. During 1656–1704, it was the Spanish presidio and Franciscan Mission San Luis. Later, it was a Creek town that Andrew Jackson burned in 1818. A new, more impressive building for conducting territorial business was built in 1826—a two-story rectangular brick building with double porches on the front gable facade, designed by Colonel Robert Butler, the first surveyor general of Florida and an aide to General Andrew Jackson.[2]

Territorial Florida's population grew, and Florida's legislative council became bicameral in 1838 and needed more space. A design competition was held, and advertisements calling for "Architects & Mechanics" to submit plans went into the newspapers of New Orleans, Mobile, Milledgeville (Georgia), Tallahassee, and St. Augustine. Cary W. Butt's design was the winner. He proposed a brick rectangular block with a monumental six-column temple-front portico. Butt was from Virginia, and he had been employed during 1836–38 in the Mobile office of the firm of Charles and James Dakin, but little else about him is known. He left the architectural business and died in July 1844. In 1839, the cornerstone was laid. In 1845, the Capitol was completed in time to celebrate Florida's admittance to the Union on March 3, as well as the election of William Moseley, the first elected governor. The first General Assembly was seated in June. Florida's total population was then 54,000, of which 27,900 were white, and 26,100 were black.[3]

The State Capitol's Classical temple-front portico has been called Greek Revival, but it is closer in style to Thomas Jefferson's Palladio-inspired Rome-based architecture than to the ancient Greek buildings. Butt's temple portico was attached to the longitudinal side of a rectangular brick block. Andrea Palladio's drawings of Roman-influenced temple-fronted buildings had been published in his *Four Books of Architecture* (1570), which was published in English in 1715 and used as an architectural guide in the southern states for plantation and public buildings. Before Palladio, Leon Battista Alberti in the fifteenth century had promoted the idea that the principal ornament in all architecture certainly lies in columns. Florida's 1845 Capitol was also a local product. Decisions and alterations were made on-site, and were influenced by the site, costs, available skills and materials, and the craftsman pattern books at hand. One of these might have been *The American Builders Companion* published by Asher Benjamin in many editions between 1773 and 1845, which popularized temple-fronted buildings across the American South.[4]

Plain and honest, the frontier 1845 Capitol is at the core of today's restored building (figs. 19.1, 19.2; plate 18). It is two stories on an elevated basement that serves as a podium (platform), the Roman and Palladian motif that was repeated on a number of Florida's early twentieth-century courthouses (chapter 18). The monumental hexastyle portico of the 1845 Capitol had six smooth-faced columns of the Tuscan or Roman Doric Order (Greek Doric columns are generally fluted) 13 feet in circumference and 34 feet tall. They supported a plain entablature and a pediment, with no reference to Greek frieze motifs—triglyphs and metopes—or the Beaux-Arts Classical cornice ornamentation of today. Cary Butt's design had Ionic capitals, like that of Jefferson's Virginia State Capitol, but Captain Richard A. Shine, who assumed the duties of supervising architect and contractor on November 12, 1839, is thought to have made the change on-site. In 1845, the portico stairs were wood, forming a graceful entry with delicately turned balusters and a handrail that curved outward as the stairs widened. Interior and exterior walls and the columns were "hard burnt brick," the "best salmon brick," supplied by Captain Shine from his brickyard. In the Classical spirit, the columns were plastered and painted white (white lead and linseed oil) to look like stone. The white color greatly emphasized their projection forward (prostyle) from the red-brick block. A cistern supplied water from 1845 to 1891; running water and indoor plumbing were added in 1891.[5]

In 1902, the Capitol was enlarged and enhanced in the current Beaux-Arts Classical taste—styled after the Classical principles taught at the École des Beaux-Arts in Paris, where a number of American architects were recently trained. Two three-story brick wings were added at the north and south ends, and a Renaissance-style dome and drum were added over its central space and interior stairway (fig. 19.2). Frank P. Milburn, the architect, was well known as a major designer of American courthouses (including Columbia County's in Lake City, Florida, shown in plate 39). His additions of the dome, lantern, modillion cornices, and balustrade reflect his training and the current popularity of the Beaux-Arts style. The dome's exterior, 136 feet above the ground, is sheathed in copper and allowed to naturally oxidize to green. Windows in the drum cast light onto an interior drum of colored "art glass," which sends a rainbow of colors into the interior stairway. Milburn added artwork in the triangular pediment tympanum, in pressed metal that depicts the state seal. It is painted white as a reference to stone sculptures in Classical pediments. Milburn stuccoed the entire salmon-red-brick Capitol with a smooth white surface. Also in Beaux-Arts style was the roof balustrade addition. In adding the wings, Milburn "strove not to change the proportions or the classical spirit of the old building." His additions in the Classical Beaux-Arts architectural

FIGURE 19.1. Florida State Capitol, 1845. Tallahassee. Leon County. Cary W. Butt, architect, with changes by Richard A. Shine, brickmaker and contractor. The two-story porticoes (with Roman- or Tuscan-style columns) attached to both the east and west facades were impressive in 1845. Rooted in Classical Greece and Rome, temple-fronts were symbolic of American democracy. They were visible across America on the most important buildings. The Capitol was finished in time to celebrate Florida's admittance to the Union on March 3, 1845, and the election of the first governor, William Moseley, and the first general assembly. Photocopy courtesy of Florida State Archives.

language, however, particularly in the dome, cornice, and white color, greatly enhanced the building's Classical effect and dignity.[6]

With the growth of the state and thus its legislature, additional wings were added by prominent Florida architects: Henry John Klutho (of Jacksonville) in 1923 to add more space to the east and west (with new entrance porticoes); M. Leo Elliot (of Tampa) in 1936 for the expanded House of Representatives

FIGURE 19.2. Frank P. Milburn's original renderings, State Capitol renovation, Tallahassee, 1902. Leon County. With Florida's growth, the Capitol needed to be expanded and improved. Running water and plumbing had been added in 1891, but the legislating body needed more rooms. Milburn was a well-known designer of American courthouses, and he was commissioned to enlarge and enhance Florida's Capitol. He added wings and a dome and ornamentation in the Beaux-Arts Classical style that was popular at the time. As years passed and Florida's growth continued, additional wings were added. During 1978–82, after a new Capitol was built, the Old Capitol was restored to Milburn's 1902 rendering. Herschel Shepard, restoration architect. Photocopy courtesy of Florida State Archives.

at the north end; and Hadley and Atkinson (of St. Petersburg) in 1947 for the Senate at the south end. In 1948, west of the Capitol, rose the new home of the Supreme Court, with a monumental portico of six columns of the Doric Order that echoed the Capitol's focal element. When the Waller Memorial Park was established between the Capitol and the Supreme Court in 1951, the complex took up an entire city block. In 1978, the twenty-two-story New

Capitol was constructed directly behind the Old Capitol (Edward Durell Stone, architect), and Waller Park was recomposed into landscaped terraces and fountains.

Meanwhile, the decision to save the Old Capitol was made. During 1978–82, it was restored to its 1902 appearance under the supervision of restoration architect Herschel E. Shepard. During the restoration, all the wings were removed, with the exception of Milburn's north and south 1902 additions. The 1845 temple-front entrance has been rebuilt with Milburn's 1902 Beaux-Arts cornice and pediment ornamentation. Much of the original fabric was conserved, including the 1902 Milburn dome and drum and along with Klutho's interior double-curved staircase and marble wainscoting. The interior dome of colored art glass was restored—workers found 103 pounds of broken glass pieces in a wall they tore down and pieced them together to find the original design. It was re-created by the Louisville Art Glass Company.[7]

Today's restored Old Capitol is that rare visible monument to the state's legislative growth, and to its nineteenth-century values, political ideals, and architectural aesthetics. It was the statehouse in which all of Florida's political business could be housed under one roof.[8] Since 2002, the restored Old Capitol has housed the Florida Center of Political History and Governance (plate 18).

Part of the Old Capitol story is that of Florida's Supreme Court Building. The first justices had taken their seats in the 1845 structure—their original tables, railings, and bench are restored to their place in the Old Capitol. Today, the buildings of the Supreme Court, Old Capitol, and New Capitol make up the Capitol Complex, the westernmost building of which is the Supreme Court (fig. 19.3). It was completed in 1948, with James Gamble Rogers II, of Winter Park, as the architect. Its temple-front portico mirrors that of the Old Capitol's east and west entrances. The court's walls are cast concrete up to 2 feet thick, their foundations resting on piles driven deeply into the red clay hill. In the walls were internal rain gutters that flowed to cisterns, but they overflowed and collapsed over the years. Originally there were spittoons, Egyptian-style chairs, and a solid aluminum front door. Security was not deemed necessary—an open-door building was considered neighborly.

The official seal of the Supreme Court is embedded in the floor in the entrance rotunda, surrounded by eight marble columns. Its symbolism is powerful: the blindfolded Goddess of Justice has a weighing scale in one hand, a sword in the other, and an eagle looking at her that is emblematic of the

FIGURE 19.3. Florida Supreme Court Building, 1948, Tallahassee. Leon County. James Gamble Rogers II, architect. The first justices took their seats in the 1845 Capitol. A century later, a new Supreme Court Building was completed west of the 1845/1902 Capitol. Its temple-front portico with six Doric columns mirrored that of the Capitol that was visible to the east. When it was built in 1848, the Supreme Court Building had an open-door policy: security at that time was not necessary. It also had internal rain gutters that fed water to a cistern. When a new Capitol rose in 1978 (Edward Durell Stone, architect) directly behind the Old Capitol, today's Capitol Complex was created, comprising the Old Capitol, the New Capitol, and the Supreme Court. Photocopy courtesy of Florida State Archives.

United States. It sends a message that Justice is paramount and impartial. (An antebellum version is said to have had the Goddess of Justice sitting on a bale of cotton.) In 1948, the cost of the building was $1.7 million; today that would not even pay for the eight columns carved from marble quarried in Maryland. When the copper roof leaked in 1988 and problems with asbestos and cork materials were discovered, the building was renovated (1990, Barnett Fronczak, architect). Security was added, a mark of changing times. Another mark of taste and time is the building's color. The courthouse's former all-white color was abandoned. Today's Supreme Court Building is light beige with architectural details highlighted in white, and windows emphasized with a red band.[9]

20 ✤ New Battles Sound

I believe that architecture has its own tasks and that its essence is the act of construction.

Peter Zumthor

Masonry coastal fortifications are no longer constructed in Florida, and those built when Florida's coastline
had to be defended against seaborne enemies have ceased
to be used as forts. Their massive stone and brick walls
loom large on Florida's built landscape with new meaning
and functions relevant to the twenty-first century. Loved
for what they stood for—American sovereignty and independence—they are preserved as they stand today, empty,
partially in ruins, to educate the public about the time when
Florida's 1,200 miles of coastline, shipping lanes, and hundreds of islands and harbors had to be defended against
the French and English, who coveted Florida, and the pirates who preyed on everyone, and about the tragedy of a
Civil War. In the 1880s, some of these U.S. coastal defenses
were upgraded with reinforced concrete and others were
abandoned. After World War II, Florida's coastal forts were
surplused; modern warfare rendered them obsolete. Cannonballs are now permanently stacked, and the sounds of
today's unsheathed swords and musket and cannon fire are
those of reenactors. The once-active parade grounds and
ramparts are in various stages of conservation and open to
the public (fig. 3). Selections of their architectural designs
and labor-intensive achievements described below immortalize those who drafted their plans, fired the bricks, quarried the coquina, constructed the ramparts, dug the moats,

stood the lonely vigils, and shed the blood, tears, and sweat that contributed to the making of the Florida we know today.

Castillo de San Marcos in St. Augustine (St. Johns County) is the premier monument of the nation's Spanish heritage, drawing almost 2 million people a year. It is symbolic of many things of first importance. Built during 1672–95 to defend the town and inlet into St. Augustine's harbor, it is the oldest masonry fort in North America, and the only extant seventeenth-century fort. El Castillo is also a landmark of military Classicism, and it marks the first large-scale use of a material given to Florida by the sea. It is called coquina, a limestone of sand and shells cemented together by calcium carbonate during the Pleistocene Epoch, when the ocean covered Florida. *Shell stones so well cemented as to appear one solid stone,* is how John Bartram described coquina in 1765.[1]

An unknown number of earlier forts had been constructed of wood. They rotted frequently, and their coastal sites were continuously undermined.[2] Their precise locations and architecture are unknown (figs. 11.1a, 20.1; plate 6) Beginning in 1672, large blocks of coquina were cut by Indians and slaves on Anastasia Island and rafted across Matanzas River and laid up with a mortar made by calcining (burning) oyster shells. Coquina walls received enemy cannonballs with a shrug—they did not splinter. Balls got stuck in the semi-soft stone, which was described as giving way like cheese stuck with a knife.[3]

The fort's initial design was staked out in 1672 by Cuban engineer Ignacio Daza. What Daza devised and a number of engineers improved upon is a square with four bastions at the corners (outward-pointing triangles) (figs. 20.2; 20.3; plate 9). This was not a new design, but his adaption of the concept to St. Augustine's location and materials was brilliant. In 1588, Bautista Antonelli and his son, Juan Bautista Antonelli, had planned similar forts for King Philip II of Spain to protect Cuba and seven other Spanish Caribbean

---

FIGURE 20.1. Two sixteenth-century defensive fort plans, St. Augustine. St. Johns County. Before the stone Castillo was begun in 1672, Spanish forts were erected with wood. They were close to the river's edge, where their cannon could reach enemy ships entering the inlet. Due to rot and storm surges, wood forts had to be continuously improved and rebuilt. The precise locations, architecture, and numbers of wood forts that preceded today's stone Castillo are unknown. These drawings represent but two of the forts mentioned in ancient documents. Photocopy courtesy of Florida State Archives.

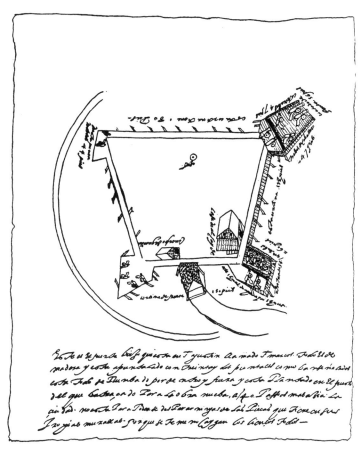

Esto se puede besso quieste en Jagustin Armado Imacus. toda Ede
madera y esta apuntalado con trinray de puntall como la refiniado
esta toda de Tumba de porque entre y fuea y esta Plantado en El puest
del que batea, en do Jora La obra nueba, a/q. o Pesso mabestia La
ciudad. no esta Jora Idaes de Puerem iya de Sab Piend que Jorem su pues
I no yeias murallas. porque se teme Cogan los licutos Todos —

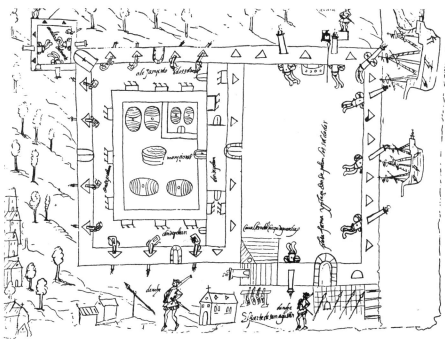

FIGURE 20.2. Aerial view, Castillo de San Marcos, St. Augustine, 2001. St. Johns County. Ignacio Daza, architect of the initial layout in 1672. Daza's plan is a square with four diamond-shaped bastions at the corners. His seventeenth-century plan was an adaptation of similar earlier layouts in the Spanish Caribbean region and Larache, Morocco, based on the designs for Spanish defenses by Juan Bautista Antonelli beginning in 1588. Photograph 2001 courtesy of Janet Goodrich.

ports, and one in Larache, Morocco. It is said that Antonelli visited St. Augustine in 1589 and gave advice on building a strong fort.[4] Did his advice lead to Governor Domingo Martínez de Avendaño's plan for a stone fort in 1594 (which was not funded)?[5]

Many talented Spanish engineers supervised El Castillo's construction, which proceeded with a multiethnic workforce of masons, lime-burners, quarry men, and carpenters. John Collins, an Englishman captured in 1670, became Juan Calens, the *Master of extracting stone and making lime at the quarry of His Majesty which is used for the construction of the Royal Fortress of this presidio*. In 1695, its first construction phase was completed, in time for the 1702 British siege. By 1740, the tall watchtower was completed and the walls were heightened in time to endure another major British assault, this time led by General Oglethorpe of Georgia. In 1755–63, engineers Pedro de Brozas y Garay and Pablo Castelló completed the vaults, the glacis, parapet, and new ravelin; they added Doric pilasters, and smoothed on the white plaster to protect the coquina walls (fig. 20.3; plate 9). With the turrets and the cordon stuccoed red, and the walls white, the fort was the color of the Spanish flag and the symbol of Spanish dominion. El Castillo was never breached, and never defeated.

During British ownership of Florida, 1763–83, the fort was called "St. Marks." When the Spanish returned in 1784, engineer Mariano de la Rocque rebuilt and embellished upon its chapel's Classical-style entrance (plate 10).[6] In 1821, Florida became a U.S. territory, and the Spanish-built castle became an American fort. It was renamed Fort Marion. The new name honored Francis Marion, the South Carolina guerrilla and hero of the American Revolution whom the British called the "Swamp Fox." In 1924, Fort Marion was designated a National Monument, on the same day that the Statue of Liberty was so designated.

One of the ironies in the story of Fort Marion is that although Indian labor had constructed this fort, Indians became its prisoners in the nineteenth century. Osceola, leader of Florida's Seminoles, was the first to be imprisoned in Fort Marion. He had been captured under a flag of truce in 1837. In the 1870s, the Kiowa, Comanche, Cheyenne, and Arapaho were removed from their western homelands and imprisoned in the fort. In the 1880s, the Apache became its prisoners. In 1933, the War Department transferred the fort to the National Park Service. In 1942, Congress restored its Spanish name.[7]

Fort Matanzas was also designated a National Monument in 1924. It is a small coquina fort that was built to guard the Matanzas River inlet south of St. Augustine and prevent a surprise back-door attack on the city. General Oglethorpe's attack on St. Augustine in 1740 prompted engineer Pedro Ruiz de Olano to design and complete the fort in 1742 on the east shore of Rattlesnake Island with a clear view of the ocean inlet. Olano sank wood pilings in the sand and marshy subsoil to create a stable foundation. However, by 1821 it was badly cracked. It was rescued in 1916, restored, and declared a National Monument (fig. 20.4). In the 1930s, a WPA-financed dock and visitors' center were added.[8]

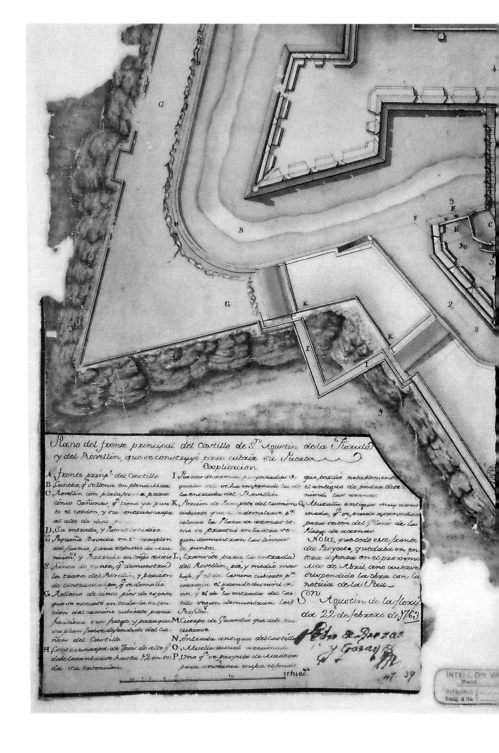

Plano del frente principal del Castillo de Sⁿ Agustín de la Florida
y del Revellin, que se construyó para cubrir su Puerta
Explicacion

A. frente prinpⁱ del Castillo
B. Cuneta, ̃ rellena en planillia
C. Revellin con plataforma para
cinco Cañones, ̃ tiene ya pues-
to el cordon, y su mamposteria
al alto de dⁱa

D. Su entrada, y Retiro de radas.
E. Pequeña Bovedα en el exemplen
del plano, para reparo de mu-
nicion, y Retirada en tⁿ noticia

F. linea de puntos, ̃ demuestran
lα trαzα del Revellin, y porcion
de contraescarpa, ̃ se demolió

G. Relleno de cinco pies de espesor
que se exercis en toda la extencion del camino cubierto para
facilitar su fuego, y para que
se pueda ser defendido del ca-
ñon del Castillo.

H. Contraescarpa de 7 pies de alto ̃
desde se arruine hasta 7 2 en toda la extencion.

I. Plazas de armas proyectadas α
quales solo se ha empezado la de
la entrada del Revellin.

K. Porcion de Parapeto del camino
cubierto que se demoleve, o se
coloca la Plaza de armas como se practis en la otra segun demuestran las lineas
de puntos.

L. transito para la entrada
del Revellin, oⁿ, y medio mas
baxo, ̃ el de Camino cubierto por
consegir el grande desnivel que
ese, y el de la entrada del Castillo segun demuestran los
Perfiles.

M. Cuerpo de Guardia que debe se
 executar.

N. Entrada antigua del Castillo

O. Muelle actual arruinado

P. Uno ̃ se proyecto de madera
para conducir mejor el fondo

que podiα notablemente
el antiguo de piedra dete-
niendo las aguas.

Q. Muralla antigua muy arru-
inada, ̃ se puede aprovechar
para razon del Placis de la
Plaza de armas.

NOTA, que todo este frente
del Proyecto, quedaba en es-
taca disposa en el proximo
mes de Abril, sino que se
suspendio la obra con la
noticia de la Paz—

Sⁿ Agustín de la florida
da 22 de febrero de 1763.

Pedro de Brozas
y Garay

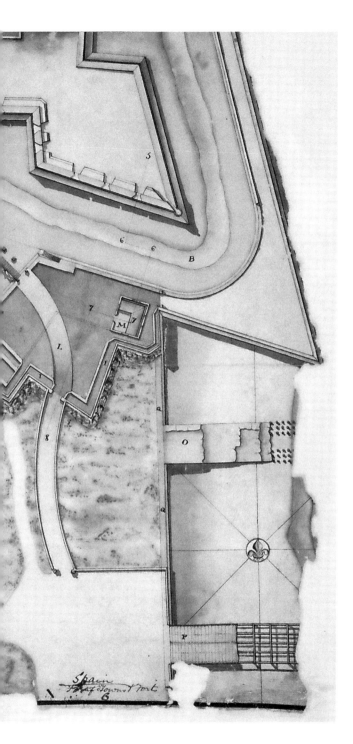

FIGURE 20.3. *Plano del frente principal del Castillo de San Agustín de la Florida,* February 22, 1763, signed by Engineer Pedro de Brozas y Garay, who had come from Ceuta (Spanish Morocco) in 1752 to complete the enormous stone fort begun a century earlier. His plans called for rebuilding the ravelin, the outer defense that would shield and protect the entrance gate and south side of the fort. Courtesy of Public Records Office, PRO: WO78/1017.

FIGURE 20.4. Fort Matanzas, 1742, St. Augustine. St. Johns County. Engineer Pedro Ruiz de Olano, architect. In 1742, following General Oglethorpe's 1740 attack on St. Augustine, a small coquina fort was built to defend the Matanzas Inlet to the south, and the river that was the back door to the Spanish capital. It was built on the east shore of Rattlesnake Island; wood pilings had to be sunk in the soft subsoil. Even so, it was badly cracked by the 1820s. It was restored in 1916, and declared a National Monument in 1924. Boat service today provides public tours to the fort. Photograph 2000 by Kenneth M. Barrett Jr.

With the growth of tourism after the Civil War, the Castillo de San Marcos has become a popular tourist destination drawing millions of visitors. Golf was once played on its glacis; its image appeared in Audubon and Tiffany paintings; and today the cannon sound off with a chilling, time-stopping sound heard throughout St. Augustine. But its 316-year-old walls and Neoclassical details are no longer plastered white, and its turrets are no longer red, and the soft shell stone is no longer protected from the weather and moisture. The fort has been in American hands for 190 years, longer than in British or Spanish hands combined. The cracks in the walls are a twenty-first-century issue, but it is thought the tourists love the antique look. Herein lies the fort's architectural story for today: how to sustain the fort's historic fabric, and how the fort will sustain the city's heritage tourism.

Experts in the field remind us that when coquina begins to fail, "the only reasonable treatment is to replace it." But "suitable replacement coquina" is difficult to find. Covering the walls with the Spanish stucco formula may not be feasible—it would necessitate whitewashing frequently at a large cost; and today's more permanent chemical coverings might have far worse consequences for the future.[9] El Castillo is an exceptional Spanish architectural landmark; in today's built landscape, it is also a monument to architectural preservation, and to future conservation issues.

Describing his childhood in St. Augustine, historian Michael Gannon writes: "I have vivid memories of climbing about the castle's cannon and letting my imagination soar as I pictured its major battles. When I rowed my boat past the old fortress to cast a net for mullet or shrimp, I envisioned gunners, musketeers, and pikemen in its embrasures, ready to fight me off if I ventured to be as foolish as the British siege forces who attempted in vain to crack those stout defenses."[10] Will tomorrow's children, and their children, be able to dream on those "stout defenses" of defending its ramparts against make-believe pirates and enemies?

In Pensacola, Escambia County, there is a Spanish-period water-battery and two U.S. forts built on Spanish beginnings. They were designed to protect Pensacola's deepwater harbor. Batería de San Antonio, Fort San Carlos de Barrancas, and Fort Pickens convey how some unusual defensive needs of their times were met with large architectural solutions at challenging waterfront locations.

Batería de San Antonio and the American Fort Barrancas occupy a site near today's Pensacola Naval Air Station. They descended from the earlier short-lived Fort San Carlos de Austria, which was erected in 1698 by the Spanish to defend the harbor they called Bahía Santa María de Galve. Fort San Carlos stood on the bluff, the Barranca de Santo Tome, and was designed by the military engineer Jaime Franck of Austria. His materials were the nearby pine, cypress, clay, and moss. It was destroyed by the French in 1719, and the Spanish moved their fortifications to Santa Rosa Island at the entrance to the bay, naming the new presidio Santa Rosa Punta de Sigüenza (fig. 10.4). It, too, was destroyed, this time by a hurricane in 1752. Santa Rosa became the site of the American Fort Pickens built during 1829–34.[11]

The Spanish left Florida in 1763 and returned in 1783 and built a new Fort San Carlos on the Barranca, and in 1796 they built the brick *medialuna* (Batería de San Antonio) below the fort at the water level (fig. 20.5). It is a large half-moon-shaped structure with a dry moat. Fort San Carlos above it was

FIGURE 20.5. Batería de San Antonio, Pensacola, 1796. Escambia County. To defend Pensacola's deep harbor, the Spanish built a brick *medialuna*, a half-moon battery at the water level below the Spanish Fort San Carlos on the bluff behind. The Spanish Fort San Carlos was destroyed by the British during the War of 1812, and the Americans built their own Fort San Carlos in 1839–44 and added a long segmental-arched brick tunnel to connect it to the water-level battery. Photocopy courtesy of Florida State Archives.

destroyed by the British during the War of 1812. On its ruins directly behind the water battery, Americans built Fort San Carlos de Barrancas (1839–44, Joseph Totten, architect-engineer). A long, segmental-arched brick tunnel connects it to the water battery. The plan was to defend the Pensacola harbor with a cross fire from Santa Rosa Island, where Fort Pickens had recently been erected—a strategy that echoed the military tactics of the Spanish a century earlier. Fort Barrancas and Batería de San Antonio present an opportunity to see exceptionally fine brickwork with long, thin, locally handmade Roman-style bricks and mortar; the complex was designated a National Historic Landmark in 1960.[12]

Fort Pickens's mammoth pentagonal walls rose in 1829–34 in the sand dunes of Santa Rosa Island across Pensacola's harbor. The vulnerable site prompted brick walls 12 feet thick and 40 feet high. Its 21.5 million bricks were locally made on the mainland and barged to the island, and twenty-six thousand casks of lime were shipped to the island from Maine. Little known is the fact that the federal workforce was comprised of slaves—skilled slaves who were supplied by Strong and Underhill Company of New Orleans, and unskilled slaves who were hired locally. Their brickwork offers an exceptional example of superb craftsmanship. In October–November 1861, Union forces at Fort Pickens and Confederate forces holding the mainland exchanged fire. Fort Pickens prevented the Confederates from using Pensacola's port, and they abandoned Pensacola in May 1862. In 1886–88, a small band of Chiricahua Apache and their chief, Geronimo, were imprisoned at Fort Pickens. Today, the fort (in Santa Rosa County) is open to the public, and is administered by the National Park System as part of the Gulf Island National Seashore.[13]

Fort Jefferson (Monroe County) is the largest coastal brick fort in the Western Hemisphere. One year after Florida's statehood (1845), the U.S. Corps of Engineers began the fort to control navigation through the Florida Straits and protect the growing Mississippi River commerce that sailed the Gulf of Mexico to the Atlantic Ocean. Even with today's technology, its undertaking is hard to imagine. Its massive hulk is anchored to an isolated coral reef named Garden Key, an island 70 miles west from the closest "mainland"— another island, Key West (plate 19). Garden Key is one of seven coral reefs originally named by the Spanish "Las Tortugas" after the sea turtles, but they were renamed Dry Tortugas to warn sailors that they held no freshwater.[14] Slaves and, later, Union deserters constructed the fort. An inventory of the architectural materials and construction features is staggering: walls 8 feet thick and 50 feet high, millions of bricks, foundations 14 feet wide, three tiers of guns, and six bastions at the angles of a six-sided plan intended to menace the enemy with 450 cannon. Fort Jefferson had barracks for 1,500 officers and soldiers, a parade ground, munition magazines, 109 cisterns, and a cast-iron lighthouse (fig. 20.6). A seawall acts like a natural reef to protect the fort from storms. It was designed to also protect it from enemy boats that a century ago might have sailed up under the guns and landed troops to scale the wall. A moat lies between the seawall (the counterscarp) and the brick fort walls (the scarp). Sharks once prowled the moat.

Before the fort and its current lighthouse were built, there was a 65-foot-tall brick (whitewashed) lighthouse and keeper's cottage (frame construction) on Garden Key that was first lighted in 1826. Within a year, the first keeper and his wife, John and Rebecca Flaherty, became depressed by life on the remote tropical key, the mosquitoes, heat, sand, gales, and lack of supplies. Seven more keepers would follow before the fort was built. Those same conditions would plague the soldiers, officers, prisoners, and slaves who built the fort. The shorter cast-iron harbor light that stands on the fort ramparts today replaced the Garden Key Lighthouse in 1877.[15]

Federal troops occupied and continued working on the fort through the Civil War and into 1873, but its tactical mission was by then obsolete. Some eight hundred to nine hundred captured deserters remained imprisoned there for ten years after the Civil War, prevented from escaping by miles of shark-infested waters. Dr. Samuel Mudd was the fort's most famous prisoner, imprisoned in 1865 after being wrongly convicted of complicity in the assassination of President Lincoln because he set the broken leg of the assassin, Johns Wilkes Booth. His life sentence was commuted in 1869 for his work during the 1867 yellow-fever epidemic that killed the fort nurses and doctor, and sickened most of the garrison. Fort Jefferson was designated a National Monument in 1935. To protect the fort and the surrounding coral reefs, and to provide a sanctuary for marine life, the Dry Tortugas National Park was created in 1992. Remote, accessible only by boat or seaplane, Fort Jefferson's magnificent and symbolic presence is a monument to Florida's and the nation's maritime greatness, and to a time when the fort was the largest link in the chain of U.S. seacoast fortifications from Maine to Texas.

Fort Clinch on Amelia Island (Nassau County), Florida's northernmost barrier island, was begun in 1847, two years after Florida attained statehood. It was constructed to protect coastal shipping, as well as the mouth of St. Marys River and the port of Fernandina. General Joseph Totten was the designing engineer; Major William Chase the supervisor. It was named after General Duncan Lamont Clinch of the Second Seminole War. After 4.5 million gray and brown bricks were laid in place (fired in Savannah, Georgia), it was still not completed, and it remained unfinished when occupied by the Confederates at the start of the Civil War. In 1862, Robert E. Lee ordered Fernandina and Fort Clinch evacuated. Union troops moved in and continued working on the construction—they brought red and orange bricks from the North. Fort Clinch was garrisoned for the last time in 1898 at the outbreak of the Spanish-American War.[16]

FIGURE 20.6. Fort Jefferson, Garden Key, Dry Tortugas, begun 1846. Monroe
County. U.S. Corps of Engineers, architects. Anchored to an isolated coral reef,
70 miles west of the nearest mainland, Fort Jefferson rose on foundations 14 feet
wide, with millions of bricks in walls 8 feet thick and 50 feet high. The six-sided
plan had 450 cannon, quarters for 1,500 men, a cast-iron lighthouse, and probably
never enough cisterns. Dr. Samuel Mudd was a prisoner here until his life sentence
was commuted in 1869 for his work during a yellow-fever epidemic. Photocopy
courtesy of Florida State Archives.

In 1964, Fort Clinch was stabilized and partially restored. Supervising architect Herschel E. Shepard describes the architecture as an irregular pentagon formed by scarp walls connecting five bastions. It has an immense sand glacis that shielded the scarp walls from cannon shot and provided a clear field of fire from the musket loopholes in the walls and parapet. Sand was also the material of the ramparts. Inside the walls is the space once called the "parade," where one finds the remains of the guardhouse, prison, latrines, lumber sheds, blacksmith shop, bakery, kitchen, and the two-story storehouse, soldiers' barracks, and the three-story officers' quarters. Water for drinking was collected in cisterns. This was a fort designed to be self-sufficient under siege. Brick was chosen for its resistance to shot and adaptability to the vaulted ceilings. Slate was chosen for the roofs and floors; and granite for the lintel and windowsills and exterior stairs. Two innovations were introduced: an unusual cast-cement lintel, and cast-iron Corinthian columns to support a second-story porch (fig. 20.7).[17]

One newspaper reporter recently described today's fort as "a small boy's dream of the perfect playground . . . long dark tunnels slice through ramparts, leading to dank, brick bastions that are climbed via narrow winding staircases. At the top, a breathtaking view of sea and sky and—best of all—rows of massive cannons bristling in the sun."[18]

It is difficult to see complicated defensive coastal architecture for what it was in the time of real life-and-death dangers, or to describe its building technologies as exciting to a generation long removed from thoughts of coastal invasions and more in tune with today's high-tech military. The behemoth constructions described above, however, might impart a sense of the immense

FIGURE 20.7. Fort Clinch, Amelia Island, 1847. Nassau County. U.S. Corps of Engineers, under General Joseph Totten, architects. Named for General Duncan Lamont Clinch of the Second Seminole War, this sand and brick fort was still unfinished at the start of the Civil War. It was occupied first by Confederate troops, and in 1862 by Union troops. The west porch of the soldiers' barracks is unique for its restored wooden gutter and roof trusses above the cast-iron beam and columns on the second floor. The window and door lintels and the brick pier capitals are solid granite. Visible in the distance are the officers' kitchens. Photograph by Wade Swicord, courtesy of Herschel Shepard, restoration architect.

amount of hard labor that was needed to layer up the walls to protect Florida from seaborne enemies. Many other coastal and river fortifications are equally important in the grand scheme of defending Florida in different places and times: Key West's Fort Zachary Taylor and its battery, East Martello Tower (Monroe County, 1845–66); and Fort San Marcos de Apalachee (Wakulla County) at the confluence of the Wakulla and St. Marks Rivers (begun 1660), occupied by Andrew Jackson and later by the Confederates. Two forts were built to protect Tampa Bay in 1898 during the Spanish-American War: Fort De Soto and Fort Dade on Egmont Key (Pinellas County). Although deactivated in 1923, Fort Dade served as a German U-boat lookout during World War II.

"Open to the public" brings a new set of architectural challenges to all these forts: maintenance, administration, preservation technologies, educational programs, the curating of museum-quality items, funding, and staying relevant with new generations. Ultimately, the forts' conservation demonstrates to the visiting public that Florida had enemies and pirates, was coveted by European powers, that war came to Florida's shores, and that coastal defenses had large roles in protecting and shaping Florida's history.

CONCLUSION

Landmarks Take Us There

One's destination is never a place but a new way of looking at things.

Henry Miller

Architecture does not just happen. It is not created haphazardly or in isolation. "Firsts" are rarely first; something always came before. We occupy buildings every day, but rarely think about how they arrived on the landscape, who drafted their designs, or what they say about our communities and about us, and about the state of Florida. *Heart and Soul of Florida* explores the built landscape to find sacred sites and historic buildings that enable us to remember Florida's past, to see Florida's cultural history in context with that of the United States, and to think about the future image of the state expressed in the built landscape. As this volume comes to a close, a few general observations seem germane.

Following a trail of discovery from 6000 B.C. to 1950 may seem excessive, but a long panoramic look offers many advantages. It enables a continuous view of landscape changes, connecting threads, and preservation achievements. An overview is the collective memory of Florida's architectural history and cultural image.

Florida's built landscape changes with generations of architectural decisions. "Nothing is permanent but change," pronounced Heraclitus, a Greek philosopher. Heraclitus understood the nature and benefits of change, but he also warned that we cannot step twice into the same river, for new waters are always flowing into it. Change therefore affords one way to look at the architectural record and the ebbs and flows of changing tastes and cultural ways affected by national architectural trends, historical events, arrivals of people with different cultural backgrounds, inventive technologies, community economies, and new styles of artistic expressions. An overview affords a sense of connections and continuities and of aesthetic diversity—provided, that is, that significant architectural landmarks are preserved as the yardsticks.

Architectural preservation, therefore, is not a luxury. Historic sites and buildings are Florida's very real three-dimensional landmarks that take us beyond the written page and latest social media screen. They are essential to the seamless Florida biography, and to conveying its story to future and younger generations with visceral impact. The preserved historic built landscape is a reservoir of perspectives and relationships. When authors write that Philadelphia is the first planned city in the United States, or that Coral Gables is the first planned community in Florida, it means they have not looked far enough into the past to see the comprehensive sixteenth-century Spanish town plan of St. Augustine, first in the nation, and first with humanistic and environmental principles. When historians north of Florida write that America began in Virginia or Plymouth, it means that Florida has not successfully promoted its own truths.

Heart and Soul of Florida is meant to show it takes centuries of diverse cultural landmarks to make a vibrant meaningful story of Florida. Those that are sacred to Florida are acquiring new roles in sustaining the heritage tourism that is now a large part of Florida's economic future. They are history in the making, with restorative makeovers and new uses. Florida has sixty-seven counties in which some historic churches, courthouses, and other public buildings have fallen under the wrecking ball, a decision later regretted. Other counties have preserved and converted their community landmarks into theaters, offices, and museums of history and art, loaded with county pride and smaller carbon footprints. "Old is the new green," and of late, the preservation of Florida's flourishing moments has brought billions of dollars to Florida's economy.[1]

Respect for Florida's Spanish architectural heritage was revived in the 1880s by Henry Flagler and his architects, Carrère and Hastings, in St. Augustine. Several decades later, South Florida developers and their architects similarly created architectural allusions to Spain and other Mediterranean countries. In this, Florida's architecture was influenced by European travels, a national trend in academic eclecticism, and a growing tourism industry. With

the arrival of thousands of Cubans beginning in the 1960s and recent immigrants from Spanish-speaking countries, it remains to be seen if the 500th anniversary of the arrival of Ponce de León and the 450th anniversary celebration of St. Augustine's founding will make better known Florida's Spanish
heritage and architectural roots.

Symbolism is a human universal with stunning connective threads. Architectural symbolism is found in the historic landmarks of the Indian, Spanish,
and American cultural periods in Florida. An architectural overview enables
us to see that it is no coincidence that circles, shells, the colors red and white,
birds, cardinal directions, domes, Classical columns, geometric proportions,
and numerology exist in Florida's sacred sites and historic architecture. Architectural symbolism is a language that enhances or transforms a building's
meaning. *Heart and Soul of Florida* makes the point that if we are not aware
of symbolism in Florida's built environment we lose sight of the human continuum in Florida.

Last is an observation about image. We live in an age defined by image.
Name recognition is essential to image. Yet the names of those who drafted
and built Florida's historic sites and buildings are little known to the public. Unlike an artist's canvas, architectural creations are not signed. Today,
the names of architects, past and present, or words of their building philoso-
phies, cultural backgrounds, and artistic training are rarely found in public
print, in those newspaper articles, guidebooks, local and state histories, and
tourist brochures meant to brand Florida as a cultural destination. Some
of America's best-known designers created Florida's historic religious and
public spaces. Among those presented in *Heart and Soul of Florida* are: Robert Mills, Richard Upjohn, Charles C. Haight, Richard Morris Hunt, John
Mervin Carrère, Thomas Hastings, Bernard Maybeck, James Renwick, Ralph
Adams Cram, Frank Pierce Milburn, J. A. Woods, the firm of Frohman, Robb
and Little, James Knox Taylor, William A. Edwards, the firm of Schultze and
Weaver, Addison Mizner, Milton B. Medary, Frederick Law Olmsted Jr., and
Frank Lloyd Wright. Victor A. Lundy, Edward Durell Stone, I. M. Pei, Arata
Isosaki, Duany Plater-Zyberk and Company, and Cannon Design are among
the many more that have expanded upon some of the historic landmarks
herein or reconfigured their historical styles into new expressions. Many
more would be added to this list if commercial, domestic, and industrial examples were included, as well as public and private schools and colleges, and
not-for-profit cultural institutions. In addition, many are the esteemed architects with statewide reputations who have received awards in recognition of
outstanding designs and preservation activities.[2] Florida's cultural richness in

the built landscape would be better known if the arts of architecture, like an artist's canvas, bore signatures and dates.

If we respect what is sacred to Florida in the architectural landscape, future generations might value what we hold sacred, and know who we are and what is special about Florida.

Appendix 1

Why the National Register of Historic Places?
Why National Historic Landmarks?

To answer the questions, "Why the National Register?" and "Why National Historic Landmarks?," Roy Hunt writes the explanation below. He is a former member of the National Trust for Historic Preservation's Board of Advisors and the National Historic Landmarks Committee (2002–8). Hunt, Distinguished Service Professor of Law Emeritus, University of Florida, also served on the Historic St. Augustine Preservation Board, and was president of the Florida Trust for Historic Preservation.

America's historic places are officially recognized by listing in the National Register of Historic Places. Their significance may occur at the national, state, or local levels. A few historic places have meaning for all Americans, and these places may be designated as National Historic Landmarks. A National Historic Landmark designation requires a demonstration that the place possesses exceptional value or quality in illustrating or interpreting the heritage of the United States in history, architecture, archaeology, engineering, and culture, and a high degree of integrity of location, design, setting, materials, and workmanship.

Neither the listing in the National Register or the National Historic Landmark designation prevents the property owners from managing the property as they choose. Often, however, federal and state laws (as in Florida) and local ordinances afford protection if the property is threatened by federal or state projects involving federal or state licensing, permitting, or funding.

Numerous economic studies have demonstrated the economic benefits of historic preservation. These benefits often take the form of tax incentives and may be provided by both federal and state law. In addition, National Historic Landmark status is required for Save America's Treasures grants, and it is a prerequisite for World Heritage Listing. Although listing is honorific in and of itself, state laws and local ordinances may impact what the property owners may do with the listed property.

[National Historic Landmarks were established by the Historic Sites Act of 1933; the National Register was established by the National Historic Preservation Act of 1966. The National Historic Landmark program is administered by the National Park Service, on behalf of the U.S. Secretary, Department of the Interior.]

Appendix 2

Introduction to the Florida Master Site File, the Florida CARL Program, and HABS/HAER/HALS Programs

The introductions below were put together with the help of Janet Snyder Matthews, Historic Preservation Scholar in Residence, University of Florida; Antoinette J. Lee, Historical Documentation Programs, National Park Service; Vincent Birdsong, administrator, Florida Master Site File, Tallahassee; and Marion Almy, archaeologist, Archaeological Consultants, Inc.

The Florida Master Site File

Florida Preservation News, the newsletter of the Florida Trust for Historic Preservation and the Bureau of Historic Preservation, describes the Florida Master Site File as the "first stop for information for anyone conducting activities in Florida that involve historic preservation" (8, no. 2 [March–April 1992]). The Master Site File is the State of Florida's official inventory of historical cultural resources—a paper file and computer database of all known archaeological and historical sites in Florida, including buildings, cemeteries, bridges, and historic districts. It also maintains copies of archaeological and historical survey reports and other manuscripts relevant to history and historical preservation. The sites described vary widely in significance, from sites that have been destroyed to sites registered as National Historic Landmarks, the nation's most prestigious historical designation. The Master Site File as of 2012 holds information on more than 180,000 cultural resources and copies of more than 17,000 manuscripts. What is recorded in the Master Site File represents an accumulation of information from a variety of sources collected. The Master Site File is maintained by the Florida Division of Historical Resources in Tallahassee, and the Master Site File staff are available to assist citizens, government agencies, and historic preservation professionals in performing searches and obtaining information from the inventory. For more information, see the Master Site File website: www.flheritage.com/preservation/sitefile/questions.cfm.

The Conservation and Recreation Lands Program (CARL)

Florida's CARL program is the largest conservation lands acquisition program in the nation. It was established in 1979 to acquire lands with natural and cultural resources that in the public interest should be protected and preserved. CARL has had a number of funding sources, from documentary stamp taxes to bond issues under the 1990 Florida Preservation 2000 Act (p–2000, 1991–2000), and the 1999 Florida Forever Act. Florida's CARL program was instrumental in purchasing and or protecting the following significant archaeological and historical landmarks presented in this book: the seventeenth-century Spanish Mission San Luis in Tallahassee, now reconstructed and designated a National Historic Landmark (chapters 6 and 10); the Key West Custom House (chapter 18); and the Miami Circle (chapter 6). Today, many sites are eligible, but only continued funding of the CARL program will assure the protection of Florida's irreplaceable extraordinary natural and historic sites and cultural heritage.

The Historic American Buildings Survey (HABS)

HABS is a Heritage Documentation Program administered by the National Park Service (NPS). It was a Depression-era program established in 1933 to document America's architectural heritage. The nation's first federal preservation program, it is national in scope. It began with a tripartite agreement between the American Institute of Architects (AIA), the U.S. Library of Congress, and the NPS. Since 1933, thousands of architects, draftsmen, writers, photographers, and students have created a comprehensive documentary record of the American builder's art. The buildings documented range from vernacular and regional designs to the monumental designs of professional architects. The HABS collection of photographs, measured drawings, and written historical information is permanently archived and protected at the Library of Congress, where it is readily accessible to the public. It is arranged in geographical order by state, county, city, or area. The measured drawings record architectural details and dimensions that would otherwise not be known in the event the historical building was damaged or destroyed. HABS documents are essential to preservationists, renovators, and restorers of historic buildings (fig. 14.5).

Recognizing the same need to document America's engineering and industrial heritage, the HAER (Historic American Engineering Record) program was formed in 1969 and, like HABS, is administered by the NPS. Also like HABS, the HAER documentation consists of measured and interpretive drawings, large-format photographs, and written histories of the historic sites, but with a focus on structure and processes, and the evolution of engineering practices. In 1973, a HAER-sponsored inventory of engineering and industrial sites in Florida listed two hundred, including forts, lighthouses, bridges, railroad stations, and local industrial buildings.

In 2000, heritage documentation was expanded from buildings and engineering sites to include landscapes in another national program, the Historic American Landscapes Survey (HALS). It is administered with HABS/HAER by the National Park Service. Its purpose is to systematically document historic American landscapes.

In Florida by 2012, some 669 sites have been documented by the HABS/HAER/HALS programs. Their collections are among the most-used online collections on the Library of Congress website. When HABS was established in 1933, Florida's population was 1.6 million. In 1960, the population was 4.9 million, and Florida was ranked by the U.S. Bureau of the Census as the fastest-growing state—since the 1920s, its growth rate was double that of the nation. By 1990, the population was 13 million; in 2012, it is slightly more than 19 million. In the context of this growth, the importance of funding and maintaining Florida's Master Site File and CARL Program, and the documenting programs of HABS, HAER, and HALS is self-evident.

Acknowledgments

There are many people to thank for making this book better.

Roy Hunt, whose tireless efforts as a founder and promoter of Florida's historic preservation and sense of place, inspired this book and continued to be its guiding light;

Meredith Babb, the director of the University Press of Florida and my sponsoring editor, who with patience encouraged this project and brought it to a conclusion; and

Charles Tingley, at the St. Augustine Historical Society research library, for generously sharing his prodigious knowledge of St. Augustine's history, his photographs, and his indefatigable interest in the architecture of historic Episcopal churches in Florida.

I cannot thank enough those readers of some early drafts of chapters who helped me develop and redirect the manuscript themes through the many versions that followed: Jerald T. Milanich, Ryan Wheeler, Bonnie G. McEwan, Jeffrey Mitchem, Janet Snyder Matthews, Roy Hunt, Charles Tingley, Michael Gannon, Herschel Shepard, Kathleen Deagan, Blair Reeves, and J. Michael Francis.

Much gratitude is owed the many authors, architects, historians, archaeologists, preservationists, and librarians whose research, unpublished and published works, lectures, and local and state activism have educated me and enabled me to see my way through an overview of architectural landmarks in context with Florida history, only some of whom could be cited in the notes and bibliography. I particularly want to thank Eugene Lyon, whose research and translations of documents have taught us to look again at the state's Spanish heritage that is "richer than we thought," and who encouraged the chapter about St. Augustine's town plan; Susan Parker for generously sharing her research drafts and translations of Spanish documents; Sherry Johnson for giving me copies of her work in Cuba and about Eligio de la Puente; Roy

E. Graham for his discoveries about early architectural plans of Caribbean defenses; Carl Halbirt, who is always ready to climb out of an archaeological trench and discuss his discoveries and "what ifs"; Blair Reeves for his guidance and never-ending support; Elizabeth Gessner for her research help and trips to Madrid; Nick McAuliffe and Janet Jordan and other members of the SAAA Board who kept me informed; the scholars of the Historic St. Augustine Research Institute, who are always exceptionally inspiring; the many friends and associates who recommended buildings to see and sent me articles and books that I treasure; Janine Farver for the copy of *Forum* (Fall 2000) with the article "Sacred Places."

To Kathleen Deagan, Bonnie McEwan, and William Marquardt, I am particularly grateful for interviews and tours of their archaeological projects in St. Augustine, at Mission San Luis, and at the Randell Research Center.

One hundred and seventy illustrations create a book within this book. To the illustrators, photographers, and curators of photographic collections, thank you for your contributions to this volume and making it visually appealing and informative. I am indebted to Susanne Hunt, who scanned the splendid photographs from *Florida Heritage* and *Florida History and the Arts,* the two award-winning publications of the Division of Historical Resources, and Division of Cultural Affairs, Florida Department of State, that should never have ceased to be published; to Roger Blackburn, whose many photographs steered the manuscript southward; to Ken Barrett, whose creative eye overcame rain and clouds where sunshine had been predicted, and who printed black-and-white images the old-fashioned way in the darkroom without manipulation to illustrate the real Florida; to Jeanie Fitzpatrick, who meticulously researched her paintings and whose artistic eye is sensitive to the natural beauty of Florida; to Adam Watson, photographic archivist at Florida State Archives, who dispatched my large order for photographs perfectly.

To Herschel Shepard, whose knowledge and creative work as a preservation architect has saved many of Florida's most important landmarks, only a few of which could be included in this book, thank you for generously sharing ideas in general about architectural arts, technologies, and preservation.

To Marthe Walters and Louise OFarrell at the University Press of Florida, and to Susan Murray, my copy editor, thank you for turning a manuscript into a work of art.

To my husband, and best friend, Mike, there will never be enough words to thank you for planning and sharing trips to architectural sites, and for your love and support that has brought joy to writing this book. And to my son, Huntly, and daughter, Beth, now you can stop asking, "When will you finish the book?"

Notes

Abbreviations Used in the Notes

AGI: Archivo General de Indias, Seville, Spain, on microfilm at SAHS-RL and at P. K. Yonge Library of Florida History at the University of Florida, Gainesville

AIA: American Institute of Architects

AME Church: African Methodist Episcopal Church

CARL: Florida's Conservation and Recreation Lands Program

EFP: East Florida Papers

FA/AIA: Florida Association of the American Institute of Architects

FAIA: Fellow, American Institute of Architects

FHQ: *Florida Historical Quarterly*

FLMNH: Florida Museum of Natural History, University of Florida, Gainesville

HABS: Historic American Buildings Survey, Library of Congress, Washington, D.C.

JSAH: Journal of the Society of Architectural Historians

NHL: National Historic Landmark

NR: National Register of Historic Places

OAH: Organization of American Historians

PRO: Public Record Office, British National Archives, Kew, Richmond, Surrey, England

SAAA: St. Augustine Archaeological Association

SAHS: St. Augustine Historical Society

SAHS–RL: St. Augustine Historical Society Research Library

WPA: Works Progress Administration

INTRODUCTION: *In Pursuit of Florida*

Epigraph source: Livio, *The Golden Ratio*, 4.

1. Shakespeare, *Measure for Measure*, 5.1.12.

2. David McCullough, "An Exchange with David McCullough," *Preservation*, March–April 2003, 48.

3. Walt Whitman, in R. Brooks Jeffery, review of *The Colonial Architecture of Mexico*, by James Early, *Preservation*, May–June 2004, 57.

4. Horwitz, *Voyage*, 387.

5. Coquina (Spanish for the tiny shellfish *Donax variabilis*) is a sedimentary limestone of shell fragments of many marine animals, mostly the *Donax*, and quartz sand cemented together from 1,800,000 to 10,000 years ago by calcium carbonate. It lies below ancient sand dunes and maritime hammocks along the east coast of Florida from Anastasia Island to Palm Beach (Fernald and Purdum, *Atlas*, 25).

6. Keller, "Wright's Stuff," 73.

7. Kaufmann, *Fallingwater*, 28; Siry, "Annie M. Pfeiffer Chapel," 499.

CHAPTER 1. *Mysteries in Water and Earth*

Epigraph source: Karaim, "Losing Sacred Ground," 32.

1. Karaim, "Losing Sacred Ground," 32.

2. Eck, "Diary Notes of Dr. Jeffries Wyman's Visit to Miami," 290, 291 n. 23.

3. Schwadron, "Archaeological Investigations," 171; Luer, "Sarasota Bay Mound," 7–15, and "The Yellow Bluffs Mound," 14; Thunen, "Grant Mound," 258; Ashley, "Introducing Shields Mound," 168.

4. Russo, "Brief Introduction," 89–92; Russo, "Why We Don't Believe," 93–108; Endonino, "Thornhill Lake," 151, 162; Hann, *Indians of Central and South Florida*, 115.

5. Doran, *Windover*. Older sacred spaces may exist beyond Florida's current coastlines, created when Florida was larger and drier and before the waters of the Gulf of Mexico and Atlantic Ocean moved inland.

6. Jackson et al., "Historical Overfishing," 629–37; Quitmyer and Jones, "Over-Exploitation of Hard Clams," 158–67; Walker, "Precolumbian Fishing," 27; MacMahon and Marquardt, *The Calusa*, 93–94; Wheeler, *Treasure of the Calusa*, 1; Milanich, *Archaeology*, 257.

7. S. Lawson, *Foothold in Florida*, 10, 11, 18, 29, 38, 164; Milanich, *Archaeology*, 92, 108, 117, 168–67, 224, 315; Milanich, *Famous Sites*, 10, 20; Milanich, *The Timucua*, 10, Milanich, *Florida Indians and the Invasion*, 28, 34, 44, 49, 62, 68, 70; Lyon, *Enterprise of Florida*, 129; Hann, *Missions to the Calusa*, 8; Hann, *Indians of Central and South Florida*, xiii, 29–31; 38–39, 68–69, 192; Larson, *Aboriginal Subsistence*, 29–31, 33–34, 66, 68, 116–17, 211–17, 124–25; MacMahon and Marquardt, *The Calusa*, 1–2, 7, 8–11, 65, 105; Hudson, *Southeastern Indians*, 76. Keith Ashley, in a paper delivered in St. Augustine in 2010, indicated that corn was not seriously cultivated in Florida before the fifteenth century.

8. Marquardt, *Calusa*, 206; MacMahon and Marquardt, *The Calusa*, 1–75.

9. Purdy, *Art and Archaeology of Florida's Wetlands*, 115.

10. Weisman, "Crystal River," 56, 58.

11. For additional reading about premodern identity and religious beliefs, see Michael Balter, "Scientist at Work: Randall White, Falling in Love with France and Its Trove of Ancient History," *New York Times*, April 10, 2007, D3; Julian Smith, "Surveying a Sacred Landscape: Archaeologists Take on the Cliffs and Caves of the Rio Grande Gorge," *Archaeology*, January–February 2008, 59; Keith Mulvihill, "On Rock Walls, Painted Prayers to Rain Gods," *New York Times*, September 19, 2008; and John Noble Wilford, "A Lost European Culture, Pulled from Obscurity," "Science Times" section, *New York Times*, December 1, 2009, D1.

12. Sears, *Fort Center*, 157.

13. Milanich et al., *Archaeology of Northern Florida*, 105–12.

CHAPTER 2. *Windover Pond*

Epigraph source: Lundquist, *The Temple*, 44.

1. Doran, "Introduction to Wet Sites," 11, 33, 34, 59 fig. 3.1; Doran and Dickle, "Radiometric Cronology," 365–80; Wentz, "Origins of American Medicine," 58.

2. Lundquist, *The Temple*, 44, 65.

3. Doran, "Introduction to Wet Sites," 4–35; Dickle, "Analysis of Mortuary Patterns," 73–96.

4. Doran, "Introduction to Wet Sites," 4–35; Dickle, "Analysis of Mortuary Patterns," 73–96; Wentz, "Origins of American Medicine," 58.

5. Lecture by bioarchaeologist Rachel K. Wentz, presented in conjunction with the SAAA and the Florida Public Archaeology Network, February 10, 2009; Wentz, "Origins of American Medicine," 57.

6. Eli Sanders, "An 8-Year Fight Ends over a 9,200-Year-Old Man," *New York Times*, July 20, 2004; John Noble Wilford, "Evidence Hints at Earlier Humans in Americas," *New York Times*, November 18, 2004; Thomas H. Maugh II, "New Evidence Suggests That Two Separate Groups Settled North America," *Los Angeles Times*, quoted in *St. Augustine Record*, March 5, 2011, 4.

7. R. L. Andrews et al. "Conservation and Analysis of Textile," 121–65; Wentz, "Origins of American Medicine," 57–58, 60–65.

8. Luer, "Archaeology of Upper Charlotte Harbor," 1, 3–18, 24; Milanich, *Archaeology*, 80–82; Purdy, *Art and Archaeology of Florida's Wetlands*, 62, 139, 141–42, 150, 153, 167–70, 177; Doran, "Introduction to Wet Sites," 35 and map 1.1.

9. S. Larsen, *Shaman's Doorway*, 85; Bownas, "Shintō," 345.

10. Hall, "Ghosts, Water Barriers," 363; Hall, *Archaeology of the Soul*, 95; Hudson, *Southeastern Indians*, 128, 133, 166.

11. Thompson, *Rise and Fall*, 27, 133–34; Romey, "Diving the Maya Underworld," *Archaeology*, May–June 2003, 16–23; *National Geographic*, November 1936, plate 17.

12. Schele and Miller, *Blood of Kings*, 282–85.

13. Ibid., 267.

14. H. Thomas, *Rivers of Gold*, 113, 129, 149.

15. Hall, "Ghosts, Water Barriers," 361, 363; Hann, *Indians of Central and South Florida*, 191.

CHAPTER 3. *Pre-Columbian Architects on Fisheating Creek*

Epigraph source: Boehm, *Conversations with I. M. Pei*, 18.

1. Sears, *Fort Center*, ix; Purdy, *Art and Archaeology of Florida's Wetlands*, 82. Seminoles and Miccosukee were Creeks who moved into Florida from Georgia and Alabama in the 1700s. The genetic relationships of the "Creeks" and Florida's Seminole Indians are discussed by Christopher M. Stojanowski in "Unhappy Trails," 38. Seminoles refused to relocate, and warfare, known as the Second Seminole War, erupted in 1835.

2. Sears, *Fort Center*, 6, 27–32, 191–92, 200; Milanich, *Florida Indians and the Invasion from Europe*, 40, 49; Hann, *Indians of Central and South Florida*, xiii, 2, 29, 31, 39; MacMahon and Marquardt, *The Calusa*, 1–3, 65–74, 113. Sears described the circular trenches near the sacred complex in terms of agriculture. Perhaps they were for fish or snail culture.

3. Milanich, *Florida Indians and the Invasion from Europe*, 28, 39–40; Fontaneda, *Memoir*, 27–28.

4. Grunwald, *The Swamp*; Milanich, *Frolicking Bears*, 151, 215–23; MacMahon and Marquardt, *The Calusa*, 113. One canal, Mud Lake Canal, in southwest Florida was designated a National Historic Landmark in 2006. See also Marjorie Stoneman Douglas, *The Everglades: River of Grass* (1947). *Map of the Seat of War in Florida*, compiled by order of General Taylor, from surveys and reconnaissance by U.S. Army officers John Mackay and Lt. J. E. Blake, copy at University of Miami Libraries.

5. Purdy, *Art and Archaeology of Florida's Wetlands*, 82–83.

6. Sears, *Fort Center*, 38–58, 157, 162–69, fig 9.14; Milanich, *Archaeology*, 294–97; Gordon, *Florida's Colonial Architectural Heritage*, 20–21; Purdy, *Art and Archaeology of Florida's Wetlands*, 86, fig. 29; Schwehm, *Carved Wood Effigies*, figs. 13 and 21.

7. Sears, *Fort Center*, 153–75; Purdy, *Art and Archaeology of Florida's Wetlands*, 82–101; Milanich, *Archaeology*, 291–98. Human remains were studied, but no report resulted.

8. Sears, *Fort Center*, 169–75; "fids" are in Walker, "Material Culture," 28, fig. 2; Sears, *Fort Center*, fig 6.1 "I" and "J."

9. Sears, *Fort Center*, 38–58; Wheeler, "Ancient Art," 85–102; Purdy, *Art and Archaeology of Florida's Wetlands*, 87–98, 101; Schwehm, "Carved Wood Effigies," 27, 29.

10. Purdy, *Art and Archaeology of Florida's Wetlands*, 66, 71–76; see also Cushing, "Exploration of Ancient Key Dwellers' Remains on the Gulf Coast of Florida"; and Kolianos and Weisman, *The Florida Journals of Frank Hamilton Cushing*.

11. Wheeler, "Ancient Art," 85–102.

12. Jerald Milanich, correspondence with the author, June 2003 and May 2004.

13. Jarrett A. Lobell, "Emblems of Empire," *Archaeology*, May–June, 2007, 34–37.

14. Joseph Campbell in S. Larsen, *Shaman's Doorway*, 66, 67, 68.

15. Hann, *Indians of Central and South Florida*, 47, 191, 196–97.

16. Sears, *Fort Center*, 45, 197; Milanich et al., *Archaeology of Northern Florida*, 99; Schwehm, *Carved Wood Effigies*, 40, 50.

17. Sears, *Fort Center*, 5, 147, 165, 191–92; Hall, *Archaeology of the Soul*, 18–19; Gibson, "Broken Circles," 25–26.

18. Hall, "Ghosts, Water Barriers," 361; Milanich correspondence with the author, June 2003.

19. Weisman, "Crystal River"; Milanich, *Famous Florida Sites*; Pluckhahn and Thompson, "Mapping Crystal River (8C11)," 5–22; Collins and Doering, "High Definition Digital Documentation at Crystal River," 23–44. See also Mainfort and Sullivan, *Ancient Earthen Enclosures*.

20. Sears, *Fort Center*, 157.

21. Ibid., 9, 59–67; 185–89, 197, 200; Milanich, *Florida Indians and the Invasion from Europe*, 29, 39, 56; MacMahon and Marquardt, *The Calusa*, 78; Jerald Milanich, communication with the author, May 2004.

22. Purdy, *Art and Archaeology of Florida's Wetlands*, 66.

CHAPTER 4. *McKeithen Mounds*

Epigraph source: Milanich, *Florida Indians and the Invasion from Europe*, 1.

1. The McKeithen Mound Site (Columbia County) was acquired by the State of Florida through its Conservation and Recreation Lands (CARL) Program. Lex McKeithen, the owner for whom the site was named, reserved a life estate in the property, but visitors with an interest in archaeology were welcomed. The 1976 and 1977 excavations were supported by funds awarded by the Wentworth Foundation, William Goza, President (Jerald Milanich, correspondence with the author, 2004).

2. Milanich et al., *Archaeology of Northern Florida*, 91–92, 97–98, 109–12, 118, 185.

3. Ibid., xvi, 21, 26, 31–34, 50, 75–76, 166, 171–72.

4. Ibid., 14–24.

5. Ibid., 94–100.

6. Ibid., 91–104.

7. Ibid., xvi, 105.

8. Ibid., xvi, 92, 105–12.

9. Ibid., 105–12.

10. Wheeler, *Treasure of the Calusa*, 17, fig. 5.4 on 133.

11. See the discussion of Cacica Doña María in chapter 11 of this book.

12. L. Thomas, "Images of Women," 321–52; Milanich, *Archaeology*, 371–78; Hudson, *Southeastern Indians*, 126.

13. Laudonnière, in S. Lawson, *Foothold in Florida*, 12.

14. Hudson, *Southeastern Indians*, 73–74; Gibson, *Poverty Point*, 186; Schele and Miller, *Blood of Kings*, 267, 285; Hall, *Archaeology of the Soul*, 138.

15. Milanich et al., *Archaeology of Northern Florida*, 112–17.

16. Hudson, *Southeastern Indians*, 122–24; Thompson, *Maya History and Religion*, 195; Lundquist, *The Temple*, 5–31; Basham, "Hinduism," 223.

CHAPTER 5. *Mount Royal*

Epigraph source: Hall, *An Archaeology of the Soul*, 169.

1. W. Bartram, *Travels*, 101.

2. Milanich, *Famous Florida Sites*, 9–11, 29–37, 56 n. 4; Waselkov and Braund, *William Bartram*, 176.

3. Schafer, "St. Augustine's British Years," 33. Egmont invested £12,000 and had seventy-three slaves working the plantation. He died in 1771 before he made a profit, and his Mt. Royal plantation was closed and his slaves sent to Amelia Island (Schafer, "Early Plantation Development," 46–48).

4. Milanich, *Archaeology*, 260; Russo, "Brief Introduction," 90; Thunen, "Grant Mound," 255, 258; Wheeler, Newman, and Mcgee, "Mount Taylor," 139–43, 153–54; Endonino, "Thornhill Lake," 147–63.

5. Worth, *Timucuan Chiefdoms*, 2:187–88; Milanich, *Famous Florida Sites*, 12–13; Purdy, *Art and Archaeology of Florida's Wetlands*, 102–36.

6. Ashley, "Archaeological Overview," 269; Ashley, "Interpretation of Shields Mound," 291, 296; Milanich, *Famous Florida Sites*, 10; Milanich, *Archaeology*, 254, 256, 263.

7. Mitchem, *East Florida Expeditions*, 23, 24; Milanich, *Famous Florida Sites*, 8–9, 11–13; Milanich, *Archaeology*, 270–72; Hann, *History of Timucua*, 141–42; Hann, *Indians of Central and South Florida*, 69, 70; Hann, *Missions to the Calusa*, 30 n. 31, 120, 130, 140, 212, 439–40; S. Lawson, *Foothold in Florida*, 94; Ashley, "Archaeological Overview," 272, 276–77, 279; "Mapa de la Ysla de la Florida," 1683, *Servicio Geografico del Ejercito*, Library of Congress, copy at SAHS-RL.

8. Milanich, *Famous Florida Sites*, 29, 30; W. Bartram, *Travels*, 101; Waselkov and Braund, *William Bartram*, 5, 45, 176–79.

9. Mitchem, *East Florida Expeditions*, 23, 24, 31, 33, 126, 154, 240, 326–28; Milanich, *Famous Florida Sites*, 1, 2–8, 29, 31, 57 n. 7. Moore's materials were later sold to the Museum of the American Indian (Heye Foundation) in New York. Much of the latter collection is now housed in the Smithsonian's National Museum of the American Indian in Washington, D.C. His field notes are in the Huntington Free Library, today part of the Hispanic Society in New York City.

10. Milanich, *Florida's Famous Sites*, 33; Thunen, "Grant Mound," 255, 258.

11. Wheeler, correspondence with the author, May 2003; Milanich, correspondence with the author, June 2003.

12. Ashley, "Interpretation of Shields Mound," 291–92; Hudson, *Southeastern Indians*, 44, 55, 127, 129, 394; Schele and Miller, *Blood of Kings*, 42; Goetz and Morley, *Popol Vuh*, 184; Thompson, *Maya History and Religion*, 269; Milanich et al., *Archaeology of Northern Florida*, 167.

13. Milanich et al., *Archaeology of Northern Florida*, 110.

14. Milanich, *Famous Florida Sites*, 11, 31, 32, 40, 50–52; Ashley, "Archaeological Overview of Mount Royal," 269, 275, 282.

15. Milanich, *Famous Florida Sites*, 29–30.

16. W. Bartram, *Travels*, 101–2; Waselkov and Braund, *William Bartram*," figs. 27–30, 240 n. 31, 241 n. 32.

17. Milanich, *Famous Florida Sites*, 31.

18. Milanich, *Archaeology*, 270; Milanich, *Florida Indians and the Invasion*, 89.

19. Ashley, "Archaeological Overview of Mount Royal," 281; Ashley, "Interpretation of Shields Mound," 267; Ashley, "Introducing Shields Mound," 153; Thunen, "Grant Mound," 255; Milanich, *Archaeology*, 270.

20. S. Lawson, *Foothold in Florida*, 94; Milanich, *Famous Florida Sites*, 12, 25; Ashley, "Archaeological Overview of Mount Royal," 279; Solís, in Kerrigan, *Barcia's Chronological History*, 77; W. Bartram, *Travels*, 104; Waselkov and Braund, *William Bartram*, 131; Ashley, "Archaeological Overview of Mount Royal," 279.

CHAPTER 6. *Round, Because the Circle Is the Perfect Symbol?*

Epigraph source: Lawler, *Sacred Geometry*, 16.

1. Scotti, *Basilica*, 51; Argüelles and Trungpa, *Mandala*, 12–14; Lundquist, *The Temple*, 16–19; Panton, "Cultural Prisms Distort," 34–35; Lakota belief system as exhibited at the National Museum of the American Indian in Washington, D.C., November 2004.

2. Weisman, Shepard, and Luer, "Origin and Significance," 342–46; Wheeler and Carr, "Miami Circle: Fieldwork, Research and Analysis," 1, 4, 6; Widmer, "Archaeological Investigations at the Brickell Point Site," 11, 19, 29, 32, 47, 54–55; Carr, "Analysis of Ceramics," 133, 156, 158; Wheeler, "Shell Artifacts from the Miami Circle," 160.

3. Carr and Ricisak, "Preliminary Report," 282; Pamela Mercer, "Miamians Tangle with Developers over Curious Tequesta Indian Ruin," *New York Times*, February 15, 1999, A13.

4. State of Florida CARL Program, a loan from the Trust for Public Land (TPL), Miami-Dade County bonds, the John S. and James L. Knight Foundation, the Metropolitan Planning organization, and private citizens.

5. Carr, "Analysis of Ceramics," 156; Collins, Doering, and Carr, "Integrated Spatial Technologies," 161, 163–65; Straight, "A. E. Douglass Cup," 187; Patricios, *Building Marvelous Miami*, 4, 111–12.

6. Eck, "Diary Notes of Jeffries Wyman," 291; Elgart and Carr, "Analysis of the Prehistoric Human Remains," 246–48; Carr and Ricisak, "Preliminary Report," 260–82; Wheeler and Carr, "Miami Circle: Fieldwork, Research and Analysis," 3–9; Widmer, "Archaeological Investigations at Brickell Point," 19, 23, 35, 39; 40, 41; Carr, "City Park Is Home to Burial Grounds," *Gainesville Sun*, July 5, 2001; Hann, *Indians of Central and South Florida*, 142, 153, 186.

7. Carr and Ricisak, "Preliminary Report," 278, 281; Wheeler and Mattick, NR Nomination, sec. 7, pp. 3, 7; sec. 8, p. 4.

8. Hall, *Archaeology of the Soul*, 95, 132–39; S. Larsen, *Shaman's Doorway*, 85; Hall, "Ghosts, Water Barriers," 362; Hudson, *Southeastern Indians*, 121, 127–28, 133, 146, 148; Goetz and Morley, *Popol Vuh*, 78; Schele and Miller, *Blood of Kings*, 181; Thompson, *Maya History and Religion*, 262.

9. Carr and Ricisak, "Preliminary Report," 276; Austin, "Chipped Stone Artifacts," 85, 128; Elgart, "Animal Interments," 179.

10. Elgart, "Animal Interments," 179–87; Carr and Ricisak, "Preliminary Report," 278; Widmer, "Archaeological Investigations at Brickell Point," 26, 29.

11. Calderón in Wenhold, "A 17th Century Letter," 13; Milanich, *The Timucua*, 136.

12. Hann and McEwan, *Apalachee Indians and Mission San Luis*, 75–77, 89, 91. Outside was a circular plaza, 410 feet in diameter.

13. Ibid., 75–77, 89, 91; on-site interviews with Dr. Bonnie McEwan, director of archaeology, Mission San Luis, 1999, 2003–5; Herschel E. Shepard, FAIA,

correspondence with the author, August 9, 1999; McEwan and Hann, "Reconstructing a Spanish Mission," 17; Calderón in Wenhold, "A 17th Century Letter," 13.

14. S. Lawson, *Foothold in Florida*, 10; Lyon, *Enterprise of Florida*, 118.

15. Hann and McEwan, *Apalachee Indians and Mission San Luis*, 35, 75–77, 80, 122–28; Hann, *Early Florida Adventure Story*, 67; S. Lawson, *Foothold in Florida*, 10–11; Hann, *Indians of Central and South Florida*, 14–15, 187, 188, 194.

16. Hann and McEwan, *Apalachee Indians and Mission San Luis*, 35, 131.

17. Hall, "Ghosts, Water Barriers," 362–63; Coe, *Sacred Circles*, 11–17; Curry, "Cherokee Holy of Holies," 74–75; Gibson, *Poverty Point*, 185; Hudson, *Southeastern Indians*, 68–69, 72, 78, 122, 126, 331–33, 135, 155–56.

18. Hall, *Archaeology of the Soul*, 170.

19. Panton, "Cultural Prisms Distort," 34–35.

CHAPTER 7. *"That's Not Just a Work of Art—That's Our Godhead"*

Author's note: The title of chapter 7 is from Charlotte Woodhead, barrister and academic convenor, Institute of Art and Law, in *Art Newspaper*, July–August 2004, Supplement: "Art and Law" (United Kingdom: Umberto Allemandi), 25.

Epigraph source: Armstrong, "Man vs God," W2.

1. Rogel, in Hann, *Missions to the Calusa*, 225, 238, 239, 242. For more about the Jesuits, see Félix Zubillaga, *La Florida: La Misión Jesuítica*, 1566–72.

2. Velasco, in Hann, *Missions to the Calusa*, 319; Hann, *Indians of Central and South Florida*, 150, 151; Hann, *Early Florida Adventure Story*, 79.

3. Fontaneda, *Memoir*, 26.

4. Governor Marquez to king, 1579, in Hann, *History of the Timucua Indians and Missions*, 69, 71, 225–27, 139.

5. Pareja, in Milanich and Sturtevant, *Pareja's 1613 Confessionario*, 25, 26, 28, 41; Alaña in Hann, *Indians of Central and South Florida*, 193; Alaña in Hann, *Missions to the Calusa*, 328, 422.

6. Weisman, "Crystal River," 54, 73–74, 185, and figs. 15, 19, 20; Milanich, *Archaeology*, 322, and *Famous Sites*, figs. 3.21, 3.24, 3.25, 4.14, 82, 120; Sears, *Fort Center*, 83–84; Wheeler, *Treasure of the Calusa*, 17, fig. 5.4 on 133; Larson, *Aboriginal Subsistence*, 115–18.

7. Hall, *Archaeology of the Soul*, 57, 161, 167.

8. Absent waterbird bones and the question of taboo were raised by Jerald Milanich, correspondence with the author, May 2004.

9. Curry, "Cherokee Holy of Holies," 70–71; Grantham, *Creation Myths*, 14, 16, 66.

10. Hudson, *Southeastern Indians*, 133–34; Jerald Milanich, communication with the author, June 2003; Gibson, "Broken Circles," 29; Gibson, *Poverty Point*, 191; Knight, "Mississippian Ritual," 47.

11. Lundquist, *Temple*, 5, 12, 31, 68, 95; Lawler, *Sacred Geometry*, 6–10; Riding, Alan, "Are Politics Built into Architecture?" *New York Times*, August 10, 2002, A13; Gibson, *Poverty Point*, 227; Schele and Miller, *Blood of Kings*, 32, 43, 266, 269, 278 n. 11, 285.

12. Lundquist, *Temple*, 12; "Maya Goods in Teotihuacan Tomb," *Archaeology*,

January–February 2003, 16; John Noble Wilford, "Inside Mexican Pyramid, Buried Clues Link Ancient Cultures," *New York Times*, November 19, 2002; Jorge Perez de Lara, "Temple of the Sun," *Archaeology*, November–December 2005, 37–41.

13. Goetz and Morley, *Popol Vuh*, 205 n. 3, 206.

14. Lundquist, *Temple*, 17, 38, 68, 83, 86–87; Severy, *Great Religions*, 18; Harris, *Illustrated Dictionary of Historic Architecture*, 533.

15. Sears, *Fort Center*, 157.

16. S. Lawson, *Foothold in Florida*, 11, 12, 89, 164; Milanich, *Florida Indians and the Invasion*, 92, 144–45.

17. Abbot, *Kingdom of the Seashell*, 174, 176, 186, 188, 190; Matos, "Imperial Tenochtitlan," 222; Schele and Miller, *Blood of Kings*, 73, 280.

18. Schele and Miller, *Blood of Kings*, 284.

19. William Marquardt, demonstration talk on-site at Randell Research Center, Pine Island, November 2011.

CHAPTER 8. *Planting Spanish Architectural Roots*

Epigraph source: Connor, *Memorial by Gonzalo Solís de Merás*, 89.

1. Connor, *Memorial by Gonzalo Solís de Merás*, 89.

2. Lyon, "First Three Wooden Forts," 130–45.

3. In 1513, Easter (as decreed in A.D. 325 by the Council of Nicea) was the first Sunday after the first full moon after the vernal equinox (*New York Times*, "Science Times" sec., October 19, 1999, D1). Slavers may have preceded Ponce de León (Milanich, *Florida Indians and the Invasion*, 107, 108; Hoffman, *Florida's Frontiers*, 22).

4. Susan Parker, correspondence with the author, May 21, 2004; Gordon, *Florida's Colonial Architectural Heritage*, 85.

5. Connor, *Memorial by Gonzalo Solís de Merás*, 88–89; Andres Gonzalez de Barcia Carballido y Zuñiga, in Kerrigan, *Barcia's Chronological History*, 81–82.

6. The author of this book visited Avilés and the Cave of Covadonga on May 16, 2007. The legend is described in *Diccionario historico de Asturias*, ed. Javier Rodríguez Muñoz (Oviedo: Editorial Prensa Asturiana S.A., La Nueva Espana, 2003), 307.

7. In the legend of the tenth-century boy saint San Pelayo, he refused to become the sex-slave of the caliph of Cordoba. Elizabeth Duran Gessner of St. Augustine researched this legend. Menéndez's flagship is described in Lyon, *Enterprise of Florida*, 26, 48, 64, 78, 93.

8. Nicolaus Copernicus published *De revolutionibus orbium coelestium* (*On the Revolutions of the Celestial Spheres*) in 1543.

9. De Bry, *Brevis narrato corum quae in Florida Ameridae*, 1591. Doubts have been raised by archaeologists Jerald Milanich and Keith Ashley in various symposiums.

10. Milbrath, "Old World Meets New: Views across the Atlantic."

11. National Park Service, "Fort Caroline," *Papers: The Jacksonville Historical Society* 4 (1960): 43; Lyon, *Enterprise of Florida*, 35; Manucy, *How Did Fort Caroline Look?*

12. Fray Juan Rogel, in Hann, *Missions to the Calusa*, 296; Grant, in Schafer, "Governor James Grant's Villa," 7.

CHAPTER 9. *The Nation's Oldest Town Plan*

Epigraph source: Quoted in "A Letter from the Publisher," *American Bungalow* 63 (Fall 2009), 1.

1. Deagan, "Archaeology of First Spanish Period," 16; Deagan, *Archaeological Strategy*; Halbirt, "Redefining the Boundaries;" Hoffman, "St. Augustine 1580," 5–19.

2. Nuttall, "Ordinances," 743.

3. Alonso de las Alas, January 12, 1600, in Lyon, "Project Historian Report," 76; Lyon, "First Three Wooden Forts," 144; Leturiondo, in Hann, "Alonso de Leturiondo's Memorial," 173.

4. Quoted translations of the Ordinances of 1573 are from Nuttall, "Ordinances," 750–51; Hoffman and Lyon, "Preliminary Report," appendix 1, 1–3.

5. Boazio, *S Augustii* (1588).

6. For more on this subject, see Lawler, *Sacred Geometry*; and Livio, *Golden Ratio*.

7. Méndez de Canzo to king in MC63, 1598–1610, AIG 54-5-9, SAHS-RL translation, 12; National Register of Historic Places Inventory Nomination Form, June 4, 1986, "Summary," p. 1, and Item Number 8, p. 1; Deagan, *Archaeological Strategy*; Halbirt, "Redefining the Boundaries"; Hoffman, "St. Augustine 1580," 16.

8. PRO CO5/553, p. 59.

9. Sexton, "Loggias," 308–11.

10. Ybarra to king, January 8, 1604, AGI, 54/5/9, SAHS-RL.

11. Captain Álvaro Flores, in Connor, *Colonial Records*, 2:189–91.

12. Bushnell, "Situado and Sabana," 88–89.

13. Carl Halbirt, city archaeologist, discussion with the author, September 2, 2010.

14. PRO CO5/549, p. 59.

15. Flagler quoted in Graham, *Flagler's St. Augustine Hotels*, 17, 19.

CHAPTER 10. *Living under Spanish Bells*

Epigraph source: Von Simson, *Gothic Cathedral*, 37.

1. Von Simson, *Gothic Cathedral*, 37. The plaza ratio of length to width is in Ordinance Nos. 112 and 113, Nuttall; "Ordinances," 750–51. Two mission churches in St. Augustine, the convent church in St. Augustine, and the church at Mission San Luis in Tallahassee may have had proportional dimensions (Gordon, *Florida's Colonial Architectural Heritage*, 47, 96, 113–14, 115).

2. Lyon, "Richer," 35; López de Mendoza, *Relacíon hecha*, 2:451; Gannon, *Cross in the Sand*, 22, 26; Lyon, *Enterprise of Florida*, 91, 107, 213, 220. All the bells might not have been unloaded.

3. Barcia, in Kerrigan, *Barcia's Chronological History*, 88.

4. Solís de Merás, in Connor, *Memorial*, 105.

5. Lyon, "Project Historian Report," 17, 111; Lyon, "First Three Wooden Forts," 144.

6. Alonso de las Alas to the Crown, St. Augustine, January 12, 1600, AGI Santo Domingo 229, in Lyon, "Project Historian Report," 76.

7. Deagan, *Archaeological Strategy*; Halbirt, "Redefining the Boundaries"; Hoffman, "St. Augustine 1580," 16.

8. Boazio, *S Augustii*; Mestas, "San Agustín."

9. Ordinance Nos. 119, 121, in Nuttall, "Ordinances," 751–52.

10. Baltasar del Castello y Ahedo, 1576 inventory, in Lyon, "Richer," 92–96.

11. Calderón, 1675, in Wenhold, "A 17th Century Letter," 7; Leturiondo, in Hann, "Leturiondo's Memorial," 185; Lyon, "Richer," 93. Elizabeth Gessner researched the *advocación* and image of Nuestra Señora de los Remedios. Hoffman, *Florida's Frontiers*, 86–87.

12. Scotti, *Basilica*, 34, 37, 51.

13. R. Scott, *Gothic Enterprise*, 106.

14. Governor Méndez de Canzo, letters, 1597–1603, AGI 54-5-9, letter to king, April 24, 1601, copy at SAHS-RL, Fl Hist, MC 63.

15. Méndez de Canzo, letter to king, February 23, 1598, in letters, 1597–1610, AGI 54-5-9/24 SD 224, copy at SAHS-RL, MC63. A "strong wind" destroyed part of the fort and guard house in September 1599, according to Fray Baltasar López, letter to Crown, 54-5-20/8 SD235. Geiger records that it was a hurricane in 1599, *Franciscan Conquest of Florida*, 122. In March 1599, the Franciscan convent and its church burned, and the friars moved into the shrine and hospital of La Soledad (Méndez de Canzo, letters of February 28, 1600, and April 24, 1601, SD 224). I have not found a reference to the parish church burning and leaving the city without a parish church, or to it being rebuilt. Bushnell wrote in "Situado and Sabana," 88, that the parish church burned. Kapitzke cites Bushnell in *Religion, Power and Politics*, 148, and adds that it was rebuilt in 1605. However, I believe the references are to the convent church, which did burn and was completed 1604, according to Fray Bermejo, Vicar.

16. AGI 58-2-2/14, Marqués de Mancera, viceroy of New Spain, to the Crown, Mexico, April 20, 1669, 90ff.; Arana, "Defenses and Defenders," 7; Hoffman, *Florida's Frontiers*, 143.

17. Calderón, 1675, in Wenhold, "A 17th Century Letter," 7.

18. Bushnell, "Situado and Sabana," 88–89.

19. Arnade, *Siege of St. Augustine in 1702*, 57–61.

20. Ibid., 41, 43, 57.

21. Gannon, *Cross in the Sand*, figure opposite p. 48; Lyon, *Richer*, 93; Coomes, "Our Country's Oldest Parish Records, 74–83.

22. Wagner, "A Draft of Town and Harbour," 1730, copy at SAHS-RL.

23. Bermejo to king, March 30, 1604, AGI 54-5-20/12.

24. Méndez de Canzo, letters to king, AGI 54-5-9, February 23, 1598, 34ff., copy at SAHS-RL, MC 63, Box 2, File 10; Leturiondo, in Hann, "Leturiondo's Memorial," 194.

25. Méndez de Canzo to king, AGI 54-5-9, February 23, 1598, 34ff.; Council of the Indies to Crown, Madrid, August 16, 1598, 11ff.; Ensign Bartolome López Gavira to the governor of Florida, AI 54-5-16/106, September 12, 1600, 4ff.

26. Méndez de Canzo, letters to king, February 28, 1600, and April 24, 1601, Stetson Collection, AGI 54-5-9/31/32/38 178ff., copy at SAHS-RL; Geiger, *Franciscan Conquest*, 122; Hoffman, *Florida's Frontiers*, 75.

27. Bermejo to king, March 30, 1604, Exhibit E, AI 54-5-20/12, copy at SAHS-RL, MC 63, Box 2. The Franciscan monastery, Convento de la Concepción Inmaculada, was built before 1587, when the first group of friars stopped there before taking up their assignments. Governor Méndez de Canzo wrote that the *body of the church is covered with palm and because fires are a frequent occurence and it is in danger* (AGI

54-5-9/24). After the 1599 fire, it was rebuilt (1601–3) with wood planks, and was more generally known as Convento de San Francisco. It was the British headquarters during the siege of 1702, and was set on fire. It was rebuilt with stone in the mid-1700s. It became the British barracks from the 1760s to 1783, and its remnants are incorporated into today's National Guard Headquarters (see Gordon, *Florida's Colonial Architectural Heritage*, 94–100).

28. Leturiondo, in Hann, "Leturiondo's Memorial," 194.

29. Calderón, 1675, in Wenhold, "A 17th Century Letter," 8.

30. Leturiondo in Hann, "Leturiondo's Memorial," 194, 217.

31. Bushnell, "Situado and Sabana," 89.

32. Bishop of Tricale to the king, April 29, 1736, AGI 58-2-14/118, copy at SAHS-RL, MC63 1736, Box 3, "Account of Auxiliary Bishop"; Gannon, *Cross in the Sand*, 79.

33. Bishop of Tricale to the king, April 29, 1736, p. 3, copy at SAHS-RL, MC63 1736, Box 3, File 36. In 1765, it was *Our Lady of Araselis* in the Memorial of Juan Chrisostomo de Acosta, January 17, 1765, copy at SAHS-RL. Elizabeth Duran Gessner researched the devotions.

34. Solana, "Report of Conditions," 1759. Solana had been chaplain of the fort since 1724 and parish priest since 1751 (Kapitski, *Religion, Power*, 153). A Spanish vara in Cuba was 33.38 inches, based on the Roman foot of 11.12 inches.

35. Chrisostomo, inventory, January 17, 1765, pp. 6 and 8, SAHS-RL; bishop of Tricale, to the king, April 29, 1736, AGI 58-2-14/122, p. 1 of translated transcription, SAHS-RL.

36. Chrisostomo, inventory, January 17, 1765, p. 7, SAHS-RL.

37. J. Bartram, *Diary*, 53.

38. Moncrief's measurements prior to its conversion were 120 feet long and 48 feet wide. After its conversion, Rocque measured it at 45 varas long by 19 varas wide, or 127 feet by 53.5 feet, based on the Cuban vara of 33.3 inches. John Bartram, a botanist from Philadelphia, estimated the church was 100 feet long. Moncrief, 1965, *Plan of the Town of St. Augustine and its Environments*, PRO, CO700 Florida 8; Rocque, Annual Report, 1784, East Florida Papers/73.

39. Dorsey, *Early English Churches*, 15–19.

40. Deagan, *Spanish St. Augustine/Colonial Creole Community*, 196–99.

41. Moultrie to Dartmouth, July 1773, PRO: CO5/553 (26), p. 33; CO5/554 (29), p. 1; W. Jones, "British Period Sawmill," 84–105.

42. PRO: CO5/553, pp. 59, 74.

43. PRO: CO5/552, pp. 121–25; CO5/559, p. 270; Gordon, *Florida's Colonial Architectural Heritage*, 118–22.

44. Millar, *Architects of the American Colonies*, 104–5, 109–10.

45. Townsend, "John Moultrie"; Gordon, *Florida's Colonial Architectural Heritage*, 205–9.

46. Schafer, "St. Augustine's British Years," 263; *Dictionary of National Biography* [England], 39: 202; Townsend, "John Moultrie"; Deagan, *Spanish St. Augustine/Colonial Creole Community*, 196–99.

47. Calderón, 1675, in Wenhold, "A 17th Century Letter," 8, 12.

48. Worth, *Timucuan Chiefdoms*, 1:113.

49. Hann and McEwan, *Apalachee Indians and Mission San Luis*, 35, 48, 11893, 150, 153–54, 162, 167; C. Jones, "James Moore and Destruction," 29–31.

50. Hann and McEwan, *Apalachee Indians and Mission San Luis*; Shapiro and Vernon, "Church Complex."

51. Herschel Shepard, FAIA, consultant to San Luis, 2003, correspondence with the author; Hann and McEwan, *Apalachee Indians and Mission San Luis*, 86–87; Gordon, *Florida's Colonial Architectural Heritage*, 47.

52. Lawler, *Sacred Geometry*, 4, 6, 10, 53; Sunderland, "Symbolic Numbers," 94–103; von Simson, *Gothic Cathedral*, 8–14, 33–35, 56, 154–55, 208–10.

53. Hann and McEwan, *Apalachee Indians and Mission San Luis*, 84–89, 119; C. S. Larsen, "Mission Bioarchaeology," 334–35.

54. Manucy, "Founding of Pensacola," 239–40; Griffen, "Spanish Pensacola," 247–56; Coker, "Pensacola, 1686–1763," 117–30; Coker, "Pensacola, 1686–1821," 8–21; Gordon, *Florida's Colonial Architectural Heritage*, 72–74; Clune, "Historical Context and Overview," 20–23; Clune et al., "Settlement, Settlers, and Survival," 27, 28, 31, 37, 39, fig. 3.1, 47, 81; Bense and Wilson, "Archaeological Remains," 150–60, fig. 4.12. The bay was named after the Virgin Mary and the viceroy of New Spain, the Conde de Galve.

55. Serres's biography was taken from descriptions at the Greenwich Maritime Museum, England, and Bryan's *Dictionary of Painter and Engravers* (London), 5:69; see also Sotheby's Auction Catalog, November 23–24, 1998, 38–40, 228.

56. Coker, "Pensacola, 1686–1821," 9; Gordon, *Florida's Colonial Architectural Heritage*, 74–77; Joy, *Colonial Archaeological Trail*, 12.

57. Gordon, *Florida's Colonial Architectural Heritage*, 75–77.

58. Cushman, *Goodly Heritage*, 8. A St. Michael's Church is noted close to the harbor on a *Plan of Pensacola and Fort San Miguel and their environs, 1816*, published in Bense, *Archaeology of Colonial Pensacola*, 41 fig. 2.10.

CHAPTER 11. *Nombre de Dios*

Epigraph source: J. Bartram, *Diary*, 53.

1. Deagan, *Historical Archaeology at the Fountain of Youth Park Site*, Final Report 2009; Deagan, "Excavations," 1, 3–7.

2. J. Bartram, *Diary*, 53.

3. Menéndez, letters to the king, September 11 and October 15, 1565, in Ruidíaz y Caravia, *La Florida*, vol. 2; Solís de Merás, in Connor, *Memorial by Gonzalo Solís de Merás*; López de Mendoza, *Relacíon hecha*, 2:431–65; Barcia in Kerrigan, *Barcia's Chronological History*, 98, 108–9; Lyon, *Enterprise of Florida*, and "First Three Wooden Forts"; Gannon, *Cross in the Sand*, chaps. 2–3; Chatelain, *Defenses of Spanish Florida*; Gordon, "From So Precious a Watering."

4. Lyon, *Enterprise of Florida*, 163, 163 n. 5.

5. Diego de Velasco to king, August 1575, in Connor, *Colonial Records*, 1:145; Geiger, *Franciscan Conquest*, 14–15, 34–38, 39, 44–47, 79; Marquéz to king, in Connor, *Colonial Records*, 2:87; Álvaro Flores, king's fort inspector, in Connor, *Colonial Records*, 2:143; Lyon, "Santa Elena," 5, 8–9; Gerónimo de Óre, in Geiger, *Martyrs*

of Florida, 33, 133 n. 4; Hoffman, *Florida's Frontiers*, 65; Bushnell, "Situado and Sabana," 42; Hann, *Early Florida Adventure Story*, 101 nn. 46 and 47; Menéndez in Connor, *Colonial Records*, 1:31, 77; Lyon, "Aspects of Pedro Menéndez," 46–47; Chatelain, *Defenses of Spanish Florida*, 136 n. 1; Gordon, "So Precious a Watering," 23–26; Gannon, *Florida Catholic Heritage Trail*, 3–4.

6. Marquéz to king, 1578 and 1579, in Hann, *History of the Timucua Indians and Missions*, 69, 139.

7. Letter to king, March 6, 1580, in Connor, *Colonial Records*, 2:279. Hoffman writes that this village was built in the governor's cornfields (*Florida's Frontiers*, 69 and 341 n. 62). The officials and the governor's strong-arm methods are noted in Lyon, "St. Augustine 1580," 24.

8. Marquéz to king, December 27, 1583, AGI SD 229, Stetson Collection; fort reconstruction is in Connor, *Colonial Records*, 2:175, 251, 252.

9. Hoffman, *Florida's Frontiers*, 69. *Visita* refers to a visiting friar teacher.

10. Deagan, *Historical Archaeology at the Fountain of Youth Park Site*, Final Report 2009, 38.

11. Geiger, *Franciscan Conquest*, 54, 56, 59; Geiger, trans., *Martyrs of Florida*; Hoffman, *Florida's Frontiers*, 41, 77; Gannon, *Cross in the Sand*, 39; Bushnell, "Situado and Sabana," 70; Hann, *History of Timucua Indians and Missions*, 68. In Florida, unlike in California, it was the practice to establish missions in preexisting Indian villages (Deagan, "St. Augustine and the Mission Frontier," 88).

12. Mestas, map, and papers, AGI 140-7-37, copy at SAHS-RL; María, letter, 1600, in Hann, *History of the Timucua and Missions*, 139; Geiger, *Franciscan Conquest*, 196; Méndez de Canzo to king, AGI 54-5-9/23 and 25, translated at SAHS-RL; Bushnell, "Situado and Sabana," 120, and "Missions and Moral Judgement," 21–22; Hoffman, *Florida's Frontiers*, 79–80; Fray Andrés, in Hann, *Early Florida Adventure Story*, 67.

13. Calderón in Wenhold, "A 17th Century Letter," 13; Dickinson, *Jonathan Dickinson's Journal*, 65; Hann, *History of the Timucua*, 271.

14. Bermejo to king, March 30, 1604, AGI 54-5-20; Geiger, *Franciscan Conquest*, 28, 54–56, 62, 87, 142 n. 70; Bushnell, "Situado and Sabana," 89, 121; Milanich, "Laboring in the Fields of the Lord," 65; Hoshower and Milanich, "Excavations in the Fig Springs Mission," 220, 235; Marrinan, "Archaeological Investigations at Mission Patale," 244, 246, 266–67; McEwan, "Spiritual Conquest," 638; Hann, *History of the Timucua*, 162.

15. Deagan, *Historical Archaeology at the Fountain of Youth Park Site*, Final Report 2009, 52; Deagan, "Summary Interpretation," 14–15, 17, 20–24; Seaberg in Deagan, *America's Ancient City*, 212; McEwan and Hann, "Reconstructing a Spanish Mission," 17.

16. Deagan, paper in preparation for a volume by the American Museum of Natural History; Deagan, "Summary Interpretation," 8, 24–25; Milanich, "Laboring in the Fields of the Lord," 65, and *The Timucua*, 201; Calderon, in Wenhold, "A 17th Century Letter," 8, 12.

17. Hita Salazar to king, AGI SD 845, quoted in Bushnell, "Situado and Sabana," 89, 120–21, and in "The Expenses of *Hidalguia*," 24. The Virgin as a Nursing Mother is a cult founded in 1598 in Madrid when an image of great devotion was placed in a small chapel (shrine) in the church of San Luis (Gannon, *Cross in the Sand*, 77, and

Florida Catholic Heritage Trail, 8; J. Michael Francis, written communication to the author, April 2011).

18. Arana, "Treading Down the Castillo," 18–19.

19. Solana, AGI 58-2-8 12931-12929, MC63 1702, Box 3, File 10, SAHS-RL.

20. Arnade, *Siege of St. Augustine in 1702*, 40–58; Hoffman, *Florida's Frontiers*, 174–83; see also "Firestorm and Ashes," *El Escribano* 39 (2002), devoted to various topics of the siege.

21. Benavides in Hann, *Missions to the Calusa*, 357–68, and *History of the Timucua*, 313–15.

22. Bullones to king, October 5, 1728, in Hann, *Missions to the Calusa*, 377–78.

23. Benavides Files, MC 63 1727–31, Box 3, Files 31–38, SAHS-RL.

24. Bullones to king, in Hann, *Missions to the Calusa*, 378–79.

25. Arana, "Defenses and Defenders," 187–200.

26. Secularization is in Kapitzke, *Religion, Power*, 134, 145; Arana, "Chapel," 118.

27. Solana to Arriaga (secretary of state for the navy and the Indies), "Report," 1759.

28. Gordon, *Colonial Architectural Heritage*, 94–99.

29. J. Bartram, *Diary*, 53.

30. S. Johnson, "Casualties of Peace," 91, 101.

31. Gannon, *Cross in the Sand*, 85. Sherry Johnson forwarded me a copy of the original document signed by Eligio de la Puente, July 20, 1764; Grant, September 3, 1766, PRO PC/1/46-57, 436; PRO CO 5/540, Col. Robertson in Maj. General Gates's letter, March 10, 1764.

32. Roworth, *Plan of the Land*, copy at SAHS-RL. Maps by Olano, Castello, and Rocque show the site of the church. Bagwell, "Evidences and Conclusions," 10.

33. Bagwell, "Evidences and Conclusions," 6–10; Mariano de la Rocque to Governor Quesada, May 22, 1793, in E. Lawson, *Correspondence of the Bishops*, vol. 1, no page or letter number.

34. St. Johns County Deed Book "R," 423–24, Warranty Deed, John McGuire to Augustin Verot, August 17, 1868; Bagwell, quoting Verot testimony of August 7, 1874, in "Evidences and Conclusions," 7, D), 2.

35. George Fairbanks in *History and Antiquities*, published in 1858, pages 115, 118–19, confused the martyr Blas de Rodriques, a Franciscan in the Guale region (Georgia) in 1595, with Blas de Montes, who was at St. Augustine in 1597 and was not martyred. See also Gannon, *Rebel Bishop*, 236 n. 25.

36. St. Johns County Deed Book "S," 114.

37. Photograph of ruined chapel is in *El Escribano* 43 (2006): 63.

38. Funds were donated by General Hardin's wife, Amelia Hardin, in memory of her husband. Bishop Curley's chapel and General Hardin's biographical data are in files at SAHS-RL. See also "Replica of Sacred Statue," *St. Augustine Record*, January 29, 1939.

CHAPTER 12. *Fort Mose*

Epigraph source: Deagan, "Runaway Slaves Establish First Fortress for Freedom," 28.

1. Hann, *History of the Timucua*, 138, 158, 312–15; Arana, "Mose Site," 78, 79; Benavides and Bullones Reports in Hann, *Missions to the Calusa*, 362, 377, 378; Bushnell, "Situado and Sabana," 198.

2. Landers, *Black Society*, 29, 294 n. 1.

3. Deagan and MacMahon, *Fort Mose*, 19, 35–36.

4. Arana, "Mose Site," 79–80; Landers, *Black Society*, 30.

5. Arana and Manucy, *Building of Castillo*, 46–48; Olano, *Plano del sitio.*

6. Deagan and MacMahon, *Fort Mose*, 22.

7. Arana, "Mose Site," 81; Deagan and MacMahon, *Fort Mose*, 20–22.

8. This creek is known as Macariz, Hospital, Cano de Leche, and Douglas at its southern end; toward the north, it is known as Robinson, Mose, and Mossy.

9. Arana, "Mose Site," 81; Landers, *Black Society*, 48.

10. Solana to Arriaga, Report of Conditions, 1759. One tuesas equals 3 varas; 1 vara equals 33.3 inches; 1 tuesas thus equals 8.3 feet, and 30 tuesas equal 249 feet.

11. Castello, *Plano del Presidio*, 1763; Landers, *Black Society*, 57.

12. Deagan and MacMahon, *Fort Mose*, 32; Deagan, "Runaway Slaves," 29; Landers, *Black Society*, 27–30, 33, 37–38, 44, 48, 49–53, map on 58, appendix 5.

13. Landers, *Black Society*, 49, 57, and map on 58; Arana, "Mose Site," 81–81; Solana to Arriaga, Report of Conditions, 1759.

14. S. Johnson, "Casualties of Peace," 95.

15. Col. Robertson in Maj. Gen. Gates's letter of March 10, 1764, PRO CO5/540, 40; Tonyn to Dartmouth, August 31, 1775, PRO CO5/555, 220.

16. J. Bartram, *Diary*, 33.

17. Schafer, "Governor James Grant's Villa," 7, 10; Schafer, "St. Augustine's British Years," 191.

18. Moultrie to Hillsborough, June 29, 1771, PRO CO5/552, 101–2.

19. PRO CO5/555, 220.

20. Patrick, *Florida Fiasco*, 107, 136, 140.

21. Deagan and MacMahon, *Fort Mose*, 24, 40–41.

22. Deagan, *Explore* (University of Florida), Fall 2004, 15; Deagan, "Runaway Slaves," 30–31.

23. Gordon, *Florida's Colonial Architectural Heritage*, chap. 8; Schafer, *Anna Kingsley.*

CHAPTER 13. *Voices in the Spanish Cathedral*

Epigraph source: Fairbanks, *History and Antiquities*, 173–74.

1. Rocque to Royal Accounting Office, St. Augustine, "List of the utensils that are needed to begin the building," August 21, 1792, in E. Lawson, *Correspondence of the Bishops*, vol. 1, nos. 91 and 99; Ysnardy to Governor Nepomuceno de Quesada, April 11, 1793, and Rocque to Governor Nepomuceno Quesada, May 22, 1793, both letters in E. Lawson, *Correspondence of the Bishops*, vol. 1, no numbers. Fairbanks's estimate in *History and Antiquities* is on 173–74.

2. Rocque, 1784 Annual Report, EFP, Reel 73; Gordon, *Florida's Colonial Architectural Heritage*, 104–10.

3. Rocque, 1790 "Plano de la Yglesia Parroquial de San Agustín de la Florida Oriental," June 2, 1790, AGI 19 and AGI 184–85, copy at SAHS-RL; Hassett to Governor

Manuel de Zespedes, August 16, 1787, and reply, same date, and Bishop Cyrillo to Governor Manuel de Zespedes, September 7, 1788, and Hassett to Governor Nepomuceno de Quesada, July 17, 1790, in E. Lawson, *Correspondence of the Bishops*, vol. 1, no number. British Statehouse conversion is in Gordon, *Florida's Colonial Architectural Heritage*, 107–8.

4. Rocque to Governor Nepomuceno de Quesada, May 22, 1793, in E. Lawson, *Correspondence of the Bishops*, vol. 1, no number; Ysnardy to Quesada, May 10, 1793, n. 101 (no signature); Ysnardy, Seguí, Fleming to governor, Mar 23, 1793, EFP Bundle 10018, Doc. 1, and governor to Rocque, EFP Bundle 171, Doc. 134—documents translated and kindly shared by Susan Parker, Jan 19, 2006.

5. Rocque, in E. Lawson, *Correspondence of the Bishops*, vol. 1, no. 101, and an undated slip of paper.

6. Rocque to Governor, June 6, 1793, EFP Bundle 171, Doc. 147; Berrio to Governor, June 17, 1793, EFP Bundle 171, Doc. 176, 179. Susan Parker found and translated these sources.

7. Quesada to Rocque, EFP Bundle 171, Doc. 134 courtesy of Susan Parker. HABS drawings, Survey No. 15–17, August 2, 1934. Rocque may have added 16 feet, not 19½ feet.

8. E. Lawson, *Correspondence of the Bishops*, vol. 1, no. 58.

9. Rocque to Quesada, in two letters both dated May 22, 1793, in E. Lawson, *Correspondence of the Bishops*, vol. 1, no number.

10. O'Reilly's house is owned by the Sisters of St. Joseph and open to the public.

11. For Hassett and O'Reilly, see Gannon, *Cross in the Sand*, 89–92, 108. For Rocque, see Ware, "Marino de la Rocque, Military Engineer: Two Files of Documents with Introduction by John D. Ware," typeset manuscript, SAHS-RL; Rocque to Quesada, June 6, 1793, EFP Bundle 171, No. 171. For Berrio, see Diaz Berrio to Quesada, June 17, 1793, EFP Bundle 171: 176, 179. For Ysnardy, see Arana, "Burials in the Cathedral," 15, 16–17, 21. Ysnardy's vault was found under the altar of St. Joseph after the church fire in 1887, but after the Renwick restoration and the 1965 alterations, the site of his burial became unknown.

12. Ysnardy to Quesada, April 11, 1793, in E. Lawson, *Correspondence of the Bishops*, vol. 1, no number; Berrio to Quesada, EFP, Bundle 171, Doc. 179.

13. O'Reilly to White, October 31, 1801, in E. Lawson, *Correspondence of the Bishops*, vol. 1, no. 207.

14. List of ornaments, August 11, 1793, and Bill of Lading, October 1, 1794, and correspondence between Don Juan Francisco Oliden y Arriola (administrator general of the Royal Company of Havana) and Governor Nepomuceno de Quesada, and Don Villanueve, from October 1794 to July 1795, in E. Lawson, *Correspondence of the Bishops*, vol. 2, nos. 117, 118, 134.

15. O'Reilly to Governor White, Dec 20, 1797, in E. Lawson, *Correspondence of the Bishops*, vol. 1, no number.

16. Florida Master Site File 8SJ63; Manucy, *Cathedral Site Report*, 5; Gannon, *Cross in the Sand*, 109.

17. Library of Congress, Manuscript Division, José Ignacio Rodríguez Papers, 1860–1907, copy at SAHS-RL. A delegation had come to St. Augustine to rent Varela a house, but they arrived too late and used the funds to build his tomb. Rodríguez

wanted an image of exactly where he died and asked the delegation for the sketch. He wrote *Vida del Presbitero Don Felix Varela* in 1878. Verot was buried in Tolomato Cemetery (the former site of an Indian mission), and reinterred in Havana, Cuba, in 1911. This information is courtesy of Charles Tingley, senior research librarian, SAHS.

18. *St. Augustine Examiner,* June 8, 1867, 3.

19. Governor White to O'Reilly, October 31, 1801, in E. Lawson, *Correspondence of the Bishops,* vol. 2, no. 207. Devil painting, ca. 1880, is in Dereck Coghlan, "Theodore Whitney: St. Augustine's Boy Publisher," *El Escribano* 44 (2007): 105; Gannon, *Cross in the Sand,* 110.

20. Graham, *Flagler's St. Augustine Hotels,* 14, 27; Graham, *Hotel Ponce de Leon,* 13; Akin, *Flagler,* 116.

21. *Florida Times-Union,* April 21, and April 23, 1887.

22. Cotter to Renwick, and Renwick to Cotter, September 1888, copies at SAHS-RL.

23. *Florida Times-Union,* April 21 and 23, 1887; HABS Survey 15–17, August 2, 1934.

24. Cotter correspondence, August, 1888, SAHS-RL; Elizabeth Kimball Oliver, "A Bostonian and His Moorish Castle," *East-Florida Gazette,* 15, no. 3 (July 1995): 3.

25. Coomes, "Basilica Cathedral," 41; Davis, *Cathedral Basilica,* 10.

26. *Florida Catholic,* March 18, 1966.

27. Arana, "Burials in the Cathedral." For Menorcan history, see P. Griffin, *Mullet on the Beach.*

28. Cathedral and Renwick files, SAHS-RL; Davis, *Cathedral Basilica,* 8–17.

29. Michael Gannon, professor emeritus of history, University of Florida, from his address to the student body at the University of Florida, September 14, 2001, following the terrorist attack on the New York City World Trade Center towers.

CHAPTER 14. *The Magic of Architecture*

Epigraph source: Hale, *The Old Way of Seeing,* 144.

1. The Adams-Onis Treaty of cession had been negotiated in 1819 but was not ratified until 1821. Flags were exchanged in St. Augustine on July 10, 1821, and on July 17 in Pensacola.

2. Map of the state of Florida, published in London, April 1, 1832, by J. T. Hinton & Simpkin & Marshall.

3. Baptist, *Creating an Old South,* 145; J. Smith, *Slavery and Plantation Growth,* 16–17, 27; Morris, *Florida Handbook, 1949–1950,* 244.

4. Tocqueville, *Democracy in America,* 1:319.

5. Carswell, *Holmes Valley,* 38, 97; Chase, *Pioneer Churches,* 4–5; Baptist, *Creating an Old South,* 236–37; Lilla Ross, "Recalling the Circuit Riders," *Florida Times-Union,* February 3, 1995, A–12; Dibble, "Religion on Frontiers," 1–23. Peniel Church is preserved and is now a Sunday school.

6. Chase, *Pioneer Churches,* 4–40; Carswell, *Holmes Valley,* 43, 53–55; Baptist, *Creating an Old South,* 146; Clark, *Historic Tour Guide,* 87; Bigelow, "Historical Sketches"; Blair Reeves, FAIA, conversation with the author, April 2009.

7. Harner, *Florida's Promoters*, 60–64; "Miami and the Story of Its Remarkable Growth, An Interview with George E. Merrick," *New York Times*, March 15, 1925.

8. Longstreth, *On the Edge*, 229, 241, 258–95; Gelernter, *American Architecture*, 203.

9. Longstreth, *On the Edge*, 243, 385 n. 34.

10. Dunlop and Schezen, *Miami: Trends*, 16–17; Curl, *Mizner's Florida*, 54–56.

11. Kathryn A. Flynn, "New Appreciation for the New Deal—and Why We Need That Now!" *Forum News*, National Trust for Historic Preservation, July–August 2009, 1–3.

12. Howey, *Sarasota School of Architecture*.

13. *Forum*, Magazine of the Florida Humanities, 28–33; Pérez and Ennemoser, *Florida Cuban Heritage Trail*, 30–31; Elizabeth Owens, *Cassadaga, Florida, Yesterday and Today*, 4th rev. ed. (Cassadaga: Pisces, 2001).

14. Fernald and Purdum, *Atlas*, 109.

15. Mike Vogel, "Big Box Worship," *Florida Trend*, December 2005, 84–89.

CHAPTER 15. *Frontier Forerunners*

Epigraph source: Tocqueville, *Democracy in America*, I, 319.

1. "Seminole" was a name applied to people of various tribes of southeastern Creeks—some had intermarried with native Timucua, Apalachee, Guale, and Black Seminoles (escaped black slaves) (Stojanowski, "Unhappy Trails," 44; Rivers, *Slavery in Florida*, 189–209).

2. Pierson, *American Buildings*, 1:206–460.

3. *Episcopal Recorder*, November 12, 1831, 132; Cushman, *Goodly Heritage*, 6, 9, and see xi, 1–2 for a brief introduction to the American Episcopal church and the Church of England).

4. *Episcopal Recorder*, November 21, 1831, 132; Cushman, *Goodly Heritage*, 6, 80; Trinity Church, Master Site File; Old Christ Church, HABS, Nr. FLA 146.

5. The committee noted in the *Herald* that it would be accepting the "lowest" bid, made by Joseph L. Smith, A. Dupont, and T. Douglass.

6. *Episcopal Recorder*, November 12, 1831, 132.

7. New York's Trinity (its second building) was torn down in 1839, and the third Gothic Revival Trinity was designed by Richard Upjohn, the architect who would become pivotal in the building of Florida's Carpenter Gothic churches after the Civil War (chapter 16).

8. E. Upjohn, *Richard Upjohn*, vi, 14, 47–67; Pierson, *American Buildings*, 2:2, 113–48, 152–53, 173; W. Andrews, *American Gothic*.

9. Knetsch and Vojnovski, "Peter Mitchel," 47.

10. *Episcopal Recorder*, November 12, 1831, 132. Regarding Peter Mitchel as a vestryman, see Strock, *By Faith*, 10. His qualifications as a church designer are not known. In Pennsylvania, Bishop John Henry Hopkins designed Pittsburgh's Trinity Episcopal Church (1825) with a crenellated Gothic tower and walls and pinnacles; Hopkins was frequently asked for church designs at this time (see Pierson, *American Buildings*, 2:170).

11. Engraved depiction of the 1830 church design in the *Episcopal Recorder*, November 12, 1831, 132; Cushman, *Goodly Heritage*, 6.

12. *St. Augustine Weekly News*, December 21(?), 1889. At this time, a new small aisle was run east-west perpendicular to the north-south aisle, and the chancel was moved to the southeast end.

13. *Florida Herald & Southern Democrat*, October 23, 1843, 2; Mrs. E. W. Lawson, ca. May 1939, for the *St. Augustine Record*, in the files of G. M. Strock and SAHS-RL; HABS FL110 drawing of the 1840s porch (date on the drawing is in error).

14. *St. Augustine Examiner*, September 29, 1866, and February 22, 1867, quoted in Cushman, *Goodly Heritage*, 61.

15. Wood, *Jacksonville's Architectural Heritage*, 48, 199.

16. *Episcopal Recorder*, November 21, 1831, 132; the former bishop's house and British Statehouse are described in Gordon, *Florida's Colonial Architectural Heritage*; foundation stones are mentioned in Mrs. Lawson's paper (see n. 13), and the coquina stone in today's walls were observed during a recent restoration and were photographed by the author of this volume.

17. Wren, 1632–1723, designed fifty-one churches after the Great Fire of 1666.

18. Handlin, *American Architecture*, figs. 22, 31; Sommer, *Old Church Book*, 15, 95.

19. Cushman, *Goodly Heritage*, 9, 80; Beverly Madison Currin, "A Brief History of Old Christ Church in the 19th Century," www.christ-church.net/oldcc.htm.

20. R. Smith, "Carpenter Gothic," 77. Haight's papers are archived at the Avery Architectural Library and the New York Public Library.

21. Beverly Madison Currin, "A Brief History of Old Christ Church in the 19th Century," typeset manuscript, copy at SAHS-RL.

22. For examples, see Asher Benjamin's *The American Builder's Companion* and *The Practical House Carpenter; Builder's Guide*. Asher Benjamin (1773–1845) published practical instructional guides and pattern books in many editions between 1806–57. Minard Lafever's *Modern Builder's Guide* had seven printings between 1833 and 1855 (Lane, *Architecture of the Old South*, 242; Scully, *Shingle Style*, xxvi).

23. J. Smith, *Slavery and Plantation Growth*, 17; Baptist, *Creating an Old South*; Rosalie Rodrigues, "Richard A. Shine," 7; Historic Marker.

24. HABS FLA 162; NR nomination, 1974.

25. Cushman, *Goodly Heritage*, 22; Chase, *Pioneer Churches*, 20; J. Smith, *Slavery and Plantation Growth*, 160, 169; Hamlin, *Greek Revival*, 151; Pierson, *American Buildings*, vol. 1, chap. 10.

26. *Distyle-in-muris* is in Brownell et al., *Making of Virginia Architecture*, 67, 442; Hamlin, *Greek Revival*, 151.

27. HABS Fla-151; Microfilm UF NA 705 H571 1920, No. 7 of 21, marked "Escambia"; Church document; "Off the Wall, Photographs and Icons, Trinity Church"; Fred Sawyer, "A Brief History of Trinity Episcopal Church, Apalachicola, Florida," manuscript (F.2 F83 A6392b), Library East, University of Florida; Cushman, *Goodly Heritage*, 55, 133.

28. Cushman, *Goodly Heritage*, 12–13, 21, 44.

29. J. Smith, *Slavery and Plantation Growth*, 114.

30. Cushman, *Goodly Heritage*, 10, 29–30, 96–97, 106–7, 126.

31. Master Site File, 8LE331, Tallahassee; NR Nomination, 1978.

32. Methodists had entered America in the Chesapeake region in the 1760s and were baptized and took communion in Anglican churches until 1784 when the

Methodist Episcopal Church was formed and began its tradition of building Methodist houses of worship designed to reflect Wesleyan egalitarianism. Until then, poorer, nonelite white Methodists sat on rough open benches at the rear of the church behind wealthy families in enclosed ornate pews (see Christopher H. Owen, "By Design: The Social Meaning of Methodist Church Architecture in Nineteenth-Century Georgia," *Georgia Historical Quarterly* 75, no. 2 [Summer 1991]: 223–24).

33. Brooks, *From Saddlebags to Satellites*, 34; NR Nomination, 1986; Historic Site Marker; Church Scrapbook, and interviews with Edna Macdonald, church historian; Lila Ross, "Recalling the Circuit Riders," *Florida Times-Union*, February 3, 1995, A–12; T. E. Ray, "History of the Middleburg Methodist Church, Middleburg, Florida, 1823–1947," manuscript, 1952.

34. Chase, *Pioneer Churches*, 4; Carswell, *Holmes Valley*, 31–59; NR Nomination, 1983; Reeves, *Guide*, 15.

35. NR Nomination, 1974; Historic Site Marker; Brooks, *From Saddlebags to Satellites*, 35.

36. *Gadsden County Times*, January 30, 1936, and May 4, 1978, 16; Florida Master Site File, Department of State, Division of Archives, History and Records Management, Tallahassee.

37. LaGrange Church website and Historic Site Marker.

CHAPTER 16. *Post Civil War*

Epigraph source: W. Andrews, *American Gothic*, 139.

1. Trinity Church in New York (1790) was an early Gothic Revival church in America. Benjamin Henry Latrobe is said to have designed the first serious Gothic structure in America—a house in 1799 known as "Sedgeley" for William Crammond of Philadelphia (see W. Andrews, *American Gothic*, 25). For additional reading about the Civil War in Florida and postwar Florida, see Gannon, *New History*, chapter 13, "The Civil War, 1861–1865," by Canter Brown Jr., and chapter 14, "Reconstruction and Renewal, 1865–1877," by Jerrell H. Shofner, and chapter 15, "Prelude to the New Florida," by Samuel Proctor.

2. Pugin, in W. Andrews, *American Gothic*, 34, 36; Pierson, *American Builders*, 2:113–205; Cushman, *Goodly Heritage*, 94–96. A recently published book is Ryan K. Smith's *Gothic Arches, Latin Crosses: Anti-Catholicism and American Church Designs in the Nineteenth Century* (Chapel Hill: University of North Carolina Press, 2006).

3. R. Upjohn, *Upjohn's Rural Architecture*.

4. W. Andrews, *American Gothic*, 63; Pierson, *American Buildings*, 2:159, 173–205.

5. Cushman, *Goodly Heritage*, 155–62. Young arrived in Florida in 1845, and ministered at St. John's in Jacksonville and Trinity in St. Augustine. In 1860, he was made assistant rector at Trinity Church in New York, the third structure by that name, a landmark Gothic Revival church designed by Richard Upjohn in 1839–45. In 1867, at age forty-seven, Young was elected the Episcopal bishop of Florida, and would soon begin his river missions.

6. NR Nomination, 1973; Bronson Files, SAHS-RL; *Historical Sketch of St. Mark's Episcopal Church*, signed M. F. P., brochure at the church; Clark, *Historic Tour Guide*, 17.

7. A list of Upjohn projects is in E. Upjohn, *Richard Upjohn*.

8. Cushman, *Goodly Heritage*, 55, 111, 112.

9. Gordon, *Florida's Colonial Architectural Heritage*, 202; NR Nomination, 1973; McKee, "St. Margaret's Church, Hibernia, Florida," 2, unpublished church history.

10. J. Griffin, "Preliminary Report," 61–66; Wood, *Jacksonville's Architectural Heritage*, 310–11.

11. Terence H. E. Webb, "St. George's Episcopal Church of Fort George Island, Florida," unpublished church history, 1–8; R. Smith, "Carpenter Gothic," 81–84; Clark, *Historic Tour Guide*, 80; WPA Records Survey.

12. Lynch, *George Rainsford Fairbanks*, 2–5, 13–14, 20; Gannon, introduction to Fairbanks's *History and Antiquities*, xxviii–xxiv; interview by the author with his granddaughter Nancy Hines, 1980.

13. Wood, *Jacksonville's Architectural Heritage*, 319 FG-7, 346 NB-1; Centennial Committee, *Trinity Episcopal Church, Melrose, Florida 1881–1891*, Committee, 1981; Reeves, *Guide*, 53; Cushman, *Goodly Heritage*, 125. A larger Grace Church was built in the 1960s in the Carpenter Gothic style by Clyde Harris (Fran Quaritius, interview by the author at Grace, 2001).

14. R. Scott, *Gothic Enterprise*, 108–9.

15. R. Upjohn, *Upjohn's Rural Architecture*; Downing, *Victorian Cottage Residences*, 13–14, 219; Pierson, *American Builders*, 2:436; Scully, *Shingle Style*, xxxiii.

16. Visit to Christ Episcopal Church, December 3, 2011.

17. Cushman, *Goodly Heritage*, 127, 178; NR Nomination, 1978; St. Mary's Church Master Site File 8C135, Tallahassee; R. Smith, "Carpenter Gothic," 77–78; *Where to Go in Florida*, by Daniel F. Tyler, pamphlet, 1881, 34; Historic Marker.

18. Cushman, *Goodly Heritage*, 167.

19. "One Hundredth Anniversary," First Presbyterian Church of Green Cove Springs, Florida, 1884–1984," unpublished church history.

20. *Holy Cross Episcopal Church 1873–1973: The Mother Church of Central Florida*, pamphlet prepared for the Centennial Celebration, 1973; Arthur E. Francke Jr., "Early Days of Seminole County, Fla.," Seminole County Historical Commission, 7–9.

21. Cushman, *Goodly Heritage*, 178, 180, and *Sound of Bells*, 43–44; Reeves, *Guide*, 94; Beatrice Wilder, "The British Connection: Central Florida's Early Colonists," *Timelines*, November 2004, 8–9, Central Florida Episcopalian, www.cfdiocese.org; site visit by Charles Tingley, Fall 2011.

22. Cushman, *Sound of Bells*, 59–60; Beatrice Wilder, "The British Connection: Central Florida's Early Colonists," *Timelines*, November 2004, 9, Central Florida Episcopalian, www.cfdiocese.org; NR Nomination, 1974.

23. Bishop Edwin Gardner Weed's address is quoted from the *Minutes of 51st Annual Council of the Diocese of Florida*, 1894, p. 9, courtesy of Charles Tingley.

24. Reeves, *Guide*, 9; NR Nomination, 1982.

25. Akron Plans facilitated the congregation with efficient traffic flow between their worship and Sunday school. The first plan appeared in Akron, Ohio, in 1872 at the First Methodist Episcopal Church, after which it was popularized in pattern books of the late nineteenth and early twentieth centuries. Winter Park's Methodist Episcopal Church was another Florida example.

26. Bishop Weed, *Minutes of 51st Annual Council of the Diocese of Florida, 1894*, p. 9; Wood, *Jacksonville's Architectural Heritage*, 260–61.

27. Printed church history by John A. Moore, obtained at the church.

28. Mandarin Museum and Historical Society.

29. Cushman, *Goodly Heritage*, 178, and *Sound of Bells*, 28–52; R.O. Jones, "Florida's Carpenter Gothic Episcopal Churches," multiple property listing, NR Nomination, 1997; Beatrice Wilder, Episcopal diocesan historiographer, "The British Connection: Central Florida's Early Colonists," *Timelines*, Central Florida Episcopalian, www.cfdiocese.org.

30. Heimovics and Zerivitz, *Florida Jewish Heritage Trail*, 17.

31. Earenfight, *A Kiowa's Odyssey*, 94 fig. 89, 130; 1884 Sanborn Map.

32. Henry Pratt Papers, MSS S-1174, Box 32: 32, Yale Collection of Western Americana.

CHAPTER 17. *Changing Directions on New Frontiers*

Epigraph source: Boehm, *Conversations with I. M. Pei*, 18, 75.

1. Flagler's "Riviera" and "Newport of the South" are in Akin, *Flagler*, 116; Longstreth, *On the Edge*, 30, 62.

2. Clark, *Historic Tour Guide*, 29; Dowda, *History of Palatka*, 172; Gladys Jacoway, Presbyterian Church historian, "Highlights of Our Church History, The Beginnings (1855–1881)." Jacoway reported that Hunt's role in the design of the Palatka church was discovered by the archivist of the Biltmore House, North Carolina, but a citation is lacking; Maddex, *Master Builders*, 88–89.

3. Graham, *Flagler's St. Augustine Hotels*, 15–16, 56–57; Conduit, "Pioneer Concrete," 128–33; E. K. Oliver, "A Bostonian and His Moorish Castle," *East-Florida Gazette*, July 1995, 3. Memorial's blueprints have been conserved, stabilized, and digitized at the University of Florida in collaboration with Flagler College. The Hotel Ponce de Leon was the first large commercial building to be built of concrete. See also Ellen W. Kramer and Aly A. Raafat, "The Ward House: A Pioneer Structure of Reinforced Concrete," *JSAH* 20, no. 1 (March 1961): 34–37. Timothy Johnson, professor of religion at Flagler College, suggests Memorial's floor plan might have been influenced by the Akron Plan (correspondence with the author, June 4, 2011).

4. "The Beautiful Memorial," *Florida Times-Union*, March 16, 1890; David Nolan, Flagler Memorial Presbyterian Church Master Site File, Tallahassee; Poppeliers, "Report on the Memorial Presbyterian Church," St. Augustine, 1965, HABS Fl-170; *The Flagler Story and Memorial Church*, 1949, by the Memorial Church Society; "Cross Back on Top," *St. Augustine Record*, December 12, 1992.

5. McKim, Mead & White, *Architecture of McKim, Mead & White in Photographs, Plans, and Elevations*, plates 31, 32.

6. Dunlop and Schezen, *Miami: Trends*, 16–17.

7. Maybeck's reputation was made in California after he left Carrère and Hastings. He received the American Institute of Architecture Gold Medal. As to his contribution in St. Augustine, see Graham, *Flagler's St. Augustine Hotels*, 34–35; Longstreth, *On the Edge*, 366 nn. 40–42; Jordy, *American Buildings*, 4: 281.

8. Mumford, *Roots of Contemporary*, 130; Reiss, *Architectural Details*, 226; Handlin, *American Architecture*, 115–16.

9. Pierson, *American Buildings*, 2:261; Handlin, *American Architecture*, 116–21; Wood, *Jacksonville's Architectural Heritage*, 11, 28–29, 45; Broward, *Architecture of Henry John Klutho*, 28–29. See also Jeanne Halgren Kilde, *When Church Became Theater: The Transformation of Evangelical Architecture and Worship in Nineteenth-Century America* (2005).

10. Author's 2010 visit to Sacred Heart Church.

11. Ordinance No. 3686-03 September 2, 2003, approving St. Ann's Roman Catholic Church Complex as a Historic District in Palm Beach; Gannon, *Florida Catholic Heritage Trail*, 39; Catholic Diocese website: www.diocesepb.org; Patricios, *Building Marvelous Miami*, 177.

12. "The Oldest Church in the U.S.A.," *Anglican Digest* (4th quarter A.D. 1979): 3–8; Patricios, *Building Marvelous Miami*, 211–12; Folsom, *More Great American Mansions*, 93–97. The developers may have been E. Raymond Moss and William S. Edgemon. Von Simson, *Gothic Cathedral*, 25.

13. Harner, *Florida's Promoters*, 15–16, 22; Grunwald, *The Swamp*.

14. Carl Fisher created Miami Beach (Harner, *Florida's Promoters*, 63).

15. Pérez and Ennemoser, *Florida Cuban Heritage Trail*, 26.

16. Ellen Uguccioni, "The City of Coral Gables," in *Florida History & the Arts* (Summer 2004): 7–9; Harner, *Florida's Promoters*, 66; Patricios, *Building Marvelous Miami*, 195–96.

17. Dunlop and Schezen, *Miami: Trends*, 17, 40: Capitman, *Deco Delights*, 34; Patricios, *Building Marvelous Miami*, 198

18. Dunlop and Schezen, *Miami: Trends*, 16–17.

19. Wood, *Jacksonville's Architectural Heritage*, 141; Curl, *Mizner's Florida*, 169–71.

20. Patricios, *Building Marvelous Miami*, 208; Heimovics and Zerivitz, *Florida Jewish Heritage Trail*, 38; St. Mary website.

21. Betsky, review of *Ralph Adams Cram*, 438; Pierson, *American Buildings*, 2:264; Gelernter, *American Architecture*, 204; Campen, *Winter Park Portrait*. For additional reading, see Cram, *My Life in Architecture* (Boston: Little, Brown, 1936). His drawings of Knowles Chapel are at the Avery Library, Columbia University.

22. William Dayton, "Pasco Pioneers: Catholic Settlements in San Antonio, St. Leo and Vicinity," *Tampa Bay History* 1, no. 2 (Fall–Winter 1979): 32–38.

23. *A Souvenir of the Abbey Church of Saint Leo in Florida* (St. Leo, Fla.: Abbey Press, 1950); www.saintleoabbey.org.

24. Bishop Weed, report, April 3, 1904, *Diocese of Florida, 60th Annual Council*, 61–62.

25. Longstreth, *On the Edge*, 259–60, 263–64.

26. Dade County Historic Survey, Site Inventory File; *The History of Plymouth Congregational Church*, church brochure; NR Nomination, 1974; Patricios, *Building Marvelous Miami*, 207–8; Pat Griffin (Harry Griffin's daughter-in-law), interview by the author, November 2010.

27. The basilica's history is quoted from its website. For St. Peter's in Rome, see Scotti, *Basilica*, 249.

28. *The WPA Guide to Florida* lists Hiss and Weekes as architects, 232; Hoffstot, *Landmark Architecture*, 37; HABS Fla 50-Palm 2.

29. Wood, *Jacksonville's Architectural Heritage*, 47.

30. *Florida Preservation News*, July–August, 1992, 3; Cushman, *Sound of Bells*, 20; Jefferson B. Browne, *Key West, The Old and the New*, facsimile ed. (1912; Gainesville: University of Florida Press, 1973), 28–33.

31. *Preservation*, November–December 2009, 7; *Florida Black Heritage Trail*, 20, 29.

32. Wood, *Jacksonville's Architectural Heritage*, 66.

33. *Florida Preservation News*, May–June 1992, 9; St. James AME NR Nomination, 1992; Winsberg, *Florida's History*, 30; St. John's NR Nomination, 1992.

34. Wood, *Jacksonville's Architectural Heritage*, 8, 224, 359.

35. See the list of buildings and their architects in Capitman, *Deco Delights*, 35.

36. Heimovics and Zerivitz, *Florida Jewish Heritage Trail*, 36, 37, 39; NR Nomination, 1980. For more on Hohauser, see Capitman, *Deco Delights*.

37. Maitland Art Center, NR Nomination, 1982; Winsberg, *Florida's History*, 87. For Mayan motifs on Art Deco buildings in Miami Beach, see Capitman, *Deco Delights*.

38. Kaufmann, *Fallingwater*, 18.

39. *WPA Guide to Florida*, 517.

40. Siry, "Frank Lloyd Wright's Annie M. Pfeiffer Chapel," 498–539; Lawrence Biemiller, "Echoes of Jefferson in a Campus Designed by Frank Lloyd Wright," *Chronicle of Higher Education*, April 15, 1992, B4, B5; Arthur Lubow, "The Triumph of Frank Lloyd Wright," *Smithsonian*, June 2009, 52–61. Annie M. Pfeiffer of New York City was its principal donor.

41. Siry, "Frank Lloyd Wright's Annie M. Pfeiffer Chapel," 498–539; Zimny, "Child of the Sun," 10; Keller, "Wright's Stuff," 74.

42. Seibert, quoted in *Sarasota Herald-Tribune*, October 27, 2001.

43. Howey, *Sarasota School of Architecture*.

44. Leedy, in Zimny, "Only Yesterday," 10–11.

45. Howey, *Sarasota School of Architecture*, 90, 95 fig. 6.44.

46. Brownell et al., *Making of Virginia Architecture*, 380.

47. Edward Bok, *America's Taj Mahal: The Singing Tower of Florida* (unpaginated); Zimny, "One Man's Gift," 12–17. The marble was quarried in Tate, Georgia (Georgia Marble Company). Frederick Law Olmsted Jr. (1870–1957) was a partner in the Olmsted Brothers firm following the death of his father in 1903 (Mumford, *Roots of Contemporary American Architecture*, 423).

48. Fay Jones won the Twenty-Five-Year Award of the American Institute of Architects in 2006 for his innovation and significant influence on American architecture.

49. Baughman was the first president of New College in Sarasota.

50. Fig. 224, in Handlin, *American Architecture*, 252

51. Amy Keller, "Leap of Faith," *Florida Trend*, September 2007, 60–66; Pierson, *American Buildings* 2:94; Ivy, *Fay Jones*, 32–65.

52. DPZ website: www.dpz.com/project/goodshepherdcatholic church; Bailey, Greer, and Howey, *Florida Architecture*, 179.

53. Pei, quoted in Gero von Boehm, *Conversations with I. M. Pei*, 18, 75. In 1965, Pei designed several buildings for the campus of New College of Florida, in Sarasota.

CHAPTER 18. *Civic Adornment*

Epigraph source: Boorstin, *The Creators*, 76.

1. As late as 1927, under its clock tower, residents could read weather and market reports on a blackboard at the Old Hendry County Courthouse in LaBelle.

2. Lake City's Old Columbia County Courthouse (1875) is wood, and was moved in 1902 and made into a rooming house (Reeves, *Guide*, 49). Lafayette County's wood courthouse in Mayo (1893) was moved in 1909. It is a large building with verandas and has been restored by several owners as a residence and bed-and-breakfast (author's 2010 conversation with Pat Griffin, a former owner with her husband, John).

3. Osceola County Courthouse NR Nomination, 1977; Winsberg, *Florida's History*, 90; Reeves, *Guide*, 92–93.

4. *The Museum of Art and History: The Custom House*, pamphlet of Key West Art and Historical Society, 1992; Key West Custom House NR Nomination, 1973; Winsberg, *Florida's History*, xii, 82; Reeves, *Guide*, 142–43; *Florida Preservation News*, March–April 1992, 1, and July–August 1992, 3.

5. Bradford County ourthouse NR Nomination, 1974; Calhoun County courthouse NR Nomination, 1980; Winsberg, *Florida's History*, 7, 13; Reeves, *Guide*, 22–23, 52–53.

6. Hamilton County courthouse NR Nomination 1983; Winsberg, *Florida's History*, 51; Reeves, *Guide*, 43.

7. See Richard Guy Wilson's introduction in McKim, Mead & White, *Architecture of McKim Mead & White*, ix–xii.

8. Broward, *Architecture of Henry John Klutho*, 31.

9. Poppeliers, Chambers, and Schwartz, *What Style Is It?*, 66.

10. Palladio, *Andrea Palladio: The Four Books of Architecture*.

11. Patricios, *Building Marvelous Miami*, 165; Nassau County courthouse NR Nomination, 1973; Fernandina Beach's Old U.S. Post Office and Courthouse NR District Nomination, 1983; Miami's Old U.S. Post Office and Courthouse NR Nomination, 1989; Winsberg, *Florida's History*, 29.

12. Reeves, *Guide*, 7.

13. Author's site visits; NR Nominations; Reeves, *Guide*, 39, 47, 97, 99, 103; Winsberg, *Florida's History*, 16; *History of Jefferson County, Florida*, a WPA project 1934–35, printed by Jefferson County in 1958, 140.

14. Pierson, *American Buildings*, 1:248–51.

15. WPA Survey, Walton County, Division of Historical Resources, Florida Department of State; NR Nominations; Reeves, *Guide*, 11; Winsberg, *Florida's History*, 132; on-site visit by Roy Hunt, November 2011.

16. Reeves, *Guide*, 7; *Florida Preservation News*, July–August 1992, 3.

17. Reeves, *Guide*, 119; Winsberg, *Florida's History*, 119; Sarasota Historical Commission Marker, 2001.

18. A photograph of the Strickland building is in Handlin, *American Architecture*, 59 fig. 52; Patricios, *Building Marvelous Miami*, 196–97.

19. Johnston, "Historic Stetson University," 295–96; *WPA Guide to Florida*, 282; FAMU Carnegie Library NR Nomination, 1978. Three of the twelve Carnegie Li-

braries have been demolished: in Gainesville, Ocala, and Bartow (Lawrence Webster and Barratt Wilkins, "A Lasting Legacy," *Florida History & the Arts*, Summer 2000, 16–19).

20. Reeves, *Guide*, 107, 117; Winsberg, *Florida's History*, 59, 99; Zimny, "Gulf Coast Culture." *Florida Heritage*, Summer 1996, photograph p. 19.

21. Broward, *Architecture of Henry John Klutho*, 29–33, 56–57, 59–61; Wood, *Jacksonville's Architectural Heritage*, 31; Clark, *Historic Tour Guide*, 24; *Florida History & the Arts*, Winter 2005, 9.

22. Tampa City Hall NR Nomination, 1974; Winsberg, *Florida's History*, 59; Capitman, *Deco Delights*, 70–71; Reeves, *Guide*, 105; Patricios, *Building Marvelous Miami*, 182–83, 271–74, 273 fig. 244.

23. Dade County Courthouse NR Nomination 1989; Winsberg, *Florida's History*, 25; Patricios, *Building Marvelous Miami*, 173, 183.

24. Reeves, *Guide*, 105. For "Old Is the New Green," see *Preservation*, March–April 2010.

25. Schultze and Weaver also designed the Rooney Plaza Hotel in Miami Beach, the Breakers Hotel in Palm Beach, the Havana Biltmore, and the Waldorf Astoria and Grand Central Station in New York.

26. NR Nomination, 1979; NHL Nomination, 2008; Matkov, "Selling City's Heritage to the Highest Bidder," 3; Uguccioni; "Uniting the Past and Future," 3; *Florida Preservationist* 4, no. 1 (Winter 2006): 1; *Florida History & the Arts* (Summer 2003): 14, and (Winter 2009): 6.

27. Krista Walton, "The Big Reveal," *Preservation*, May–June, 2009, 36–37.

28. Flynn, "New Appreciation," 1–3; Florida Memory website: New Deal WPA Architecture, "A Guide to New Deal Records at the State Archives;" Zimny, "New Art, New Deal," 14–19.

29. Willoughby Marshall of Apalachicola kindly supplied the name of the architect, builder, and date. A photograph of the old Romanesque courthouse is in the state archives.

30. Reeves, *Guide*, 49, 107; Winsberg, *Florida's History*, 49; Capitman, *Deco Delights*, 66; *WPA Guide to Florida*, 109; Patricios, *Building Marvelous Miami*, 183; *Preservation*, July–August 2008, 45.

31. Capitman, *Deco Delights*, 95; Bass Museum website.

32. Daytona Beach Post Office NR Nomination, 1988; Winsberg, *Florida's History*, 126.

33. Susan R. Parker, "Overview of Use and Residents," draft manuscript, May 1994; personal correspondence with Jean Parker Waterbury, 2001; unpublished writings and correspondence by Janet Snyder Matthews, 2011; Gordon, *Florida's Colonial Architectural Heritage*, 89–94, 129–31; Schafer, "St. Augustine's British Years," 44–45.

34. Douglas, autobiography, 69–70, in Gordon, *Florida's Colonial Architectural Heritage*, 129.

35. Contract, John Rodman and Elias Wallen, House Report Number 223, 25th Cong., 3rd sess., copy at SAHS-RL.

36. Mellen C. Greeley to Bradley Gwinn Brewer, August 25, 1968, copied to author by Janet Snyder Matthews from the University of Florida Digital Collections, October 31, 2011.

37. See chapter 9 of this book.

38. Gordon, *Florida's Colonial Architectural Heritage*, 89–94, 129–30, figs. 4.36, 4.37; plate 13.

39. It is also known as the "Key West Extension" of Flagler's Florida East Coast Railway. P. Scott, *Hemingway's Hurricane*, 20–30; Akin, *Flagler*, 210–24; *WPA Guide to Florida*, 200.

40. P. Scott, *Hemingway's Hurricane*, 31–34, 43, 60, 200, 223, 227.

41. Ibid., 227.

CHAPTER 19. *Rescuing the Old State Capitol*

Epigraph source: Cather, *Death Comes for the Archbishop*, 270.

1. *Florida's Historic Capitol: A Status Report, 1978*, prepared by Division of Archives History & Records Management, Bureau of Historic Sites & Properties, Historic Preservation Section, Miscellaneous Project Report Series, No. 42, April 1978, 7–10.

2. It is depicted in a drawing by a French artist, Francis, Conte de Castelnau, in *Vues et souvenirs de l'Amerique du Nord*, Library of Congress; Morris, *Florida Handbook 1965–1966*, 33–35; Schafer, "U.S. Territory and State," 210; Ewen, "Anhaica" 112–13; Warner, "Florida's Capitols," 245; Hann and McEwan, *Apalachee Indians and Mission San Luis*; Womack, *Gadsden*, 14.

3. Morris, *Florida Handbook 1949–1950*, 244; Morris, *Florida Handbook 1965–1966*, 35; Warner, "Florida's Capitols," 246–49; Morris, *Florida Handbook 1949–1950*, 244, 150–51, 160; Lane, *Architecture of the Old South: Louisiana*, 102–11; Galbraith and Miller, *Historical Documentary Research Project*, 97–99, 222–24, 229, 234; Brownell et al., *Making of Virginia Architecture*, 41; Charles Dakin, 1811–39, was in Mobile while James Dakin, 1806–52, managed the New Orleans office.

4. See chap. 15, n. 22.

5. Galbraith and Miller, *Historical Documentary Research Project*, 54, 219–29, 234; Warner, "Florida's Capitols," 244; Warner and Eastland, *Tallahassee: Downtown Transitions*, 64–66; Rodriguez, "Richard A. Shine," 13–14; brochure, Museum of Florida History, Division of Historical Resources, Florida Department of State.

6. *Florida's Historic Capitol: A Status Report, 1978*, 1–6. Milburn's wooden stairway to the dome and interior dome of art glass set in white iron frame were removed in the 1923 remodeling by Henry John Klutho.

7. Sam Miller, *Capitol*, a report for the Florida Department of State, 1982. For its report of restoration, see the Herschel E. Shepard, Jr. Collection at the University of Florida.

8. *Florida's Historic Capitol: A Status Report, 1978*, 1–6. Nothing remains of the enormous wings to the north and south, which were for the House of Representatives (1936) and the Senate (1947).

9. Morris, *Florida Handbook 1965–1966*, 104; McClane and McClane, *Architecture of James Gamble Rogers II*, 38–39; www.supremecourt.org.

CHAPTER 20. *New Battles Sound*

Epigraph source: Quoted in Diana Ketcham, "In the Studio with Peter Zumthor, Architecture's Swiss Mystic," *New York Times*, January 7, 1999. Zumthor won the 1998 Carlsberg Prize for Architecture, and the 2009 Pritzker Prize.

1. J. Bartram, *Diary*, 53; Waterbury, *Coquina*, booklet published by SAHS; *Old Spanish Quarry*, pamphlet published by the National Park Service and Florida Department of Environmental Protection.

2. Lyon, "First Three Wooden Forts"; Gordon, "From So Precious a Watering."

3. Waterbury, *Coquina*, booklet published by SAHS; *Old Spanish Quarry*, n. 1.

4. Roy Graham, director of the Center for World Heritage, Research and Stewardship, University of Florida, in "Pre-Submission Report to include the Castillo de San Marcos in the San Juan, Puerto Rico World Heritage Site," a draft of which, with his research, was shared with the author, on March 23, 2011.

5. Papers of Hernando de Mestas, AGI 140-7-37, copies at SAHS.

6. For Juan Calens, see the papers of Governor Juan Marques Cabrera, 1682, AGI 54-5-11/80; Arana and Manucy, *Building of Castillo*, 17–20, 26–29; Arana, "Defenses and Defenders," 27, 54, 56, 119, 152, 174; Chatelain, *Defenses*, 66; Gordon, *Florida's Colonial Architectural Heritage*, 238–45; Arnade, *Siege of St. Augustine in 1702*.

7. Arana, "Fort at Matanzas Inlet," 87, 133; Arana, "Notes on Fort Matanzas," 45.

8. Arana, "Notes on Fort Matanzas," 45–73.

9. David Ferro, preservation administrator, Florida Department of State, in *Florida History & the Arts* 9, no. 3 (Summer 2001): 21; Herschel Shepard, conversation with the author, October 25, 2011.

10. Gannon, "Florida's Seashell Castle," 18.

11. Coker, "Pensacola 1686–1763," 117–30. Fort San Carlos was named after the thirteen-year-old Charles of Austria, who became Charles VI of the Holy Roman Empire.

12. Gordon, *Florida's Colonial Architectural Heritage*, 73, 258–60; Faye, "British and Spanish Fortifications," 277–92, 286; McAlister, "Pensacola," 282, 291; Anderson, "Pensacola Forts," 1–25, 32, 36–61; Bearss, *Fort Barrancas*, 4–21; Newton and Reeves, *Historic Architecture*; Gauld, "A Survey of the Bay of Pensacola with part of Sta Rosa island etc., 1766," by Geo Gauld, PRO CO700/32; PRO CO5/597, pp. 29–31; Wm. Brasier *fecit*. T. Sowers, Engineer, PRO MPG 9 and MPD 194 (4), "Plan of the Entrance of Pensacola Harbour Shewing the Situation of the New Batteries," 1771, enclosure to General Gage's letter, August 5, 1772, T 1/493, f.230, and C.O. 5/89f.291; HABS No. Fl144 Batería de San Antonio.

13. Anderson, "Pensacola Forts," 72–131; Coleman and Coleman, *Pensacola Fortifications, 1698–1980*; National Park Service pamphlet; Pollock, "Fort Pickens, Guarding Pensacola Bay," *Florida Heritage*, Summer 1996.

14. Fort Jefferson's story is based on the author's visit to the fort and information collected at the site and in publications by and for the National Park Service. Carlos Harrison, "The Fort That Time Forgot," *Preservation*, November–December 2009, 31–32, 52–53.

15. T. Taylor, *Territorial Lighthouses*, 103–23, 292.

16. Shepard, "Construction," 6; NR Nomination, 1972; Reeves, *Guide*, 70; Bicentennial Commission of Florida, *The Florida Bicentennial Trail: A Heritage Revisited*, http://ufdc.ufl.edu/AM00000172/00001, 78–79.

17. Shepard, "Construction," 6. A copy of the complete research document from which this article is abstracted, titled "The Construction of Fort Clinch 1965, Herschel E. Shepard Jr., Architect" (unpublished), is at the P. K. Yonge Library, University of Florida, Gainesville.

18. Charlie Patton, "March Peacefully to Fort Clinton," *Florida Times-Union*, April 5, 1996.

CONCLUSION: *Landmarks Take Us There*

Epigraph source: Quoted in Mayes, *Every Day in Tuscany*, 183.

1. "Economic Impacts of Historic Preservation in Florida," *Trend Magazine*, www.flheritage.com, documents the amount to be $4.2 billion annually. Mclendon and Klein, "The Benefits of Historic Preservation," 12.

2. The awards are found in Bailey, Greer, and Howey, *Florida Architecture: A Celebration, The History of the Florida Association of Architects, A.I.A. 1912–2000.*

Bibliography

Published books and articles and unpublished primary materials cited in this book are listed below. Newspaper articles, unpublished church and county histories, and various government pamphlets cited in the text are documented in the endnotes.

Abbott, R. Tucker. *Kingdom of the Seashell.* New York: Bonanza, 1982.

Akin, Edward N. *Flagler: Rockefeller Partner and Florida Baron.* Gainesville: University Press of Florida, 1992.

Anderson, Robert L. "A History and Study of the Pensacola Forts." Master's thesis, Auburn University, 1969.

Andrews, R. L., J. M. Adovasio, B. Humphrey, D. D. Hyland, J. S. Gardner, and D. G. Harding. "Conservation and Analysis of Tactile and Related Perishable Artifacts." In *Windover*, edited by Glen H Doran. Gainesville: University Press of Florida, 2002.

Andrews, Wayne. *American Gothic.* New York: Vantage, 1975.

Arana, Luis Rafael. "Burials in the Cathedral." *El Escribano* 3, no. 1 (1966): 15–21.

———. "The Chapel of Castillo de San Marcos." *El Escribano* 9, no. 3 (1972): 114–26.

———. "Defenses and Defenders at St. Augustine: A Collection of Writings by Luis Rafael Arana," edited by Jean Parker Waterbury. *El Escribano* 36 (1999).

———. "The Fort at Matanzas Inlet 1740–1821." *El Escribano* 36 (1999): 87–113.

———. "The Mose Site." *El Escribano* 36 (1999): 78–86.

———. "Notes on Fort Matanzas National Monument." *El Escribano* 18 (1981): 45–73.

———. "Treading Down the Castillo, 1675–1680." *El Escribano* 41 (2004): 13–22.

Arana, Luis Rafael, and Albert Manucy. *The Building of Castillo de San Marcos.* Eastern National Park and Monument Association for Castillo de San Marcos National Monument. 1977.

Argüelles, José, and Chögyam Trungpa. *Mandala.* London: Shambhala, 1972.

Armstrong, Karen. "Man vs God, Two Prominent Thinkers Debate Evolution, Science and the Role of Religion." *Wall Street Journal*, September 2009.

Arnade, Charles W. *The Siege of St. Augustine in 1702.* Gainesville: University of Florida Press, 1959.

Ashley, Keith H. "Archaeological Overview of Mt. Royal." *Florida Anthropologist* 58, nos. 3–4 (2005): 265–86.

————. "Introducing Shields Mound (8DU12) and the Mill Cove Complex." *Florida Anthropologist* 58, nos. 3–4 (2005): 151–73.

————. "Toward an Interpretation of Shields Mound (8DU12) and the Mill Cove Complex." *Florida Anthropologist* 58, nos. 3–4 (2005): 287–99.

Austin, Robert J. "Chipped Stone Artifacts from the Miami Circle Excavations at Brickell Point." *Florida Anthropologist* 57, nos. 1–2 (2004): 85–131.

Bagwell, Charles C., Jr., "Evidences and Conclusion in Re Site of La Leche—Nombre de Dios." Manuscript at SAHS-RL. June 1938.

Bailey, S. Keith, Diane D. Greer, and John Howey. *Florida Architecture, A Celebration: The History of the Florida Association of Architects, A.I.A. 1912–2000.* Florida Association of the American Institute of Architects, 2000.

Baptist, Edward E. *Creating an Old South, Middle Florida's Plantation Frontier before the Civil War.* Chapel Hill: University of North Carolina Press, 2002.

Bartram, John. *Diary of a Journey through the Carolinas, Georgia, and Florida.* Annotated by Francis Harper. Philadelphia: Transactions of the American Philosophical Society 33. 1942.

Bartram, William. *Travels of William Bartram.* Edited by Mark Van Doren. New York: Dover, 1955.

Basham, A. L. "Hinduism." In *Encyclopedia of the World's Religions,* edited by R. C. Zaehn. New York: Barnes and Noble, 1997.

Bearss, Edwin C. *Fort Barrancas, Gulf Islands National Seashore, Florida, Historic Structure Report and Historic Resource Study.* Denver: U.S. Department of the Interior, National Park Service.

Benjamin, Asher. *The American Builder's Companion.* Reprint of 6th ed. (1827). New York: Dover, 1969.

Bense, Judith A., ed. *Presidio Santa María de Galve.* Gainesville: University Press of Florida, 2003.

Bense, Judith A., and H. James Wilson. "Archaeological Remains." In *Presidio Santa María de Galve,* edited by Bense. Gainesville: University Press of Florida, 2003.

Berrio, Pedro Díaz. *Plano general de la Ciudad de Sn. Agustín en la Florida, 1797.* Copy at SAHS-RL.

Betsky, Aaron. Review of *Ralph Adams Cram—An Architect's Four Quests: Medieval, Modernist, American, Ecumenical,* by Douglass Shand-Tucci. *JAHS* 65, no. 3 (2006): 438.

Bigelow, Lee Eugene. "Historical Sketches of Some of the Churches and Missions of Duval County and Jacksonville, 1937." Typewritten carbon copy prepared for the Federal Writers' Project at SAHS-RL.

Boazio, Baptista. *S Augustii pars est terrae Florida sub latitudine 30 gradora vero maritimta humilior est, lancinata et insulosa.* Engraved map attributed to a drawing by Boazio that accompanied an account of Drake's privateering raids 1585–86 in the West Indies, *Expeditio Francisci Draki Equitis Angli in Indias Occidentales A.M.D. LXXXV,* by Captain Walter Bigges and Lieutenant Croftes, published in Leiden (1588). An English edition of Walter Bigges's *A Summarie and true discourse of Sir Frances Drakes West Indian Voyage,* 2nd ed. (London: R. Ward, 1589) also has an engraving of the map with slight variations. Copies of both are at the British Library, London, and copies of the copies can be seen at SAHS-RL.

Boehm, Gero von. *Conversations with I. M. Pei.* New York: Prestel, 2000.

Bok, Edward W. *America's Taj Mahal: The Singing Tower of Florida.* 1929. Lake Wales: Bok Tower Gardens Foundation, 1989.

Boorstin, Daniel J. *The Creators.* New York: Vintage Books, 1993.

Bownas, G. "Shintō." In *Encyclopedia of the World's Religions*, edited by R. C. Zaehn. New York: Barnes and Noble, 1997.

Bretos, Miguel A. "Nuestra Senora de la Leche" (Our Lady of the Milk) (in Spanish). *El Nuevo Herald*, January 22, 1991, 1C.

Brooks, William Erle. *From Saddlebags to Satellites: A History of Florida Methodism.* Nashville: Parthenon Press, 1969.

Broward, Robert C. *The Architecture of Henry John Klutho.* Gainesville: University Presses of Florida, 1983.

Brownell, Charles E., Calder Loth, William M. S. Rasmussen, and Richard Guy Wilson. *The Making of Virginia Architecture.* Richmond: Virginia Museum of Fine Arts, 1992.

Bushnell, Amy Turner. "The Expenses of *Hidalguía* in Seventeenth-Century St. Augustine." *El Escribano* 15 (1978): 23–36.

———. "Missions and Moral Judgement." *OAH Magazine of History* (Summer 2000): 21–22.

———. "Situado and Sabana." *Anthropological Papers of the American Museum of Natural History* 74 (September 21, 1994).

Cabeza de Vaca, Alvar Nuñez. *The Shipwrecked Men, or The Journey of Alvar Nuñez Cabeza de Vaca and His Companions from Florida to the Pacific 1528–1536.* Trans. Fanny Bandelier. Rev. Harold Augenbraum. London: Penguin, 2002.

Campen, Richard N. *Winter Park Portrait: The Story of Winter Park and Rollins College.* Beachwood, Ohio: West Summit Press, 1987.

Capitman, Barbara Baer. *Deco Delights.* New York: Dutton, 1988.

Carr, Robert S. "Analysis of Ceramics from Brickell Point, 8DA12." *Florida Anthropologist* 59, nos. 3–4 (2006): 133–59.

Carr, Robert S., and John Ricisak. "Preliminary Report on Salvage Archaeological Investigations of the Brickell Point Site (8DA12), Including the Miami Circle." *Florida Anthropologist* 53, no. 4 (2000): 260–84.

Carswell, Elba Wilson. *Holmes Valley: A West Florida Cradle of Christianity.* Bonifay: Central Press, 1969.

Castello, Pablo. *Plano del Presidio de Sn Agustín de la Florida y sus contornos . . . 1763.* Copy at SAHS-RL.

Cather, Willa. *Death Comes for the Archbishop.* New York: Modern Library, 1993.

Chase, Elizabeth, ed. *The Pioneer Churches of Florida.* Chuluota, Fla.: Mickler House, 1976.

Chatelain, Vern Elmo. *The Defenses of Spanish Florida 1565 to 1763.* Publication 511. Washington, D.C.: Carnegie Institution, 1941.

Clark, Susan. *A Historic Tour Guide of Palatka and Putnam County, Florida.* Putnam: Putnam County Historical Society and Glanzer Press, 1992.

Clune, John James. "Historical Context and Overview." In *Presidio Santa María de Galve*, edited by Judith A. Bense. Gainesville: University Press of Florida, 2003.

Clune, John James, R. Wayne Childers, William S. Coker, and Brenda Swann. "Settlement, Settlers, and Survival: Documentary Evidence." In *Presidio Santa María de Galve*, edited by Judith A. Bense. Gainesville: University Press of Florida, 2003.

Coe, Ralph T. *Sacred Circles*. Exhibition catalogue. Kansas City: Nelson Gallery of Art, Atkins Museum of Fine Arts, 1976.

Coker, William S. "Pensacola, 1686–1821." In *Archaeology of Colonial Pensacola*, edited by Judith A. Bense. Gainesville: University Press of Florida, 1999.

———. "Pensacola, 1686–1763." In *The New History of Florida*, edited by Michael Gannon. Gainesville: University Press of Florida, 1996.

Coleman, James C., and Irene S. Coleman. *Pensacola Fortifications, 1698–1980: Guardians on the Gulf*. Pensacola: Pensacola Historical Society, 1982.

Collins, Lori D., and Travis F. Doering. "High Definition Digital Documentation at the Crystal River Archaeological Site (8Cl1)." *Florida Anthropologist* 62, nos. 1–2 (March–June 2009): 23–44.

Collins, Lori D., Travis F. Doering, and Robert S. Carr. "Integrated Spatial Technologies: High Definition Documentation of the Miami Circle and Royal Palm Circles." *Florida Anthropologist* 59, nos. 3–4 (2006): 161–77.

Conduit, Carl W. "The Pioneer Concrete Building of St. Augustine." *Progressive Architecture*, September 1971, 128–33.

Connor, Jeannette Thurber. *Colonial Records of Spanish Florida*. DeLand: Florida State Historical Society, 1930.

———. "The Nine Old Wooden Forts of St. Augustine, I." *FHQ* 4, no. 3 (January 1926): 103–11.

———. "The Nine Old Wooden Forts of St. Augustine, II." *FHQ* 4, no. 4 (April 1926): 170–80.

———. *Pedro Menéndez de Avilés: Memorial by Gonzalo Solís de Merás*. Gainesville: University of Florida Press, 1964.

Coomes, Charles S. "The Basilica Cathedral of St. Augustine, Florida, and Its History." *El Escribano* 20 (1983): 32–44.

———. "Our Country's Oldest Parish Records." *El Escribano* 18 (1981): 74–83.

Curl, Donald W. *Mizner's Florida*. Cambridge: MIT Press, 1984.

Curry, Andrew. "Cherokee Holy of Holies." *Archaeology* (September–October 2002): 70–75.

Cushing, Frank Hamilton. "Exploration of Ancient Key Dwellers' Remains on the Gulf Coast of Florida." *Proceedings of the American Philosophical Society* 35, no. 153 (December 1896): 329–448.

Cushman, Joseph D., Jr. *A Goodly Heritage*. Gainesville: University of Florida Press, 1965.

———. *The Sound of Bells*. Gainesville: University Presses of Florida, 1976.

Davis, Albina M. *The Cathedral Basilica of St. Augustine and Its History*. St. Augustine: Cathedral Basilica, 1994.

Deagan, Kathleen A. *America's Ancient City: Spanish St. Augustine 1565–1763*. New York: Garland, 1991.

———. *Archaeological Strategy in the Investigation of an Unknown Era: Sixteenth-*

Century St. Augustine. Project report submitted to the St. Augustine Foundation, Inc., St. Augustine, Florida, January 1978. On file at FMNH.

———. "The Archaeology of First Spanish Period St. Augustine 1972–1978." *El Escribano* 15 (1978): 1–22.

———. "Archaeology of Sixteenth-Century St. Augustine." *Florida Anthropologist* 38 (1985): 6–34.

———. "Downtown Survey: The Discovery of 16th-Century St. Augustine in the Urban Area." *American Antiquity* 46, no. 3 (1981): 626–33.

———. "Excavations at the Menéndez Fort and Campsite, 1565–1572." *SAAA* 10, no. 2 (April 1995): 1, 3–6.

———. *Historical Archaeology at the Fountain of Youth Park Site (8SJ31) St. Augustine, Florida 1934–2007.* Final Report on Florida Bureau of Historical Resources Special Category Grant #SC 616, Draft 3, July 1, 2008, revised June 15, 2009.

———. "Runaway Slaves Establish First Fortress for Freedom." *Forum* (Winter 2001): 28–31.

———. *Spanish St. Augustine: The Archaeology of a Colonial Creole Community.* New York: Academic Press, 1983.

———. "St. Augustine: First Urban Enclave in the United States." *North American Archaeologist* 3, no. 3 (1982): 183–205.

———. "St. Augustine and the Mission Frontier." In *The Spanish Missions of La Florida*, edited by Bonnie E. McEwan. Gainesville: University Press of Florida, 1993.

———. "Summary Interpretation of Archaeological Field Work at the Fountain of Youth Park Site (8SJ31) 1951–2002." Florida Museum of Natural History Miscellaneous Projects Reports in Archaeology No. 56. Gainesville: University of Florida, 2004.

Deagan, Kathleen, and Darcie MacMahon. *Fort Mose: Colonial America's Black Fortress of Freedom.* Gainesville: University Press of Florida, 1995.

Dibble, Ernest F. "Religion on Florida's Territorial Frontiers." *FHQ* 80, no. 1 (Summer 2001).

Dickinson, Jonathan. *Jonathan Dickinson's Journal or, God's Protecting Providence.* Edited by Evangeline Walker Andrews and Charles McLean Andrews. New Haven: Yale University Press, 1861.

Dickle, David N. "Analysis of Mortuary Patterns." In *Windover*, edited by Glen H. Doran, 73–96. Gainesville: University Press of Florida, 2002.

Doran, Glen H. "Introduction to Wet Sites and Windover (8BR246) Investigations." In *Windover*, edited by Doran. Gainesville: University Press of Florida., 2002.

———, ed. *Windover.* Gainesville: University Press of Florida, 2002.

Doran, Glen H., and David N. Dickle. "Radiometric Chronology of the Archaic Windover Archaeological Site (8Br246)." *Florida Anthropologist* 41, no. 3 (September 1988): 365–80.

Dorsey, Stephen P. *Early English Churches in America, 1607–1807.* New York: Oxford University Press, 1952.

Dowda, Robert Black. *A History of Palatka and Putnam County.* Palatka: Putnam County Archives and History Commission, 1976.

Downing, Andrew Jackson. *Victorian Cottage Residences.* New York: Dover, 1981.

Dunlop, Beth, and Roberto Schezen. *Miami: Trends and Traditions.* New York: Monacelli Press, 1996.

Earenfight, Phillip. *A Kiowa's Odyssey.* Seattle: University of Washington Press, 2007.

Eck, Christopher R. "A Picturesque Settlement: The Diary Notes of Dr. Jeffries Wyman's Visit to Miami and the First Archaeological Excavations in South Florida, 1869." *Florida Anthropologist* 53, no. 4 (December 2000): 286–93.

Elgart, Alison A. "The Animal Interments at the Miami Circle at Brickell Point Site (8DA12)." *Florida Anthropologist* 59, nos. 3–4 (September–December 2006): 179–89.

Elgart, Alison A., and Robert S. Carr. "An Analysis of the Prehistoric Human Remains Found at the Miami Circle." *Florida Anthropologist* 59, nos. 3–4 (September–December 2006): 241–49.

Endonino, Jon C. "The Thornhill Lake Archaeological Research Project: 2005–2008." *Florida Anthropologist* 61, nos. 3–4 (September–December 2008): 147–65.

Ewen, Charles R. "Anhaica: Discovery of Hernando de Soto's 1539–40 Winter Camp." In *First Encounters,* edited by Jerald T. Milanich and Susan Milbrath. Gainesville: University Press of Florida, 1989.

Fairbanks, George R. *The History and Antiquities of the City of St. Augustine.* Facsimile reproduction of the 1858 edition. Gainesville: University Presses of Florida, 1975.

Faye, Stanley. "British and Spanish Fortifications of Pensacola, 1781–1821." *FHQ* 20, no. 2 (October 1941): 277–92.

Federal Writers' Project of the Works Progress Administration for the State of Florida. *The WPA Guide to Florida: The Federal Writers' Project Guide to 1930s Florida.* 1939. New York: Pantheon, 1984.

Fernald, Edward A. and Elizabeth D. Purdum, eds. *Atlas of Florida.* Gainesville: University Press of Florida, 1992.

Flynn, Kathryn A. "New Appreciation for the New Deal and Why We Need that Now!" *Forum News* 15, no. 6 (July–August 2009): 1–3.

Folsom, Merrill. *More Great American Mansions.* New York: Hastings House, 1967.

Fontaneda, Hernando de Escalante. *Memoir of Do. d.' Escalante Fontaneda Respecting Florida, Written in Spain, About the Year 1575.* Trans. Buckingham Smith, 1854. Edited by David O. True. Coral Gables, Fla.: Glade House, 1945.

Galbraith, Christine, and Barbara Miller. *Historical Documentary Research Project, 1902 Florida Capitol Restoration Reports.* Tallahassee: Historic Tallahassee Preservation Board, 1979.

Gallay, Alan. *The Indian Slave Trade.* New Haven: Yale University Press, 2002.

Gannon, Michael. 1965. *The Cross in the Sand.* Gainesville: University Presses of Florida, 1989.

———, ed. *The Florida Catholic Heritage Trail.* Sun City Center, Fla.: Florida Catholic Heritage Trail, 2005.

———. "Florida's Seashell Castle." *Forum* (Spring 2005): 18–19.

———, ed. *The New History of Florida.* Gainesville: University Press of Florida, 1996.

———. *Rebel Bishop.* Milwaukee: Bruce, 1964.

Geiger, Maynard J., O.F.M. *The Franciscan Conquest of Florida 1573–1618.* Washington, D.C.: Catholic University of America Press, 1937.

———, trans. *The Martyrs of Florida 1513–1616,* by Luís Gerónimo de Oré, O.F.M. Franciscan Studies 18. New York: Joseph F. Wagner, 1936.

Gelernter, Mark. *A History of American Architecture: Buildings in Their Cultural and Technological Context.* Hanover, N.H.: University Press of New England, 1999.

Gibbs, James. *Book of Architecture, Containing Designs of Buildings and Ornaments.* London: 1728.

Gibson, Jon L. *The Ancient Mounds of Poverty Point.* Gainesville: University Press of Florida, 2001.

———. "Broken Circles, Owl Monsters, and Black Earth Middens: Separating Sacred and Secular at Poverty Point." In *Ancient Earthen Enclosures of the Eastern Woodlands,* edited by Robert C. Mainfort Jr. and Lynne P. Sullivan. Gainesville: University Press of Florida, 1998.

Goetz, Delia, and Sylvanus G. Morley. *Popol Vuh: The Sacred Book of the Ancient Quiché Maya.* Norman: University of Oklahoma Press, 1950.

Gordon, Elsbeth. *Florida's Colonial Architectural Heritage.* Gainesville: University Press of Florida, 2002.

———. "'From So Precious a Watering': In Pursuit of Mission Nombre de Dios, 1565–1595." *El Escribano* 43 (2006): 1–54.

Graham, Thomas. *Flagler's Magnificent Hotel Ponce de Leon.* Reprinted from *FHQ* 54 (July 1975).

———. *Flagler's St. Augustine Hotels.* Sarasota: Pineapple Press, 2004.

Grantham, Bill. *Creation Myths and Legends of the Creek Indians.* Gainesville: University Press of Florida, 2002.

Griffen, William B. "Spanish Pensacola, 1700–1763." *FHQ* 37, nos. 3–4 (January–April 1959).

Griffin, John W. "Preliminary Report on the Site of Mission of San Juan del Puerto, Fort George Island, Florida." Papers of the Jacksonville Historical Society 4. 1960.

Griffin, Patricia C. *Mullet on the Beach: The Minorcans of Florida 1768–1788.* Jacksonville: University of North Florida Press, 1991.

Gritzner, Janet Bigbee. "Tabby in the Coastal Southeast: The Cultural History of an American Building Material." Ph.d. diss., Louisiana State University, 1978.

Grunwald, Michael. *The Swamp.* New York: Simon and Schuster, 2006.

Gyure, Dale Allen. *Frank Lloyd Wright's Southern College.* Gainesville: University Press of Florida, 2010.

Halbirt, Carl D. "Redefining the Boundaries of 16th-Century St. Augustine." *SAAA* 14, no. 1 (March 1999).

Hale, Jonathan. *The Old Way of Seeing.* Boston: Houghton Mifflin, 1994.

Hall, Robert L. *An Archaeology of the Soul.* Urbana: University of Illinois Press, 1997.

———. "Ghosts, Water Barriers, Corn and Sacred Enclosures in the Eastern Woodlands." *American Antiquity* 41, no. 3 (1976): 360–64.

Hamlin, Talbot. *The American Spirit in Architecture*. New Haven: Yale University Press, 1926.

———. *Greek Revival Architecture in America*. New York: Oxford University Press, 1944.

Handlin, David P. *American Architecture*. London: Thames and Hudson, 1985.

Hann, John H. *An Early Florida Adventure Story by Fray Andrés de San Miguel*. Gainesville: University Press of Florida, 2001.

———. *A History of the Timucua Indians and Missions*. Gainesville: University Press of Florida, 1996.

———. *Indians of Central and South Florida, 1513–1763*. Gainesville: University Press of Florida, 2003.

———. *Missions to the Calusa*. Gainesville: University of Florida Press, 1991.

———. "Translation of Alonso de Leturiondo's Memorial to the King of Spain." *Florida Archaeology*. Florida Bureau of Archaeological Research 2. 1982.

Hann, John H., and Bonnie G. McEwan. *The Apalachee Indians and Mission San Luis*. Gainesville: University Press of Florida, 1998.

Harner, Charles E. *Florida's Promoters: The Men Who Made It Big*. Tampa: Trend House, 1973.

Harris, Cyril M., ed. *Illustrated Dictionary of Historic Architecture*. New York: Dover, 1977.

Harrison, Carlos. "The Fort That Time Forgot." *Preservation* 61, no. 6 (November–December 2009): 30–32, 52–56.

Heimovics, Rachel B., and Marcia Zerivitz. *Florida Jewish Heritage Trail*. Tallahassee: Florida Department of State, Division of Historical Resources, 2000.

Hoffman, Paul E. *Florida's Frontiers*. Bloomington: Indiana University Press, 2002.

———. "St. Augustine 1580: The Research Project." *El Escribano* 14 (1977): 5–19.

Hoffman, Paul E., and Eugene Lyon. "A Preliminary Report on the Layout of St. Augustine, Florida, ca. 1580. Manuscript prepared for St. Augustine Restoration, Inc., January 5, 1976.

Hoffstot, Barbara D. *Landmark Architecture of Palm Beach*. Pittsburgh: History and Landmarks Foundation, 1974.

Horwitz, Tony. *A Voyage Long and Strange on the Trail of Vikings, Conquistadors, Lost Colonists, and Other Adventurers in Early America*. Picador Edition. New York: Harry Holt, 2009.

Hoshower, Lisa M., and Jerald T. Milanich. "Excavations in the Fig Springs Mission Burial Area." In *The Missions of La Florida*, edited by Bonnie G. McEwan. Gainesville: University Press of Florida, 1993.

Howey, John. *The Sarasota School of Architecture 1941–1966*. Cambridge: MIT Press, 1995.

Hudson, Charles. *The Southeastern Indians*. Knoxville: University of Tennessee Press, 1976.

Ivy, Robert Adams, Jr. *Fay Jones*. New York: AIA, 1992.

Jackson, Jeremy B. C., Michael X. Kirby, Wolfgang H. Berger, Karen A. Bjorndal, Louis W. Botsford, Bruce J. Bourque, Roger H. Bradbury et al. "Historical Overfishing and the Recent Collapse of Coastal Ecosystems." *Science* 293 (July 27, 2001): 629–37.

Johnson, Kenneth W. "Mission Santa Fé de Toluca." In *The Spanish Missions of Florida*, edited by Bonnie G. McEwan. Gainesville: University Press of Florida, 1993.

Johnson, Sherry. "Casualties of Peace: Tracing the Historic Roots of the Florida-Cuba Diaspora, 1763–1800." *Colonial Latin American Historical Review* (Winter 2001): 91–125.

Johnston, Sidney. "The Historic Stetson University Campus in DeLand, 1884–1934." *Florida Historical Quarterly* (January 1992): 281–304.

Jones, Calvin. "Colonel James Moore and the Destruction of the Apalachee Missions in 1704." Bureau of Historic Sites and Properties Bulletin No. 2, 25–33. Tallahassee: Division of Archives, History, and Records Management, Florida Department of State, 1972.

Jones, Robert O. "Florida's Carpenter Gothic Episcopal Churches." National Register of Historic Places Multiple Property Documentation Form. Department of State, Bureau of Historic Preservation, Tallahassee, Florida, February 1997.

Jones, William M. "A British Period Sawmill." *El Escribano* 18 (1981): 84–105.

Jordy, William H. *American Buildings and Their Architects*. Vol 4. New York: Oxford University Press, 1972.

Joy, Deborah. *The Colonial Archaeological Trail in Pensacola: Phase 1*. Report submitted to the Bureau of Historic Preservation, Division of Historical Resources, Florida Department of State, 1989.

Kapitzke, Robert L. *Religion, Power, and Politics in Colonial St. Augustine.* Gainesville: University Press of Florida, 2001.

Karaim, Reed. "Losing Sacred Ground." *Preservation*, March–April 2003, 30–35.

Kaufmann, Edgar, Jr. *Fallingwater.* New York: Abbeville Press, 1986.

Keller, Amy. "Leap of Faith." *Florida Trend*, September 2007, 60–66.

———. "Wright's Stuff." *Florida Trend*, October 2007, 70–75.

Kelsey, Harry. *Sir Francis Drake, The Queen's Pirate.* New Haven: Yale University Press, 1998.

Kerrigan, Anthony. *Barcia's Chronological History of the Continent of Florida.* Gainesville: University of Florida Press, 1951. Translation of *Ensayo chronológico para la historía general de la Florida*, by Barcia Carballido y Zúñiga (under anagram of Don Gabriel de Cardenas z Cano, Madrid 1723).

Knetsch, Joe, and Pam Vojnovski. "Peter Mitchel: Frontier Speculator, Developer and Entrepreneur." *El Escribano* 47 (2010): 43–69.

Knight, Vernon J., Jr. "Mississippian Ritual." Ph.D. diss., University of Florida, 1981.

Kolianos, Phyllis E. and Brent R. Weisman, eds. *The Florida Journals of Frank Hamilton Cushing.* Gainesville: University Press of Florida, 2005.

Landers, Jane. *Black Society in Spanish Florida.* Urbana: University of Illinois Press, 1999.

Lane, Mills. *Architecture of the Old South: Louisiana.* New York: Abbeville Press, 1990.

Larsen, Clark Spencer. "On the Frontier of Contact: Mission Bioarchaeology in *La Florida.*" In *The Spanish Missions of La Florida*, edited by Bonnie G. McEwan. Gainesville: University Press of Florida, 1993.

Larsen, Stephen. *The Shaman's Doorway.* Rochester, Vt.: Inner Traditions, 1998.

Larson, Lewis H. *Aboriginal Subsistence Technology on the Southeastern Coastal Plain during the Late Prehistoric Period.* Gainesville: University Presses of Florida, 1980.

Lawler, Robert. *Sacred Geometry.* London: Thames and Hudson, 1982.

Lawson, Edward W. *Correspondence of the Bishops and Curates.* 2 vols. Manuscript. Transcribed and translated from microfilm, Library of Congress, East Florida Papers, LC Reference Aug 2-44-000586 AMF 1568. Copy at SAHS-RL.

Lawson, Sarah. *A Foothold in Florida.* East Grinstead, West Sussex, England: Antique Atlas, 1992.

Lepper, Bradley T. "Archaeology of the Newark Earthworks." In *Ancient Earthen Enclosures of the Eastern Woodlands,* edited by Robert C. Mainfort and Lynne P. Sullivan. Gainesville: University Press of Florida, 1998.

Livio, Mario. *The Golden Ratio.* New York: Broadway, 2002.

Longstreth, Richard. *On the Edge of the World.* Cambridge: MIT Press, 1989.

López de Mendoza Grajales, Francisco. *Relacíon hecha por el Capellán de Armada Francisco López de Mendoza, del viaje que hizo el Adelantado Pedro Menéndez de Avilés a la Florida.* In *La Florida, su conquista y colonización por Pedro Menéndez de Avilés,* edited by Eugenio Ruidíaz y Caravia. Madrid: Hijos de J. A. García, 1893.

Luer, George M., ed. *Archaeology of Upper Charlotte Harbor, Florida.* Florida Anthropological Society Publication No. 15. September 2002.

———. "Sarasota Bay Mound: A Safety Harbor Period Burial Mound, with Notes on Additional Sites in the City of Sarasota." *Florida Anthropologist* 58, nos. 1–2 (March–June 2005): 7–55.

———. "The Yellow Bluffs Mound Revisited: A Manasota Period Burial Mound in Sarasota." *Florida Anthropologist* 64, no. 1 (March 2011): 5–23.

Lundquist, John M. *The Temple: Meeting Place of Heaven and Earth.* London: Thames and Hudson, 1993.

Lynch, Arthur Joseph. *George Rainsford Fairbanks.* Los Altos, Calif.: Shambles Press, 1999.

Lyon, Eugene. "Aspects of Pedro Menéndez the Man." *El Escribano* 24 (1987): 39–52.

———. *The Enterprise of Florida.* Gainesville: University Presses of Florida, 1976.

———. "The First Three Wooden Forts of St. Augustine, 1565–1571." *El Escribano* 34 (1997): 130–47.

———. "Project Historian Report: Excavations at the Menéndez Site St. Augustine, K. Deagan, P.I." Manuscript, 1997.

———. "Richer Than We Thought: The Material Culture of Sixteenth-Century St. Augustine." *El Escribano* 29 (1992).

———. "Santa Elena: A Brief History of the Colony 1566–1587." Research Manuscript Series 193. Institute of Archaeology and Anthropology, University of South Carolina, 1984.

———. "St. Augustine 1580: The Living Community." *El Escribano* 14 (1977): 20–34.

MacMahon, Darcie A., and William H. Marquardt. *The Calusa and Their Legacy.* Gainesville: University Press of Florida, 2004.

Maddex, Diane, ed. *Master Builders.* New York: Preservation Press, 1985.

Mainfort, Robert C., Jr., and Lynne P. Sullivan, eds. *Ancient Earthen Enclosures of the Eastern Woodlands*. Gainesville: University Press of Florida, 1998.

Manucy, Albert C. *The Cathedral of St. Augustine*. Historic Site Report. 1946.

———. "The Founding of Pensacola—Reasons and Reality." *FHQ* 37, nos. 3–4 (January–April 1959): 223–42.

———. *The Houses of St. Augustine 1565–1821*. St. Augustine: St. Augustine Historical Society, 1978.

———. *How Did Fort Caroline Look? A Report on the Feasibility of Reconstructing Fort Caroline*. National Park Service, 1960.

Marquardt, William H. "Calusa." In *Handbook of North American Indians*. Vol. 14, *Southeast*, edited by R. D. Fogelson. Washington: Smithsonian Institution, 2004.

Marrinan, Rochelle A. "Archaeological Investigations at Mission Patale, 1984–1992." In *The Spanish Missions of La Florida*, edited by Bonnie G. McEwan. Gainesville: University Press of Florida, 1993.

Matkov, Becky Roper. "Selling City's Heritage to the Highest Bidder." *Florida Preservationist* 3, no. 4 (Fall 2005): 3.

Matos, Moctezuma Eduardo. "Imperial Tenochtitlan." In *Mexico: Splendors of Thirty Centuries*. New York: Metropolitan Museum of Art, 1990.

Mayes, Frances. *Every Day in Tuscany: Seasons of an Italian Life*. New York: Broadway Books, 2010.

McAlister, L. N. "Pensacola during the Second Spanish Period." *FHQ* 37 (January–April 1959): 281–327.

McClane, Patrick, and Debra McClane. *The Architecture of James Gamble Rogers II in Winter Park, Florida*. Gainesville: University Press of Florida, 2004.

McEwan, Bonnie G., ed. *The Spanish Missions of La Florida*. Gainesville: University Press of Florida, 1993.

———. "The Spiritual Conquest of La Florida." *American Anthropologist* 103, no. 3 (September 2001): 633–44.

McEwan, Bonnie G., and John H. Hann. "Reconstructing a Spanish Mission: San Luis de Talimali." *OAH Magazine of History* 14, no. 4 (Summer 2000): 16–19.

McKim, Mead & White. *The Architecture of McKim, Mead & White in Photographs, Plans, and Elevations*. New York: Dover, 1990.

Mclendon, Timothy, and Joann Klein. "The Benefits of Historic Preservation." *Florida History & the Arts* 11, no. 1 (Winter 2003): 12–15.

Mestas, Hernando de. "Map ca. 1594, San Agustín." Papers of Hernando de Mestas, AGI, Seville, Spain.

Milanich, Jerald T. *Archaeology of Precolumbian Florida*. Gainesville: University Press of Florida, 1994.

———. *Famous Florida Sites: Mount Royal and Crystal River*. Gainesville: University Press of Florida, 1999.

———. *Florida Indians and the Invasion from Europe*. Gainesville: University Press of Florida, 1995.

———. *Frolicking Bears, Wet Vultures, and Other Oddities*. Gainesville: University Press of Florida, 2005.

———. "Laboring in the Fields of the Lord." *Archaeology* (January–February 1996): 60–67.

———. *The Timucua*. Cambridge: Blackwell, 1996.

———. "Water World." *Archaeology*, September–October, 2004, 46–50.

Milanich, Jerald T., Ann S. Cordell, Vernon J. Knight Jr., Timothy A. Kohler, and Brenda J. Sigler-Lavelle. *Archaeology of Northern Florida a.d. 200–900: The McKeithen Weeden Island Culture*. Gainesville: University Press of Florida, 1997.

Milanich, Jerald T., and Susan Milbrath, eds. *First Encounters: Spanish Exploration in the Caribbean and the United States, 1497–1570*. Gainesville: University of Florida Press, 1989.

Milanich, Jerald T., and William C. Sturtevant. *Francisco Pareja's 1613 Confessionario*. Tallahassee: Florida Department of State, Division of Archives, History and Records Management, 1972.

Milbrath, Susan. "Old World Meets New: Views across the Atlantic." In *First Encounters*, edited by Jerald T. Milanich and Milbrath. Gainesville: University Presses of Florida, 1986.

Millar, John Fitzhugh. *The Architects of the American Colonies*. Barre, Mass.: Barre Publishers, 1998.

Mitchem, Jeffrey M. *The East Florida Expeditions of Clarence Bloomfield Moore*. Tuscaloosa: University of Alabama Press, 1999.

Moncrief, James. "Plan of the Town of St. Augustine and Its Environs." PRO: 700, Florida 8.

Morris, Allen. *The Florida Handbook 1949–1950*, and *The Florida Handbook 1965–1966*. Tallahassee: Peninsular.

Mumford, Lewis. *Roots of Contemporary American Architecture*. New York: Dover, 1972.

Newton, Earle W., and Blair Reeves. *Historic Architecture of Pensacola*. Pensacola Historic Restoration and Preservation Commission. N.d.

Nuttall, Zelia. "Ordinances Concerning the Laying out of New Towns." *Hispanic American Historical Review* 4, no. 4 (November 1921): 743–53.

Olano, Pedro Ruis de. *Plano del sitio de la Florida, August 8, 1740*. Copy at SAHS-RL.

Palladio, Andrea. *Andrea Palladio: The Four Books of Architecture*. New York: Dover, 1965.

Panton, Daniel T. "Cultural Prisms Distort." *Forum* (Winter 2001): 34–35.

Patricios, Nicholas N. *Building Marvelous Miami*. Gainesville: University Press of Florida, 1994.

Patrick, Rembert W. *Florida Fiasco: Rampant Rebels on the Georgia-Florida Border 1810–1815*. Athens: University of Georgia Press, 1954.

Pérez, Elizabeth P., and Rusty Ennemoser. *Florida Cuban Heritage Trail*. Tallahassee: Florida Department of State, Division of Historical Resources, 1994.

Pierson, William H., Jr. *American Buildings and Their Architects*. Vols. 1–2. New York: Oxford University Press, 1986.

Pluckhahn, Thomas U., and Victor D. Thompson. "Mapping Crystal River (8Cı1): Past, Present, Future." *Florida Anthropologist* 62, nos. 1–2 (March–June 2009): 5–22.

Poppeliers, John C., S. Allen Chambers Jr., and Nancy B. Schwartz. *What Style Is It? A Guide to American Architecture*. Washington D.C.: Preservation Press, 1983.

Puente, Juan Joseph Elixio de la. *Plano del Pressidio de Sn Agustín de la Florida que*

poscen a la sason los Yngleses con las Barras Rios Terranos . . . 16 Febrero de.1769.
Museo Naval, Madrid.

———. *Plano de la Real Fuerza, Baluartes, y Linea de la Plaza de Sn Agustín de Flor-ida, Con . . . Henero 22 de 1764.* Museo Naval, Madrid.

Purcell, Joseph. "A Plan of St. Augustine Town and Its Environs in East Florida from an Actual Survey made in 1777." Copy at SAHS-RL.

Purdy, Barbara A. *The Art and Archaeology of Florida's Wetlands.* Boca Raton, Fla.: CRC Press, 1991.

Quitmyer, Irvy R., and Douglas S. Jones. "The Over-Exploitation of Hard Clams (Mercenaria spp.) from Five Archaeological Sites in the Southeastern United States." *Florida Anthropologist* 53, nos. 2–3 (June–September 2000): 158–67.

Reeves, F. Blair, FAIA, ed. *A Guide to Florida's Historical Architecture.* Gainesville: University of Florida Press, 1989.

Reiss, Marcia. *Architectural Details.* San Diego: Thunder Bay Press, 2004.

Rivers, Larry Eugene. *Slavery in Florida.* Gainesville: University Press of Florida, 2000.

Rocque, Mariano de la. *Plano Particular de la Ciudad de Sn Agustin de la Florida . . . 25 de Abril de 1788.*

Rodriguez, Rosalie. "Richard A. Shine, 1810–1862: Tallahassee's Premier Ante-bellum Builder." Typescript. December 1995.

Romey, Kristin M. "Diving the Maya Underworld." *Archaeology* (May–June 2004): 16–23.

Roworth, Sam. "A Plan of the Land Between Fort Mossy and St. Augustine in the Province of East Florida, Sam Roworth, Dept. Surv. Gen'l." N.d. Copy at SAHS-RL.

Ruidiaz y Caravía, Eugenio. *La Florida, su conquista y colonization por Pedro Menen-dez de Avilez.* Vols. 1–2. Madrid: Hijos de J. A. Garcia, 1893.

Russo, Michael. "A Brief Introduction to the Study of Archaic Mounds in the Southeast." *Southeastern Archaeology* 13, no. 2 (Winter 1994): 89–92.

———. "Why We Don't Believe in Archaic Ceremonial Mounds and Why We Should: The Case from Florida." *Southeastern Archaeology* 13, no. 2 (Winter 1994): 93–108.

Schafer, Daniel L. *Anna Kingsley.* St. Augustine: SAHS, 1994.

———. "Early Plantation Development in British East Florida." *El Escribano* 19 (1982): 37–53.

———. "Governor James Grant's Villa: A British East Florida Indigo Plantation." *El Escribano* 37, 2000.

———. "St. Augustine's British Years 1763–1784." *El Escribano* 38 (2001).

———. "U.S. Territory and State." In *The New History of Florida,* edited by Michael Gannon. Gainesville: University Press of Florida, 1996.

Schele, Linda, and Mary Ellen Miller. *The Blood of Kings: Dynasty and Ritual in Maya Art.* New York: George Braziller and Kimbell Art Museum, Fort Worth, 1986.

Schwadron, Margo. "Archaeological Investigations at De Soto National Memorial: Perspectives on the Site Formation and Cultural History of the Shaw's Point

Site (8MA7), Manatee County, Florida." *Florida Anthropologist* 53, nos. 2–3 (June–September, 2000): 168–89.

Schwehm, Alice Gates. "The Carved Wood Effigies of Fort Center: A Glimpse of South Florida's Prehistoric Art." Master's thesis, University of Florida, 1983.

Scott, Phil. *Hemingway's Hurricane: The Great Florida Keys Storm of 1935.* New York: International Marine/McGraw-Hill, 2006.

Scott, Robert A. *The Gothic Enterprise.* Berkeley and Los Angeles: University of California Press, 2003.

Scotti, R. A. *Basilica, The Splendor and the Scandal: Building St. Peter's.* New York: Plume, 2007.

Scully, Vincent J., Jr. *The Shingle Style and the Stick Style.* New Haven: Yale University Press, 1971.

Sears, William H. *Fort Center: An Archaeological Site in the Lake Okeechobee Basin.* Gainesville: University of Florida Press, 1982.

Severy, Merle, ed. *Great Religions of the World.* Washington, D.C.: National Geographic Society, 1978.

Sexton, Kim. "Loggias and Ethnicity in Early Medieval Italy." *JSAH* 68, no. 3 (September 2009): 308–37.

Shapiro, Gary, and Bonnie G. McEwan. "Archaeology at San Luis: The Apalachee Council House." *Florida Archaeology* 6, pt. 1. Florida Bureau of Archaeological Research, Florida Department of State (1992): 1–173.

Shapiro, Gary, and Richard Vernon. "Archaeology at San Luis: The Church Complex." *Florida Archaeology* 6, pt. 2 (1992): 177–277. Florida Bureau of Archaeological Research, Florida Department of State.

Shepard, Herschel E., Jr. "The Construction of Fort Clinch." *Florida Architect*, January 1965.

———. "The Construction of Fort Clinch, 1965, Herschel E. Shepard, Jr., Architect." 1965. Manuscript in the Herschel Shepard Collection, P. K. Yonge Library, University of Florida, Gainesville.

Siry, Joseph M. "Frank Lloyd Wright's Annie M. Pfeiffer Chapel for Florida Southern College." *JSAH* 63, no. 4 (December 2004): 498–539.

Smith, Julia Floyd. *Slavery and Plantation Growth in Antebellum Florida 1821–1860.* Gainesville: University of Florida Press, 1973.

Smith, Ryan. "Carpenter Gothic: The Voices of Episcopal Churches on the St. Johns River." *El Escribano* 32 (1995): 65–90.

Solana, Juan Joseph. "Report of Conditions in St. Augustine, April 22, 1759." Enclosure of April 9, 1760 to Ex. mo Sr. Bo. Fr. D. Julian de Arriaga, Secretario de Estado y del Despacho Universal de estas Indias, AGI 86-7-21/41, transcribed and translated copy at SAHS-RL.

Solís de Marás, Gonzalo. *Memorial.* In *Pedro Menéndez de Avilés, Memorial by Gonzalo Solís de Merás,* edited by Jeannette Thurber Connor. Gainesville: University of Florida Press, 1964.

Sommer, Robin Langley. *The Old Church Book.* New York: Barnes and Noble, 1999.

Stanton, Phoebe B. *The Gothic Revival and American Church Architecture.* Baltimore: Johns Hopkins University Press: 1968.

Stojanowski, Christopher M. "Unhappy Trails." *Natural History,* July–August, 38–44.

Stowell, Daniel W. "Timucuan Ecological and Historic Preserve: Historic Resource Study." Manuscript at Kingsley Plantation, National Park Service, 1996.

Straight, William M. "The A. E. Douglass Cup from the Brickell Mound." *Florida Anthropologist* 57, nos. 1–2 (March–June 2004): 187–90.

Strock, G. Michael. *By Faith with Thanksgiving: A History of Trinity Episcopal Parish 1821–1996.* St. Augustine: Trinity Episcopal Parish, 1996.

Sunderland, Elizabeth Read. "Symbolic Numbers and Romanesque Church Plans." *JSAH* 18, no. 3 (October 1959): 94–103.

Taylor, Thomas W. *Florida's Territorial Lighthouses 1821–1845.* Allandale, Fla.: Thomas W. Taylor, 1995.

Thomas, Hugh. *Rivers of Gold.* New York: Random House, 2005

Thomas, Larissa A. "Images of Women in Native American Iconography." In *Interpretations of Native North American Life,* edited by Michael S. Nassaney and Eric S. Johnson. Gainesville: University Press of Florida, 2000.

Thompson, J. Eric S. *Maya History and Religion.* Norman: University of Oklahoma Press, 1972.

———. *The Rise and Fall of Maya Civilization.* 1954. Norman: University of Oklahoma Press, 1973.

Thunen, Robert L. "Grant Mound: Past and Present." *Florida Anthropologist* 58, nos. 3–4 (September–December 2005): 255–63.

Tocqueville, Alexis de. *Democracy in America, I.* 1835. New York: Vintage, 1957.

Townsend, Eleanor Winthrop, M.D. "John Moultrie, Junior, M.D. 1729–1798." Read before the Medical History Club, Charleston, S.C., December 9, 1937. Manuscript. Bound copy at P. K. Yonge Library, University of Florida, Gainesville.

Uguccioni, Ellen. "Uniting the Past and Future." *Florida Preservationist* 3, no. 4 (Fall 2005): 3.

Upjohn, Everard M. *Richard Upjohn: Architect and Churchman.* New York: DaCapo Press, 1968.

Upjohn, Richard. *Upjohn's Rural Architecture: Designs, Working Drawings and Specifications for a Wooden Church, and Other Rural Structures.* New York: Putnam, 1852.

Vesilind, Priit J. "Watery Graves of the Maya." *National Geographic,* October 2003, 82–101.

von Simson, Otto. *The Gothic Cathedral.* New York: Harper and Row, 1964.

Vorsey, Louis de, Jr. "A Colonial Resident of British St. Augustine: William Gerard de Brahm." Manuscript at SAHS.

Walker, Karen J. "The Material Culture of Precolumbian Fishing: Artifacts and Fish Remains from Coastal Southwest Florida." *Southeastern Archaeology* 19, no. 1 (Summer 2000): 24–45.

Warner, Lee H. "Florida's Capitols." *FHQ* (January 1983): 245–59.

Warner, Lee H., and Mary B. Eastland. *Tallahassee: Downtown Transitions.* Tallahassee: Historic Tallahassee Preservation Board, 1976.

Waselkov, Gregory A., and Kathryn E. Holland Braund, eds. *William Bartram on the Southeastern Indians.* Lincoln: University of Nebraska Press, 1995.

Weisman, Brent R. "Crystal River: A Ceremonial Mound Center on the Florida Gulf Coast." *Florida Archaeology,* no. 8 (1995).

Weisman, Brent R., Herschel E. Shepard Jr., and George Luer. "The Origin and Significance of the Brickell Point Site (8DA12), Known as the Miami Circle." *Florida Anthropologist* 53, no. 4 (December 2000): 342–46.

Wenhold, Lucy L. "A 17th-Century Letter of Gabriel Diaz Vara Calderón, Bishop of Cuba, Describing the Indians and Indian Missions of Florida." *Smithsonian Miscellaneous Collections* 95, no. 16 (1936).

Wentz, Rachel K. "The Origins of American Medicine." *Archaeology*, May–June 2011, 57–58, 60–65.

Wheeler, Ryan J. "Ancient Art of the Florida Peninsula: 500 B.C. to A.D. 1763." Ph.D. diss., University of Florida, 1996.

———. "Shell Artifacts from the Miami Circle at Brickell Point (8DA12)." *Florida Anthropologist* 57, nos. 1–2 (March–June 2004): 159–86.

———. *Treasure of the Calusa: The Johnson Wilcox Collection from Mound Key, Florida.* Tallahassee: Rose Printing, 2000.

Wheeler, Ryan J., and Robert S. Carr. "The Miami Circle: Fieldwork, Research and Analysis." *Florida Anthropologist* 57, nos. 1–2 (March–June 2004): 3–10.

Wheeler, Ryan J., Christine L. Newman, and Ray M. McGee. "A New Look at the Mount Taylor and Bluffton Sites, Volusia County, with an Outline of Mount Taylor Culture." *Florida Anthropologist* 53, nos. 2–3 (June–September 2002): 132–57.

Widmer, Randolph J. "Archaeological Investigations at the Brickell Point Site, 8DA12, Operation 3." *Florida Anthropologist* 57, nos. 1–2 (March–June 2004): 11–57.

Winsberg, Morton D. *Florida's History through Its Places: Properties in the National Register of Historic Places.* Tallahassee: Bureau of Historic Preservation, Division of Historical Resources, Florida Department of State. August 1995.

Womack, Miles Kenan, Jr. *Gadsden.* Gadsden County Historical Commission, 1976.

Wood, Wayne W. *Jacksonville's Architectural Heritage.* Jacksonville: University of North Florida Press, 1999.

Worth, John E. *The Timucuan Chiefdoms of Spanish Florida.* 2 vols. Gainesville: University Press of Florida, 1998.

Wright, Frank Lloyd. *Frank Lloyd Wright on Architecture: Selected Writings.* Edited by Frederick Gutheim. New York: Grosset and Dunlap, 1941.

Zimny, Michael. "Child of the Sun." *Florida Heritage*, Fall 1996, 10.

———. "New Art, New Deal." *Florida Heritage*, Winter 1998, 14–19.

———. "One Man's Gift." *Florida Heritage*, Spring 1998, 12–17.

———. "Only Yesterday: The Sarasota School of Architecture." *Florida History & the Arts*, Summer 2000, 10–11.

Index

Page numbers in *italics* refer to illustrations.

Gezu Catholic Church, Miami, 193, *194*

Ghost-busting magic, 27–28

Gibbs, James, 91, 156

Giller, Ira (architect), 208

Glades I–II culture, 48

Goggin, John M., 42

Golden section (Golden Ratio), xvii, 86, 95. *See also* Sacred geometry

Gonzalez, Rick, 241

Good Shepherd Catholic Church, Miami, 215–16

Gothic Revival style, 138–39, 149–55, 158, 159, 163–64, 170, 177, 197, 202, 204–8. *See also* Carpenter Gothic style; Jones, Fay; Ozark Gothic

Governors, Spanish colonial. *See specific names*

Governor's House (Government House), St. Augustine, 6, 7, 71, 74, *81*, 248–54, *249, 251, 252, 254*

Grace Episcopal Church, Orange Park, 168

Grace United Methodist Church, St. Augustine, 144, 182–83, *184*

Graham, Billy, 137

Granada Site/Royal Palm Circle, 48

Granaries (hórreos), 101, 102

Grant, Stuart, and Randall Sender, 235

Grant, James (governor, East Florida), 41, 71, 108, 115

Grant Mound, 17, 46

Greek Revival architecture, xv, 137, 157–58, 227, 245, 258, 259

Greeley, Melvin Clark, 250

Green Cove Springs, 171

Griffin, Harry M., 202, 247–48

Guard house/armory, St. Augustine, 7, 78, 87

Gulf Island National Seashore, 275

HABS (Historic American Building Survey), 71, 121, 127, 144, 145, 242, 288

Hadley and Akinson, 261

Halbirt, Carl, 77, 78

Hale, Jonathan, 135

Hall, Robert, 27, 41, 58

Hamilton County Jail, Jasper, 220

Hampton, Martin Luther, 235

Hann, John, 95

Hannibal, Joseph (Key West architect), as son of Shadrack, former slave, 205

Harding, Warren, 140

Hardman, Charles, 245

Harris, Clyde E., 250

Hassett, Father Thomas, 119, 121

Hearst, William Randolph, 190

Heisenbottle Architects, 241

Herrera, Juan de, 125

Hewitt, John, 91

Hill, George Snow, 242

Hillsborough County Courthouse, Tampa: 1892, 172, 237–38, *238*; 1955, 238, *239*

Hindu Temple Shiva Mandir, Oakland Park, 146

Hita Salazar, Pablo de (governor), 104

Hoffman, Paul, 86

Hohauser, Henry (architect), 208

Holy Cross Church, St. Leo Abbey, 200

Holy Cross Episcopal Church, Sanford, 175

Holy Trinity Episcopal Church, Chetwynd, 175

Honeycott, A. James, 245

Hontoon Island, 20, 42

Hornabecque (defensive barrier), 107

Horwitz, Tony, 3

Hosford, Edward C., 224

Hospital, Spanish, Santa Barbara, 7, 80, 88

Hospital Creek, 108. *See also* Macariz Creek

Hubbard, M. H. (architect), 204, 205

Hunt, Richard Morris (architect), 182

Hunt, Roy, 285, 287

Hunter-gatherers, 24, 42. *See also* McKeithen Mounds Complex; Mount Royal Burial Mound; Water harvests

Hurley, Joseph P. (Archbishop, St. Augustine), 131

Hurricane, 96, 97, 98, 104, 140, 178, 205, 255

Immaculate Conception Catholic Church, Jacksonville, 190, 204, *206*

Indian canals, 30

Indian Removal Act, 29

Indian River, 24, 214

Indians, Florida, mentions of, 5, 17, 20, 24–28, 95, 97, 266, 269. *See also* Apalachee council house; Calusa; Fort Center; McKeithen Mounds; Miami Circle; Mission Nombre de Dios; Mount Royal Burial Mound; Tequesta; Timucua

Indians, North American, mentions of, 24, 27, 40, 45, 58, 93, 269, 275. *See also* Seminoles

Indian trade routes, 30, 42, 50

Indian women, status of, 38–40

Inlets: St. Augustine, 72, 99; Matanzas Inlet, 65, 269

International style, 210, 235

Islamorada WPA Memorial, 255

Isosceles triangle, 29

Isozaki, Arata, 245

Jackson, Andrew, 258, 280

Jackson, Helen Hunt (author), 201

Jacksonville, 1901 Great Fire, 170, 205, 232

Janley, J. C., 169

ELSBETH (BUFF) GORDON is a writer and artist-photographer specializing in architectural history. Her interest in the subject began with graduate studies in pre-Columbian architecture and iconography at archaeological sites in Mexico, at Tulum, and in Veracruz, where as a graduate student she was the artist/photographer for a University of Florida–National Geographic project. As a partner of Adaptive Restoration, Inc., she restored a number of Florida buildings listed in the National Register of Historic Places. Gordon is currently a research associate at the Historic St. Augustine Research Institute and a board member of the St. Augustine Archaeological Association. She has written for *El Escribano* and *Forum*, and she is the author of *Florida's Colonial Architectural Heritage*.

The University Press of Florida is the scholarly publishing agency for the State University System of Florida, comprising Florida A&M University, Florida Atlantic University, Florida Gulf Coast University, Florida International University, Florida State University, New College of Florida, University of Central Florida, University of Florida, University of North Florida, University of South Florida, and University of West Florida.

MAR · 2013